The Church-State Debate

Also available from Bloomsbury:
Building a Just and Secure World, Amy C. Schneidhorst

Rethinking U.S. Labor History, edited by Donna T. Haverty-Stacke and Daniel J. Walkowitz

Forthcoming:
The History of the United States Supreme Court, George Conyne

In Search of the City on a Hill, Richard M. Gamble

The Church-State Debate
Religion, Education and the Establishment Clause in Post War America

Emma Long

BLOOMSBURY
LONDON • NEW DELHI • NEW YORK • SYDNEY

Bloomsbury Academic
An imprint of Bloomsbury Publishing Plc

50 Bedford Square	1385 Broadway
London	New York
WC1B 3DP	NY 10018
UK	USA

www.bloomsbury.com

Bloomsbury is a registered trade mark of Bloomsbury Publishing Plc

First published 2012
Paperback edition first published 2013

© Emma Long, 2012

Emma Long has asserted her right under the Copyright, Designs and Patents Act, 1988, to be identified as Author of this work.

All rights reserved. No part of this publication may be reproduced or transmitted in any form or by any means, electronic or mechanical, including photocopying, recording, or any information storage or retrieval system, without prior permission in writing from the publishers.

No responsibility for loss caused to any individual or organization acting on or refraining from action as a result of the material in this publication can be accepted by Bloomsbury or the author.

British Library Cataloguing-in-Publication Data
A catalogue record for this book is available from the British Library.

ISBN: HB: 978-1-4411-3446-2
PB: 978-1-4725-2252-8
ePDF: 978-1-4411-1144-9
ePUB: 978-1-4411-5853-6

Typeset by Deanta Global Publishing Services, Chennai, India

Contents

List of Tables	vi
Acknowledgements	vii
A Note on Sources	viii
Introduction	1

Part One: School Aid

Chapter 1: The Beginnings: *Everson* and *Allen*	15
Chapter 2: Reassessing the Burger Court	33
Chapter 3: Accommodation Triumphant? The Rehnquist Court	61

Part Two: School Prayer

Chapter 4: *Engel* and *Schempp*: Controversy and Compliance	86
Chapter 5: School Prayer and the Reagan Era	114
Chapter 6: All Change? The Rehnquist Court	139

Part Three: Equal Access

Chapter 7: The Issue Emerges: *Widmar* and the Equal Access Act	159
Chapter 8: The Court United and Divided: The Path to *Rosenberger*	174
Conclusion	191
Notes	207
Bibliography	255
Index	276

List of Tables

Table 1: School Aid Cases: Dates, Rulings, Authors   77
Table 2: School Prayer Cases: Dates, Rulings, Authors   154
Table 3: Equal Access Cases: Dates, Rulings, Authors   189

Acknowledgements

My sincere thanks to Dr. George Conyne, Dr. Karen Jones and Professor David Turley for their encouragement, support, and advice throughout this project. I would also like to thank Professor Mark Connelly, Professor David Welch and Dr. Andy Wroe (thanks for the political science perspective) for their help and support along the way. Particular thanks also to Jackie Waller (for everything).

Financial support was provided in the early stages of my research by the Arts and Humanities Research Board (now Council) and by the School of History at the University of Kent. My thanks to both for providing the resources to enable me to start and then to continue with this project. I would also like to thank Ian Bolt and the panel of the Christine Bolt Scholarship who provided the opportunity for a final research trip to the Library of Congress. Thanks also to the staff of the Manuscript Division and the Law Library at the Library of Congress, the British Library and the Templeman Library at the University of Kent for helping me with my requests for both mundane and rather odd information.

Thanks also to the following people for advice and support along the way: Jonathan Beer, Dr. David Budgen, Aurelie Carpenter, Alison Chapman, Mary Dagg (I miss those late night chats about the Burger Court), Ann Hadaway, Nicola Huxtable, Tim Keward, Dr. Emily Payne, Sarah Rock, and Steve Van-Hagen. Thanks to the staff of the School of History and the Department of Politics and International Relations at the University of Kent for keeping me motivated with their interest and encouragement.

Finally, deepest gratitude to those who put up with me while I was writing: Jane and John Buckley, Chris and Viv Long, Olly and Lisa Long, Matthew Buckley and Ian Buckley.

A Note on Sources

The following papers are all lodged with the Manuscript Division of the Library of Congress, Washington DC:
  Justice Hugo Black Papers
  Justice Harry Blackmun Papers
  Justice William Brennan Papers
  Justice Harold Burton Papers
  Justice William Douglas Papers
  Justice Thurgood Marshall Papers
  Justice Wiley Rutledge Papers

Introduction

Congress shall make no law respecting an establishment of religion, or prohibiting the free exercise thereof; or abridging the freedom of speech, or of the press; or the right of the people peaceably to assemble, and to petition the Government for a redress of grievances.[1]

The First Amendment to the United States' Constitution protects freedoms which are considered basic to the American way of life: freedom of speech and the press, the right to peaceably assemble and thus protest, and the ability to petition government. The Amendment begins, however, with what are known as the Religion Clauses: the Establishment Clause and the Free Exercise Clause. The Establishment Clause governs the relationships between the institutional forms of religion and government: churches, schools, religious groups and organizations as institutions of the 'church' and governments, state or federal, and their representatives as institutions of the 'state'. At minimum, the state is forbidden from establishing its own church or designating one denomination as more favoured than others. Beyond this, there is widespread debate as to the exact scope of the Clause: does it forbid all aid to religion or just that with a religious purpose? Must the institutions of the churches and the state remain entirely separate and, if not, what degree of interaction can be allowed before cooperation becomes support? These questions are of importance in a nation where 90 per cent or more of citizens declare a belief in God or a Higher Power, religious organizations and charities are active in social welfare provision and several faiths maintain extensive religious school systems. As the arbiter of the Constitution, the Supreme Court has been responsible for determining the meaning of the Establishment Clause and thus where the acceptable line between church and state should fall. While its rulings have not always been popular, they remain the controlling principles in modern church-state relations by which organizations of both churches and the state must abide.

By contrast, the Free Exercise Clause protects individuals from government coercion in matters of faith and belief. Individuals are free to choose religion or no religion without interference from the government. In this sense, both Religion Clauses operate with a similar intent. However, in practice, the Free Exercise Clause works by allowing exceptions to be carved out of applicable laws for people of faith whose beliefs are unduly burdened by the laws' operation. Thus, students may not be required to salute the flag, a Seventh Day Adventist may not be denied unemployment compensation for refusing to accept work on the Sabbath, the Amish may not be required to send their children to school beyond the eighth grade and Jehovah's Witnesses may not be prevented from public proselytizing and door-to-door canvassing.[2] However, the right is not absolute. In 1940, the Court stated: 'The First Amendment embraces two concepts – freedom to believe and freedom to act. The first is absolute but, in the nature of things, the second cannot be. Conduct remains subject to the regulation of society'.[3] As a result, Sunday closing laws were upheld over the objection of Orthodox Jews, Amish parents cannot refuse to send their children to school before the eighth grade, the government may use social security numbers despite religious objections and forest service road construction and timber harvesting in areas of national parks traditionally used by Native American tribes for religious purposes have been permitted.[4] The Free Exercise Clause differs from the Establishment Clause not in intent, which is to protect the religious choices of Americans from coercion or control, but in focus: the Free Exercise Clause concentrates on the rights of individuals and the Establishment Clause restricts the actions of the state. If the former allows exceptions to generally applicable policies for people of faith, the latter dictates the type of policies that can even be considered. As such, the Free Exercise Clause concerns the place of faith in American society, while the Establishment Clause addresses how religious and secular institutions interact in a religious nation with a secular state. It is the latter with which this book is concerned.

The Establishment Clause did not become a major part of constitutional jurisprudence until the mid-twentieth century. As written, the Clause restricted only *federal* government action 'respecting an establishment of religion' and, by the terms of the Constitution, the federal government was small with limited powers; most power resided in state governments that were not bound by the terms of the First Amendment and maintained their own church establishments.[5] The Court heard only two major Establishment Clause cases before the mid-twentieth century. In *Bradfield v. Roberts* (1899), the Court upheld federal funding for the care of indigent patients in a Catholic hospital on the grounds that the funding benefited the patients and not the Church, and in *Quick Bear v. Leupp* (1908) allowed the use of federal funds appropriated for the Sioux to pay for tuition payments at religious schools because the funds belonged to the tribe and were only managed by the federal government.[6] Two changes in the twentieth century brought the Establishment Clause to greater prominence. First, as the federal government grew in size and scope as a result of the New Deal and World War II, public perceptions about, and expectations of, government activity at all levels altered to include social welfare provision, an area traditionally occupied by private, mainly religious, groups. With church and state organizations increasingly performing similar tasks, the need arose for guidance about the proper relationship between them to prevent violations of the Constitution.

The second development had bigger consequences for the Establishment Clause and for church-state relations across the United States: known as 'incorporation', it involved the process of making the provisions of the Bill of Rights applicable to the states. As written, the Bill of Rights applied only to the federal government, and in 1833, Chief Justice John Marshall concluded: 'These amendments contain no expression indicating an intention to apply them to the state governments. This court cannot so apply them'.[7] The ratification of the Fourteenth Amendment in 1868, however, laid the foundations for later legal change, forbidding states from violating 'due process' and 'equal protection of the laws'. Although the Court continued to maintain into the twentieth century that the Bill of Rights was not applicable to the states, it was required to define and give meaning to these key provisions; without reference to the Bill of Rights, the Court was required to create its own standards.[8] Then, in *Gitlow v. New York* in 1925, Justice Edward Sanford noted: '[W]e may and do assume that freedom of speech and of the press . . . are among the fundamental rights and "liberties" protected . . . from impairment by the States'.[9] *Gitlow* thus began the process of selective incorporation of the Bill of Rights that continued throughout the twentieth century. In 1947, in *Everson v. Board of Education*, the Supreme Court made the Establishment Clause applicable to the states through the Fourteenth Amendment.[10] Not only was the Clause applicable to a new range of federal government activities, *Everson* held that state activities would also be held to the same standard. Without a long history of Establishment Clause interpretation, in *Everson*, the Court accepted the task of determining what the Clause meant and how it should be applied to the mid-twentieth-century United States.

Interpreting the Establishment Clause

Much of the difficulty and controversy surrounding the Court's application of the Establishment Clause has come from the inherent lack of clarity of its key terms, 'respecting' and 'establishment'. After 1833 when Massachusetts ended its support of churches within the state, no traditional form of church establishment existed in the United States. The continued relevance of the Clause rests on the term 'respecting': laws respecting an establishment of religion may be those which fall short of a traditional establishment but have some similar characteristics and, by implication, dangers. The Clause itself, however, makes no attempt to determine what such laws may be, and records of the First Congress contain sparse information about the thoughts of the ratifiers.[11] As such, the legal and academic debate surrounding 'original intent' has entered Establishment Clause debate. Originalists assert that the Constitution is the supreme law of the land and should be followed to the letter; where clauses and phrases are unclear, it should be the words, ideas and intentions of the Founding Fathers that provide the answers. The theory rests on the assumption that it is possible to discover 'what the Framers meant'. But the debate on the Bill of Rights in the First Congress occurred at a level of superficiality that might be considered indecent given the importance attached to it in the modern United States. Historians seeking lengthy philosophical discussions about the relation of belief to government, or the meaning of the terms 'respecting' and 'establishment', will be gravely disappointed.[12] Although these problems do not render a jurisprudence of original intent impossible, they show that an unquestioning reliance on contemporary sources is not sufficient justification. Advocates must 'seek the intention of the Framers in the words of the Constitution, as the Framers themselves intended'.[13]

In opposition, interpretivists argue that the Constitution was a blueprint for a government that the Founding Fathers understood would need to change over time in order to endure, the vagueness of the wording intended to ensure that the spirit of the provisions survived but that they could be applied in different ways to account for new situations. The intentions of the Framers, where discernible, were deserving of deference but not unquestioning devotion. 'Preoccupation by our people with the constitutionality, instead of the wisdom, of legislation or executive action is preoccupation with a false value', wrote Justice Felix Frankfurter.[14] There is a danger that lawyers, judges, legal scholars, politicians and historians become so caught up in the search for the 'true meaning' of the words of Jefferson and Madison and others that they become blind to the issue of whether the challenged action or legislation is suitable for modern society. Interpretivists argue that the meaning and purpose of other constitutional provisions have changed with the social evolution of the American nation and thus it would be foolish to suggest that the Establishment Clause is in any sense different.[15]

With regard to the Establishment Clause, the Court has never followed the route of original intent. It has thus accepted the task of determining what the Clause means in the context of the modern world. As a result, a number of different theories have developed addressing how the Establishment Clause should most properly be interpreted.

Among legal commentators there are three main schools of thought concerning Establishment Clause analysis. Strict separationists regard as absolute and inviolable the 'wall of separation' that Justice Black wrote into constitutional law: the Establishment Clause created a complete and total separation of the spheres of civil authority and religious activity. The government, advocates assert, must maintain an entirely secular public sphere and be firmly committed to a position of official agnosticism. Separationists frequently praise the Court for the school prayer rulings and criticize decisions in the realm of school aid or equal access.[16] Accommodationists criticize other theories of interpretation for relying too heavily on the practices of the past and being blind to the consequences of such practices in modern society. Excluding religion from any governmental consideration simply because it is religion impermissibly disadvantages religion in a society where government is so active in social welfare. Nothing in the Establishment Clause, they argue, prevents government favouring religion over secular alternatives so long as no denomination or religious group is favoured over others. President Ronald Reagan and his Attorney General, Edwin Meese, were prominent advocates of this approach, as Justice Antonin Scalia has been on the Court.[17] Accommodationists strongly oppose the Court's prayer rulings but largely approve of later school aid and equal access cases from the Rehnquist Court.[18] Neutrality theory, the third approach to Establishment Clause interpretation, argues that while strict separation is not possible in modern society, there are limits to the activities in which church and state may cooperate. Advocates reject absolutism in either form and argue the Court should weigh the demands of the Establishment Clause against the rights of the individual in each case based on the particular alignment of facts and circumstances. The government may neither advance nor inhibit religion or religious belief, advocates assert; in particular, government may not prefer religion over non-religion, but an indirect benefit from a neutrally administered government programme is not *per se* unconstitutional.[19]

These theories have competed for acceptance among scholars and Justices since 1947 and the incorporation of the Establishment Clause into the Fourteenth Amendment. The debates on and before the Court in Religion Clause cases highlight that all three theories of interpretation remain controversial and continue to have their devotees. That the Court has never explicitly accepted one approach over the others, intimating that all three approaches have validity in certain circumstances, has provided even greater fuel for this academic debate.

The debate between strict separationists, accommodationists and neutrality theorists has been lively and controversial and has revealed the potential consequences of employing one theory over another. It has helped illustrate more clearly the path chosen by the Court by suggesting alternatives.[20] Yet in asserting what the Court *should* have done or trying to claim the Court's affinity with a particular approach, these advocates often overlook the question of *why* the Court took the approach it did and what factors beyond theory played a role in the Court's decisions. By seeking to explain the Court's actions in terms of a particular interpretation of the Establishment Clause such approaches also overlook comments and interpretations which do not help their cause: thus their interpretations provide only a partial explanation of the ruling. In addition, by focusing on how the Court employed precedent the question of why and for what purpose is less often addressed. The historical approach employed here addresses the questions that are so often overlooked by such theories as a way to explain and understand the Court's actions.

Although not addressing the Establishment Clause specifically, a wide body of political science literature has addressed the questions often overlooked by the legal literature. Looking to consider why the Court acts as it does and what factors influence the justices' decision making, this literature offers the possibility of greater understanding of the Court's Establishment Clause jurisprudence by looking beyond traditional legal theories. Political science presents three main models of Supreme Court behaviour. The Legal Model shares some characteristics of strict separationist theory and asserts that the primary influences on Court behaviour are legal norms, principles and methods such as original intent and *stare decisis*.[21] The Attitudinal Model presents Justices as policy-oriented individuals influenced primarily, if not solely, by their desire to see their preferred outcomes written into opinions. The institutional protections afforded to the justices by their position on the Court leaves them free to vote based purely on their preferred outcomes; opinions are little more than justifications for these outcomes. Advocates reject the Legal Model as little more than rhetorical cover for judicial policy making.[22] Rational Choice, the third model of Court activity, has two strands. Internal Rational Choice Theory holds that the influences of other justices and the need for justices to gain and hold a majority for a binding opinion fundamentally influences how the Court operates. A clear understanding of any Court opinion must therefore consider the bargaining and discussion between the justices in the period between the conference vote and announcement of the Court decision.[23] The second strand of Rational Choice Theory asserts that external factors such as lower courts, public opinion and the other branches of government fundamentally influence Court activity.[24] While some see this as a cooperative relationship, others perceive it to be an antagonistic one.[25] Despite these differences, those supportive of External Rational Choice Theory seek to place the Court as an institution in its political and social context and argue that failure to do so overlooks key influences on Court behaviour. Thus, although not directly addressing the Court's Establishment Clause jurisprudence, such studies provide an alternative framework within which to view the Court's actions in this area of constitutional law.

Yet taken individually, the Legal, Attitudinal and Rational Choice Models exhibit some of the same weaknesses of the more traditional legal approaches represented by strict separation, accommodation and neutrality. The Legal Model ensures that the importance of the law and legal norms and practices are not entirely overlooked, yet focuses on them to the exclusion of other potential influences. The Attitudinal Model is weakened by a similar narrowness of view, though its assertion that the justices themselves are of central importance in understanding Court activities demands that the individuals comprising the Court are given due consideration. Of the three models, the Rational Choice approach takes the broadest view, requiring that the Court be considered as the legal and political institution it actually is and that it be viewed as a branch of government, governed by similar rules to those of the legislative and executive branches. It also demands that the collegial nature of the Court be taken into account. Yet Rational Choice also has its weaknesses, often assuming a level and clarity of knowledge that is rarely possible outside the realms of hindsight or theory while not always fully recognizing that different branches of government carry different weight in certain circumstances, especially when interpreting the Constitution. Thus, individually, these models explain only part of what the Court does; taken together, however, they present the possibility of a fuller, clearer understanding of the Court.

In analysing the first fifty years of the Supreme Court's Establishment Clause jurisprudence, the intention here is not to test which legal or political science theory best explains the Court's decisions. All the approaches offer something of value to the student of the Court and the Establishment Clause, but devotion to any individual theory is unnecessarily limiting. For decades now the Supreme Court's Establishment Clause jurisprudence has been criticized as incoherent and inconsistent, lacking an overall structure and failing to provide clear guidance about the proper relationship between church and state in the modern United States. What follows challenges this all-too-easily accepted interpretation, in part by challenging the traditional frameworks in which the Court is viewed. It does this by stepping outside of those structures and taking a deliberately historical approach towards the subject matter, taking the broadest possible view. As a result, it is hoped that we may come to a clearer understanding of both the modern meaning of the Establishment Clause and of the Supreme Court and its decisions in this area of constitutional law.

Beyond the Court

While the Supreme Court and its cases are crucial to understanding the church-state debates in the United States since the mid-twentieth century, other factors also require consideration. The decisions of the Court interpreting the Establishment Clause provide the outer limits of acceptable church-state interaction and thus the framework within which much of the debate has taken place, but the nature of these debates has been influenced by more than just legal opinion. What brings cases to the Court in the first place? What makes an issue sufficiently controversial that individuals or groups are willing to invest the time and effort to argue it through the court system until they reach the Supreme Court? Focusing solely on the Court and its opinions often means such important questions are overlooked and, as a result, the full scale and scope of the debate remains unexplored.

The aim of this book is to integrate the legal discussion with these broader factors and to understand how, in the area of church-state relations, one influenced the other. Broadly speaking, four major non-legal factors are identified as playing a role in shaping, informing and inflaming church-state issues in the second half of the twentieth century. First are the dominant political views of the time. The school prayer decisions of the early 1960s, for example, reflected the growing liberalism in American society. The re-emergence of attempts to overturn those decisions in the early 1980s cannot be fully understood without first recognizing the growth of conservative politics and the links between the Republican Party and the emerging Religious Right. The national political mood created the backdrop against which local practices, new laws or old issues were perceived. A change in that mood can heighten or lessen tensions, making litigation more or less likely. Linked to this, individuals played a key role. Representative Frank Becker, Francis Cardinal Spellman, Senator Jesse Helms, Dr Billy Graham and Presidents Reagan and Bill Clinton, among others, had a significant impact on the timing and nature of key church-state debates. Their roles, in the context of broader political circumstances, are important in understanding church-state debates. Second, international political trends, in particular the Cold War, also shaped Americans' understanding of the place of religion in American life. The importance placed on faith as a means to fight the international Communist threat from the late 1940s into the 1960s had a huge impact on perceptions of issues relating to religion and churches, whether public demonstrations of devotion, the place of religious education, or religious exercises in schools. Thus the earliest church-state debates need to be considered in the context of the Cold War mindset that permeated American society. Third, economic circumstances played a large role in shaping attitudes towards public funds and education. Economic difficulties in the 1940s and again in the 1970s were responsible for stimulating major debates about school aid programmes and the importance of religious schools as part of the nation's system of education. State attempts to cut budgets in the 1970s brought the role of such schools to public attention in a context very different to that of the 1940s. The massive expansion in the number of school aid cases being heard across the country in the 1970s, and the growing prominence of policy debates surrounding the issue, cannot be fully understood without consideration of the economic circumstances surrounding them. The fourth factor to be considered is the role and situation of religious groups within the United States. Changing attitudes towards Catholics and Catholic schools as a result of the Second Vatican Council of the early 1960s are important when considering different reactions to school aid programmes of the 1940s and 1950s, as well as those of the 1970s and 1980s. Growing numbers of religious schools run by Jews, Muslims and conservative Christians from the late 1970s onwards also affected perceptions of school aid. The activities of the Religious Right in the 1980s, meanwhile, provide an important factor in understanding both school prayer debates and the move for equal access legislation in that decade. Churches and their members were active participants in church-state debates, their participation adding alternative views of the place of faith and religion in American society to those advocated in secular arguments. Such views, and their impact on church-state debates, also need to be taken into consideration if a full understanding of those debates is to be developed.

Education and the Church-State Issue

In analysing church-state controversies of the second half of the twentieth century, this book focuses on debates and Court cases involving schools and education policy. While such issues do not encompass the entirety of Establishment Clause debate, they do account for a significant majority of the Court's Establishment Clause jurisprudence. There are three main areas of controversy: school aid and the provision of government benefits to religious schools and their students, school prayer and other school-sponsored religious exercises on public school grounds and equal access, the question of voluntary student-initiated religious activities on public school premises. Analysis begins with *Everson* and the Court's original statements about the meaning of the Clause and traces its jurisprudence through to *Agostini v. Felton* (1997), concerning the provision of remedial educational services to religious school students in New York City. In *Agostini*, half a century after incorporating the Establishment Clause, the Court for the first time explicitly overruled itself in this area of constitutional jurisprudence, overturning two long-standing principles of Establishment Clause jurisprudence: that aid to religious school students could not be provided on religious school grounds and that religious schools were so pervasively religious that any indirect benefit to them must be immediately suspect. In rejecting these positions, the Court effected a fundamental shift in the underlying principles of Establishment Clause interpretation and thus the meaning of the Establishment Clause.[26]

What follows is a discussion of how and why these changes occurred, considering the roles of constitutional interpretation, the Court and the Justices, as well as non-legal factors such as politics, economics and religious belief. What emerges is the complex interplay of these legal and non-legal factors which shape our understanding of the history and modern meaning of the Establishment Clause.

Part One

School Aid

Introduction

'When a Religion is good, I conceive that it will support itself; and when it cannot support itself, and God does not care to support it, so that its Professors are oblig'd to call for the help of the Civil Power, it is a sign, I apprehend, of its being a bad one', asserted Benjamin Franklin in 1780.[1] Franklin's views were echoed by his contemporaries James Madison and Thomas Jefferson in their fight for religious liberty in Virginia between 1785 and 1786.[2] By the time of the Constitutional Convention in 1787, the issue of the 'proper' relationship between religion and government had been debated in the majority of states, spurred in part by the experiences of religious minorities during the colonial period. Of particular concern were religious tests for holding office and financial support of churches by the state. By 1789, six states provided for governmental financial support of religion; in three, funds were directed to Protestants, in the others, 'Christian' groups were the recipients.[3] Gradually, even these were altered or repealed, and in 1833 Massachusetts became the last state to abolish its establishment. Although the First Amendment was applicable only to Congress, the issues it raised were prompted by debates in the states and in turn its passage prompted further discussion. As the states became more religiously diverse it became clear that in a nation dedicated to religious liberty, state funding of particular denominations could not be justified. At the very least establishment equated to providing funds to a church or churches. Abandoning this practice at a time of limited government ensured limited contacts between church and state.

The emergence of education as an issue of concern for the states in the early nineteenth century revived debates about the relationship between religion and the government. The public school movement was spurred on by Protestant Christian groups, mainly Baptists and Methodists, who believed in making education available to all. Although not intended as places of religious dogma, elements of Protestant religious belief and practice permeated the schools, whether intended to preserve order in the classroom, mould the good character of their (largely Protestant) students or simply to recognize the wonder and power of God.[4] Horace Mann, widely regarded as the father of the public school system in the United States, believed in 'secular' public schools to the extent that the Gospels should not be preached but also advocated knowledge of and reverence for God and the Bible. While the country remained largely Protestant, these practices remained relatively uncontroversial; as the nation's Roman Catholic population began to expand, however, instances of conflict surrounding the public schools increased in number. Catholics objected to what they saw as open bias against their faith in institutions funded by the states, and in several states advocated public funds for Catholic schools. Open bias against Catholicism in the New York City schools prompted Governor William Henry Seward in 1839 and in 1840 to propose, at the urging of the city's Catholics, legislation that would provide state funds to the city's Catholic schools. The public reaction nearly lost Seward the election in 1840 and led to bitter public debate, heavily influenced by nativism and anti-Catholic sentiment. Similar proposals led to equally heated, sometimes violent, conflicts in states, including Indiana, Kansas, Massachusetts, Michigan, Minnesota and Wisconsin.[5] The public schools thus became a symbol of the history of anti-Catholicism in the United States, an image which persisted into the twentieth century.

The Depression and the New Deal introduced a new element into the debate about education. Until the 1930s most church groups tended to oppose the idea of federal aid to education, charging, along with educators, that such proposals would result in the nationalization of schools and an intrusion by the federal government into an area of policy reserved to the states. Early efforts between 1870 and 1890 were opposed by Catholics and Protestants, while proposals made between 1918 and 1926 to provide aid to education aimed at 'Americanizing' new immigrants and to reduce the widespread illiteracy discovered during World War One were decried by a wide range of religious groups.[6] The New Deal programmes did not benefit schools and education policy directly, but instead drew on the 'child benefit' theory that had been expressed by the Supreme Court in 1930. In *Cochran v. Louisiana State Board of Education* the Court held that Louisiana could provide free textbooks to students in private schools as well as public schools on the grounds that they benefited the children and not the institutions. By 1936, the 'child benefit' principle had been used to provide bus transportation, free hot lunches and medical, dental and public health services to children in non-public schools.[7]

More generally, the New Deal emphasized that active government, through subsidies and regulation, could work to the advantage of the nation at a time when Catholics found it increasingly difficult to continue to fund and operate religious schools. Hesitantly, Catholic opinion towards federal aid to education, including religious schools, became more favourable, based on the idea that if Congress could aid the 'general welfare', then it could extend funds to all schools equally without violating the traditional church-state relationship.[8] Protestant groups had taken little active notice of or role in federal education bills throughout the decade until the 1938 report of President Roosevelt's Advisory Committee on Education recommended a major programme of federal aid to education, including non-public schools in certain portions of the proposed grants. Some in the Protestant press portrayed the report as little more than a veiled attempt by Catholics to obtain federal funds, while others implied pressure was brought to bear on the committee by Catholic organizations.[9] Critics of the bills that developed from the *Report*, both religious and secular, demanded that federal aid be specifically limited by Congress to public schools, defined as free, tax-supported institutions. Whether intended or not, the implication was that this was an attempt to prevent aid being diverted to Catholic schools. Combined with Protestant-Catholic splits over similar state programmes, particularly in Maryland, New York and Ohio, the issue of government aid to religious schools threatened to revive the divisions of the nineteenth century. It was against this background that the Court agreed to hear *Everson v. Board of Education of Ewing Township*, the case in which the Justices would incorporate the Establishment Clause into the Fourteenth Amendment and make it applicable to the states for the first time.

With the Supreme Court's acceptance of *Everson* for oral argument in 1946 began the Court's task of expounding the meaning of the Establishment Clause in the modern world. For much of the nation's history, Franklin's concerns held little relevance for the relationship between government and religion: with a small federal government limited in its powers and social welfare provided largely through private, charitable organizations, the realms of church and state remained mostly separate. The New Deal brought a fundamental change, moving the state closer to areas of influence traditionally occupied by religious organizations and churches, increasing the likelihood of contact between them. As the federal government became increasingly active in these areas, the Establishment Clause of the First Amendment gained greater prominence. At the same time, debates over the place of religious schools in states' education programmes were expanded by discussions about federal funding for the nation's educational enterprise. With the end of World War Two and the coming of the Cold War, education for individual development and national strength seemed crucial in the fight for freedom. The existence of a significant religious school system in many states, predominantly Roman Catholic schools, implicated the Establishment Clause further.

The vastly changed nature of American society and government competed with the use of history and the framers' intent for consideration in discussions about what the First Amendment 'meant'. Establishment, aid, government action and even religion required defining in the context of mid-twentieth-century church-state relations. The Court's accepted task was to untangle the threads and enunciate a clear interpretation of the Establishment Clause, within the confines of specific cases. This task was complicated by the consequences for social welfare legislation of the Court's interpretations. Funding cases did not involve theoretical interpretations of constitutional provisions but affected legislation enacted by the federal and state governments that reflected broader policy decisions. When the Supreme Court accepted *Everson* and later cases for consideration, the resulting opinions had practical consequences for education policy, even when the Court's opinions focused solely on the religious elements.

The broad implications of the Supreme Court's school aid decisions ensured that the resulting commentary would be social and political as well as legal.[10] However, it has been the latter which has been most damning of the Court's actions. Critics have accused the Court of inconsistency, lack of clarity and blatant attempts to reach politically desirable results through spurious reasoning. Focusing particularly on the period of the Burger Court (1969–86), legal scholars have argued that the Court's jurisprudence was confused and lacked any consistent philosophy leading to disparity in results and consequent confusion about the meaning and scope of the Establishment Clause. However, analysing the Court's opinions and placing them in their broader social and political context reveals a more complex situation than most critics have allowed. The decisions of the Burger Court reflected both ideas that had been discussed in earlier opinions and the influence of the changing political, economic and educational circumstances from which the cases had arisen. The Rehnquist Court (1986–2005) drew on the precedents established by the Burger Court in finding its own direction in school aid cases. Placing the Court's decisions in this broader context allows for a different perspective, which may account for many of the Court's alleged 'inconsistencies'.

Chapter 1

The Beginnings: *Everson* and *Allen*

Laying the Foundations: *Everson v. Board of Education*

The case which set the Court on its path of Establishment Clause jurisprudence began in 1943 when Arch Everson, a New Jersey taxpayer, filed suit against Ewing Township alleging that the practice of reimbursing parents for the cost of using public transport to take their children to non-public schools violated five provisions of the New Jersey Constitution and the Fourteenth Amendment of the United States Constitution. On the surface the case seemed straightforward, but it touched on deeper currents of history and emotion which combined to make *Everson v. Board of Education* a difficult and potentially explosive case. Debates about federal financing of education in the years before World War II had renewed old tensions between Catholics and Protestants over the issue of education. The perception of public schools as anti-Catholic institutions was reinforced by heavily Protestant opposition to federal aid legislation and similar state funding plans in the 1930s. With the case of Arch Everson this was reinforced by the participation of the Junior Order of United American Mechanics (JOUAM) who sponsored and paid for Everson's lawsuit. By the 1940s JOUAM was a fraternal benefit life insurance society, but its origin in the 1840s was as a secret nativist organization, gradually developing throughout the century into a broader anti-radical, anti-immigrant, anti-Catholic organization.[1] This history made it anathema to Catholics and further reinforced the mistaken image that Everson's lawsuit was an attack on the Catholic school system, an image that persisted even after the American Civil Liberties Union intervened on Everson's behalf in 1943.

This potential for religious divisiveness may have been one of the reasons the Supreme Court accepted *Everson* for oral argument in late 1946. If the issue could be turned from a political issue into a legal one, or, better yet, a constitutional one, the argument about religious discrimination might be averted. Although not mentioned in conference, the justices could not have been unaware of the religious angle of the political dispute and both Justice Hugo Black's majority opinion and the dissent by Justice Wiley Rutledge avoided references to any particular religious denomination or sect.[2] The activity of, and disagreement among, the states regarding statutes similar to New Jersey's also appears to have motivated the Court. The growing nature of the debate across the country suggested some guidelines were necessary to ensure all conformed to the federal Constitution.[3] In addition, *Everson* provided the Court with the opportunity to complete what had begun with *Cantwell v. Connecticut* (1940): the incorporation of the Religion Clauses into the Fourteenth Amendment.[4] That all the justices present in conference on 23 November 1946 discussed *Everson* in First Amendment terms suggests a tacit understanding that irrespective of the final result in the case, the Court would incorporate the Establishment Clause.[5] Thus a combination of factors aligned to make *Everson* an acceptable case for contemplation by the Supreme Court.

'The First Amendment has erected a wall between church and state. That wall must be kept high and impregnable. We could not approve the slightest breach. New Jersey has not breached it here', wrote Justice Black for the five justice majority in *Everson*, beginning a long-running debate in Establishment Clause commentary: exactly what did *Everson* mean?[6] The wall metaphor, taken from Roger Williams and Thomas Jefferson, and the clear passages in the opinion referring to a strict separation between church and state led the majority of commentators to see in *Everson* the embodiment of the strict separationist argument. But this immediately raised a conflict with the result in the case, which allowed New Jersey's law to remain in operation, leading many of the same individuals to decry Black's opinion for its ambiguity. *Everson* is, however, better understood as a clash of competing interpretations: strict neutrality as expressed for the Court by Black versus strict separation as argued by Rutledge in dissent. Frequently overlooked in the rush to find strict separation in Black's opinion is that Rutledge's dissent provides arguably the clearest expression of that position ever articulated in a Court opinion. Failure to recognize this does a disservice to Rutledge and his opinion, which provided a template for those looking to make separationist arguments in the future. Such an interpretation also allows for a more coherent understanding of Black's majority opinion.

Often overlooked or simply dismissed when trying to show that Black wrote the wall of separation into constitutional law is the passage that stated: 'That Amendment requires the state to be neutral in its relations with groups of religious believers and non-believers; it does not require the state to be their adversary.'[7] The opinion was permeated with similar ideas and references. Often criticized as inaccurate and misleading, Black's use of colonial and early American history served not as a comprehensive introduction to the period, but as a tool to show how unrelated to the traditional idea of 'establishment' the New Jersey law was. The examples he used of oppression and forced belief were so alien to mid-twentieth-century American sensibilities that the bus transportation statute appeared to be in a completely different category, barely related to an 'establishment' of religion. The approach was also visible in Black's comparison of bus transportation with the provision of other public services such as police and fire protection, sewage disposal and sidewalks. Religious institutions and individuals could not be excluded from public benefits simply because of their religion, Black argued, therefore they could be included should a state wish to do so, so long as they were not eligible solely because of their religion. Equally, services provided by the state to religious institutions which did not touch on their religious function were also acceptable under the newly incorporated Establishment Clause. In no way can these passages be reconciled with a strict separationist position.

There were elements of strict separation in Black's opinion but they were neither pervasive nor central to the ruling; they were simply dicta. Although Black's use of history emphasized the Founding Fathers' desire for a separation of church and state, it was limited in its advocacy of this position by its ultimate aim of distancing mid-twentieth-century New Jersey from the founding period. The strict separationist reading rests on two particular passages: the use of the wall metaphor and the oft-quoted description of practices forbidden under the Establishment Clause. The first is little more than two sentences and seems designed to catch attention, to end with a flourish rather than providing a convincing argument. The second is more substantial:

> Neither a state nor the Federal Government can set up a church. Neither can pass laws which aid one religion, aid all religions, or prefer one religion over another . . . No tax in any amount, large or small, can be levied to support any religious activities or institutions, whatever they may be called, or whatever form they may adopt to teach or practice religion . . . In the words of Jefferson, the clause against the establishment of religion by law was intended to erect 'a wall of separation between Church and State'.[8]

The passage appears unambiguous and, separated from the final ruling, its implication is clear: no state aid, financial or otherwise, should reach religion or religious institutions. That the passage was intended as an espousal of strict separation is clear from earlier drafts which provided for far less stringent restrictions on government aid to religion.[9] A comparison of these earlier expressions with the final passage indicates that the latter was far closer to a position of strict separation, arguably reinforcing the tone of the entire opinion. However, these passages still do not comport with *Everson*'s ruling. Black reportedly told his friends that he made the victory 'as tight' as possible in order to render it a 'pyrrhic victory' for aid proponents.[10] This statement, and Black's *Everson* opinion more generally, have been interpreted as evidence of strict separationism and a product of the justices' mistrust of Catholicism, reflecting similar attitudes in the population of the country.[11] However, the separationist dicta can alternatively be viewed as a warning to Catholics that the Court's ruling was not *carte blanche* for the complete aid that they were advocating. From this perspective, the dicta operated to limit the granting of aid to those forms represented by New Jersey's statute: non-financial, indirect and part of a general programme of aid which made no reference to religion. In this way the ruling was still 'tight' since it implied that other forms of aid being sought by the Catholic Church, whether the paying of teachers' salaries or the provision of funds for building work, would not be acceptable, or would at least require close judicial scrutiny.

The social and political context of *Everson* provides some explanation for the position of the majority and the arguments made by them. 'Changing local conditions create new local problems which may lead a state's people and its local authorities to believe that laws authorizing new types of public services are necessary to promote the general well-being of the people', wrote Black.[12] In 1947, the constitutions of 46 states contained provisions that prevented an intermingling of church and state; 37 of them made explicit reference to sectarian institutions, the so-called Blaine Amendments.[13] Yet at the same time, at least 340 arrangements were in place across the states to provide public support to private, mostly Catholic, schools in forms ranging from tax exemption to salary reimbursement.[14] Across the country by 1947, states with Blaine Amendments far stricter and more specific than the First Amendment were providing some form of public financial assistance to religious schools. Such state practices suggested that programmes such as that in *Everson* did not violate the idea of separation of church and state: Black's language in the opinion and his emphasis on deference to the New Jersey legislature's decision suggests that this was a factor of significant influence for the majority.[15] State court decisions also influenced the majority however: Black's carefully constructed argument that religious schools perform a public purpose and so fall within the public domain had been expressed in at least one earlier state court opinion; likewise, Justice William Douglas's conference comment that bus transportation was a 'service indirectly benefiting' the schools.[16]

The justices in the minority were aware of legislative activity in this area but for them it meant something different. 'Neither so high nor so impregnable today as yesterday is the wall raised between church and state . . . New Jersey's statute sustained is the first, if indeed it is not the second breach to be made by this Court's action. That a third, and a fourth, and still others will be attempted, we may be sure'.[17] It was infused from beginning to end with separationist references and key arguments. For the dissenters, statutes similar to that in New Jersey and the Court's apparent acceptance of them signalled the abandonment of the principle of separation of church and state established by James Madison. '[O]nce [the] door is opened [there] is no telling where it will end', argued Rutledge, the author and driving force behind the dissenting opinion, in conference, '[Y]ou can't draw a line between a little and a lot of pregnancy. If you can justify these you can [go] much further'.[18] Black wanted to avoid causing immediate upheaval with his opinion, but Rutledge and his three colleagues were focused on the longer term and wider scale. They feared, as had Madison, that allowing religious groups to compete for public financial benefits would ultimately lead to social fragmentation and religious disharmony in the nation. Rutledge's detailed discussion of the history of the First Amendment and the views of its framers was intended to reinforce this image.[19] For the dissenters, current practice was less important than the separationist intent of the Founding Fathers: 'Now as in Madison's day it is [a matter] . . . of principle, to keep separate the separate spheres as the First Amendment drew them; to prevent the first experiment on our liberties; and to keep the question from becoming entangled in corrosive precedents.' [20]

The opinion was important to Rutledge: he worked at length on the dissent – an opinion significantly longer and more detailed than Black's – and the dissenters consulted frequently among themselves as the opinion took shape. The original conference vote was 6:2 in favour of allowing the statute to stand, with Rutledge and Justice Felix Frankfurter in the minority, but shortly after first drafts were circulated Justices Harold Burton and Robert Jackson joined Rutledge's position.[21] In his post-*Everson* correspondence Rutledge indicated disappointment that he had been unable to convince a fifth vote to his position but hoped that a reversal would not be long in coming. His experience between conference and final opinion indicated that his optimism was not without foundation and may have motivated him to write what could, at some future date, become the foundation for a majority opinion. In a 1948 letter to Harold Meek, editor of the *St. Louis Post Dispatch*, Rutledge expressed this sentiment: 'Just among us girls, perhaps I can say that there are times when it pays to yell like hell even if one is licked, on the chance that the yelling may have some effect toward retrieving a victory for the future'.[22]

Federal Aid to Education: The Political Context, 1947–1965

Everson came at an awkward time for the debate on government aid to education. Between 1900 and the end of World War Two approximately a dozen federal aid to education bills came before Congress, each defeated by a combination of educators, states' rights supporters and a variety of religious groups. The issue of federal aid to education was controversial: education was traditionally the province of the states, and states and local school boards feared a loss of autonomy, especially after the experiences of centralization during the New Deal and the War. In addition, educators were divided between the old fear that in the wake of federal funds would come federal control and a loss of local control and flexibility, and the new problems of a critical teacher shortage, lack of facilities and limited financial resources. Educators thus found themselves caught in a dilemma: while they did not want federal government scrutiny, they did need greater financial resources.[23] However, by mid-1947, leading educational organizations, including the National Education Association (NEA), American Association of School Administrators (AASA) and the American Council on Education (ACE), had shifted to support federal aid to education, influenced by a recognition of low teacher morale, lack of adequate facilities, the need to increase salaries and the necessity of maintaining the United States' leadership in the world.[24] Congress responded with a series of bills between 1946 and 1949 that sought different ways to provide federal financial support without restrictive controls or regulations. However, the contentious issue of the participation of religious schools defeated all attempts at school aid.

In July 1946, the Representative Assembly of the NEA signalled a change of opinion within the organization when it adopted as a statement of legislative objectives that: 'Congress should provide federal aid without federal control to assist the states in more nearly equalizing educational opportunity through public elementary and public secondary schools in the United States'.[25] In March 1947, the first post-war meeting of the AASA agreed, adopting a resolution declaring education the shared responsibility of the local community, the state and the federal government, and accepting in principle the need for federal financing.[26] However, the conference also made clear that it would not accept federal controls as a consequence of federal funds. In May 1947, the ACE added its support to the move for federal aid. Thus by mid-1947 the contemporary financial and political situation of schools and teachers led a majority of the nation's educators towards a recognition that federal aid, under the right circumstances, was necessary to maintain and improve American education.

By 1947 there was also renewed congressional interest in aid to education. In 1946 the Senate Committee on Education and Labor reported favourably on a bill proposing a permanent programme of federal grants to the states for the purpose of equalizing educational opportunity across the country. S.181 lapsed when the Senate took no action regarding the bill. In 1947, Senator Robert Taft (R-Ohio), one of S.181's sponsors, introduced a second bill, S.472, providing federal grants to the states for the support of education. Also aimed at equalizing opportunity, the bill guaranteed a minimum of $40 per year for each school child; if after making more than the average effort a state could not provide the minimum level of funding, the federal government would make up the shortfall. Indicating the severe problems facing American education, Taft estimated that at least 33 states would fall under the provisions of the bill.[27] In an attempt at compromise, S.472 provided that states could distribute funds received in accordance with their own existing policies; in effect, states which provided some form of aid to religious schools could continue to do so with federal funds. Portrayed as an exercise to make the bill acceptable to Catholics, the provision was also an attempt to allay fears of federal control: by leaving decisions about the distribution of funds to the states, Taft's bill ensured that federal intervention would be kept to a minimum. Speaking in support of the bill in March 1947, Taft reinforced this point: 'It is based on sound principles. It recognizes the obligation of the national Government to see that each child has an adequate education. It recognizes and avoids the dangers of Federal control and leaves to the states the responsibility and the power to work out their own salvation'.[28]

Long before S.472 reached the Senate floor, the provision of funds to states that would use them to aid religious schools had been widely debated by religious and secular interest groups. In House hearings on eleven federal aid to education bills during April and May 1947, the issue of church-state separation was raised at least as frequently as concerns over federal control of education.[29] Throughout the summer the Southern Baptist Convention, the Presbyterian Church in the United States and the United Lutheran Synod of New York passed resolutions at their annual conventions opposing the Taft Bill and state aid to religious schools generally. Although explicitly denying that they were motivated by the likelihood that the bill would largely benefit Catholic institutions, elements of anti-Catholicism were evident in some pronouncements. 'If the schools to be aided were run by Protestants, the same kind of opposition would be in order', stated the report of the Presbyterian Church, emphasizing, 'this is [not] a position to which we are driven by prejudice against the Roman Catholic church'. However, the report also argued that enactment of the Taft Bill would be accepted as 'an open invitation to go on tapping tax money for other Roman Catholic activities whenever its political power permits'.[30] In an editorial in December 1948, *Christian Century* also warned of the continuing struggle of the Catholic hierarchy to obtain a share of federal funds for their schools.[31] The confusion wrought by *Everson* and the majority's failure to clearly state where the 'high wall of separation' should be placed fuelled these debates. Concern about the lack of clarity in *Everson* led the NEA in July 1947 to call for a test case to be brought before the Supreme Court to clarify the issue, to be brought jointly by the NEA and the Catholic Church.[32] Although never initiated, the NEA's call for a test case revealed more clearly the problems caused by *Everson*, problems which fed into the congressional debates.

The religious issue combined with concerns about federal interference to defeat federal aid to education in 1948. When S.472 reached the full Senate for debate, Taft and his supporters fought off two opposing amendments: the first would have excluded religious schools from receiving any benefits provided under the bill and was defeated 80:5; the second, defeated by an equally bipartisan 66:14, sought to allow religious schools to appeal directly to the federal government for funds in states where constitutional provisions prevented state financing of such schools.[33] Although S.472 passed the Senate 58:22 in April 1948, attempts to enable federal aid to education stalled when the House Education and Labor Committee failed to take action on a similar bill.

The Supreme Court also added to the debate when, in March 1948, it handed down *McCollum v. Board of Education*. In an 8:1 decision, the Court held that so-called 'released time' programmes, in which public school students were released from regular classes during the school day to receive religious instruction on school grounds, violated the Establishment Clause.[34] Reaction to the ruling varied from support on the grounds that it upheld the principles inherent in the First Amendment to fears that the Court was attempting to secularize American education and, by default, the whole of American society. The decision divided religious groups and fuelled discussions about the proper place of religion in American society, both of which affected the aid to education debate. First, the decision appeared contrary to *Everson*, taking a position less favourable to religion than the 1947 case, raising questions about the meaning of the 1947 decision. Second, Catholic and some Protestant groups saw *McCollum* as an attack on religion generally, making them far more sensitive to perceived slights, such as proposals to exclude religious schools from any federal aid bills. Third, the debate about religion in society established a precedent for religiously motivated arguments that, while not new, added further intensity to the debates which followed.

In March 1949, the Senate Labor and Public Welfare Committee unanimously voted for Senate consideration a new federal aid to education bill authorizing annual grants of between $5 per pupil to twenty-five high-income states to $26.58 per pupil to Mississippi, the lowest-income state. The bill aimed to 'assist the states and territories in financing a minimum foundation education program of public elementary and secondary schools and in reducing the inequalities of educational opportunities through public elementary and secondary schools'.[35] Similar to the Taft Bill, S.246 permitted but did not require states to use funds to provide textbooks, transportation and additional auxiliary services to private and religious school pupils. The bill was passed by the Senate 58:15 with relatively little controversy. The consequence of the earlier debates and the impact of *McCollum* became clear, however, when Representative Graham Barden (D-NC) introduced into the House a bill similar to S.246 but which restricted federal funds to tax-supported schools. Opposition to both bills came from religious and secular groups, the latter including such diverse groups as the United States Chamber of Commerce, the Pennsylvania and Indiana State Chambers of Commerce, the Pro-America Organisation and Daughters of the American Revolution. Protestant groups largely opposed the Senate bill as violating the First Amendment and opening the way for diversion of other funds for religious schools while supporting the House bill, HR.4643, which they described as 'sound, honest, and consistent with the Constitution'.[36] Catholic groups generally opposed the Barden Bill and supported S.246 on the grounds that it treated Catholic schools as equal educational establishments, providing a public service by educating a significant number of children across the country. Despite the Chairman of the House Labor Committee claiming he would block all Administration bills until action was taken on federal aid, by December 1949 the issue remained deadlocked, and by February 1950 it was clear that a compromise could not be reached. The House rejected S.246 in March and, as no alternatives could be agreed on, the issue was shelved. By mid-1950, proponents and opponents had argued themselves to a political stalemate, helped in large part by the divisive religious debate.

The activities of Francis Cardinal Spellman played a significant role in the failure of S.246 and HR.4643. In an address at Fordham University in June 1949, Spellman denounced Barden as a 'new apostle of bigotry', and asked the audience to pray for 'one who, because of his sponsorship of un-American, anti-Catholic legislation, deserves . . . to be linked in American history with the names of others guilty of disservice to our country and the multiple people and principles that make our nation consecrate'.[37] The following month he attacked Eleanor Roosevelt for her 'anti-Catholic campaign', and accused her of 'discrimination unworthy of an American mother' for having opposed federal aid to religious schools in a newspaper column.[38] Spellman's attacks on such leading figures inflamed already heated feelings of discrimination while doing little to further the Catholic cause. By arguing in such sectarian terms Spellman made any challenge to his position appear anti-Catholic. While this was most likely his intention, it served only to damage the movement for federal aid, portraying those with a secular interest in opposing federal aid as anti-Catholic, and denying any possibility that the bill could be debated calmly and without religious undercurrents. A significant subsidiary effect was to create a political bandwagon onto which politicians seeking re-election could easily jump: oppose the Barden Bill, gain the Catholic vote, support the bill and gain the Protestant vote.[39] By creating such a situation, Spellman and those who vociferously opposed him, ensured the subject became too divisive for Congress to debate and ensured that any attempt to gain federal aid for education would result in failure.

With the shelving of any attempt at federal aid to education, the heat of the debate passed and more cordial interdenominational relations were re-established. Two main factors account for this development: anti-Communism and the Second Vatican Council. With the Cold War – and the portrayal of the 'bad guys' as 'atheistic Communists' – came a belief that the best way to fight the influence of Communism at home was by strength of faith. Elements of a civil religion, a generalized expression of Judeo-Christian traditions, had been present in American society since its founding, but as the Cold War deepened the perceived need for a strengthened civil religion increased. The Supreme Court contributed to this development. In 1952 the Court handed down *Zorach v. Clauson*, a second released time case in which the Court ruled that such programmes would be acceptable if conducted off campus. Finding New York's programme did not violate the Constitution, Justice Douglas wrote: 'We are a religious people whose institutions presuppose a Supreme Being ... When the state encourages religious instruction or cooperates with religious authorities by adjusting the schedule of public events to sectarian needs, it follows the best of our traditions'.[40] Irrespective of the problems this dictum has caused for scholars since 1952 in trying to decipher the Court's philosophy of Establishment Clause interpretation, it is clear that Douglas was referring to the nation's civil religion while seeking to avoid inflaming the religious debate. Two years later Congress added 'under God' to the Pledge of Allegiance, made 'In God We Trust' the national motto and added the phrase to paper currency. In addition, generalized prayers and Bible readings officially sponsored in the public schools were a fundamental element of the civil religion of the 1950s. In all of these elements Catholics were free to participate; in fact their participation was welcomed. Catholic schools might be perceived by Protestants and secular groups as divisive forces endangering national unity, but Catholicism shared some common values with Protestantism which made it a welcome partner in the anti-Communist fight. At a time when atheism was considered dangerous, the strength of Catholic belief made it a valuable force.[41]

The second factor changing relations between Catholics and other religious groups was the Second Vatican Council (Vatican II) of 1963–5, which modernized the Church and opened it up to modern trends. Significantly, the Council's Declaration on Religious Freedom recognized the freedom of belief and practice of all people, Catholic or not. In addition, the Declaration pointed towards greater cooperation with other faiths, an increased role in worship and administration for the laity and generally reduced the authoritarianism exercised by the clergy.[42] Taken together, these changes addressed many of the concerns expressed by non-Catholic Americans during debates on state aid throughout the century. The breaking down of the Church's own walls of separation reduced much of the suspicion and mistrust that had surrounded the faith. With regard to Catholic schools, Vatican II allowed for increased participation of lay teachers, both in education and administration, bringing new perspectives to the schools which complemented the opening of the curricula. Catholic schools were no longer intended to be insular, doctrinaire defenders of the faith, but 'enlivened by the gospel spirit of freedom and charity', becoming less separatist and engaging more with the communities within which they were situated.[43] The changing nature of the Catholic Church (and of Catholicism generally), combined with the impact of John F. Kennedy's presidency, allowed Catholics to feel more integral to American society and non-Catholics to perceive the Catholic Church as less alien and suspect.

As religious antagonisms declined, one barrier to federal aid was removed and several bills were passed providing limited, indirect aid to pupils attending religious schools and colleges.[44] These programmes, along with silence from the Supreme Court on school aid issues until 1968, indicated favourable conditions for a new, comprehensive bill. However, the Court's 1954 ruling in *Brown v. Board of Education* introduced a new factor into the debate on government and private schools: race. In Congress, Southern segregationists united in opposition to any federal aid to schools, fearing federal government interference in school segregation patterns.[45] After defeats on education bills in 1955, 1956 and 1957, criticism of the Administration and Congress, even in Protestant and Catholic journals, centred on the race issue rather than religion.[46] The position of Catholic schools as private schools also complicated the issue since more than one state attempted to circumvent *Brown* by subsidizing private schools. As the Supreme Court struck down state subsidies for private schools it seemed unlikely that Congress would provide similar subsidies, even if the motivation was different.[47] A third factor working against federal aid to Catholic schools was that as so few blacks were Catholic, Catholic schools faced the danger that they might unintentionally end up racially segregated. In 1967, Dr Eugene Reed, president of the New York State branch of the National Association for the Advancement of Colored People, announced a fundraising drive to oppose aid to religious schools, stating, '[w]e are against aid in any way, shape, or form, because it only helps those who would skirt legislation on desegregation'.[48] Thus race became an additional obstacle for school aid advocates to overcome.

Kennedy's candidacy for the presidency in 1960 brought a resurgence of the religious issue and debate about how Catholicism and civic duty could coexist. Kennedy's response during the campaign to fears about a Catholic in the White House – that he would make decisions as a president, not as a Catholic – reflected his awareness of the broader national concern about his religion as well as discomfort with being identified solely as a Catholic congressman promoting parochial interests.[49] Although successful in overcoming the public's fear about a Catholic in the White House, Kennedy could not overcome the religious issue in relation to aid to education. The Administration's 1961 attempt to aid public schools directly through grants for salary and construction costs while expanding the scope of the 1958 National Defense Education Act to benefit religious schools was defeated by a familiar triumvirate of Republicans, Southern Democrats and the religious issue. Republican opposition rested on the federal nature of the aid, fearing loss of autonomy and more federal interference in education, an argument that predated Kennedy's presidency. Southern opposition rested on the belief that federal aid would be used to enforce desegregation throughout the region, a concern exacerbated by Kennedy's apparent support for the Civil Rights Movement. Kennedy's attempts to find a compromise in the religious debate convinced no-one: opponents of school aid saw the extension of the NDEA for what it was, expanded federal aid to religious schools, while Kennedy's public opposition to including such schools in a general aid programme alienated Catholics, including the eighty-eight Catholics in the House whose votes would be necessary for success.[50] Further attempts the following year were defeated by the same problems, fuelled additionally by the Supreme Court's prayer ruling in *Engel v. Vitale* on 25 June, the Administration's proposed ban on literacy tests in federal elections and the growing controversy surrounding the admission of James Meredith to the University of Mississippi.[51] The Administration's two successes, the Higher Education Facilities Bill, which provided construction loans for all colleges, and extension of the NDEA combined with greater funding of vocational education, were both signed into law by President Lyndon Johnson in December 1963. Although providing necessary financial benefits for schools and colleges, the two Acts were limited successes for the Kennedy Administration: most of the controversial or innovative provisions had been defeated or excluded based on earlier experience, their scope and application far smaller than those envisioned in 1961. The Kennedy era thus indicated the continued divisiveness of the religious issue and its ability, in combination with other factors, to defeat federal aid bills.

However, on Sunday 11 April 1965, in front of the former one-room schoolhouse in which he began his own schooling, President Johnson signed into law the Elementary and Secondary Education Act (ESEA). Two years after the defeat of Kennedy's third aid to education bill in Congress, Johnson presided over the single largest federal aid to education bill that Congress had ever passed. The ESEA's success was due to a combination of skilful political manoeuvring, lessons learnt and a confluence of events. Johnson was committed to education as an issue, believing as he did that it had made his own rise from poverty possible and that it was a logical extension of the New Deal.[52] In fact Johnson's linking of poverty with education proved to be the key in overcoming the political and religious divisions that had defeated earlier bills. Few disputed the need to do something about the increasingly documented poverty problem in the country: linking school aid to this aim helped overcome earlier objections In December 1964, Commissioner of Education Francis Keppel suggested exactly this in a brief sent to Johnson suggesting that a programme of aid directed to children of the poor in urban slums and rural areas might overcome religious objections by employing the child benefit rationale and political objections by giving money to state agencies to administer as they saw fit.[53] The Economic Opportunity Act of 1964 indicated the approach and rationale was possible. Johnson agreed, and in speeches throughout the election campaign consistently tied the improvement of education to the goals of the Great Society.

In addition, a series of events altered the political context to the Administration's advantage. In the 1964 elections, the Democrats won thirty-eight new seats in the House; new members provided a potential seventy-six votes to break the previous stalemate, making legislative passage potentially easier. Equally, the 1964 Civil Rights Act prevented segregated institutions from participating in federally funded programmes: the Act thus deflected the racial issue away from any education bill the Administration might advocate. Meanwhile, the Civil Rights Movement created greater public awareness of the inequalities faced by black and other minority children in the United States, bringing pressure for greater federal involvement in education. Johnson's skilful handling of the outpouring of congressional and public goodwill in the aftermath of Kennedy's death, combined with his political experience, proved a third factor making federal aid to education easier. However, none of these elements could counteract the religious issue. While Johnson as a Protestant had arguably more leeway than Kennedy to move on school aid, no bill could be successful without some movement in the religious stalemate that had developed during the previous Administration. '[B]e sure that whatever you do you don't come out with something that's going to get me right in the middle of this religious controversy. I don't want to have the Baptists attacking me from one hand and the Catholics from another', Johnson told his advisers.[54] However, the defeat of Kennedy's bills showed that if aid to education was to be successful, some compromise would be necessary. A glimmer of hope appeared in 1963 when the NEA did not oppose federal aid to religious colleges but there was little reason to believe the Association's stance on aid to religious schools had changed. After lengthy conversations with the NEA and the National Catholic Welfare Conference (NCWC), however, Keppel observed, 'a genuine desire on everyone's part to solve the educational problem of the children'.[55] Hard work by Keppel and a new spirit of compromise combined with the child-oriented emphasis of the bill to resolve, at least temporarily, the religious debate: religious school supporters would accept that some, but not all, of their schools would receive indirect aid through their students while aid opponents could claim that it was the needy students who benefited and not the schools. Although tenuous, the agreement between the NEA and NCWC helped Johnson and his staff to overcome the biggest of the obstacles to federal aid. The ESEA was a remarkable political achievement. Circumstance, political manoeuvring and the ability of the individuals involved combined to ensure passage of one of the most significant pieces of Great Society legislation.

School Aid Returns to the Court: *Board of Education v. Allen*

In 1968 the Supreme Court heard oral argument in its first school aid case since *Everson*. With the calming of the political debate over school aid at national level and the development of a degree of consensus about the position of religious schools in general education programmes, it seemed unlikely that a Court ruling would result in the debate seen at the time of *Everson*. *Board of Education v. Allen* involved a challenge to a New York law requiring local public school authorities to lend textbooks free of charge to all students in grades seven through twelve, including students attending religious schools. Under the terms of the statute, books were requested by and loaned to students but the schools consolidated the requests, submitted them to the state authorities and stored the books provided. The textbook issue had come before the Court in 1930 when in *Cochran v. Louisiana* the Court upheld Louisiana's textbook loan statute under the Fourteenth Amendment, arguing that the state's interest in the secular education provided by religious schools justified their equal treatment. The case suggested little about the result in *Allen*, however, as the contemporary case involved an Establishment Clause challenge, an option not available to participants in *Cochran*. The Court's rulings in *Engel v. Vitale* and *Abington School District v. Schempp* earlier in the decade also served to obscure the Court's leanings: both were perceived as strict separationist opinions yet the most direct precedent for *Allen*, *Everson*, had, in result at least, allowed the aid statute to stand.[56] With apparently conflicting precedents and a Court containing only two of the *Everson* justices, the outcome of *Allen* was unpredictable.

The justices' conference discussions and the opinions that developed from them indicated a Court unsure of the grounds on which to proceed. In conference, Chief Justice Earl Warren argued that the *Allen* statute was a welfare measure for students, similar to that in *Everson*, and so should stand. Justice Abe Fortas objected to the programme's operation and the significant role of the religious schools in requesting and maintaining the books on loan. Justices Black and Douglas, the only remaining members of the *Everson* Court, sought to distinguish between lunches and bus transportation and books, the latter being far more fundamental to the educational process than the former.[57] Lacking a clear test for constitutionality, the justices also lacked agreement on the issues of central importance to school aid cases.

Writing for the 6:3 majority, Justice Byron White drew heavily on the few available precedents as if drawing strength from them to uphold the statute and offset the lack of a clear test within the opinion. *Everson*, White noted, was 'most nearly in point for today's problem': textbook loans raised different Establishment Clause questions than school prayer and Bible reading and thus required a different approach to that taken by the Court in *Engel* and *Schempp*.[58] The crux of the Court's opinion contained strong echoes of Black's *Everson* opinion: the programme was general and provided to all children, and the benefit was to parents not the schools. White thus strengthened the precedential value of *Everson*, which had been in some doubt after *Engel* and *Schempp*, while employing it to strengthen his own argument. As Black had done, White also drew on the existing political situation for support: if politicians and school boards decided that including religious schools in general education programmes was a permissible and effective way to strengthen education, he argued, then the Court was not prepared to suggest they were wrong, at least on the 'meagre record' presented in *Allen*.[59]

In dissent, Black lambasted the majority opinion and its interpretation of *Everson*.[60] Defending the 'wall of separation' and arguing against 'compelled tax support' of religious institutions there was no ambiguity about the separationist stance of the author, in stark contrast to *Everson*. Black sought to distinguish between the 'general and nondiscriminatory transportation service' he had written to uphold in 1947 and the textbook loan now at issue, suggesting '[b]ooks are the most essential tool of education' and, if allowed, there was no limit to where the claims might end, an argument supported by Justices Douglas and Fortas.[61] Despite the passion of the opinion and attempts to distinguish his *Everson* opinion, nothing could disguise that Black's arguments were almost direct repetitions of those made by Rutledge in 1947. His suggestion that a distinction could be made between different types of general aid based on whether the educational function of the schools was aided, an argument forcefully supported by Douglas in separate dissent, introduced a further element of subjectivity to the issue: not only would legislatures and courts need to decide whether a programme was a 'general' one, under Black's approach they would also be required to distinguish between educational and non-educational aid. Although used in dissent and therefore not binding, Black's opinion was widely analysed because of his role in *Everson*; the *Allen* opinion was retrospectively applied to try and understand an already ambiguous opinion leading only to greater confusion.[62]

Allen indicated that despite an increase in the number of Establishment cases in the nation's courts, the Supreme Court had not formulated a clear approach to school aid cases. The debate in conference and within the opinions suggested a lack of agreement on what constituted the important facts in such cases: should it be the final recipient of the aid or that statutes were facially neutral and defined recipients without reference to religion, as Warren suggested? Should the form of the aid be considered, as Douglas and Black argued, or was it more important that the students attended religious schools, that fact alone to be sufficient? Without agreement on these issues no clear test could be formulated: a test cannot be created if it is unclear what needs to be tested. White's opinion, closely tied to the specific facts of the case, answered none of these questions beyond the scope of New York's textbook loan programme. Black's dissent, challenging a majority opinion which claimed *Everson* as its foundation, made the situation more complex by seemingly providing a reinterpretation of his own opinion. Such opacity came at an awkward time. As enrolment in religious schools fell from their height in the mid-1960s and criticisms of public schools increased, states were seeking new ways to aid the religious school endeavour. Without clear guidelines as to the constitutionality of such statutes, the spectre of increased litigation and lower court confusion loomed.

Concluding Thoughts

With the decision in *Everson*, the five justices of the majority guaranteed the Court's continued participation in debates concerning the 'proper' relationship between church and state. That task was made more difficult by a number of factors. First, because the Establishment Clause as written applied only to the federal government, states had experienced their own history of church-state debates that had shaped that relationship. There was little unanimity of approach, which made any attempt to create a federal position likely to conflict with that taken in at least some states. Second, the history of heated – and occasionally violent – clashes between Catholics and Protestants over schools and state funding made both sensitive to further debates in this area. Any Court decision held the potential to reignite old tensions. Third, debates over federal aid to education, spurred by a growing sense of inequality throughout the nation and the financial difficulties of some states after the World War Two, raised the public profile of the church-state issue and of the religious conflict it created. Tensions were thus already heightened, making a more volatile situation for the Court to engage with. Fourth, the division within the Court itself, as revealed in *Everson*, resulted in an opinion that was less than clear on the grounds for its holding. The opacity of Black's opinion and the resulting debates about its 'true' meaning exacerbated rather than resolved the conflict.

Broader political trends, rather than Court decisions, worked to calm much of the earlier tension. A combination of the Cold War, the Second Vatican Council, the experience of a Catholic president and a growing desire to address social inequalities within the nation worked to move previously antagonistic participants towards greater cooperation. But while the tensions had subsided, the Court was no closer to a clear definition of the requirements and limitations of the Establishment Clause. As *Allen* revealed, the justices were still divided on the issue of how to approach such cases. Without clear guidelines, the potential for future conflict remained a very real possibility.

Chapter 2

Reassessing the Burger Court

By 1969, when Chief Justice Earl Warren retired from the Court and was replaced by Chief Justice Warren Burger, the Court had heard and decided only two major school aid cases. The majority opinion in *Everson v. Board of Education* had caused confusion because of Justice Hugo Black's use of the 'wall of separation' metaphor at the same time as upholding New Jersey's programme of bus transportation of students to religious schools as well as public schools. What was more important, asked commentators, the high wall of separation or the fact that the programme was held not to breach that wall? Twenty-one years later, the Court's second case provided few answers. The majority opinion in *Board of Education v. Allen* drew on *Everson* and its indirect benefit theory to uphold textbook loans to religious school students while Black in dissent lambasted the Court for misreading his opinion in *Everson*. While the published opinions provided little guidance as to what, if anything, beyond busses and books was constitutional, the private discussions of the justices revealed disagreement over how Establishment Clause cases should be approached. As Burger came to the Supreme Court, lower courts were facing an increasing number of school aid cases, making it likely that the issue would soon return to the Court for consideration.

The Emergence of a Test: *Lemon v. Kurtzman*

Lemon v. Kurtzman, along with companion cases *Earley v. DiCenso* and *Robinson v. DiCenso*, represented the type of litigation resulting from the confusion over the Court's opinions and the forms of legislation being employed in states to address growing educational problems. Pennsylvania permitted the state Superintendent of Public Instruction to 'purchase secular educational services' from non-public schools. Such schools were reimbursed from state funds for the costs of teachers' salaries, textbooks and instructional materials.[1] The case differed from *Everson* and *Allen* insofar as it involved financial aid provided directly to religious schools rather than services or materials provided to individual parents or students. In Rhode Island, the salaries of non-public school teachers providing instruction in secular subjects were supplemented by up to 15 per cent by public funds so long as the resulting salary did not exceed that of public school teachers. In practice, all teachers involved in the programme taught at Catholic schools.[2] After detailed consideration of the operation and intention of both programmes, the Court, in an opinion written by Chief Justice Burger, struck down both statutes as violating the Establishment Clause.

Lemon's most enduring significance was in the eponymous three-part test Burger formulated against which Establishment Clause violations could be judged: 'First, the statute must have a secular legislative purpose; second, its principal or primary effect must be one that neither advances nor inhibits religion . . .; finally, the statute must not foster an excessive government entanglement with religion'.[3] The test was not new, Burger culled parts one and two from *Abington School District v. Schempp* (1963) and the entanglement 'prong' from *Walz v. Tax Commission of the City of New York* (1970), but for the first time the Court had a specific test to employ in school aid cases. However, Burger warned against unqualified adherence to tests and argued that the main aim was to guard against the 'three main evils' the Establishment Clause was formulated to prevent: 'sponsorship, financial support, and active involvement of the sovereign in religious activity'.[4] Significantly, *Lemon* and the test it spawned did not adhere to the strict separationist position. Burger explicitly rejected this approach early in the opinion: 'Our prior holdings do not call for total separation between church and state; total separation is not possible in an absolute sense. Some relationship between government and religious organisations is inevitable'.[5] The *Lemon* test was, then, a balancing test, designed to weigh the benefits of an aid programme against the danger of Burger's 'three main evils'. However, with strict separation supporters on the Court in Justices Black, William Brennan and William Douglas, *Lemon* did not offer the opportunity to expand the scope of accepted aid programmes. Instead, Burger sought to consolidate the existing position and lay foundations for future developments.[6]

In ruling the Pennsylvania and Rhode Island statutes unconstitutional, Burger employed a series of considerations which worked to expand the meaning of the rather vague terms laid down in the three-part test. Burger's first concern was the nature of the aid provided. 'In terms of potential for involving some aspects of faith or morals in secular subjects, a textbook's content is ascertainable, but a teacher's handling of a subject is not': 'secular, neutral, or nonideological services' could be provided to religious schools, any possible danger that religion might be supported by public funds and the aid violated the Constitution.[7] This connected to Burger's second concern that aid should not take the form of direct financial grants. This had been implicit in *Everson* and *Allen* and few were willing to go so far as to advocate the direct provision of public money to religious schools: the image of religious education funded by tax dollars seemed far closer to the eighteenth-century definition of 'establishment' than either textbooks or bus transportation. In light of concern about the potential misuse of benefits, concern about financial aid may also have been influenced by the difficulty of monitoring how it was employed, Burger's third concern and the foundation for the entanglement prong of the *Lemon* test. Having concluded that church and state must interact at some point, Burger's intention was to ensure those connections were no more extensive than necessary. He also recognized that the line between the permissible and the unacceptable was not an obvious one: '[j]udicial caveats against entanglement must recognize that the line of separation, far from being a "wall", is a blurred, indistinct and variable barrier depending on all the circumstances of a particular relationship'.[8] In Burger's opinion, entanglement could only be uncovered after a thorough consideration of the challenged programme's operation, including the nature of the institutions benefited, the kind of aid provided and the resulting relationship between the government and religious institutions. Finding that Pennsylvania's programme involved a direct financial subsidy to religious schools and Rhode Island's salary supplement could be easily misused, Burger concluded for the majority: 'the cumulative impact of the entire relationship arising under the statutes in each State involves excessive entanglement between government and religion'.[9] It was not the monitoring alone that violated the Constitution, but the very fact that such a requirement was necessary.

On the surface, the Court in *Lemon* appeared to have overcome the divisions of *Allen*. *Lemon* itself was decided by an 8:0 vote and *Earley* and *Robinson* were decided 8:1, Justice Byron White, the author of *Allen*, the lone dissenter. The change in personnel in the intervening years had little impact: Chief Justice Warren and Justice Abe Fortas had retired, one in the *Allen* majority, the other in dissent, leaving the basic split unaltered. The positions of Chief Justice Burger and Justice Harry Blackmun on Religion Clause cases were unknown but appeared unlikely to shift the balance significantly. The original conference vote, however, indicated that the problems of *Allen* continued: four justices voted to strike down the laws, two voted to uphold and three justices declined to vote.[10] Burger assigned the opinion to himself, despite his ambiguous vote in conference, a tactic for which he would become well known, and forged the consensus expressed in the *Lemon* ruling. *Lemon* was thus a compromise opinion written to secure the broadest possible concurrence within the Court. However, for Douglas, Black, Brennan and White, the opinion did not go far enough. Brennan and Douglas filed separate concurrences that expressed strict separationist sentiments. Douglas, joined by Black, concentrated primarily on the argument that religious schools served no significant public purpose and so government should not involve itself with them. Brennan drew heavily on his own opinions in *Schempp* and *Walz v. Tax Commission*, restating briefly a broad range of arguments for ensuring limited church-state contacts, making a particular point of the danger to religious schools of government control. White criticized the majority for dismissing legislative findings and the ability of schools themselves to reject government funds should they wish to do so. These concurrences and White's partial dissent indicated the tenuous nature of *Lemon*'s nearly unanimous opinion. *Lemon* brought a degree of clarity to school aid jurisprudence and the test provided lower courts with more definitive guidelines than had existed to that point, but under the surface fundamental disagreements existed about the practical implications of the Establishment Clause.

The Political and Economic Significance of School Aid

Lemon v. Kurtzman proved to be the beginning of a flood of Establishment cases to the Supreme Court which lasted for at least fifteen years. It was a rare term that saw the Court without such a case on its docket. Two major factors stimulated this trend. First, the Court itself had indicated clearly that it did not view all government aid to religious institutions as unconstitutional, leaving open the way for states to devise programmes of aid that fell within the limits imposed by the Court's rulings. The narrow nature of the rulings also meant that new approaches and forms of aid were not necessarily encompassed within existing doctrine and thus were open to challenge. Second, the economic situation of the 1970s highlighted both the contribution made by religious schools to keeping education costs to the state low and the financial burden placed on parents who chose a religious education for their children as tax rates rose and private tuition costs increased. Unwilling to challenge the Supreme Court's rulings, many states and legislators nevertheless increasingly saw the benefit to public education provided by religious schools and sought to ease their financial positions, and that of parents, in small, if significant, ways. Portrayed by critics as attempts to subvert the wall of separation or to 'get round' Court rulings, state law sought generally to abide by their dictates while expanding their application to new areas.

The school aid debate of the 1970s was much different to that of the late 1940s and 1950s. In the 1970s Americans experienced what President Jimmy Carter famously termed the 'crisis of confidence'. The result of a combination of factors, including the loss of the Vietnam War and the fall of Saigon to the Communists, the effects of the social upheaval of the late 1960s, Watergate, OPEC price rises and the energy crisis, and inflation and unemployment, the impact of the 'crisis' was as much financial as emotional. Economists termed the economic situation 'stagflation' – a combination of high unemployment, inflation and lack of growth that defied orthodox laws of economics. Such economic problems affected many areas of public policy, and education was no exception. States could not turn to the federal government for help as they had done in the 1940s and 1950s. As part of his plan of 'New Federalism', President Nixon instituted block grants to the states in 1972 as part of a five-year revenue-sharing plan designed to reduce the centralization of power that he perceived had resulted from the New Deal, World War Two and the Great Society. As a consequence, education was returned firmly to the sphere of the states.

A debate about how to fund education efficiently and effectively emerged in most states as they struggled financially throughout the decade.[11] Inflation affected schools and school budgets severely. Basic education costs soared, consuming allocated funds faster than anticipated. Inflation also reduced state aid: in many states school finance was provided partly on the basis of real estate wealth; as local property values soared districts became 'wealthier' and thus eligible for less state aid. The combination of inflation and unemployment made many Americans unwilling and unable to pay increased taxes instituted to cover spiralling costs. The most extreme reaction was California's Proposition 13 in 1978 which limited property tax to 1 per cent of market value. States sought new ways to finance education that might offset some of the cost increases. New Jersey instituted an income tax in 1976 that had been widely resisted, Maine enacted a state-wide property tax in 1973 that was repealed four years later after arousing bitter resentment, and Cleveland and other Ohio school districts were forced to borrow against the following year's tax receipts in order to pay their staff.[12] These and other initiatives had little impact as costs spiralled and budgets suffered real as well as proportional cuts. In the Gallup annual survey of public attitudes towards education, 'lack of proper financial support' rated among the top five 'major problems confronting the public schools' for most of the decade.

The financial crisis coincided with a growing disenchantment with the public school system. Desegregation in the 1950s and 1960s and bussing in the 1960s and 1970s disillusioned many parents across the country. In addition, the Court's decisions in *Engel* and *Schempp* in the early 1960s led to fears of growing secularism in the public schools. Studies showing high dropout rates, falling standards as measured by standardized tests, increased truancy, poor discipline and high suspension rates raised questions about the effectiveness of the nation's public schools. The problems were worst in inner-city schools.[13] Financial cuts forced on schools by reductions in state aid only reinforced perceptions of the decline of the public schools as enrichment programmes – including music programmes, school trips and team sports – were cut as being non-essential to the education function, the number of guidance counsellors was reduced and class sizes increased as teachers were made redundant. Schools were it appeared, increasingly unable to provide a well-rounded education, moving instead to concentrate only on the basics which, while necessary, resulted in narrower, duller programmes. Educators feared that for those students for whom a basketball programme or violin instructor provided the motivation to take school seriously, the cutting of 'frills' might do irreparable damage.[14]

Like public schools, religious schools struggled financially throughout the decade for many of the same reasons. Catholic schools in particular faced a number of problems. From a high of 5.6 million in 1965, Catholic school enrolment fell to 3.8 million in 1973 and 3.29 million by 1978.[15] As numbers fell tuition increased as schools attempted to cover their operating expenses. Simultaneously, the effect of the ecumenism of Vatican II led to an exponential increase in the number of lay teachers. In 1971, for the first time, a majority of faculty members were laymen, a trend which continued unabated.[16] Lay staff took no vows of poverty and, although they frequently served at lower-than-average salaries, they demanded remuneration that would cover their living costs, putting pressure on schools' salary budgets.[17] Increased financial demands on parishes and raised tuition fees came at a time when Catholic schools' traditional constituency – blue collar, urban families – were suffering as a result of the nation's economic troubles and many could no longer afford the cost of the schools. In addition, in making the Catholic Church less insular, Vatican II prompted many Catholics to question whether church schools were necessary or viable. As Catholic culture became less distinctive the need to defend and protect such a culture through schools came into question.[18] If Catholic schools were no longer as unique as in the past, what should be their mission? This question occupied Catholic educators throughout the 1960s and 1970s. Father Paul Reinert, President of St Louis University, concluded that: 'If we as Catholic educators cannot transmit an additional quality to our graduates beyond the accumulation of knowledge, then we should give up our mandate as Catholic educators. It is not enough that Johnny should learn to read and write or become a biochemist in an institution which is different solely because it is supported by Catholic dollars'.[19] 'When Pope John opened the windows at Vatican II', commented one Catholic school teacher, 'he let in a hurricane'. 'All we can do', responded another, 'is to try and weather the storm while we find a definitive solution'.[20]

Despite these problems, Catholic schools in the 1970s were, politically at least, in a stronger position than in previous decades. As the Jewish Day School Movement flourished and some Protestant denominations established their own schools, Catholic educators acquired valuable allies.[21] In August 1971, President Nixon announced through the President's Panel on Non-Public Education that the Administration would be favourably disposed towards federal tax credit schemes. While no bill passed Congress, Nixon's support added weight to the push for some form of government aid to religious schools. At state level, Catholic educators also found allies among politicians seeking to ease the burdens on public schools or simply looking for the best educational alternatives available. Governor William T. Cahill of New Jersey and Governor Nelson A. Rockefeller of New York were leading advocates of the cause of the religious schools within their states. Throughout the 1970s, as state courts, federal courts and the Supreme Court struck down a variety of programmes intended to provide aid to religious schools, Cahill and Rockefeller continued to advocate, support and sign into law new ways of funding education, whether public or private.

While religious and political motivations played their part, defences of state aid programmes most frequently followed the route laid down by Black in *Everson*: religious schools provided a public service and so should be eligible for public aid. Speaking in 1973, Cahill defended a recently defeated aid proposal on these grounds: 'We believe that it is in the overall public interest to provide the financial assistance needed to ensure the continued viability of the non-public schools. If these schools were forced, one by one, to close their doors the burden of educating these children would be shifted to the state public school system.'[22] Across the country states with large non-public school systems sought to enact legislation that would ease the financial burden of such schools, ensuring their survival and thus easing the potential financial burden on public schools. Unlike the debates of the immediate post-war period, in many instances religious schools were not advocated as alternatives because they were religious, but because they provided effective education at no higher cost than that provided by the state. Opponents of tuition grants, tax credits or voucher plans just as frequently objected that such plans were not effective education measures as they did to the fact that religious schools were included; religion was only part of a broader debate about effective education policy, a fact easily overlooked as a result of the new Establishment Clause cases reaching the Supreme Court in the 1970s.

The broad range of programmes instituted by states and school boards throughout the 1970s explains the variety of cases heard by the Supreme Court. The Court's tendency to write narrow, fact-specific opinions meant that the constitutionality of innovative programmes was not always clear to legislators writing laws or courts hearing challenges to them. The frequency with which school aid cases were litigated led to the perception that legislators were trying to 'get around' the Court's rulings, to circumvent the Establishment Clause in order to win electoral favour.[23] A brief consideration of the statutes that found their way to the Supreme Court indicates that this was generally untrue. In *Meek v. Pittenger* (1975) the Court noted that Pennsylvania's statute providing textbooks, instructional equipment and auxiliary services to public and religious school students had a secular purpose and was extended to all students within the state: two years earlier, in *Committee for Public Education and Religious Liberty v. Nyquist* (1973), the Court had specifically noted that if a programme only benefited religious school students then it was constitutionally suspect.[24] In *Wolman v. Walter* (1977) Justice Blackmun's plurality opinion noted that the Ohio law in question 'was enacted after this Court's May 1975 decision in Meek v. Pittenger . . . and obviously is an attempt to conform to the teachings of that decision'.[25] The aid provided by Ohio covered all students, did not involve direct financial aid to the religious schools and placed certain limits on the manner in which the aid could be used, all concerns raised by the Court in *Nyquist* and *Meek*. In all cases heard by the Court, defenders of the challenged programme could make a reasonable attempt at showing how the statute conformed to the *Lemon* test, even if the Court eventually rejected the arguments based on the operation of the programmes in question. This does not imply that *all* statutes passed by the states were genuine attempts to conform to the Court's rulings – at least one notable case from New Jersey indicated they were not – but it does suggest that a larger number were honestly structured and not blatant attempts to circumvent the Court's rulings for political gain.[26]

The Burger Court's Jurisprudence

Between *Lemon* and *Aguilar v. Felton* and *Grand Rapids School District v. Ball* in 1985, the Supreme Court addressed a broad range of issues that stemmed from the social and political debate over education policy and aid to religious schools. Over the course of fourteen years the Burger Court upheld loans of textbooks to religious school students;[27] provision of funds for standardized testing and scoring in religious schools;[28] diagnostic hearing and speech services on religious school grounds; therapeutic, guidance and counselling services to religious school students provided off campus;[29] general purpose funds for non-sectarian uses to religiously affiliated colleges and universities;[30] and tax deductions for educational expenses for all parents.[31] In the same period the Court struck down grants to religious schools for maintenance and repair costs;[32] reimbursement of tuition costs to low income parents;[33] income tax benefits to parents of children attending private (including religious) schools;[34] loans of instructional materials including maps, tape recorders and overhead projectors;[35] auxiliary services, including remedial education, guidance counselling and speech and hearing services to students on religious school campuses;[36] reimbursement for the cost of field trips;[37] and direct reimbursement to religious schools for the costs of record-keeping and testing required by state law.[38]

A cursory glance at such a list raises a number of questions. For example, what is the practical difference between textbooks and other 'instructional materials'? Why is reimbursement of tuition less acceptable than income tax deductions? How could the Court make so many seemingly contradictory rulings in such a short period of time? The orthodox view suggests that this period in the Court's history of Establishment Clause jurisprudence was confused, inconsistent and symptomatic of a Court without strong leadership or clear guidelines for deciding cases. Justice Lewis Powell's majority opinion in *Nyquist* appeared to reinforce this image, arguing that 'the Court ... recognise[s] its inability to perceive with invariable clarity the lines of demarcation in this extraordinarily sensitive area of constitutional law'.[39] Powell's statement seemed to predict the nature of the decisions which followed. However, those who criticize the Burger Court for its inconsistency and lack of clarity frequently fail to consider the reasoning offered in the opinions of the justices. These opinions reveal the importance of the specific circumstances in which the programme was created and in which it operated. They also show that the Court was far more consistent than critics have allowed.

Within the Burger Court a series of concerns became an informal framework for analysing Establishment cases. These significant but unstated questions were whether the aid provided was direct or indirect aid, financial or non-financial in form, whether a challenged programme took place on or off religious school campuses and whether a programme was specifically aimed at individuals or institutions because of religious concerns. This was a fluid, functional set of guidelines that, while rarely stated explicitly by the justices in opinions, was nevertheless highly influential in deciding cases. These were not new concerns, possibly one of the reasons why they remained significant for so long: *Allen* upheld textbook loans to students on the grounds that books were not financial aid and were an indirect benefit to the schools; *Lemon* struck down additional salary payments because they were direct, financial and used on religious school campuses. Any attempt to understand the Establishment Clause jurisprudence of the Burger Court as it related to school aid must take these approaches into account.

Black established the direct-indirect aid distinction in *Everson* when the Court held that New Jersey could not provide aid to religious schools but that reimbursing parents for the cost of bus transportation provided only an indirect benefit to the schools concerned. This was reinforced by White's reasoning in *Allen* and further underscored in *Lemon* when Burger struck down the programmes because the aid went directly to the schools. In none of these cases was it the sole consideration, but it was a significant one. Direct aid related closely to the concerns of the Founding Fathers that one way to establish a religion was to finance it. In the case of school aid this analysis rested heavily on the perception of church-affiliated schools as 'pervasively sectarian' institutions, permeated to such an extent by the doctrines of the church that they could be perceived as nothing other than religious institutions. Such concerns were expressed about religious dominance in church-related schools throughout the Burger Court era but were articulated most clearly by Justice Potter Stewart for the Court in *Meek v. Pittenger*. Having established the nature of the schools in question, Stewart stated: 'We agree ... that the *direct* loan of instructional material and equipment has the unconstitutional primary effect of advancing religion because of the *predominantly religious character of the schools* benefiting from the Act'.[40] In one sentence Stewart cogently summarized the link in the majority's mind between direct aid and the religious nature of the schools in question; the message to legislators and school districts was that in order to pass constitutional muster, programmes of aid must not be aimed at the religious schools themselves but at easing the burden of parents or children.[41]

The second of the informal considerations addressed by the Court involved differentiating between programmes which provided, or appeared to provide, financial aid and programmes which provided materials or equipment. Government programmes exhibiting signs of transferring public funds to religious schools incurred far greater scrutiny from the Court. Implicit in Chief Justice Burger's argument for the Court in *Lemon* was the concern that controlling the use of money is far more difficult than controlling the use of a textbook. In *Committee for Public Education and Religious Liberty v. Nyquist* (1973), the Court employed a similar argument to rule unconstitutional maintenance and repair grants to non-public schools in low-income areas: not only did the grants directly subsidize the religious function of the school, there were no practical restrictions which could be imposed upon their use.[42] Striking down the tuition reimbursement statute also challenged in *Nyquist*, the Court employed a similar argument. Rejecting a statute that provided financial benefits to parents, not to schools, challenged two arguments made previously by the Court: that parents form a break in the chain between church and state, and that indirectly influencing parents' decision to choose religious schools does not *per se* constitute a constitutional violation, both of which had been advanced in *Everson* and *Allen*. The effect was to impose much greater scrutiny on financial aid programmes and to require far stricter limits on them than on alternative forms of aid.[43] The message from the Court was clear: financial benefits were far more likely to be considered direct aid to the religious function of the school simply because the use of such benefits was virtually impossible to regulate and any attempt to do so would have to be so extensive that it would raise entanglement concerns.

This, however, does not address the most common criticism of the Burger Court's jurisprudence: that the distinctions drawn between different types of non-financial aid made little sense. At first glance there is little discernible difference between the tuition reimbursement grants of *Nyquist* and the income tax benefits of *Mueller v. Allen*, between textbooks and 'periodicals, documents, pamphlets, photographs . . . maps, charts, globes, sound recordings . . . [and] films' in *Meek v. Pittenger* (1975). The distinctions appear meaningless until they are viewed in light of the Court's concerns regarding financial aid: the aid provided must be of a kind which cannot be diverted or subverted to religious purposes. The most striking example of this train of thought was *Meek v. Pittenger* (1975). In *Meek*, the Court addressed challenges to Pennsylvania's programmes of textbook loans, loans of instructional materials, provision of auxiliary services and the loan of instructional equipment to religious schools and their students.

A fractured Court upheld the textbook loans by a 6:3 majority and struck down the remaining three programmes by the same margin but with different justices forming the opposing sides.[44] Textbook loans had already been upheld by the Court in *Allen*, a fact relied on heavily by Justice Stewart for the Court, in addition to noting that the books were lent to the students and not to the schools. In contrast, the instructional materials and equipment were loaned directly to the non-public schools, which to the majority equated to the aiding of the religious function of the school, thereby violating the First Amendment. The lack of restrictions on the use of the materials and the equipment was also determinative for the majority, as it had been in *Nyquist*. Two years later, in *Wolman v. Walter*, the distinction became clearer when the Court addressed Ohio's programmes of textbook loans; testing and scoring services; the provision of diagnostic, therapeutic, guidance and remedial services; loans of instructional materials and equipment; and reimbursement for the cost of field trips. For a Court more fractured than in *Meek*, Justice Blackmun wrote for the shifting majority.[45] Limited by their medical, health-related nature, diagnostic hearing, speech and psychological services could take place on religious school campuses because the content was effectively self-regulating. In contrast, therapeutic services, including those provided as a result of the testing services, allowed the therapist to 'establish a relationship with the pupil in which there might be opportunities to transmit ideological views' and, as such, could only be upheld if conducted by state-employed staff at 'truly religiously neutral locations'.[46]

Reading between the lines in these cases it is possible to see the Court's fear that overhead projectors paid for with public funds might be used to show biblical images and texts, that tape recorders would be used to play hymns and sermons and that maps, globes and photographs might be employed in theology or religious studies classes. Because there was no way, without unconstitutional entanglement, to limit the use of the aid, the possibility that it might be misused was sufficient to render the loans unconstitutional. The auxiliary services, including remedial instruction, guidance counselling and speech and hearing services, suffered a similar fate. Unlike books which, arguably, could be read once and the religious content determined, teachers, guidance counsellors, healthcare professionals and the equipment used by them, could not be simply and easily monitored, and thus no way existed to ensure that those benefits would not be employed for religious purposes, particularly when the religious environment was so pervasive. Benefits whose use was known were thus acceptable; any uncertainty about that use and the immediate presumption was of unconstitutionality.[47]

The on-campus/off-campus distinction was originally drawn by the Court in two cases dealing not with the provision of public aid to religious institutions, but with the use of public institutions to provide religious instruction: *McCollum v. Board of Education* (1948) and *Zorach v. Clauson* (1952). In *McCollum*, the religious education classes were conducted on the public school campus; in *Zorach*, students were taught at 'religious centers' off-campus. Holding that '[t]his is beyond all question a utilization of the tax-established and tax-supported public school system to aid religious groups to spread their faith', Justice Black struck down the Illinois programme with only Justice Stanley Reed dissenting.[48] Only four years later, Justice Douglas, writing for a 6:3 majority, upheld New York's programme, largely rejecting the applicability of *McCollum* because the programme in question 'involves neither religious instruction in public school classrooms nor the expenditure of public funds'.[49] Given the similarities in all other respects of the programmes, Douglas's opinion seems disingenuous in the least, and it is with some sympathy that one reads Black's pointed dissent: 'I see no significant difference between the invalid Illinois system and that of New York here sustained[,] [e]xcept for the use of the school buildings in Illinois'.[50] Despite its controversial beginnings, however, the on-campus/off-campus distinction remained an integral part of the Court's analytic framework. Closely linked to the belief in church-affiliated schools as pervasively sectarian institutions, the argument shared many similarities with the direct-indirect distinction as interpreted by the Burger Court: aid provided on campus, such as auxiliary and therapeutic services, was frequently considered closer to direct than indirect aid. The distinction had a significant symbolic element too. The image of teachers or others entering religious schools or setting up mobile classrooms on school grounds implied a relationship between the two, a relationship less obvious when aid was provided to individuals or at alternative locations. Concerned to avoid actual 'entangling' relationships between church and state, the Court was unwilling to allow the appearance of improper ties.

Established by Black in *Everson*, the issue of eligibility criteria remained part of the Court's informal standards for constitutionality throughout the Burger era. Essentially, if a programme was available to all who met the eligibility criteria, and those criteria were not religiously based, then the benefit could not be ruled unconstitutional without further consideration. In *Nyquist*, the Court employed this analysis to strike down New York's tuition reimbursement programme and income tax benefits on the grounds that they were available only to parents with children attending non-public schools, approximately 85 per cent of which were religiously affiliated. For the plurality, that the benefits were not also available to parents of public school children suggested that the programme was not general and that the result was a favouring of religious schools. In *Meek* two years later, the Court found neutral eligibility criteria crucial in upholding Pennsylvania's textbook loan initiative. Eligibility for challenged programmes was elevated to a more influential position by Justice Rehnquist in *Mueller v. Allen* (1983). Central to his opinion was that 'the [tax] deduction is available for educational expenses incurred by *all* parents, including those whose children attend public schools'.[51] For the bare majority, the programme was sufficiently broad to avoid the concerns raised by *Nyquist* because the benefit to religious parents was only incidental to a benefit provided to all parents. The dissenters accused Rehnquist of exalting form over substance, noting that although the benefit was technically available to all parents, 'the vast majority of the taxpayers who are eligible to receive the benefit are parents whose children attend religious schools'.[52] *Mueller* signalled a change in emphasis: broad eligibility criteria were no longer simply a baseline requirement but were now a factor in a programme's favour.

Mueller also elevated to greater prominence the 'child benefit' theory. Positing that if government provides benefits to an individual and that individual chooses to use those benefits to attend, or when attending, a religious school, the chain between the secular and the religious is broken, this mode of analysis suggests that it is the individual who is the beneficiary of the government aid and not the religious institution. The genesis of the theory was in *Cochran v. Louisiana*, where Chief Justice Charles Evans Hughes held that the state's policy of providing textbooks to students in religious schools benefited the students, not the schools they attended. Justice Black wrote the theory into Establishment Clause jurisprudence in *Everson*, and in *Allen* the Court upheld New York's textbook loan programme specifically on the grounds that the aid was provided to the student and not to the school.[53] *Meek* and *Wolman* firmly embedded the child benefit theory into the Court's jurisprudence. In *Mueller*, however, Rehnquist extended the reach of the theory to encompass, for the first time, financial benefits to parents in addition to materials and services. As with the use of eligibility criteria, Rehnquist followed precedent by employing the child benefit theory; however, by ignoring the differences between financial and non-financial benefits in its application, he weakened the restrictions on state aid to religious schools that had been established by the Burger Court since *Lemon*.

The approaches and analysis employed by the justices in school aid cases explains some of the most obvious 'inconsistencies' between the cases heard through the 1970s. However, the results were only one aspect for concern among scholars, critics and members of the legal profession. Equally disconcerting was the inability of the Court to form and maintain a stable majority: on Establishment Clause issues the justices appeared to shatter into voting blocs, and alliances between them appeared as fluid and inconsistent as the results they produced. The Court had divided before – *Everson* and *Allen* were decided by the smallest of majorities – but the frequency with which plurality opinions were handed down, or opinions in which different justices signed to different sections, was unprecedented. The explanation, however, lay in consistency rather than its opposite.

Vincent Blasi's description of the 'rootless activism' of the Burger Court, the control exerted by moderate, pragmatic men at the Court's political centre, was nowhere more evident or apt than in the school aid cases.[54] Analysis of the voting patterns of the justices on the Court between 1969 and 1985 in Establishment cases shows three distinct voting blocs: Rehnquist, White, Burger and Sandra Day O'Connor voted for 'accommodationist' results in more than 73 per cent of cases they heard; Black, Marshall, Brennan, Stevens and Douglas voted for 'separationist' results in more than 80 per cent of cases. This left a centre bloc of Powell, Harlan, Stewart and Blackmun, who voted slightly more frequently for separationist results than accommodationist ones but who were clearly the swing votes.[55] Between 1973 and 1977, the period between *Nyquist* and *Wolman*, these voting blocs remained steadiest: Brennan, Marshall and Stevens voted together in 100 per cent of cases, as did Burger, White and Rehnquist: the separationist and accommodationist camps were clearly established.[56] The centre grouping of Powell, Blackmun and Stewart agreed in 83 per cent of cases, only marginally less than the 90 per cent agreement rate in the pre-1973 period.[57] Significantly, in three of the most important and controversial cases of this period, the majority opinions were written by these swing voters.[58]

The consequences of this control by the centre were narrowly written opinions, closely related to the specific facts of the case. In *Nyquist*, Powell drew on the jurisprudence of Oliver Wendell Holmes, stating: 'Our Establishment Clause precedents have recognised the special relevance in this area of Mr. Justice Holmes' comment that "a page of history is worth a volume of logic"'.[59] The sentiment was echoed by Stewart in *Meek*, who suggested that while the *Lemon* test was the proper mode of analysis, the Court should be wary of unquestioned adherence to such tests.[60] For the justices of the centre, the Constitution required pragmatism, not dogma, and their respective approaches to the cases reflected this clearly. Echoing his *Nyquist* opinion, Powell offered in partial concurrence in *Wolman* a statement that serves to challenge those who accuse the Court of inconsistency and a lack of clarity. He wrote: 'Our decisions have sought to establish principles that preserve the cherished safeguard of the Establishment Clause without resort to blind absolutism. If this endeavor means a loss of some analytical tidiness then that too is entirely tolerable'.[61]

Neither so widespread nor so influential as traditional thinking suggests, inconsistencies and problems nevertheless existed in the Court's jurisprudence. Two elements of opinions were particularly problematic for clarity of meaning: poorly reasoned, weak opinions and the use of dicta. Powell's opinion for the Court in *Nyquist* was arguably the weakest of the Court's Establishment Clause cases up to that point. Trying to distinguish New York's maintenance and repair grants from earlier aid cases by arguing that those programmes were channelled to the separate secular educational function of the schools while the maintenance grants were not was the sort of 'hair-splitting' for which critics attacked the Court.[62] Rehnquist's opinion for the Court in *Mueller* suffered from similar problems. In trying to distinguish *Nyquist*, Rehnquist argued that Minnesota's tax deduction fell under the exception left open in the earlier case for laws benefiting all students. Elsewhere, however, he appeared to suggest that the difference between the cases was that Minnesota's programme involved a 'genuine tax deduction' while *Nyquist* did not, a claim equally in danger of being labelled 'hair-splitting'.[63]

Mueller was also full of non-decisive but prominent dicta which embodied both Rehnquist's commitment to federalism and his political conservatism. The opinion appeared to tie the Court more closely to the political arena in the area of religion than at any time before. Although the subject had been debated for nearly two decades, tax credits or deductions as an education policy had been rejected in the wake of the Court's 1973 *Nyquist* ruling. However, the issue returned to Congress in 1981 as a result of continued disenchantment with public schools, continued financial problems and the Reagan Administration's attempt to shift responsibility from the government to the private sector. Those supporting credits argued that they would provide effective competition for the public schools (thus encouraging their improvement), that private schools provided a public service and parents should not be penalized for making that choice and that credits would promote diversity and freedom. Opponents of tax credits, including a majority of public school educators as well as secular organizations supporting a strict separation of church and state, argued that such a policy would damage the public schools, turning them into repositories for those students that other schools refused to take, that public schools served as unifying forces in American society while private schools did not and could not, and that if religious schools were to be included a violation of the Establishment Clause would occur.[64] Although not mentioned in the opinions, the justices were aware of the controversy surrounding tax credits.[65] Rehnquist's majority opinion, however, appeared at times to be advocating policy decisions favourable to school aid. The combination of these problems in *Mueller* with confusion about the Court's other school aid cases ensured the issue would return to the Court.

The *Lemon* Test Confirmed: *Aguilar* and *Ball*

By the early 1980s religion had become a more prominent political issue, driven in part by the rise of conservative evangelicals and the Religious Right, and the presidency of Ronald Reagan. The congressional battle in the early 1980s over so-called 'court stripping' bills, which were intended to restrict the Supreme Court's jurisdiction over school prayer and abortion cases, stimulated debate about the Supreme Court's Establishment Clause jurisprudence. Reagan's vocal, if not practical, support for a school prayer amendment to the Constitution, combined with forceful professions of his own religious beliefs, provided impetus to the Religious Right and those who opposed it. Secular advocacy groups such as the American Civil Liberties Union, Americans United for the Separation of Church and State, and People for the American Way undertook legal and political campaigns to challenge what they saw as 'the moral majoritarians['] ... crusade to impose their beliefs on everyone'.[66] The prayer debate politicized all areas of church-state relations: previously uncontroversial accommodations, such as legislative chaplains challenged in *Marsh v. Chambers* (1983) and New York's remedial education programmes, suddenly became battlegrounds between those who viewed them as legitimate government recognitions of religion and those who perceived them as unconstitutional government favouritism. Statutes and programmes became more than statutes and programmes – they became substitutes for discussions about the 'proper' place for religion in American life.

The debate had been a particular factor in the 1984 presidential election. At the Republican National Convention in Dallas, fundamentalist Protestants played a prominent role and stressed links between patriotism, morality and religion. At a prayer breakfast the day after the Convention, Reagan suggested that religion and politics were inseparable and those who argued otherwise were 'intolerant of religion'. Although the Religious Right had been a significant force in the 1980 election, the perception in 1984 was that it was more proactive and visible, and that Reagan had been more assertive in embracing its leaders and its causes. Other events at the same time reinforced the perception of an ever-increasing religious influence in politics: Reverend Jerry Falwell gave a benediction at the Republican National Convention in which he referred to Reagan and Vice President George Bush as 'God's instruments for rebuilding America'; a 'report card' published by Christian Voice gave Democratic vice presidential candidate Geraldine Ferraro a low mark because she supported a nuclear freeze; the emergence of the Presidential Biblical Scorecard, maintained by advisors within the Religious Right, to 'score' politicians based on their support for religious and 'moral' causes; a speech by Reagan to the convention of National Religious Broadcasters when he made twenty-four references to God and Jesus. The activism was not limited to Protestants. In June, Archbishop John O'Connor of New York stated, 'I don't see how a Catholic in good conscience can vote for a candidate who explicitly supports abortion', sparking strong criticism from Catholic politicians such as Governor Mario Cuomo of New York and Senator Edward Kennedy (D-Mass).[67]

The apparent influence of the Religious Right in the Republican campaign and Reagan's frequent professions of faith stimulated others to comment in opposition. In early September, a joint statement by the American Jewish Committee, Baptist Joint Committee on Public Affairs, National Council of Churches, National Coalition of American Nuns and the Synagogue Council of America, condemned recent events and called on Democrats and Republicans to 'reject categorically the pernicious notion that only one brand of religion meets with God's approval and that others are necessarily evil'.[68] At the same time, Norman Lear, founder of People for the American Way, a group organized specifically to combat fundamentalist influence in politics, released letters between himself and President Reagan discussing the church-state issue. Nothing in Reagan's replies to Lear was particularly controversial, nor were they new to those familiar with his speeches, but publication of the letters fuelled the existing debate, as Lear no doubt intended. Democratic presidential candidate Walter Mondale used the occasion of a speech to B'nai B'rith, a non-partisan Jewish service organization, to respond to Reagan and comment on the church-state debate.[69] The debate rumbled on throughout the autumn, reinforcing the sense that religion and politics were becoming intimately intertwined. A CBS/*New York Times* poll found that 42 per cent of respondents felt that the candidates were misusing religion and only 22 per cent believed candidates should discuss religion in the campaign.[70] Although unlikely to affect the justices' deliberations in *Aguilar* and *Ball* directly, the controversy of the election raised the visibility of church-state issues, politicizing the positions in a very public way. The lengthy and frequently emotional debate increased public sensitivity to the potential consequences of a Court ruling and threatened to increase the political divisiveness the Court had warned of in earlier opinions.

Aguilar v. Felton and *Grand Rapids v. Ball* resulted, in part, from the growing sensitivity about church-state relationships. In many cases, challenges to statutes or programmes were brought before they went into effect, or at least while their history was relatively brief. The lack of an adequate record on which to judge constitutional violations was noted by justices in *Nyquist, Meek* and *Wolman*. In contrast, Grand Rapids' Community Education and Shared Time programmes were first instituted in the 1976–7 school year, operating for at least three years before being challenged, while New York's programme had been in operation for fourteen years. In comparison to earlier cases both programmes were well established. However, both programmes were victims of the increased politicization of church-state debates in the early 1980s.

Aguilar developed from New York City's provision of remedial educational services to students in private (including religious) schools using Title I funds, the largest such programme in the country. Title I of the Elementary and Secondary Education Act of 1965 authorized the provision of funds to local educational agencies to meet the needs of educationally deprived children from low-income families.[71] Using such funds, New York implemented a programme whereby private school pupils would be transported to public schools after school hours for instruction. Concern for the safety of the students, poor attendance and tired pupils and staff led the Board of Education to move after-school instruction on to private school campuses. The programme yielded equally mixed results and led the Board to implement the programme challenged in *Aguilar* where Title I services were provided by public school teachers on private school premises during school hours. Only public school teachers were eligible to participate, assignments were made on a voluntary basis and an extensive system of monitoring was established.[72] *Ball* involved similar programmes – but funded by state resources, not federal funds. Grand Rapids established two programmes: Shared Time and Community Education. The former provided remedial and enrichment reading and mathematics classes, in addition to other subjects intended to supplement the core curriculum of the schools, and took place during school hours, on religious school grounds, but were taught by full-time public school teachers. The Community Education Program, which was offered to children and adults after school hours, on religious school grounds, provided a wider range of subjects and classes, and were taught by employees of the particular school who were designated as 'part-time public employees' for the duration of the classes. Unlike the New York programme, Grand Rapids had not provided for any monitoring of the programmes. The result in each case was the same, the programmes violated the Establishment Clause because they created too close a link between church and state.[73]

Aguilar and *Ball* took much of the legal community by surprise. Although believing that 'to uphold the programs, the Supreme Court will either have to draw some exquisitely fine lines or disavow the key precedents that have placed tight limits on parochial aid', this was exactly what the Court had been criticized for and was not considered beyond possibility.[74] An additional factor was the Court itself. In *Mueller*, Rehnquist's dicta had suggested a more accepting attitude towards religious schools, a perception reinforced in 1984 when the Court handed down *Lynch v. Donnelly* upholding a city-sponsored display of a crèche in a public park as part of a Christmas celebration. Writing for the 5:4 majority in *Lynch*, Burger argued that the nativity scene was acceptable as part of Pawtucket's broader recognition of Christmas as it formed only part of a predominantly secular display. In the weeks before the *Aguilar* and *Ball* opinions were announced, the Court ruled against positions favoured by accommodationists in two other cases, but because they were not specifically school aid cases the perception of growing accommodationism on the Court prevailed.[75]

To understand *Aguilar* and *Ball* they must be viewed as companion cases. Argued together and handed down together, Brennan explicitly stated the link in his *Aguilar* opinion.[76] Considering these cases together addresses the most common criticism of the *Aguilar* opinion: its almost exclusive reliance on the entanglement prong of the *Lemon* test. Rather than representing an expansion of entanglement beyond its natural bounds, *Aguilar* was one part of a much broader argument; considered with the purpose and effects analysis of *Ball*, the cases served not to undermine the *Lemon* test, but to reinforce its centrality to Establishment Clause jurisprudence. If *Aguilar* undermined the *Lemon* test, it is difficult to understand how in *Ball*, the case which precedes it in the Court reports, Brennan could assert:

> We have particularly relied on *Lemon* in every case involving the sensitive relationship between government and religion in the education of our children ... The *Lemon* test concentrates attention on the issues – purpose, effect, entanglement – that determine whether a particular state

action is an improper 'law respecting an establishment of religion.' We therefore reaffirm that state action alleged to violate the Establishment Clause should be measured against the *Lemon* criteria.[77]

For those expecting inconsistency from the Court in light of earlier cases, *Aguilar* and *Ball* simply reinforced existing preconceptions, but to overlook the clear link between the two cases is to misunderstand what the justices were trying to do.

Viewed in this way there was little remarkable or unpredictable about the *Aguilar* and *Ball* opinions. In *Ball*, Brennan found 'no reason to disagree' with the lower court's finding that the Community Education and Shared Time programmes had a secular purpose.[78] In analysing 'effect', the role of the teacher was again crucial: that the teachers could not be easily controlled because of the nature of the teacher-student relationship raised concerns about the 'misuse' of the aid provided. Equally, because state provision of the courses relieved the schools of the financial burden of running such courses themselves, the state freed funds which the school could use elsewhere, potentially for religious instruction. Brennan wrote: '[t]his kind of direct aid to the educational function of the religious school is indistinguishable from the provision of a direct cash subsidy to the religious school that is most clearly prohibited by the Establishment Clause'.[79] In this way the aid was both direct and financial, the two types of aid traditionally receiving closest scrutiny and least support from the Court.

More unusual was Brennan's use of 'symbolic union' analysis. More akin to a balancing of church-state interaction, the test implied a greater openness to accommodation than Brennan's history of separationist opinions reflected. Its inclusion was most likely an attempt to win Justice Sandra Day O'Connor's vote for the majority. In her relatively short time on the Court, O'Connor had shown a tendency towards pragmatism in Establishment cases, based on close reading of the factual records and a willingness to question existing tests.[80] However, the intention behind 'symbolic union' was not new to the Court's jurisprudence. Both the on-campus/off-campus distinction and the direct-indirect aid division included symbolic elements and Brennan's reference to *McCollum* and *Zorach* as part of his analysis served to reinforce the link. In *Ball*, the majority was concerned that because the remedial and supplementary education classes were taught by employees of the religious school in which the instruction took place, the children participating would be unable to distinguish between the religious and secular providers, thereby creating in their minds a union of church and state. The combination of the religious affiliation of the teachers and the religious schools in which the classes were taught presented far too great a danger of a constitutional violation for the justices who, it might be supposed, would have felt far more comfortable had the programme been offered anywhere but on the religious school premises.

Elements of these arguments also appeared in Brennan's *Aguilar* opinion. However, the first two prongs of the *Lemon* test were fully addressed in *Ball*; the only significant difference in *Aguilar* was that a system of monitoring had been established, providing the Court with a forum to discuss the least used of the Court's *Lemon* test concerns. The entanglement test was initially formulated in *Walz v. Tax Commission of the City of New York*, a 1970 case in which the Court addressed the constitutionality of New York's tax exemption for buildings used solely for religious purposes. Upholding the programme, Chief Justice Burger not only suggested that 'there is room for play in the joints productive of a benevolent neutrality', but went a step further by suggesting that government support of religion was permissible as long as there was no 'excessive government entanglement with religion'.[81] In *Lemon*, Burger established categories for entanglement analysis and warned that the test should not become an end in itself but a means to the end of upholding the Constitution: 'This is not to suggest, however, that we are to engage in a legalistic minuet in which precise rules and forms must govern. A true minuet is a matter of pure form and style, the observance of which is itself the substantive end. Here we examine the form of the relationship for the light that it casts on the substance'.[82] Entanglement, as Burger noted in *Lemon*, was implicitly tied to other concerns in Establishment cases. Without the belief in religious schools as pervasively sectarian institutions, monitoring would be unnecessary and the concern would be irrelevant, as in the religious college cases. If direct aid to religious schools had been accepted by the Court, monitoring of the kinds of aid provided and how it was used would have been equally obsolete. Thus, although *Aguilar* appeared to involve only entanglement, it rested heavily on well-established concerns.

This interlinking is important not only for the opinion in *Aguilar*, but for the entanglement test in general. In dissent, Rehnquist accused the majority of 'tak[ing] advantage of the "Catch-22" paradox of its own creation . . . whereby aid must be supervised to ensure no entanglement but the supervision itself is held to cause an entanglement'.[83] The argument became a popular one for attacking the entanglement test in the aftermath of *Aguilar*. Yet Rehnquist's attack fundamentally misread precedent. Especially in *Meek* and *Wolman*, programmes of aid that were not considered self-governing were struck down because they could easily be put to illegitimate religious uses. The Court never said that monitoring would make a programme constitutional, only that if a programme would require supervision to ensure no transgressions then it was likely the aid violated the Establishment Clause. This was the argument advanced by the *Aguilar* majority in its relatively brief opinion. Taken in context with this and the opinion in *Ball*, entanglement was a part of these additional concerns, not separate from them. Thus *Aguilar* and *Ball* were neither major changes in Establishment Clause doctrine nor evidence of entanglement gone mad.

The majority's unwillingness to consider the detailed records of the operation of both the New York and Grand Rapids programmes was unusual, however. In the majority of the Court's earlier cases there had been no history to consider: the laws and programmes were recent attempts to deal with new problems affecting public and religious schools and were challenged either before they went into effect or very soon after. In both *Aguilar* and *Ball* extensive histories were submitted to the Court for consideration. The majority's failure even to address the existing record signalled a weakening of the control of the pragmatists on the Court. As in *Mueller*, the Court divided largely along ideological lines, the Court's liberals, Brennan, Marshall, Blackmun and Stevens, voted for a strict separationist result, the conservatives, Burger, Rehnquist and White, favoured accommodationism. Powell and O'Connor thus held the balance but their influence was not so strong that they could shape the final opinion. Powell provided the liberals with their fifth vote but the tone and structure of Brennan's opinion reflected little of the balancing evident in Powell's *Nyquist* and *Wolman* opinions. In both majority opinions, the heavy emphasis on the 'pervasively sectarian' nature of the schools involved and the dominant role it played in determining the outcome signalled a far greater concern for the symbolic nature of the relationship between religion and government than had been evident in other cases. Combined with a similar ideological division in *Mueller*, *Aguilar* and *Ball* signalled that the pragmatism of earlier years was coming to an end.

Significant among the *Aguilar* dissents was that of Justice O'Connor. As the newest member of the Court, her view of church-state relations and the Establishment Clause was least well known. Appointed by Reagan in 1981 to fill the seat left vacant by Potter Stewart's resignation, O'Connor was viewed as 'a sometime conservative with a moderate, even progressive streak'.[84] Initially sceptical, the conservative right embraced O'Connor over the course of her first year as she voted with Rehnquist in 123 of 139 cases, a closer relationship than that between Rehnquist and Burger.[85] In Religion Clause cases, however, O'Connor appeared closer to the pragmatists of the early Burger years than to the conservatives. Given her position as a potential swing vote on the Court, two particular elements of O'Connor's opinion were significant. The first was her rejection of the idea expressed so clearly by the majority that the 'pervasively sectarian' nature of religious schools made them constitutionally suspect. Removing this initial hurdle of suspicion made defending programmes of aid less difficult. The second was her challenge to the on-campus/off-campus distinction.[86] By identifying a potential inconsistency in the argument rather than simply attacking it as wrong, O'Connor offered the first significant challenge to the long-standing category. For justices looking to secure her support in future cases, these two areas were potential starting points, either of which could alter fundamental thinking about the Establishment Clause.

Reaction to *Aguilar* and *Ball* was mixed but largely predictable. Education groups such as the American Federation of Teachers, liberal Jewish groups, and secular organizations such as the American Civil Liberties Union (ACLU) and People for the American Way lauded the decision as both a strengthening of the separation of church and state and a reaffirmation of the Court's 'determination to protect our nation's public schools'.[87] Brother James Kearney, superintendent of schools for the New York diocese, called the rulings 'a blow to fairness and justice for poor and needy children', a sentiment echoed by the US Catholic Conference, whose spokesman, Richard Duffy, responded: 'The Court with remarkable ease has nullified legislative judgments aimed to assist the education of school children in Grand Rapids and New York City'.[88] Amid the political debates, school boards across the country began the process of finding alternative ways to supply remedial services to religious school students as mandated by Title I. Off-site services, educational television and mobile vans were among the earliest suggestions. 'We'll have to come up with some new ways of doing it', commented Gwen Gregory, deputy legal counsel to the National School Boards Association, who also indicated that she would prefer Congress to eliminate the religious school requirement entirely.[89] The Reagan Administration's reaction was twofold. Education Secretary William Bennett and Attorney General Edwin Meese both publicly denounced the Court and the two rulings, promising to find new ways to get Title I funds to religious school students that did not violate the Court's requirements.[90] In addition, the Administration renewed its efforts to pass through Congress a bill providing school vouchers for poor families, a new approach to the 'choice' debate. After *Aguilar*, the Reagan Administration repeatedly attempted to legislate for school vouchers, partly as a way to circumvent the Court's decision, but also as an integral part of a long-standing campaign to broaden educational choice to all parents. Congress showed little interest and another of Reagan's plans for American education faded away as states adjusted to newly organized methods of providing Title I services to students within their borders.

Concluding Thoughts

The era of the Burger Court is crucial for any understanding of the history of the Establishment Clause. In the years between *Lemon* in 1971 and *Aguilar* and *Ball* in 1985 the Court heard more school aid cases than the combined total of the Vinson and Warren Courts before it and the Rehnquist Court after it. The Court under Burger inherited a fledgling constitutional issue for which no previous Court had developed a clear approach and not only developed a test for constitutionality, but then applied that test more or less consistently for more than a decade. The Burger Court is also important because of the impact of economic problems on the overall perception of the role played by religious schools. The first has all too often been misjudged, the second too frequently neglected as a contributing factor.

Much of the criticism of the Burger Court rests on two foundations: that the Court shifted from a jurisprudence of strict separation to one allowing greater interaction between church and state, and that the decisions reached by the Court were inconsistent and incoherent. However, contrary to separationist belief, the Supreme Court never held to the idea that church and state must be completely separate. In nearly every major school aid case the Court made clear that complete separation was not possible in the modern United States. Representations of Court decisions implying that by striking down aid programmes the Court was supporting strict separation were fundamentally misleading and led to as much confusion about the Court's jurisprudence as did the lack of clarity in the opinions themselves.

The criticism of inconsistency comes from a comparison of results, or outcomes, of the Court's cases. Looking beyond the results to consider the justices' approach to such cases presents a fundamentally different picture. From this perspective, the Court's opinions from *Everson* in 1947 to *Aguilar* and *Ball* in 1985 show that the justices adhered to a series of firm, yet uncodified, considerations when assessing the constitutionality of statutes: whether the aid was direct or indirect, financial or material, provided on or off religious school campuses, or was provided to individuals or institutions. In every major school aid case one, and usually more, of these requirements was considered by the justices. Rather than superseding these elements, the *Lemon* test embraced them and loosely codified them into a coherent test that could be applied by lower courts. One consequence of such an approach was a need to undertake a detailed consideration of the exact operation of the challenged programme. The result was a series of narrowly tailored opinions that spoke little to programmes similar, but not identical, to those challenged in the case under consideration and a jurisprudence based heavily upon specific factual situations where a minor change in a programme's operation could lead to a significantly different result.[91] An additional consequence was frequent disagreement over the 'relevant' facts of the case; yet rather than evidence of inconsistency, such disagreements appear to be little more than the normal disagreements found between nine individuals on any subject.

Crucial to the development of the Burger Court's jurisprudence was the influence of the justices at the Court's centre. Particularly noticeable as the Burger Court sought to construct a coherent approach to Establishment cases was the influence of factions within the Court, the development of predictable groups based on individual justices' philosophies and approaches to interpreting the Establishment Clause.[92] Between 1969 and 1985 clear separationist and accommodationist blocs developed on the Burger Court, neither able to form a majority without the concurrence of one or more of the swing voters: Harlan, Stewart, Blackmun and Powell. This gave these four justices substantial influence over the structure and content of opinions where they guaranteed the majority. Although all four had different views and approaches to deciding cases, their jurisprudence was characterized by pragmatism and a wariness of unquestioned adherence to tests, arguably the dominant characteristics of the Burger Court's school aid jurisprudence. More than any other, Powell symbolized the pragmatism of the Burger Court era, voting with the majority more times than any other justice with whom he sat. Moderating the more extreme views of either the accommodationists or separationists, the justices of the centre bloc accounted for much of the tenor and shape of the Burger Court's Establishment cases.

Equally important in understanding the development of the Establishment Clause and in thinking about the church-state relationship in this era are the economic difficulties faced by the country and the political debates that emerged as a result. The Court's decisions set the parameters of the Establishment Clause, the outer edges of permissibility, but those limits were tested, challenged and clarified because the economic climate pushed legislators to consider new options for funding education. The frequency with which the Court was asked to address or clarify Establishment issues was a direct result of states seeking alternative funding arrangements. The combination of economic pressures and a general sense of public disillusionment with public schools created the conditions within which educators and politicians began to search for ways in which to improve education. The presence of religious schools was not new, but the social and economic circumstances put their contributions in a new, more favourable light. Across the country, legislators began to see that religious schools provided education at a frequently lower per pupil cost than public schools, and that for relatively small amounts of additional funding such schools relieved state budgets and public schools of a significant burden. Religious schools thus came to be seen as providing a public good at more than one level.

Politicians and educators were able to view religious schools in this way as a result of two major changes: the greater integration of Catholics into American society and the changing nature of the religious school universe. Earlier school aid debates had been hindered by a persistent anti-Catholicism, or at least a view of Catholics and their schools as insular, different and divisive. As the twentieth century concluded its third quarter that perception had changed as a result of factors internal and external to the Catholic Church and community. At the same time, other faith groups began to invest in their own schools, spurred on by an increased desire for religiously influenced education and a growing sense of dissatisfaction with the nation's public schools. As the number of Jewish and Protestant schools increased, the religious school universe became less a metaphor for Catholic schools and more a reflection of an increasingly diverse group of educational institutions. Catholic schools were still in the majority, but were nothing like as dominant as before. Thus school aid could be discussed as a benefit to members of different faith groups, and earlier criticisms of such policies being a cover for payments to Catholic schools became less frequent and less valid.

The Court's decisions both shaped and reflected this changing image. By allowing indirect benefits to religious schools through parents or pupils, the Court allowed states to experiment with school aid programmes and consider religious schools valid participants. Had the Court taken the path of strict separation such debates would have been unlikely or impossible. Equally, the justices were aware of, and often sympathetic to, the situation in which states and schools found themselves. In conference on *Lemon*, Chief Justice Burger commented, 'I am troubled by these cases ... I am influenced by the financial crisis that exists'.[93] Though the justices were unlikely to blatantly write such sympathies into constitutional law, the Court's deference to legislative decision-making in cases where clear Establishment Clause violations were absent is suggestive of a willingness to accept new arrangements given the existing circumstances. Thus the full scope and significance of the Burger Court's decisions cannot be understood separate from their political, economic and social context.

Chapter 3

Accommodation Triumphant? The Rehnquist Court

By the mid-1980s the nature of school aid debates had changed significantly from those of the 1940s. No longer were school aid programmes immediately suspected of being 'Catholic school aid programmes', and discussion of such policies rarely resulted in the kinds of religious division seen in earlier eras. The coming of the Cold War, encouraging Americans to turn to faith as a form of protection against the dangers of Communism, the greater openness of the Catholic Church after Vatican II and the experience of the Kennedy Administration combined to change public perception about the place of Catholics in American life and to calm the anti-Catholicism that had driven many of the earlier debates. The nation's economic problems in the 1970s led politicians to see in religious schools, now comprised of significant numbers of Jewish and Protestant as well as Catholic schools, a public benefit rather than a divisive threat. Politicians such as Governor Nelson Rockefeller in New York and Governor William Cahill in New Jersey openly advocated aid to religious schools, asserting their educational achievements and their benefit to stretched state budgets. And, as Americans lost faith in their public schools, especially in the inner cities, religious schools appeared to offer better education, better discipline and a more attractive option to many parents.

The role of the Supreme Court was also important in shaping debates on school aid. In case after case between *Everson v. Board of Education* in 1947 and *Grand Rapids School District v. Ball* in 1985 the Court held that school aid programmes could be acceptable under certain conditions. The Establishment Clause did not, the Court consistently argued, require the complete separation of church and state in the field of education programmes. By upholding those programmes which met the criteria of the *Lemon* test, the Court gave legitimacy to state programmes aimed at benefiting students or parents which indirectly also benefited religious schools. In its cases the Court established the outer limits of the Establishment Clause, indicating that there was room for experimentation within those boundaries. In doing so the Court also granted legitimacy, where it was necessary, to the educational role played by religious schools. While strict separationists continued to criticize the Court and its rulings in this area, after more than forty years of debate the separationist and accommodationist arguments were well rehearsed, their respective advocates well known and familiar with one another: they were no less divided but the familiarity of the arguments made took much of the earlier heat out of the debates.

Much of the Burger Court's jurisprudence, however, rested on the role of the Court's centrist justices as swing votes between the separationist and accommodationist blocs on the Court. But, as *Aguilar* and *Ball* had hinted, the control of the centre was declining as the Burger Court came to an end. A change of personnel, or a change of thinking by one or more of the justices, held the potential to significantly alter the direction of the Court's Establishment Clause jurisprudence.

Laying the Foundations for Change

In 1986, the final year of the Burger Court, the justices addressed the extension of state financial assistance to a blind student pursuing a Bible studies degree at a Christian college under a Washington state statute providing rehabilitation assistance to the blind. *Witters v. Washington Department of Services for the Blind* (1986) allowed the aid to continue with all nine justices, in a rare moment of Establishment Clause unity, agreeing that this aid could in no way be considered a benefit to the religious institution. The case undermines the argument of those who suggest *Aguilar v. Felton* (1985) was evidence of the Court's 'return' to strict separation: the American Civil Liberties Union, Americans United for the Separation of Church and State and the Anti-Defamation League, all long-standing advocates of strict separation, filed *amicus* briefs opposing the statute. Equally, *Witters* is disappointing for those who argue that *Aguilar* was evidence of the emergence of entanglement as the most significant part of any *Lemon* analysis: the Court rejected any entanglement analysis on the grounds of an insufficient record and no lower court decision on the matter, hardly evidence of entanglement gone mad.[1] In many ways, *Witters* was similar to the opinions in *Allen, Nyquist, Meek* and *Wolman* in that the opinion was narrowly tailored to the specific facts of the case and made no sweeping statements of doctrine or principle.[2] The content of the Court's opinion in

Witters was unremarkable: it restated the applicability of *Lemon*, found a valid secular purpose in promoting the 'well-being of the visually handicapped through the provision of vocational rehabilitation', and found the aid was provided to individuals and not institutions, thereby falling under the long-standing direct-indirect aid distinction.[3] The opinion appeared designed to avoid any potential area of doctrinal controversy.

In terms of its actual impact on Establishment Clause doctrine, *Witters* was relatively unimportant. However, differences highlighted by the three concurrences signalled a new debate on the Court. The debate began in December 1985 when Justice Lewis Powell responded to circulation of the first draft of Justice Thurgood Marshall's majority opinion with a suggestion that *Mueller v. Allen* provided better support for the argument being made. Marshall refused the suggestion, responding: 'I continue to believe that the Mueller [in original] case was wrongly decided, and am concerned that extensive discussion of it would only muddy the waters here'.[4] In *Mueller*, Marshall had objected to the tax deduction for educational expenses because, he argued, it provided a direct financial subsidy to religious schools since the deduction in reality only benefited religious parents and thus subsidized a religious choice. *Witters* differed because no greater aid was received by individuals attending religious colleges, thus ensuring the funds went to a religious college because of the free, unfettered choice of Larry Witters. In both cases, Marshall's analytical starting point was the institution receiving the aid. For Powell, *Mueller* meant that if a programme was directed towards individuals, the institution receiving the aid was less important than whether those eligible for the programme were defined according to religion. Because this was not the case in either *Mueller* or *Witters* the effect was to aid the individual and any aid reaching religious schools or colleges was no longer state-provided: the individual broke the link between church and state. In this approach, the focus of attention was on the eligibility criteria. The debate was not new: eligibility criteria played a part in decisions in *Nyquist* and *Meek*. What made *Witters* significant was that Justices Sandra Day O'Connor, Lewis Powell, William Rehnquist and Byron White and Chief Justice Burger, the *Mueller* majority, all concurred with the latter approach, effectively reaffirming *Mueller* even though the ostensible majority opinion made no reference to the case.[5] The balance on the Court also showed post-*Aguilar* and *Ball* claims of a 're-emergence' of strict separation in Establishment Clause jurisprudence were premature. The concentration on the issue of neutral eligibility criteria in *Witters*, combined with the *Aguilar* dissenters' views of religious institutions, indicated potential for a fundamental shift in the Court's approach to school aid cases.

The change came seven years later in *Zobrest v. Catalina Hills School District*, although because of the limited scope of the case the full significance of the shift did not become evident until later. *Zobrest* involved Arizona's refusal to provide a sign-language interpreter to a profoundly deaf student, James Zobrest, under the Individuals with Disabilities Education Act (IDEA) on the grounds that he attended a Roman Catholic high school. Providing an interpreter in such a situation, argued appellees and the four dissenting justices, amounted to a state subsidy of the religious function of the school since James Zobrest could not learn without such aid and would 'authorize[. . .] a public employee to participate directly in religious indoctrination' in an 'ongoing, daily, and intimate' fashion.[6] The majority rejected such claims and in doing so authorized the presence of a public employee with a significant role to play in the education of a child on religious school grounds for the first time.[7] Although the majority opinion rested on the understanding that an interpreter was little more than a conduit for information, adding nothing of substance in the transmission from teacher to student, the precedent was set: publicly financed aid to students attending religious schools no longer automatically had to be provided at off-campus locations. Combined with the ruling in *Witters* and a shift away from the 'pervasively sectarian' portrayal of religious schools, *Zobrest* provided the foundation upon which the Court rested to reject its longest standing line of demarcation.

Justice Rehnquist's opinion for the majority contained two key arguments. First was the issue of broad eligibility criteria. In suggesting past concern with eligibility, Rehnquist accurately drew on the Court's jurisprudence but his emphasis on that issue over the religious nature of the institution involved was a reversal of earlier opinions. Relying solely on *Mueller* and *Witters*, the two school aid cases which exhibited a similar preference for the issue of eligibility, Rehnquist suggested that facial neutrality alone might be sufficient to withstand an Establishment Clause challenge, a remarkable shift from the Court's holdings in *Meek v. Pittenger* (1975) and *Wolman v. Walter* (1977) that eligibility was only a threshold issue.[8] The apparent lack of concern about James Zobrest's attendance at a Catholic school was reinforced by the absence of any explicit mention of the *Lemon* test. The test was premised on the understanding that as religious institutions, religious schools were immediately suspect and only limited types of aid could flow to them. Rejecting this as 'smacking of antiquated notions of taint' and ignoring the traditional *Lemon* criteria, Rehnquist implied that the majority were no longer concerned with institutions but with the operation of the programmes of aid.[9] The second area of concern, the role of the individual in Establishment Clause cases, had been addressed by Rehnquist in *Mueller*; in *Zobrest* the argument was much the same but easier to make since the programme was challenged with respect to one individual, unlike *Mueller* where a whole class of people was implicated. That the aid in *Zobrest* was provided to an individual was uncontroversial and the dissent did not challenge it: in *Everson*, *Allen*, *Nyquist* and *Meek* the Court had accepted that aid genuinely provided to individuals did not create an impermissible link between church and state. In that respect, Rehnquist continued the Court's approach. The significance of the role of the individual in *Zobrest*, however, lay in its combination with the Court's rejection of immediate suspicion of religious schools; together they shifted the Court's focus away from religious schools and towards a programme's eligibility criteria, a far more lenient standard for allowing aid under the Establishment Clause.

Brief consideration of the central disagreement between the majority and dissent highlights this change.[10] In earlier cases the Court had distinguished between neutral forms of aid that could not be diverted to religious purposes and aid that conceivably might require monitoring to ensure no Establishment Clause violation: the former was constitutional, the latter constitutionally suspect. For the majority, the signer was nothing more than a conduit for information, no less neutral than the textbooks or auxiliary services staff the Court had previously allowed. In a thoughtful and compelling dissent, Blackmun challenged such an interpretation. 'In an environment so pervaded by discussions of the divine, the interpreter's every gesture would be infused with religious significance', Blackmun asserted, arguing that the interpreter was not a neutral conduit but an aid to religious education.[11] For Blackmun and Souter, who joined the dissent, the fact that the signer must pass on religious teachings, possibly including Catholic mass, was sufficient to violate the Constitution: it was irrelevant that the religious message did not originate with the signer since he or she must transmit it to the student, thereby implicating them in the religious mission of the school. When paid for with state funds this equated to state financing of religious indoctrination. In this debate the signer became either a religiously neutral aide through whom religion was passed or an active participant in religious indoctrination. The dissenters were influenced by the fact the signer was present on religious school grounds and that the school was pervasively sectarian. The majority, however, ignored this and concentrated on eligibility criteria. The debate over the role fulfilled by the signer thus became an extension of the debate about where the Court's attention should be focused: the programme or the institution. The dissenters' position was far closer to that advocated by the Burger Court; the majority opinion showed the shift the Court had taken.

The Court's shift was the result of a number of factors. First, the change of personnel on the Court between *Witters* and *Zobrest* had a significant impact. Between the two cases, William Brennan, Marshall and Powell retired from the Court to be replaced by Anthony Kennedy, Antonin Scalia, David Souter and Clarence Thomas. The Burger Court's leading liberals and consistent strict separationists, Brennan and Marshall, had gone, along with Powell, arguably the epitome of the Burger Court's pragmatism. Scalia and Thomas were known conservatives and favourable towards accommodation in religion cases; Souter was a relative unknown; and Kennedy, although a moderate conservative, had shown evidence of a balancing approach to the Establishment Clause when he switched votes during the consideration of *Lee v. Weisman* the year before *Zobrest*.[12] With the loss of two strict separationists and the arrival of two accommodationists, the balance of the Court tipped more favourably towards the latter, especially in those cases where the swing votes of O'Connor and Kennedy could be won. Thus, only clear violations of the Establishment Clause were likely to be struck down by the Court.

Second, the Court's approach to equal access cases increasingly appeared in school aid cases. Because equal access usually involved use of public school facilities, the question of the religious nature of the institution did not arise, and the Court had generally taken an approach closer to that of free exercise and free speech cases: religious and secular groups had to be treated equally unless there was good reason not to do so. This approach placed a greater burden on those seeking limits on school aid to prove why religion should be treated differently, a factor in *Zobrest* and, to a lesser extent, in *Witters*. While the approach made sense in the context of equal access, in the arena of school aid it undermined traditional principles of wariness about religious institutions, a principle upon which the Court's Establishment Clause jurisprudence was originally founded. The overall effect was to create an easier test for constitutionality which focused on the point of entry to the programme while downplaying the importance of potential church-state interaction within the programme itself.

Third, the role of precedent was also a factor. *Witters* and *Zobrest* rested on the role of the individual and facially neutral programmes of aid, both of which had been Establishment concerns since *Everson*. The danger inherent in the Court's use of uncodified guiding principles was that with changed personnel there might be a shift in the relative importance of those principles. This is what happened with *Zobrest*: the accommodationists did not discard past approaches, they simply modified them. In *Zobrest*, Rehnquist found a majority for bringing eligibility criteria to greater prominence, as he had advocated in dicta in *Mueller* a decade earlier. While not entirely discarding the rest of the Burger Court's concerns, by making eligibility the threshold issue other factors were held to be unnecessary or irrelevant unless recipients were identified by religion. These were fundamental changes in the Court's approach, achieved within existing modes of analysis.

An additional factor in the Court's shifting perception was the changing nature of the religious school universe. Major changes occurred within the realm of religious schools between the early 1970s and the 1990s that effected a shift in public perception about benefits to such institutions. Arguably the biggest change came within Catholic schools. Originally the epitome of the 'pervasively sectarian', insular parochial school, by the 1990s Catholic schools served large numbers of poor, minority, non-Catholic students. In 1970, non-Catholic enrolment stood at 2.7 per cent, by 1990 this had increased to 14.3 per cent nationally. In the nation's inner-city schools the figures were frequently higher: in Chicago, non-Catholic enrolment stood at 40 per cent, in individual schools in Harlem and Chinatown in New York the figure was as high as 70 per cent.[13] The trend was the result of increased enrolment generally in religious schools, fuelled in part by continued disillusion with the public schools. Research by Andrew Greeley, James Coleman and others in the 1980s showed that Catholic schools could provide better educational results than public schools at a lower cost per student, mainly because of effective discipline, lack of bureaucracy and an atmosphere of spiritual commitment.[14] Despite criticisms of these studies they appeared to reflect wider public opinion. 'My three children in the sixth, fourth, and third grades at St. Aloysius started in the public schools. They are getting a better education here, learning the fundamentals. I believe religion is the lesser evil when you think of what's out there', one atheist father told the *New York Times* in 1988. A Muslim mother with two children in Catholic schools told the same reporter, 'It is organised. I like the close supervision. With any religion one's beliefs may differ, but are not the principles the same? They all teach honesty, humility'.[15] As Catholic schools served increasingly large non-Catholic student populations, the perception of them as religious enclaves dedicated solely to the perpetuation of the faith could no longer be maintained. Although some Catholic educators expressed doubts about the continued mission of Catholic schools serving large numbers of non-Catholics, the majority of schools maintained elements of Catholic religious instruction to which few parents, Catholic or otherwise, objected, considering it an integral part of the schools' mission. Catholic schools remained recognizably 'Catholic', but the change in staff and student composition ensured they were not the dogmatic, insular schools of an earlier era.[16]

Also influencing the world of the religious schools was the rise throughout the 1970s and 1980s of Jewish day schools, Christian schools and fundamentalist Protestant schools.[17] Of the three, the fundamentalist schools represented the fastest growing and most politically influential. Ironically, they also closely resembled the Catholic schools of the nineteenth century in terms of mission and outlook. For many of the same reasons that parents had earlier turned to Catholic schools, fundamentalist parents began establishing their own schools to teach their own religious beliefs and to counteract their perceived growth of 'secular humanism' in public school curricula. German Baptists, Nazarenes and Assembly of God congregations were among those involved in the movement. By 1980, enrolment in such schools reached one million for the first time.[18] Thus, by the 1990s opponents of school aid could no longer claim that it would benefit only one religious group at the expense of others. Approximately 50 per cent of private school students in 1991 attended Catholic schools compared to 90 per cent in 1971, while Catholic schools constituted only 30 per cent of religious schools, compared to 65 per cent when *Lemon* was decided.[19]

In addition, religious schools could no longer be accused of perpetuating racial segregation. Catholic schools in inner-city areas served increasing numbers of minority students leading one scholar to note, '[w]hen religious preference[s] [are] taken into account ... blacks attend Catholic secondary schools in higher proportions than do whites or Hispanics'.[20] Equally, Black churches began extending their traditional mission of serving the community by soliciting money from private foundations and government sources to establish educational programmes of their own.[21] By the mid-1990s, National Center for Education Statistics' figures showed the number of African-Americans attending conservative Christian schools had reached 12 per cent, nearly double the 1991 figure, and significantly higher than the first years of such schools when they were often established to be bastions of segregation.[22]

Such diversity within and among religious schools made more traditional arguments against school aid harder to make. While schools provided a religious education, some more strictly than others, public funds directed to all students attending religious schools could no longer be portrayed as benefiting one religious group or expressing favouritism towards a particular belief. Given that the Supreme Court's precedents rested heavily on such arguments, these changes suggested the possibility of a fundamental change in Court doctrine.

The Court Changes Direction: *Agostini v. Felton*

The consequences of the changes seen in *Mueller, Witters* and *Zobrest* became clear in the Supreme Court's 1997 ruling in *Agostini v. Felton*. The case was, in effect, an appeal from the Court's *Aguilar* decision twelve years earlier, involving the same programme and many of the same schools. As a result of *Aguilar*, New York City's Board of Education modified its Title I programme so that it could continue serving students in private religious schools. The solution was to provide remedial educational services on public school campuses, at leased sites or in mobile instructional units parked near the religious schools, often simply across the street. In part, the shift was merely a return to a pre-*Aguilar* practice, but it reflected the Court's stance in *Aguilar* that it was not the programme *per se* which violated the First Amendment, but how and where that programme operated. By the time *Agostini* reached the Supreme Court, it was estimated that a decade of '*Aguilar* costs' had cost the school board more than $100 million, costs which were deducted from Title I funds, reducing by an estimated 28,000 the number of New York City students aided by Title I.[23] Noting that these costs were anticipated in *Aguilar*, Justice O'Connor's opinion for the Court in *Agostini* nevertheless took pains to note the negative impact of the *Aguilar* ruling, suggesting it was an issue of some importance to the justices.[24] This was reinforced at the end of the opinion:

> Indeed, under these circumstances, it would be particularly inequitable for us to bide our time waiting for another case to arise while the city of New York labors under a continuing injunction forcing it to spend millions of dollars on mobile instructional units and leased sites when it could instead be spending that money to give educationally disadvantaged children a better chance at success in life by means of a program that is perfectly consistent with the Establishment Clause.[25]

In a 5:4 decision, in *Agostini* the Court, for the first time in Establishment Clause cases, overruled itself and held that New York's Title I programme did not violate the Constitution.

For those who already held doubts about the consistency, durability and logic of the Supreme Court's Establishment Clause jurisprudence, *Agostini* confirmed their worst fears. Not only had the Court overruled previous cases, an event notable in itself, it had apparently done so, critics argued, by explicitly rejecting the premises on which Establishment Clause jurisprudence had stood since *Everson* in 1947.[26] For the first time the Supreme

Court had allowed significant numbers of public employees to enter religious schools and rejected the long-standing belief that this created an impermissible commingling of the functions of church and state, outraging strict separationists both on and off the Court. The changing perception of the nature of religious schools and the function of teachers was also a striking characteristic of the *Agostini* ruling and one that the Court subsequently applied in later cases.[27] What critics of the decision singularly failed to note, however, was that these changes had not occurred suddenly or without warning.[28] What was different about *Agostini* as compared to *Witters* or *Zobrest* was that it applied to a much larger group of people; what was not significantly different was the reasoning employed. *Agostini* did not constitute a change in Supreme Court jurisprudence; it simply consolidated in a high-profile case changes that had already occurred.

In *Zobrest*, Chief Justice Rehnquist criticized the Court's prior holdings as 'smacking of antiquated notions of "taint"'.[29] *Agostini* unequivocally rejected the possibility that the atmosphere of a religious school was so potent that all who entered would be influenced by it.[30] O'Connor's matter-of-fact statement of this position for the Court belied the striking nature of the argument in light of the Court's own precedent. Concern for the 'uncontrollable' nature of certain types of aid had frequently been evident in the Court's opinions. Despite the Court's objection to Stanley Geller's assertion in oral argument of the 'unprofessionalism' of teachers, that was exactly the concern of the majority in *Meek*; that the 'pervasively sectarian' atmosphere of the school would overcome the professionalism and training of those same teachers.[31] *Agostini* thus appeared anomalous; public school employees were permitted to interact freely with religious school staff and students, there were minimal monitoring procedures and access to religious school classrooms was unrestricted within the procedures laid down in the Title I programme. Justice O'Connor explained the reason for the apparent shift with a single sentence repudiation of the Court's traditional portrayal of the all-pervasive force of religion in religious schools: 'we have abandoned the presumption erected in *Meek* and *Ball* that the placement of public employees on parochial school grounds inevitably results in the impermissible effect of state-sponsored indoctrination'.[32]

O'Connor's statement carried a significance belied by its brevity. Virtually all the Court's previous cases had been underpinned by the understanding that religious schools were representatives of the church and could thus only be in receipt of state aid indirectly if the Establishment

Clause was to be maintained. The effect and entanglement prongs of the *Lemon* test were premised on exactly these grounds. Although not stated explicitly, by rejecting this assumption the majority effectively held to be irrelevant, or at least of significantly less importance, all but the purpose prong of *Lemon*. This was reinforced by other arguments in the majority opinion which clarified themes which had been present in *Witters* and *Zobrest*.

Signalling the demise of the on-campus/off-campus test, the Court stated: 'cooperation between Title I instructors and parochial school faculty is the same no matter where the services are provided'.[33] If there is no difference in the level of contact between staff of the respective institutions, whether the classes are taught at the religious school or elsewhere, then there is no real foundation for distinguishing between the two; if the contact violates the First Amendment it does so no matter where the instruction takes place and should be stopped completely; if it does not then it should be freely allowed. O'Connor's opinion also addressed the issue of entanglement. 'Regardless of how we have characterized the issue . . . the factors we use to assess whether an entanglement is "excessive" are similar to the factors we use to examine "effect" . . . Thus, it is simplest to recognize why entanglement is significant and treat it . . . as an aspect of the inquiry into a statute's effect'.[34] Until *Agostini*, entanglement was technically an Establishment Clause violation in its own right, O'Connor's opinion reduced it to no more than one of a number of factors to be considered. In doing so O'Connor did little more than state the approach the Court had generally taken towards entanglement analysis. Its strength, however, was in ending the idea, perpetuated by the Court's own language, that entanglement alone was sufficient to warrant a finding of unconstitutionality. Whereas previous opinions had foundered under the weight of rhetoric or legalisms, O'Connor's opinion sought to be clear and unambiguous. Avoiding the problems of earlier Courts, O'Connor made clear what the Court was looking for in its effects analysis: 'It does not result in governmental indoctrination; define its recipients by reference to religion; or create an excessive entanglement'.[35] The three elements she pointed to expressed the Court's concern for the nature and operation of the programmes and statutes in question and nowhere reflected the now defunct concern about the types of institutions receiving the aid: a new period of Establishment Clause jurisprudence was being ushered in.

Although these changes indicated a greater acceptance by the majority of closer links between government and religion, the Court also made clear that this was not an entirely unrestricted relationship. The use of three particular arguments by the *Agostini* majority linked the opinion to those of an earlier era and highlighted the restraints. As with New Jersey's bus transportation reimbursement programme in *Everson*, the majority argued that the benefit to religious schools of New York's Title I programme was only a result of the children in receipt of the benefit attending such schools; no money was provided to the schools, and the likelihood that more parents might choose a religious school for their children as a result of the programme was considered negligible.[36] Thus, unrestricted grants of aid, whether financial or in kind, remained unconstitutional under *Agostini*. Equally, defining beneficiaries by religious criteria remained unacceptable to the Court: eligibility requirements must remain neutral and secular to pass constitutional scrutiny. Third, the child benefit theory continued to play a significant role in the Court's analysis. *Aguilar*'s critics emphasized that the only real impact of the Court's ruling was to disadvantage further those children already labouring under significant social and economic disadvantages. The effect of the *Agostini* ruling, although not emphasized in the Court's opinion, was to free a significant proportion of Title I funds for providing places for greater numbers of children.[37] Although criticized by some as a smokescreen to cover otherwise blatant benefits to religious institutions, the child benefit theory ensured that programmes must provide some appreciable improvement in the lives and/or education of the individuals involved and that the benefit was received by the individuals, even if there were large numbers of them, and not just the schools. In combination with neutral eligibility criteria it operated to ensure that programmes did not simply provide large grants of aid to religious schools without secular motivations. These limitations were neither as strict nor as pervasive as those of earlier eras, but while the relationship between churches and the state became freer, it was not entirely unrestricted.

The immediate effect of *Agostini* was the end of mobile vans for teaching and the return of public school teachers to religious school classrooms. The $14 million a year charge to the city of New York for the lease and running costs of the 114 mobile classrooms was released to be used to provide places for more disadvantaged students. 'We finally got some common sense', said one high school principal, voicing the complaints of many others about the inconvenience of the *Aguilar* arrangements.[38] Among commentators two issues were raised: the problem of church-state separation in which traditional lines were drawn and familiar arguments repeated, and the procedural issue by which the case had been decided. Because the Court had not specifically overruled *Aguilar* in cases prior to

Agostini, many saw in the Court's approach a 'willingness to sidestep normal procedures' in order to provide relief in New York City and allow a greater accommodation between church and state. The argument had strong support: it was the focus of the dissent filed by Justice Ruth Bader Ginsburg, in which Justices John Paul Stevens, David Souter and Stephen Breyer joined.[39] Support for the ruling came from those who saw common sense and pragmatism in the Court's opinion. 'The Court correctly understood that it was absurd for New York City . . . to have to spend $100 million in Federal education money to lease vans for use as classrooms so that public school teachers would not have to set foot in religious schools to teach remedial students', argued one defender.[40] Although *Agostini* was controversial and much political and academic comment followed the announcement of the opinion, the debate was not as heated as it had been in earlier cases. Two reasons in particular account for this. First, fifty years of Establishment Clause debate had refined arguments on every side of the issue: reactions from the American Civil Liberties Union, Committee for Public Education and Religious Liberty and various Catholic groups were predictable and well rehearsed. There were no surprises to cause tension. Second, the decision had been widely anticipated in the wake of *Witters*, *Zobrest* and a 1994 decision in *Board of Education of Kiryas Joel v. Grumet* in which five justices had expressed dissatisfaction with *Aguilar*.[41] While these factors did little to lessen the divisions between separationists and accommodationists, they did ensure a more moderate, thoughtful debate between the groups that was far less politically divisive than debates of an earlier era.

Agostini gave new impetus to the school choice debates that had been in existence since the early 1980s. As perception of urban public schools as places of low academic achievement, poor discipline and limited resources continued, so did discussion about alternatives to public schools. Under Reagan, tax credits or deductions had been the proposed method of broadening private school availability; by the early 1990s, choice advocates were looking for additional ways to provide alternatives to the public schools. By far the most frequently advocated proposal was for school vouchers: governments would provide to parents a 'voucher' for a predetermined value that could be put towards tuition costs at public or private schools. Rarely did the voucher cover the full cost of non-public school tuition, and only occasionally did voucher plans include religious schools. By the time the Supreme Court handed down its decision in *Agostini*, California, Colorado, Connecticut, New York, Ohio, Oregon, Vermont, Washington DC and Wisconsin had all debated voucher plans, although only in Cleveland and

Milwaukee had plans been put into operation. *Agostini* did not speak to the voucher debate but the Court's greater openness to large-scale programmes of aid to religious school students, along with the perceived abandonment of strict separation, held out hope to voucher supporters that they might receive a more sympathetic hearing. Against that, *Agostini* involved non-financial aid to individuals whereas vouchers raised the spectre of direct financial grants to religious schools nominally provided to parents. The openness of the legal issue combined with a continuing search for improved education suggested that new relationships between religion and government in the area of education would require the continued mediation of the Supreme Court.

Concluding Thoughts

The Court's position in *Agostini* echoed through the Rehnquist Court's subsequent school aid decisions. In *Mitchell v. Helms* (2000), the Court in a 6:3 decision upheld Louisiana's practice of providing instructional materials to students in public and religious schools. In doing so the Court overturned parts of *Meek v. Pittenger* (1975) and *Wolman v. Walter* (1977). With the decline of the nature of the institution as an issue of importance in school aid cases the result was anticipated: the grounds on which *Meek* and *Wolman* were decided had been eroded by *Zobrest* and, specifically, by *Agostini*. In 2002, the Court rejected a challenge to Cleveland's school voucher programme in an opinion narrowly tailored to the specifics of the city's statute in *Zelman v. Simmons-Harris*. Again, the criteria for participation in the programme outweighed the nature of the institutions involved for the 5:4 majority. In addition, *Zelman* confirmed the Rehnquist Court's move away from the financial versus non-financial aid distinction of the Burger Court that had been hinted at by Rehnquist in *Mueller v. Allen* in 1983. The trend seen in *Witters*, *Zobrest* and *Agostini* was thus continued by the Rehnquist Court.

The Rehnquist Court accepted far closer links between church and state than previous Courts. Crucial to understanding this shift was the changing personnel on the Court. The larger number of justices personally and philosophically sympathetic to accommodation was as central to the Rehnquist Court's jurisprudence as the centrist justices had been to the Burger Court. Rehnquist, Scalia and Thomas joined White in advocating closer church-state relations. Also O'Connor and Kennedy were more sympathetic to the inclusion of religious school students in government aid programmes than the swing voters of the Burger Court, and only one of them was required for the accommodationists to secure a majority.[42] However, Justices Breyer, Ginsburg, Souter and Stevens formed a reliable separationist bloc more than capable of attracting O'Connor or Kennedy if the circumstances were right. Although sympathetic to accommodation, Kennedy and O'Connor never accepted the constitutionality of all aid programmes and O'Connor in particular required the presence of restrictions and limitations. Those seeking a majority were required to adapt and modify approaches to attract the votes of either one or both justices. Neither *Witters, Zobrest* nor *Agostini* advocated an unlimited, unregulated relationship between church and state. But while claims of the demise of the Establishment Clause are somewhat exaggerated, it is clear that the conservative majority of the Rehnquist Court accepted far more church-state interaction in education than any previous Court had permitted.

As in the Burger era, the educational circumstances also played a role in shaping the Court's approach to school aid cases. By the mid-1980s the religious school universe was changing; increasing numbers of Jewish and Protestant schools diversified the range of religious schools in many states while continued dissatisfaction with inner-city public schools saw a vastly increased non-Catholic population attending Catholic schools. The religious school of 1990 was significantly different from the religious school of 1950, allowing for the rejection of the earlier suspicion that the religiosity of religious schools was so high that the provision of any aid violated the Establishment Clause. A majority of the justices on the Court recognized this change as significant to Establishment Clause jurisprudence, altering, as it did, the circumstances in which challenged programmes operated. This adaptation to broader circumstances had precedent: Black had considered state practices on bus transportation in *Everson*. As immediate suspicion of links with religious schools declined, so did the need for the on-/off-campus distinction and the direct/indirect test. Instead, the majority's concern shifted to eligibility criteria: were a programme's participants chosen as a result of religious criteria, if so the programme was constitutionally suspect, if not, the programme was valid.

A minority of the Court disagreed, especially Justices Stevens and Souter, seeing in the majority's altered emphasis a desire for greater accommodation not a genuine reinterpretation of the Establishment Clause. For this group, religious schools remained suspect because they were religious: changed circumstances, they argued, did not extend to a decline in the schools' religious mission and so they remained religious institutions with which government must maintain only limited contacts. The inability of the minority to regularly win the votes of Kennedy or O'Connor emphasized the importance of both the Court's composition and the impact of the changing perception of the role of religious schools. Division on those grounds was also significant for the fact that it represented, for the first time, a significant disagreement about the basic principles for deciding Establishment cases.

Accommodation Triumphant? The Rehnquist Court 77

Table 1 School Aid Cases: Dates, Rulings, Authors

Year	Case	Court Holding	Vote	Author	Concurrences (Author in bold)	Dissents (Author in bold)
1947	*Everson v. Board of Education of Ewing Township* 330 US 1	New Jersey policy of reimbursing parents for cost of sending children to religious schools did not violate the Constitution. (Affirmed the New Jersey Court of Errors and Appeals).	5:4	Black		**Jackson** with Frankfurter **Rutledge** with Frankfurter, Burton and Jackson
1948	*McCollum v. Board of Education* 333 US 203	Released Time for religious instruction on public school grounds unconstitutional. (Overturned Illinois Supreme Court ruling that the programme did not violate the Constitution).	8:1	Black	**Frankfurter** with Rutledge, Burton and Jackson **Jackson**	Reed
1952	*Zorach v. Clauson* 343 US 306	Released Time for religious instruction conducted off public school campuses does not violate the Constitution. (Affirmed New York Court of Appeals ruling on similar grounds).	6:3	Douglas		**Black** **Frankfurter** **Jackson**
1968	*Board of Education v. Allen* 392 US 236	Loan of secular textbooks to students attending religious schools constitutional. (Affirmed New York Court of Appeals' ruling that textbook loan was neutral with respect to religion and therefore did not violate the Establishment Clause).	6:3	White	Harlan	**Black** **Douglas** **Fortas**
1970	*Walz v. Tax Commission of the City of New York* 397 US 664	Tax exemptions for property owned by churches do not violate the Establishment Clause. (Affirmed ruling of New York Court of Appeals).	7:1	Burger	Brenman Harlan	Douglas

(*Continued*)

Table 1 (Continued) School Aid Cases: Dates, Rulings, Authors

Year	Case	Court Holding	Vote	Author	Concurrences (Author in bold)	Dissents (Author in bold)
1971	Lemon v. Kurtzman (including Earley v. Di Censo and Robinson v. DiCenso 403 US 602)	Pennsylvania's reimbursement of religious schools for cost of secular books, instructional materials and teachers' salaries violated the Constitution (*Lemon*). Rhode Island policy of supplementing religious school teachers' salaries by up to 15% for those teaching secular subjects also found unconstitutional (*Earley* and *Robinson*). (Marshall does not participate in case). (Overturned District Court ruling in *Lemon* that found no constitutional violation; affirmed District Court finding of unconstitutionality in *DiCenso*)	8:0 (*Lemon*) 7:1 (*Di Censo*)	Burger	**White** (in *Lemon*) **Douglas** with Black **Brennan**	**White** (in *Di Censo*)
1973	*Committee for Public Education and Religious Liberty (CPERL) v. Nyquist* 413 US 756	Striking down a New York statute providing maintenance and repair costs to religious schools. (Affirmed decision of District Court).	8:1	Powell	**Rehnquist** with Burger and White	**White**
		Striking down a New York statute providing tuition reimbursement and tax deduction for parents of children attending non-public schools. (Overturned District Court's ruling that such programmes did not violate the Constitution).	6:3	Powell	**Burger** with White and Rehnquist	**Rehnquist** with Burger and White **Burger** with White and Rehnquist

Accommodation Triumphant? The Rehnquist Court

1975	*Meek v. Pittenger* 421 US 349	Upholding loan of secular textbooks to students attending religious schools. (Affirmed ruling of District Court).	6:3	Stewart	**Burger Rehnquist** with White	**Brennan** with Douglas and Marshall
		Striking down loan of instructional materials, including maps, tape recorders and overhead projectors to religious schools. Also holding unconstitutional remedial education, guidance counselling and hearing and speech therapy services provided on religious school grounds. (Affirmed District Court with regards to instructional materials and overturned ruling regarding auxiliary services).	6:3	Stewart	**Brennan** with Douglas and Marshall	**Burger Rehnquist** with White
1977	*Wolman v. Walter* 433 US 229	Ohio programme of aid to religious schools and their students challenged with regard to six separate programmes (all programmes held not to violate the Constitution by the Ohio District Court):				
		Loan of secular textbooks to religious school students held constitutional.	6:3	Blackmun		**Marshall Brennan Stevens**
		Provision of funds to cover costs of standardized tests and scoring services required by the state held to not violate the Constitution.	6:3	Blackmun		**Marshall Brennan Stevens**
		Provision of diagnostic speech and hearing services on religious school grounds held constitutional.	8:1	Blackmun	**Marshall Stevens**	**Brennan**

(*Continued*)

Table 1 (Continued) School Aid Cases: Dates, Rulings, Authors

Year	Case	Court Holding	Vote	Author	Concurrences (Author in bold)	Dissents (Author in bold)
		Therapeutic, guidance and remedial services provided by state employees at neutral locations or on public school grounds for public and religious school students held not to violate the Constitution.	7:2	Blackmun	Stevens	**Marshall** **Brennan**
		Loans of instructional materials (other than books) to non-public school students held unconstitutional.	6:3	Blackmun	**Marshall** **Stevens** Powell (in judgement only)	Burger Rehnquist White
		Payment of cost of field trips and transportation held unconstitutional.	5:4	Blackmun	**Marshall** **Stevens**	Burger Powell White Rehnquist
1983	*Mueller v. Allen* 463 US 388	Upholding Minnesota law allowing parents to make tax deductions for cost of tuition, textbooks and transportation for their children regardless of whether attending public or religious schools. (Affirmed Eighth Circuit ruling that statute was facially neutral and thus did not violate the Establishment Clause).	5:4	Rehnquist		Marshall with Brennan, Blackmun and Stevens

Accommodation Triumphant? The Rehnquist Court 81

1985	*Grand Rapids School District v. Ball* 473 US 373	Shared Time programmes providing remedial and enrichment classes to religious school students on religious school grounds taught by public school teachers and Community Education programmes providing classes for pupils and adults after school hours on religious school grounds taught by religious school teachers both found to violate the Establishment Clause. (Affirmed Sixth Circuit ruling finding an unconstitutional effect and entanglement).	7:2 (Community Education) 5:4 (Shared Time)	Brennan Brennan	**Burger O'Connor**	**Rehnquist White** **Burger O'Connor Rehnquist White**
1985	*Aguilar v. Felton* 473 US 402	New York's Title I funded programme to provide remedial education services to children of poor families during school hours and on religious school grounds held unconstitutional. (Upholding Second Circuit finding that the Court's prior cases established an insurmountable barrier between state funds and religious schools).	5:4	Brennan	Powell	**Burger Rehnquist White O'Connor** with Rehnquist
1986	*Witters v. Washington Department of Services for the Blind* 474 US 481	State disability assistance provided to a blind student could be used for the student to attend a Christian college. (Overturned Washington State Supreme Court ruling that provision of aid in such circumstances would have the primary effect of aiding religion).	9:0	Marshall	White O'Connor Powell with Burger and Rehnquist	

(Continued)

Table 1 (Continued) School Aid Cases: Dates, Rulings, Authors

Year	Case	Court Holding	Vote	Author	Concurrences (Author in bold)	Dissents (Author in bold)
1993	*Zobrest v. Catalina Hills School District* 509 US 1	Holding state provision of a sign language interpreter for a deaf student did not violate the Establishment Clause when that student attended a religious school. (Overturned a Ninth Circuit ruling that such provision would result in state promotion of the religious development of the student, in violation of the Constitution).	5:4	Rehnquist		**Blackmun** with Souter **O'Connor** with Stevens
1997	*Agostini v. Felton* 521 US 203	New York's Title I funded programme to provide remedial education services to children of poor families can take place on religious school grounds without violating the Establishment Clause (overturns *Aguilar*). (Overturned Second Circuit ruling that the Supreme Court had not yet overruled *Aguilar* and therefore the principles established in the earlier case still applied).	5:4	O'Connor		**Souter** with Stevens and Ginsburg **Ginsburg** with Stevens, Souter and Breyer

Part Two

School Prayer

Introduction

Battles over prayer and Bible reading were not new to American education when the Supreme Court agreed in 1962 to hear oral arguments in *Engel v. Vitale*. In the nineteenth century, the emergence of the public school movement led to deep, and occasionally violent, conflicts between Protestants and Catholics. Although advocates did not intend for public schools to be sectarian in teaching or orientation, the aim of the schools – to develop children to be good citizens, willing, able and ready to meet the challenges of the rapidly changing society around them – relied on the local communities to determine what made children good citizens. Schools were not expected to promote or enforce sectarian dogma but neither were they expected to undermine the teachings of the home and the Church. In the 1830s, this meant predominantly Protestant beliefs and practices dominated in the nation's developing public schools. Daily devotionals, Bible reading and prayer activities occurred in most schools. Even the most popular school readers contributed to the development of Christian morality: written by William Holmes McGuffey, a professor of moral philosophy and Presbyterian minister, the McGuffey readers were infused with Protestant morality.[1]

Increased immigration from Ireland in particular in the late 1830s and 1840s challenged this Protestant dominance and led to conflict in areas in which Irish Catholics settled in significant numbers. In New York City, Catholics objected to school activities including the use of Protestant prayers and hymns, exclusive use of the King James Bible and the use of religious, literary and historical texts which showed anti-Catholic bias, including regular use of the term 'popery'. Such activities, they argued, made it impossible for them to send their children to public schools. Attempts by Governor

William Henry Seward, who was sympathetic to the Catholic perspective, to obtain public funds for diocesan schools resulted in petitions, editorials and anti-Catholic tracts sent to the legislature in opposition. After a bitter public battle, many of the activities were removed or altered, but daily Bible reading continued; Catholics exhausted from the fight accepted partial victory and the readings continued unchallenged.[2] In Philadelphia, Catholics protested against the dismissal of Catholic teachers for refusal to participate in daily readings from the King James Bible and the chastising and harassment of Catholic children who refused to participate. Led by Bishop Francis Kendrick, they sought to change the practices within the schools. Virulently anti-Catholic political groups formed, while editorials, sermons, tracts and posters warned of the Catholic 'threat' to the city. Heightened tensions resulted in riots between Protestant and Catholic mobs on 3 May 1844: at least one Protestant youth was killed, dozens of homes were destroyed and Catholic churches and schools were burned to the ground. A report on the riots published a little over a month later blamed those it claimed were seeking to exclude the Bible from public schools, failing to calm the remaining tensions, and, on 4 July, riots erupted again, resulting in 'mob action, gunfire, and the storming of a Catholic church'.[3] Tensions declined only when the city's Catholics abandoned attempts to press schools into greater sensitivity to their beliefs and practices and turned instead towards developing the diocesan schools in the area.

Such events were symptomatic of a broader nativist and anti-Catholic sentiment across the United States in the nineteenth century. Although less violent, similar anti-Catholic debates were stimulated by school aid proposals in states including Kansas, Michigan, New Jersey, Ohio and Wisconsin. Gradually, Catholics either withdrew into the developing Catholic school system or remained silent about practices in the public schools their children attended. However, the image of public schools as antithetical to Catholic beliefs was a consequence of these bitter battles. Without continued scrutiny, practices such as daily prayers and Bible reading continued throughout the nineteenth century and into the twentieth, although with less frequency in some areas of the country than in others, reinforcing the image of public schools as unwelcoming to Catholics. The emergence of a movement advocating greater recognition of religion in the nation's schools which emerged in the aftermath of World War II and the coming of the Cold War potentially threatened a return of these older, divisive debates.

Initially, the subject seemed outside the purview of the Supreme Court: although the Establishment Clause had been incorporated into the Fourteenth Amendment by the Justices in *Everson v. Board of Education* in 1947, the Court had shown little interest in considering religion in the context of public schools. Although the striking down of on-campus released time programmes in 1948 had been a cause for concern among advocates of school prayer, the Court's 1952 decision allowing off-campus programmes appeared to redress the balance: the silence that followed suggested that the Court was no longer concerned with such practices. *Engel* served notice that the Court *was* concerned, an interest that continued throughout the following decades, committing the Court to decisions in an area of historical and contemporary sensitivity.

'I have a feeling of sadness because these are so-called Godly people . . . If their God teaches them to wish my kids get polio and my house be bombed, then I think He hasn't done a very good job with them', commented Frances Roth, one of the plaintiffs in *Engel v. Vitale* shortly after the decision was handed down.[4] In *Engel*, the Supreme Court ruled unconstitutional school-sponsored prayer activities; a year later, in *Abington School District v. Schempp*, Bible reading was also struck down.[5] Reaction to the cases was diverse but the commentary was vocal and passionate. For many, *Engel* and *Schempp* signalled the banning of God from school classrooms and from the lives of children, leading ultimately to the secularization of society: arguments which had also been heard during the debates of the nineteenth century. For those who supported the decisions, this was nonsense: the Court had not barred religion from public schools at all; it had simply ensured that the schools could not organize religious activities or require participation. The issue of prayer remained a sensitive one: as a fundamental part of so many religions, allowing the individual to communicate with their God or Gods, prayer went to the heart of religious faith for many Americans, and any comment regarding prayer appeared as a comment on religion itself. In a nation significantly more religiously diverse than in the nineteenth century, any comment from the Court risked the possibility of greater religious division. Involvement with the issue thus drew the Supreme Court into a highly emotional, sensitive area of American life, requiring the Justices to seek a correct balance between the demands of the Constitution and the faith of the American people. The manner in which the Court responded to this challenge, and the public and political reaction to the Court's rulings in this area of constitutional law, form a significant part of the modern debate over the proper relationship between the Church and the State in the United States.

Chapter 4

Engel and *Schempp*: Controversy and Compliance

Religion and Education After World War II

'The shattering power of the atomic bomb has focussed our sense of need for a kind of education which gives first place to making a life rather than a living', wrote Erwin Shayer, member of the International Council of Religious Education in December 1946.[1] As Americans sought to comprehend the consequences of a second world war, the growing understanding of the Holocaust and the implications of the new atomic age, state and national attention turned to the country's schools and the question of education. As Congress debated the need for federal aid to education to attract more teachers and improve resources and facilities, educators were also re-evaluating the purpose and function of education. Since the days of Jefferson and Madison a function of education had been to create good citizens in order to maintain a healthy democracy; in the late 1940s and 1950s educators and interested others engaged in a debate about how best to achieve this aim. The nation's emergence as the leading international economic power after 1945 and the development of the Cold War later in the decade lent urgency to the discussion: in fighting an ideological war a nation's greatest strength was its citizens, and good citizens required effective schools. Spurred on by national and international factors as well as pedagogical concerns, educators began to debate and study methods to improve the citizenship education provided by America's schools.

The greater use of religion was one method explored by educators after World War Two to strengthen the citizenship education of students. The national political debate gave impetus to the movement. As the Cold War deepened and politicians frequently represented the Soviet Union and Communism as atheistic, religion increasingly became the cornerstone for defence of the nation and the American way of life. In 1954, Congress endorsed the perceived link between democracy and faith when it added the words 'under God' to the Pledge of Allegiance. The House UnAmerican Activities Committee and the McCarthy hearings reinforced the connection by implying that atheists were immediately suspect either as dangerous subversives, or worse, as potential Soviet spies. In such a climate, where religion and education were both considered fundamental to the survival of American democracy, the likelihood of greater emphasis on religion in public education increased significantly.[2]

Educators themselves called for greater recognition of religion in the school environment. In June 1947, the American Council on Education published a report entitled *The Relation of Religion to Public Education*. Based on a three-year study, the Council called upon schools and colleges to give more curricula recognition to the place of religion in the spiritual and cultural life of the American people. Fearful of inviting sectarianism into their schools, educators had nevertheless 'gone too far' in studiously avoiding any mention of religion in their educational programmes, argued the report. Greater care should be taken to ensure that the role of religion in history, literature, the arts and other areas of life was neither overlooked entirely nor treated in 'an inadequate and superficial manner' that might appear to devalue religion.[3] Suggestions included using Bible verses in character education, studying the Ten Commandments and the Beatitudes as well as Hitchins' Good American Code in discussions of law and civics, employing religious art in studies of culture and artistic development, religious music in music classes and the Bible and other religious writings in literature classes. In addition, history classes should include discussions of religious motivations and the faiths of historical figures.

For a small group of educators these suggestions did not go far enough. 'When religion is left out of education then secularism by default, if not by intent, is the resulting frame of reference', they argued.[4] 'What schools have recently been calling their responsibility for "character education" is essentially the same thing that the church and the home call religious education', asserted one educator: in order to mould the whole child, the home, church and school should all reinforce the same message, making religion a natural addition to the curriculum.[5] In addition, some educators, in conjunction with religious leaders, believed, 'we cannot inculcate spiritual values by employing solely the method or content of humanism and pure science'.[6] Only religiously grounded values and morals were sufficiently strong, enduring and relevant to influence the individual student, mould his or her character and ensure his or her continued good citizenship.[7] For advocates of such a position, secular values were insufficient to maintain a strong nation and moral individuals. If education was to create the strong, moral citizens that circumstances required, they argued, religion should not be overlooked because to do so was to ensure weaker secular values dominated.

However, the trend towards greater inclusion of religion in public school curricula was rarely accompanied by demands for sectarian use of religion, at least explicitly.[8] Among many in the fifteen years after World War Two was a concern to avoid the dangers of classroom proselytizing while simultaneously attempting to raise awareness of religious tenets and their applicability to modern life. The use of religion in public schools was not intended to deepen divisions between those of different faiths, but to emphasize those values perceived as being fundamental to good character and good citizenship while teaching and encouraging tolerance and respect for the beliefs of others. Suggesting the use of devotionals or Bible reading as part of a programme for character education, Henry Lester Smith noted: '[i]n this rather controversial field the type and amount of religious education must be determined by local opinion and conditions'.[9] Although it is likely that in some schools blatant attempts to inculcate religion as dogma occurred, there is little more than anecdotal evidence for this. Discussions among educators, however, suggested that the motives of the majority were benign, representing genuine attempts to encourage tolerance of and respect for different beliefs while drawing on religion to encourage good character development. Most educators appeared to agree that, '[t]he problem of moral nihilism cannot be solved by a return to Puritanism. *Goodness cannot be coerced; morals cannot be established through categorical commandments.*'[10]

For opponents of the greater use of religion in public schools the difficulties of teaching about religion outweighed any possible benefits. V. T. Thayer, former superintendent of Wisconsin schools, advocate of Progressive education and one of the leading critics of released time and Bible reading programmes, argued, 'secular education today is under severe attack from individuals and groups who would transform its traditional character'.[11] Thayer and others perceived several key dangers. First, the variety of faiths and beliefs in the United States made it almost impossible to teach elements of religion that did not conflict with someone's faith. The secular public school developed to ensure that education provided to all would offend no-one on the grounds of their religion; the introduction of religion into schools thus threatened the very foundation of the public school. Second, attempts to find common ground between religions only offended those with genuine faith by picking and choosing certain elements that were 'acceptable' and those that were not. The separation of church and state had been intended to avoid both dangers and should thus be adhered to strictly. Third, teaching about religion without indoctrination required careful balancing that, critics asserted, most teachers were unequipped to handle as a result of insufficient training or personal bias. Whether intended or not, more religion in classrooms would lead to religious advocacy, violating the separation of church and state.

An alternative to introducing religion into the public school classroom was character education, and later, moral education. For supporters, values and virtues should be taught through students' active involvement and participation in a range of activities. Field trips and excursions, studies of the local community and its problems, attempts to develop solutions to local problems, participation in community activities and projects and involvement with established youth groups were among the suggestions to encourage students to take responsibility for community matters and thus develop civic virtue. Active participation and creative thinking were crucial to this approach, things rarely associated with religious instruction classes of the era. In Los Angeles, a study of character education programmes in several schools revealed that religion and religious practices were rarely employed by the teachers surveyed.[12] A classroom assignment to secretly abide by the Golden Rule of consideration for others with regard to their families found students reporting experiences and attitude changes which supported advocates' belief. Although eventually falling out of favour, character education programmes revealed that educators were looking at alternatives to religion as a solution to good citizenship. Given the potential pitfalls of introducing religion into the public school curriculum, the apparent lack of evidence for religion or against character education, and the concerns about church-state separation, many educators looked to more secular means of character training.

Thus, by the time *Engel v. Vitale* reached the courts there was no broad agreement among educators concerning the best or most effective way to instil American values into their students. Despite a slight favouring of religious exercises, among those responsible for educating the nation's children there was no consensus on the question of the proper place for religion in the public schools. Throughout the period, educators made suggestions for programmes of character education, posed questions to be considered when religious exercises were introduced into the curriculum and advocated further study of the issue to more fully understand the options and their consequences. Concentration on state laws conceals the significance of local practice that was often commented on but rarely studied, but indicates the breadth of opinion on the subject of religious exercises in the public schools. A 1948 report on the Golden Rule experiment in California indicated a relatively small number of teachers employed the Bible or religion in their classes, yet a 1955 study noted that religious teaching 'is going on quietly and effectively and with the full knowledge and support of parents in many school systems'.[13] In 1950, in one of the few detailed studies of the subject, Andrew Edington reported that four states prohibited Bible reading in schools while twenty-seven states had no law regarding the practice.[14] Four years later it was estimated that thirteen states required Bible reading and eight prohibited it entirely, the other states maintaining no law.[15] 'There is', one commentator concluded, 'no consistent policy among states, among communities within a state, or even among public schools within a single public school system'.[16] In 1955, Rolfe Lanier Hunt, executive director of the Department of Religion and Public Education for the National Council of Churches in Christ argued: 'There will be no national solution answering questions of how the public schools should deal with religion . . . There will be no one solution . . . The solution we seek should observe the voluntary principle so far as possible'.[17] His argument embodied the opinion of many educators, although not all, who did not appear unhappy at the lack of a national policy and accepted that different communities would come to their own arrangements at a time when no position could attract a majority and no evidence could conclusively prove the success of either religious or purely secular teaching. The Supreme Court's intervention in the debate in 1962 brought federal involvement for the first time and with it something approaching a national requirement.

First Principles: *Engel v. Vitale*

In April 1962 the Supreme Court heard oral argument in *Engel v. Vitale*. *Engel* involved a challenge to a twenty-two word prayer composed by the members of the Board of Education of New Hyde Park, New York, adopted by the State Board of Regents as an exercise to be performed daily in the public schools. The prayer read: 'Almighty God, we acknowledge our dependence upon Thee, and we beg Thy blessings upon us, our parents, our teachers, and our country'.[18] As part of the Regents' 'Statement on Moral and Spiritual Training in the Schools', the prayer, they alleged, was intended not as a religious exercise but as a spiritual one, pointing to its non-denominational character in support for their assertion. The use of the Regents' Prayer was challenged by the parents of ten pupils of the school district as a violation of the Establishment Clause; rejecting the officials' claim that this was an exercise designed purely to inculcate school children into the moral values of society, the parents alleged that this was a blatant example of state support for religious belief forbidden by the Establishment Clause. The Supreme Court agreed. In an opinion written by Justice Hugo Black, the Court stated, 'the State of New York has adopted a practice wholly inconsistent with the Establishment Clause', rejecting the claim that non-denominationalism made the prayer any less religious. In arguably the most famous passage from the opinion, the the Court made clear the way it viewed the issues raised by *Engel*: 'the constitutional prohibition against laws respecting an establishment of religion must at least mean that in this country it is no part of the business of government to compose official prayers for any group of the American people to recite as part of a religious program carried on by the government'.[19]

Black's opinion for the six-justice majority rested heavily on two basic principles: that prayer, whether sectarian or non-denominational, was an intrinsically religious activity and that the First Amendment at its most basic prevented government officials composing, conducting or endorsing such religious exercises. The rest of the opinion was designed to reinforce these two fundamental points. On these the justices showed a degree of consensus remarkable in the light of the deep divisions present on later Courts. For Justices Black, Felix Frankfurter, John Marshall Harlan and Chief Justice Earl Warren, that the case involved prayer was virtually sufficient by itself, irrespective of the deity invoked, to violate the Constitution.[20] As far as religious exercises in public schools were concerned, the Court's position was one of strict separation. In this clarity of interpretation, Black's *Engel* opinion stands alone: in later cases, although the Court reinforced the principles laid down in *Engel*, it did so in the language of 'neutrality', a term which blurred the Court's interpretations and motivations.[21] Black's assertions that the Court and government were not and should not be hostile to religion prefigured the Court's use of 'neutrality', but his opinion, supported by five other justices, rested firmly on the foundations of strict separation.

Equally firmly, the majority placed the issue of religious exercises in public schools within the purview of the Establishment Clause. The need to do so was created by the School Board's use of excusal remedies as a defence. Excusal remedies were not a new issue for the Court in 1962; however, *Engel* was the first time they had been raised as a means of counteracting an alleged Establishment Clause violation.[22] As defined by the New York District Court: 'Nonparticipation may take the form of either remaining silent during the exercise, or if the parent or child so desires, of being excused entirely from the exercise'.[23] Drawing heavily on free exercise cases, the School Board argued that as long as no child was compelled to participate in the activity, no establishment could be discovered. The Court rejected the argument. While the Religion Clauses of the First Amendment may both be aimed at protecting religious liberty within the United States, stated the Court, they do so in very different ways: the Free Exercise Clause operates by protecting the individual specifically; the Establishment Clause by acting as a restraint on government. While excusal remedies may protect the rights of the dissenting individual, they cannot in any way act to limit the role of the government and therefore are insufficient against Establishment Clause challenges. This was a hugely significant argument: in dissent, Justice Potter Stewart argued that *Engel* was really a free exercise issue, critics from outside the Court argued that it was a free exercise issue and advocates have continued to maintain that school prayer is a free exercise issue, but Black and the majority made clear that they considered it an Establishment issue.[24] In doing so, the Court established that certain rules now applied to similar cases: excusal remedies alone would not be sufficient to withstand a challenge, and coercion to participate would not be a decisive test for unconstitutionality. Unless or until the Court chose to alter them, these were the terms in which future challenges must be discussed; thus *Engel* constituted the basic framework for the analysis of future cases.

Bernard Schwartz has argued that in *Engel*, the justices, 'uncharacteristically overlooked the political and public implications' of the ruling.[25] However, close reading of Black's opinion suggests a justice, and a Court, aware of the reaction the case would cause. Although criticized by Stewart and others, Black's extensive use of history served a dual purpose: in direct response to claims made by the Board of Regents that a recognition of God was part of the country's national heritage, it showed that such 'recognition' had, throughout history, led to the persecution of those who did not conform to the beliefs of the majority, and that the aims of the Framers of the Constitution were to prevent the continuation of this oppression in the new nation by separating the secular from the religious. It also established that the values of toleration of dissenters and the prohibition of governmental support for religious exercises were equally long-standing American traditions. The Court was not simply creating new law, but was in fact following a long tradition, that of the Founding Fathers. By laying claim to such distinguished lineage, Black sought to assuage criticism by arguing that this ruling conformed to the best traditions of the nation, that of true freedom and choice:

These men knew that the First Amendment, which had tried to put an end to governmental control of religion and of prayer, was not written to destroy either. They knew rather that it was written to quell well-justified fears which nearly all of them felt arising out of an awareness that governments of the past had shackled men's tongues to make them speak only the religious thoughts that government wanted them to speak and to pray only to the God that government wanted them to pray to.[26]

Equally important were Black's repeated assertions that neither the Supreme Court nor the ideas underpinning the ruling were hostile to religion or religious belief. '[R]eligion is too personal, too sacred, too holy, to permit its "unhallowed perversion" by a civil magistrate', wrote Black, quoting from James Madison's paean to religious freedom, *Memorial and Remonstrance*. Later in the opinion he commented, 'It is neither sacrilegious nor antireligious to say that each separate government of this country should stay out of the business of writing or sanctioning official prayers'.[27] Had the Court believed that *Engel* would be easily accepted by the public, then these would have been unnecessary assertions to make, certainly with such frequency. However, the tone of earlier debates about school prayer or curriculum recognition of religion suggested that claims of anti-religious bigotry, or at least of growing secularism, might result from the striking down of the Regents' Prayer.[28] The contemporary debate surrounding government aid to religious schools had also resulted in similar claims. Both made it likely that the *Engel* ruling would be interpreted in this manner by some groups. In these circumstances the frequency of Black's rejection of religious hostility on the part of the Court showed a clear awareness of these concerns by arguing that the striking down of school prayer should be interpreted only as a rejection of the practice itself and not as a rejection of the belief or beliefs held by those involved.

Black faced a difficult task in writing for the *Engel* majority. Aware of the political and social repercussions, he was denied recourse to legal tradition by the lack of controlling precedent in this area. Although lower courts had ruled in prayer cases since the nineteenth century, such opinions were based on state law or state constitutions, not the First Amendment.[29] As such, they could provide support for a particular approach but not a definitive meaning of the Establishment Clause. Of the Court's Establishment rulings, *McCollum v. Board of Education* (1948) and *Zorach v. Clauson* (1952) were the closest precedents, but released time programmes did not involve the schools and their staff to the anything like the extent Black argued was involved in *Engel*.[30] While a weakness of Black's opinion, the omission of legal precedent in *Engel* was deliberately designed. Even accepting the limited range of legal precedent open to him, Black's use of history and sweeping language implied an argument that was broader than the law. Black conjured images of men searching for fundamental principles, a nation steeped in the tradition of tolerance, the positive good of belief and the evil of its corruption in any form, thus turning the debate over school prayer into one of right and wrong, tolerance versus bigotry, an argument beyond law, about the very nature of the society in which Americans live.[31] Black thus sought to turn the weakness of limited precedent to his advantage, crafting a broad opinion that spoke to fundamental values and American traditions and applying them specifically to the Regents' Prayer. If the majority believed that a limited, narrow legal opinion would be unlikely to quell the dissatisfaction of the public with the ruling, then a broad, sweeping opinion would be unlikely to cause any greater criticism, and might win greater support.[32] Thus, far from being unaware of the implications of *Engel*, both the structure and content of Black's majority opinion were designed with the consequences in mind.

However, the arguments made by Justices Harlan and William O. Douglas in concurrence, and Stewart in dissent, inadvertently worked to undermine Black's efforts and brought out areas of disagreement that foreshadowed problems in future cases. Harlan held an almost reverential attitude towards *stare decisis* and judicial restraint; a striking aspect of his jurisprudence was that he would often follow precedents with which he disagreed, even dissenting from Court opinions which failed to adhere to a precedent in which he had initially dissented. This is key to understanding Harlan's approach to *Engel*: although troubled by the result, he 'reluctantly' joined the majority 'in light of the direction the cases have taken'.[33] Harlan's tentative support for the ruling in *Engel* reflected concern for specific facts of the case and the precise circumstances in which it had arisen: under different circumstances Harlan's position may have been different.

Douglas struggled to a greater degree, to the extent that as late as 11 June he had not decided whether he would concur or dissent. His difficulty, though, was not so much with the final result as with its implications.[34] As with at least two earlier opinions, Douglas was primarily concerned with another issue very much on the political agenda at the time: public financing of religious schools.[35] Early drafts of his opinion show the difficulty Douglas faced when trying to reconcile his views with those of the majority in this case. In failing to address the financial issue, Douglas believed that the Court was not facing or dealing with the reality of *Engel*'s implications, relying too heavily on abstractions and raising the spectre of major doctrinal inconsistencies in the future.[36] That Douglas raised an issue not discussed at conference and that he concurred separately and alone was as much a part of his jurisprudence as Harlan's approach was symbolic of his, but Douglas's concern with the financial issue broadened the scope of the issue beyond that addressed by Black for the majority. As such, Douglas's positions remained unanswered and the consequences of *Engel* for activities other than school prayer remained unclear. The suggestion that the Pledge of Allegiance and 'In God We Trust' might be under threat raised subjects outside the scope of the case, which Black had deliberately tailored narrowly to the facts, and arguably intensified reaction to *Engel* by creating uncertainty.

Stewart took the opposite direction to Harlan and Douglas and became the sole dissenter in *Engel*. That he was less sure of the result in the case than the others was obvious in conference where he commented that he was 'not at peace' and 'still in doubt', a discomfort which manifested itself in his opinion.[37] Given the agreement among the justices at the ideological extremes of the Court, Stewart's dissent appeared, at first glance, to be something of an anomaly. However, a preference for pragmatism over ideology and concern for the 'fairness' of decisions led him to dissent in *Engel*.[38] For Stewart the central issue before the Court was the free exercise rights of the majority: 'I cannot see how an "official religion" is established by letting those who want to say a prayer say it. On the contrary, I think that to deny the wish of these school children to join in reciting the prayer is to deny them the opportunity of sharing in the spiritual heritage of the nation'.[39] For Stewart, fairness required consideration of the views of the majority over a small minority of students; any requirement for the protection of individual rights contained in the Free Exercise Clause was provided by the existence of excusal remedies. Stewart's affinity for pragmatism led him to reject the relevance of sixteenth-century British and eighteenth-century American history in favour of 'the history of the religious traditions of our people, reflected in countless practices of the institutions and officials of our government'.[40] However, Stewart's pragmatism served to confuse the Establishment and Free Exercise doctrine by suggesting that school prayer involved the free exercise rights of the majority rather than the establishment limitation on government. The argument provided ammunition to religious groups supporting school prayer and challenged the majority's insistence that it was clearly an Establishment issue. Stewart's dissent gave impetus to the argument about the relationship between the Religion Clauses of the First Amendment which the Court would be required to address in future cases.

Here lay at least part of the problem of the misconception of *Engel*'s ruling and the widespread misinterpretation of its underlying principles. In the absence of a clear test, attention turned to what information was available within the opinions that could provide guidelines. Black's opinion, with its sweeping statements of principle and history, provided little in terms of concrete advice and so scrutiny was directed towards the concurrence and dissent. Stewart's interpretation of the majority's holding suggested that 'state and federal governments are without constitutional power to prescribe any particular form of words to be recited by any group of the American people *on any subject touching religion*'. Following this with a discussion of religious references in the national anthem and the Pledge of Allegiance, Stewart argued by association that these things would now come within the purview of the Court's holding.[41] More influential in inflaming public reaction was Douglas's opinion. By suggesting that the prayer at issue in *Engel* involved unconstitutional state financial aid, then going on to equate the Regents' Prayer with the Pledge of Allegiance, congressional and military chaplains, 'In God We Trust' on the nation's currency and the Court's own invocation at opening, Douglas appeared to suggest that all these things were unacceptable too. Although Black had explicitly refuted claims along these lines, he had done so only in a footnote near the end of the opinion, and it is not surprising that this was so easily overlooked, or deliberately ignored.[42] Thus, although the majority attempted to reassure the public that the Court was not hostile to religion and that the Constitution did not require hostility on the part of government, the lack of any clear test led many to exactly this conclusion.

Establishing Battle Lines: Reaction to *Engel* and *Abington School District v. Schempp*

The initial reaction to *Engel* was swift and overwhelmingly critical, although the Court was not without its supporters. Reverend Dr Martin Luther King, Jr called *Engel* 'a sound and good decision reaffirming something that is basic in our Constitution, namely separation of church and state'.[43] Leo Pfeffer, general counsel for the American Jewish Congress, stated: 'I am highly gratified by the decision which I believe is consistent with the earlier position of the Supreme Court that the Constitution requires an absolute separation of church and state and a secular public school system'.[44] Isaac Frank, executive director of the Jewish Community Council of Greater Washington, believed *Engel* 'is good for religion, public education, and democracy', and the *Washington Post* praised the decision as, 'an act of liberation. It frees school children from what was in effect a forced participation by rote in an act of worship that ought to be individual, wholly voluntary, and devout'.[45] Support also came from the Baptist Joint Committee on Public Affairs, the United Church of Christ and a group of Protestant leaders including the dean of Harvard Divinity School, in addition to the American Civil Liberties Union and Protestants and Other Americans United for the Separation of Church and State (Americans United). The dominant themes running throughout supporters' reactions included support for the Court as having upheld fundamental constitutional principles and values, the importance of freedom of choice and voluntariness, and a strong belief that *Engel* protected religion. 'When the positive content of faith has been bleached out of a prayer, I am not too concerned about retaining what is left', stated Dr Franklin Clark Fry, president of the Lutheran Church of America.[46]

More common was the reaction of Senator Herman Talmadge (D-Ga) who denounced *Engel* as 'unconscionable . . . an outrageous edict', and that of Representative Frank Cheef (D-Ky) who suggested that the majority 'ought to be ashamed and ought to resign'.[47] Representative John Bell Williams (D-Miss) insisted that the decision constituted 'a deliberate and carefully planned conspiracy to substitute materialism for spiritual values'; Senator John Sparkman (D-Ala) called it 'a tragic mistake'; and Representative Frank Becker (R-NY), who would become the leader of the opposition to the Court on this issue, suggested that *Engel* was 'the most tragic decision in the history of the United States'.[48] Among members of Congress, some of the most vocal of the Court's critics, two themes dominated. First, any opposition to religious activities in the public schools was an attack upon religion and upon God Himself. Senator Eugene McCarthy (D-Minn) claimed that the Court had promoted 'not only a secularised government, but a secularised society'; Senator A. Willis Robertson (D-Va) considered it the most extreme ruling the Court had ever made in favour of atheists and agnostics; and Senator Robert Byrd (D-W.Va) argued, 'somebody is tampering with America's soul'.[49] Second, the Court had opened the United States to attack by the Communists. 'These men in robes are doing everything possible to help Khrushchev bury us', argued Representative Alvin O'Kinski (R-Wis), while Representative William Colmer (D-Miss) asked, 'is this another step toward the adoption of Communist philosophy?'[50] In addition, critics accused the Court of stepping beyond its legitimate bounds and the justices of putting themselves above God. Shortly after *Engel* was handed down, twenty-two Senators and fifty-three Representatives had introduced constitutional amendments to overturn the Court's decision and 'return God' to the nation's public schools.[51]

Support for the idea that the Court had banished God from the classrooms came from a variety of religious groups and leading individuals, dominated by Catholics and a number of mainstream Protestant denominations. Francis Cardinal Spellman declared himself 'shocked and frightened' by the decision, arguing, 'the decision strikes at the very heart of the Godly tradition in which America's children have for so long been raised'.[52] Cardinal Francis James McIntyre found the situation 'positively shocking and scandalising . . . it is not a decision according to law but a decision of licence', and the Roman Catholic Bishop of Dallas-Fort Worth predicted, 'American public schools will have to start bootlegging religion into the classroom'.[53] Reverend John Wesley North, Methodist Bishop of Washington, stated, '[I]t seems to me in this decision one of the ancient landmarks of our American culture and tradition is being removed', a sentiment echoed by his Georgia colleague, Reverend John Owen Smith, who said, 'it's like taking a star or stripe off the flag'.[54] Dr Billy Graham, one of the nation's best-known fundamentalist clergymen, claimed, 'this is another step toward the secularisation of the United States', proceeding to link school prayers to other church-state interactions, stimulating fear for what the Court might do next, as well as fundamentally misinterpreting the majority's decision.[55]

Such reaction, despite its predictability due to denominational activity in support of school prayer, may in part explain the vehemence of congressional reaction. As representatives of some of the largest religious groups in the United States, Congressmen may well have considered the stance of Spellman, Graham and others to be representative of the views of the majority of the population. Concerned with the need for re-election in the 1962 mid-term elections, failure to be seen to 'stand up for God' could have been political suicide. As one contemporary commentator noted, copies of anti–*Engel* statements mailed to constituents 'will be worth their weight in ballots [in the South]'.[56] Political motivations also partially account for the severe misrepresentation of the meaning and consequences of Black's opinion. Equating *Engel*'s supporters with agnostics, atheists, Communists and other 'un-American' ideas made for unambiguous soundbites that could be easily reported and which touched on concepts and fears already familiar to the American people. Such simplistic equations were also easier to communicate than the more complex, but more correct, concepts of separation of church and state, the dangers of coercion and the benefit to religion of being free from state interference. In hearings undertaken by the Senate Judiciary Committee in late July and early August 1962, the misrepresentation continued. Written statements by groups including the ACLU, the

Anti-Defamation League, American Ethical Union, American Jewish Congress, National Association for the Advancement of Colored People and the Baptist Joint Committee, as well as a letter signed by 110 deans and professors of law and political science, were opposed by the near unanimous oral testimony criticizing the Court's action.[57] No report was issued and no legislation was proposed as a result of the hearings; they were little more than an opportunity for opponents to attack the Court on the record, achieving cheap political advantage, while not being required to take any concrete action that might endanger political support.

However, at least part of the reaction against the ruling was because it showed a level of judicial activism that was unexpected. Frequently forgotten amid the legacy of *Brown v. Board of Education* and the Warren Court's later civil rights and civil liberties rulings is that the early years of Warren's tenure on the Court differed little from the moderate positions assumed by the Court under his predecessor, Fred Vinson. Several years before Warren's appointment to the Court, journalist John Gunther wrote: '[he] is honest, likeable, and clean, [characterized by] decency, stability, sincerity, and a lack of genuine intellectual distinction. He will never set the world on fire or even make it smoke'.[58] The early years of Warren's tenure as chief justice did little to dispel these initial assessments of his influence on the Supreme Court: when interpreting the Constitution, Warren's decisions were cautious and generally reflected mainstream values.[59] Writing in 1957, legal scholar Robert McCloskey observed: 'The Supreme Court is in a period of transition and at the moment it is difficult to know whether it will continue along the path taken since 1937 of limited activism, or once again take on the role of bringing the central problems of American political life under close surveillance'.[60] Against this background, the negative reaction to *Engel* is more understandable. First, the Court's intervention and application of the First Amendment to the states required a national approach to an issue that, until *Engel*, had been decided by communities themselves. Second, the issue of school prayer had not been a major part of political debate for several decades but fell at its first significant challenge, struck down by what was perceived to be a restrained, cautious Court. Both gave the impression of far greater judicial activism than was the case.

Despite the restrained approach to much of its constitutional jurisprudence, by the time the Court decided *Engel* in 1962 it had already developed a small but vocal and politically influential opposition that was willing to challenge what it considered to be the Court's overarching activism. The vast majority of this opposition consisted of southerners, alienated by the Court's opinion in *Brown* and subsequent rulings outlawing Jim Crow and insisting on desegregation. A series of internal security cases in which the Court upheld the rights of the individual over the rights of the state brought southerners allies in the form of national security conservatives and turned regional disaffection for the justices into a national phenomenon.[61] In the summer of 1957, the National Association of Attorneys General offered a resolution condemning the Red Monday opinions; and in 1957, and again in 1959, the American Bar Association expressed disagreement with the Court's decisions.[62] In 1958, Congress entered the fray holding hearings on House Resolution 3 and the Senate equivalent, the Jenner Bill, designed to limit the influence of the Court in internal security cases. Both resolutions were quickly defeated but the challenge to the Court was unmistakable. By 1962, Walter Murphy observed that there was a 'quiet but unmistakable undertone on Capitol Hill, a fear not only among conservatives but among moderates as well as some liberals that the justices had gone too far in protecting individual rights and in doing so had moved into the legislative domain'.[63] The Court's decisions on segregation and internal security, in the words of one commentator, 'turn[ed] the Court from a hero into a harridan, and its Chief Justice from prospective President to public pariah'.[64]

In the midst of the storm, in late 1962, the Supreme Court announced that it would hear argument in *Abington School District v. Schempp*. That it did so came as little surprise; it had been widely predicted over the intervening months during congressional hearings into the *Engel* ruling. But much had changed in the intervening year, both on and off the Court, that would impact on the Court's ruling. If in 1962 the Court was less activist, less radical and generally more circumspect than 'history's Warren Court' suggests, by 1963 it was clear that the Court was moving towards the position for which it has so rightly been remembered, and within a few years a whole plethora of cases would expand civil rights and liberties beyond any imagining.[65] A change of personnel on the Court both stimulated this development and added to the sense of shifting foundations. Felix Frankfurter, the Court's leading advocate of judicial restraint, retired from the Court in 1962. His ability to influence colleagues and secure majorities made him an influential figure on the Court and a key vote; with his retirement came the opportunity for other justices to influence the outcome of cases. Frankfurter's replacement, Arthur Goldberg, told his wife before taking his seat that he intended to be a liberal justice, and quickly settled in to provide the liberal bloc of Warren, Douglas, William Brennan and Black with a majority-securing fifth vote.[66] Likewise, the moderate conservative Charles Whittaker was replaced by Kennedy nominee Byron White in 1962, thus adding to the sense of change.[67] Justice Tom Clark's shift to support the liberal majority in *Mapp v. Ohio* has been credited as signalling the collapse of the conservative bloc, and, although not quite so dramatic, it added to the growing sense of liberal activism on the Warren Court.[68] Although this process was only beginning in 1963, it was already significant enough to affect not only the justices of the Court, but also public perception of *Schempp*.

Schempp consolidated two challenges to the daily practice of reading passages from the Bible, one from Pennsylvania and one from Maryland. Unitarians Edward Schempp and his family challenged the practice as violating the Establishment Clause on the grounds that it forced his children to participate in a ritual which contravened their religious belief. In *Murray v. Curlett*, the Maryland case, a similar law was challenged by atheist Madalyn Murray and her son, who argued that equating moral and spiritual values with religion rendered alternative views suspect, alien and sinister, and made outcasts of those holding them. Potentially the impact of the case was more wide ranging than *Engel*: while school prayer was predominantly, although not exclusively, a southern phenomenon, Bible reading was practised widely throughout the states.[69] Undeterred, the Court found no greater difficulty in *Schempp* than it had in *Engel*, striking down the practice with an 8:1 majority, stating: 'We agree with the trial Court's findings as to the religious character of the exercises. Given that finding, the exercises and the law requiring them are in violation of the Establishment Clause'.[70]

Establishing the practice of Bible reading as a religious exercise, and not simply a moral or spiritual one with religious overtones, was crucial to the opinion. Whereas the prayer challenged in *Engel* was a religious exercise and was recognized as such by both parties, in *Schempp* attempts were made to suggest that the Bible was used for its 'educational and moral value for the students'.[71] *Engel* had appeared to rule that no religious exercises were permitted in the public schools and so defenders of the practice needed to show that Bible reading was not an inherently religious practice. The centrality of the issue was indicated by the parties' submissions to the Court: in *Schempp* and *Murray* opponents spent a combined twenty-two pages of their briefs addressing how and why the Bible and the Lord's Prayer were religious and sectarian documents.[72] In response, supporters argued that Bible reading had transcended its religious origins to become part of the traditional practices of the state and discussed perceived pedagogical reasons for continuing the practice.[73] The Court gave short shrift to the argument. In his opinion for the majority, Clark quoted at length from testimony given at trial in *Schempp* concerning the religious and sectarian nature of the Bible before concluding, 'in both cases the laws require religious exercises', thus bringing the case under the control of *Engel* and to all intents and purposes determining the outcome of the case.[74] In terms of the final ruling, the political furore surrounding the Court had no impact. The major points of Clark's opinion closely reflected those made by Black the previous year. The justices' near consensus regarding the sectarian nature of the Bible reading practices challenged reflected their belief that *Engel* remained good law, and their commitment to the legal precedent established there, which remained unshaken by the broader political debate.[75]

However, much about the *Schempp* opinions showed that the Court was aware of the controversy surrounding *Engel* and took steps to address it. The legal principles of *Schempp* were the same, but the tone and structure of the majority opinion were sufficiently different from the earlier case to show that the opinion was about more than simply establishing legal precedent.[76] The most obvious difference was Clark's extensive use of legal references and analysis of the Court's previous holdings in Establishment cases. No explicit attempt was made to link this discussion to the issue in question, but it appeared to have several functions. First, Clark used the cases to illustrate that the Court had always recognized the importance of religion and its role in society, reinforcing arguments made elsewhere in the opinion and echoing Black's concern in *Engel*. Second, in light of criticism of Black specifically after *Engel*, and the Warren Court more generally, Clark showed that the Court was aware of this legal history and was prepared to make use of it, challenging those who accused the justices of being unscholarly. Third, and more significantly, the use of legal precedent returned the issue of religious exercises in public schools to the legal arena. Black's appeal to larger principles of tolerance and freedom convinced those who supported the ruling but opened the Court to criticism that it was imposing its own views on society and engaging in 'judicial legislation'. By returning the issue to purely legal foundations, Clark's opinion sought to narrow the discussion before the Court to those areas with which it was primarily concerned. In doing so, the opinion attempted to cut off the route for such criticism and return the Court, in the eyes of the public, to a position as a purely legal institution.

Clark's authorship of the majority opinion also had broad political significance. It is unlikely that the assignment was given to Clark in order to keep him as part of the majority. Even without Clark's vote a majority existed to strike down the Pennsylvania and Maryland practices. Besides, Clark had voted with the majority in *Engel* the year before. But the Texan had two advantages for the Court: first, he was publicly identified as a conservative on the Court, in contrast to Black; second, Clark had felt so strongly about *Engel* that in the summer of 1962 he had publicly defended the ruling, and the Court, from the criticism it received.[77] It had seemed fitting that Black should write for the majority in *Engel*; as the Court's leading expounder of the theory of constitutional absolutes, *Engel* was a perfect fit for his personal philosophy. But a year later circumstances had changed. Avoiding the rigidity of *Engel*, Clark carefully skirted discussion of the 'wall of separation' in favour of the language of neutrality. The result was the same, but the tone was less strident and less confrontational.

Clark's opinion also sought to address two notable omissions from the *Engel* ruling that had opened the Court to criticism: clarifying the foundations of the opinion and providing a test for future cases. In *Schempp*, the majority opinion was clearly anchored in the concept of neutrality: 'In the relationship between man and religion', wrote Clark, 'the State is firmly committed to a position of neutrality'.[78] That Clark himself firmly believed in this concept is illustrated by his assertion in conference on *Murray* that 'it would be OK to open schoolrooms to all religious exercises by all religious groups', an assertion a strict separationist would never make.[79] In this light, his concentration at the beginning of the opinion on the sectarian nature of the Bible and Bible reading served to show that the practices at bar could not be considered neutral *between* religions, violating the Establishment Clause even before considering whether religion was favoured over non-religion. The definition of neutrality found expression through Clark's two-part test: 'what are the purpose and primary effect of the enactment? If either is the advancement or inhibition of religion then the enactment exceeds the scope of legislative power as circumscribed by the Constitution . . . there must be a secular legislative purpose and a primary effect that neither advances nor inhibits religion'.[80] With this the Court provided the structure and clarity that had been lacking in *Engel*, a window into the thinking of the Court and guidelines for future challenges.[81]

The significance of Clark's use of the language of neutrality was reinforced by the concurring opinion of Justices Goldberg and Harlan. In conference on *Schempp*, Goldberg had argued, 'schools can't be opened to every sect – how about Black Muslims? How about screwball groups? You can't draw a line that is a viable one – it would mean drawing lines that would interfere with true exercise'.[82] For Goldberg, as for Clark, the problem was not only that religious exercises were conducted in the public schools, but that such exercises could not feasibly reflect all beliefs and all religious groups. As a result, certain ideas, beliefs or denominations were favoured over others, thus violating the principle of religious neutrality embodied in the First Amendment. In combination, the opinions of Goldberg and Clark challenged critics who accused the Court of being hostile to religion and its place in public life. The intent of the First Amendment, and thus the aim of the Court, was to protect church and state by ensuring that one did not interfere with the other; the Court was not rejecting religion by barring Bible reading, but preventing state interference with or endorsement of an inherently religious exercise. The same argument had been made in *Engel*; in *Schempp* the justices made it clearer.

Congress, Constitutional Amendments and the Public: 1963–1980

As with *Engel*, the result in *Schempp* accounts for only part of its significance. Superficially, *Schempp* took the principles laid down in *Engel* and applied them to Bible reading with little or no regard for the political and legal debate which surrounded the case and did so with only one dissent. Closer consideration, however, reveals a Court clearly aware of the legal and political context and willing to address it, but not directly. In *Brown*, Warren had worked hard to ensure the Court's consensus, understanding that in such a controversial case the full force of the Court would be important in gaining acceptance of the ruling and enforcing compliance.[83] In *Schempp*, despite the heated nature of the surrounding political debate, unanimity was not discussed. In fact, more significant differences about the grounds for the decision appeared in *Schempp* than had been evident in *Engel*. Stewart continued to dissent, largely on free exercise grounds, Douglas again raised the issue of state financing as relevant to schooltime religious activities, while Brennan wrote a 73-page treatise on what was and was not permissible, a legal guidebook for those affected by *Engel* and *Schempp*.[84] Short of explicitly rejecting the relevance of the political debate, the Court could not have indicated more clearly how insignificant it was to the final ruling.

The Court's dismissal of the relevance of the surrounding political debate did not deter politicians and religious groups from continuing their campaigns to overturn the Court. Although the constitutional amendments introduced into Congress in 1962 came to nothing, in the aftermath of *Schempp*, 146 prayer amendments in 35 forms were introduced during the 88th Congress, all but ensuring committee hearings. Although initially supporters of *Engel* and *Schempp* believed that the dominant proposal – the so-called Becker Amendment – would die in committee as previous amendments had done, significant congressional support for Becker's discharge petition forced Emanuel Celler, chairman of the House Judiciary Committee, to schedule hearings which ran from 22 April to 3 June 1964.[85] Support for the amendment came from 97 congressmen, led by Frank Becker; a number of evangelical Christian groups, including the National Association of Evangelicals and the International Council of Christian Churches; state officials including Governors Farris Bryant of Florida and George Wallace of Alabama; a range of interest groups from the American Legion, the Concerned Citizens' Committee and the newly formed Constitutional Prayer Foundation to the American Farm Bureau Federation and Project America. Opposition came from Protestant groups including the American Baptist Convention, the Baptist Joint Committee and the General Council of Seventh Day Adventists; Jewish groups representing Orthodox, Conservative and Reform Judaism from the Anti-Defamation League to the Rabbinical Assembly; and several secular groups including the ACLU, the American Humanist Association and Americans United; a joint statement issued by over two hundred constitutional law professors and legal practitioners; and four Congressmen.[86] Despite strong rhetoric at the opening of the hearings, it became clear that Becker and his supporters could neither agree on the consequences of the amendment nor produce an effective substitute, while opponents methodically exposed the weaknesses of the proposed amendment. Becker's 'one man crusade' thus ended in committee without ever reaching the floor of the House.

Despite its failure, testimony provided for and against the Becker Amendment revealed much about the nature of the political debate over school prayer and Bible reading, trends which shaped the debate for several years afterwards. Most significantly, the testimony of advocates illustrated the symbolism with which they were trying to associate the prayer issue. Becker opened the hearings with reference to a 'fraternity of secularists' and 'atheists and unbelievers', and concluded, 'I find my enthusiasm increased by the nature and personnel of the opposition'.[87] Connecting supporters of the Court's rulings with atheism or Communism was not a new means of attack, but its continued employment in the face of testimony from a range of religious groups and individuals indicated how deeply ingrained the proposition was and how crucial an element to the pro-prayer movement. Other familiar arguments appeared repeatedly throughout the hearings: that the Court had misinterpreted the history of the Establishment Clause, favouring separation over the true intent of religious neutrality; that *Engel* and *Schempp* denied the majority the free exercise of their religion; that the Becker Amendment would return control over schoolroom religious exercises to states and local communities, more in keeping with US federalism; that religion promoted morality; and that since the majority of the public favoured school prayer, the unelected Supreme Court should be overturned by the democratically elected representatives of the people. Defenders of school prayer sought to present themselves as advocates of the true American way, as defenders of morality and goodness, representatives of the majority voice and protectors of real religious freedom. They were the good guys, defending Americanism from the immoral, the atheists, the unbelievers and the Communists. That states' rights, local control, morality and majority rule were issues unrelated to interpretation of the Establishment Clause suggested that ensuring the most accurate constitutional interpretation was not the primary concern of Becker and his supporters. The political and electoral consequences of identification with these issues were, however, significant: politicians in particular sought to associate prayer with those electoral issues most significant in their constituencies. Thus the prayer debate was not just about prayer; it encompassed subtexts that varied depending on region and circumstance.

Equally significant was the testimony of opponents of the Becker Amendment and its impact on the Judiciary Committee. Slanting their campaign as 'protecting the sanctity of the First Amendment', opponents' major aim was to mobilize religious leaders to make it 'safe' and 'respectable' for Congressmen to oppose the Becker Amendment.[88] Providing religious spokesmen who could present the case for the danger posed to faith from mandated school prayer helped to counteract the Becker forces' suggestion that they stood on the side of God and that anyone who opposed them must be Godless.[89] Throughout the hearings, witnesses testified to the problems and dangers facing faith and religion should the amendment pass. Harvard law professor Paul Freund challenged the free exercise approach of the Becker forces, arguing that mandated prayers discriminated against the minority; others challenged the true voluntariness of prayer exercises, asserted that faith coerced was no faith at all, argued that the very blandness of a prayer that would offend no-one made it irrelevant as an expression of faith, and challenged their opponents to show who would decide what prayer and Bible passages would be read and with what consequences in religiously diverse communities – a challenge Becker and others failed to meet. By raising these issues, witnesses revealed that the simplicity of 'returning God to America's classrooms' claimed by Becker was not simple at all, and that the consequences of a national school prayer went far beyond anything acknowledged by Becker and his supporters.[90]

Legal scholars and practitioners reinforced the sense of the issue's complexity. Especially potent was the assertion made by Leo Pfeffer and others that, 'if you open the door for constitutional amendment because a particular decision at a particular time is unpopular, the entire purpose of the Bill of Rights to ride out periods of passion will have been destroyed'.[91] The danger, they asserted, was that by amending the Bill of Rights once, the structure was so weakened that it would be unable to withstand future attacks. The sentiment was reinforced on the final day of the hearings when a memorandum entitled 'Our Most Precious Heritage' was submitted to the Committee, signed by 223 constitutional lawyers, including the deans of some of the nation's leading law schools.[92] The impact of the submission was summarized by one committee member who remarked, 'we have just been hit by 223 bricks'.[93] The methodical approach of analysing the consequences of the Becker Amendment used by its opponents worked to overcome the populist rhetoric employed by Becker and others. By rejecting easy soundbites which would sell well to the public through the media, and focusing instead on detailed analysis addressed to the committee members, opponents illustrated the real, practical problems posed by the measure, turning it into an issue of pragmatism rather than emotion. The ultimate failure of the Becker Amendment to pass through the Committee was testament to the success of this approach.

Similar patterns of debate occurred in subsequent battles over prayer amendments to the Constitution. In 1966, Senate Minority Leader Everett Dirksen (R-Il) introduced a new amendment, arguing 'prayer is the roadmap to God. It should become the greatest adventure for young minds'.[94] Opposition of a similar character to that in the 1964 House hearings focused again on the problems of language and application and the dangers of prayer activities that were not truly voluntary.[95] Similar patterns were reflected in Senator Howard Baker's (R-Tenn) proposed amendment in 1971, and again in 1978 when Senator Jesse Helms (R-NC) sought to circumvent the unsuccessful amendment process by proposing a bill that would deny the Supreme Court jurisdiction to act on any state law, ordinance, rule or regulation relating to voluntary prayer in public schools.[96] Continued lack of success, frequently ensured by the measured, analytical testimony of lawyers, legal scholars and religious representatives, as seen in the Becker Hearings, did not stop repeated legislative attempts to overturn *Engel* and *Schempp*, but made each new attempt as unlikely to succeed. Politicians, however, continued to use the issue to gain maximum political exposure with the minimum amount of work. The guaranteed publicity and commentary surrounding each new proposal ensured for politicians a high profile and the opportunity to win favour with the electorate or other party members, but, since the bills were unlikely to pass, the politically difficult task of putting them into practice could be avoided.

Public opinion polls conducted several years after Becker's campaign indicated that politicians' concern to represent the popular will had strong foundations. In the Sixth Annual Gallup Poll of Public Attitudes Towards Religion in 1974, the first to explicitly ask about school prayer, 77 per cent of respondents favoured a constitutional amendment and 17 per cent opposed one.[97] Considering the Supreme Court had made no ruling on the issue for more than a decade and the last major congressional attempt at amendment was three years previously, such high levels of support suggested strong feelings among the public on the issue of school prayer. However, the experiences of the House Judiciary Committee during the Becker Hearings suggests that these figures do not reveal the whole truth. In April 1964, the *New York Times* reported, 'it is conceded widely in Congress that Congressional mail on this issue has grown to flood proportions, exceeding the mail of the civil rights controversy'.[98] Representative Lionel Van Deerlin (D-Cal) wrote that his colleagues 'are being inundated with constituent mail, the great bulk of which favors such an amendment', and Representative Alec Olson (D-Minn) wrote to a constituent, 'I have received correspondence which is at least 200 to 1 in favor of such an amendment'.[99] Had public pressure continued at this level it was unlikely that any Congressman seeking re-election would have jeopardized his campaign by opposing Becker.

However, as John Laubach's study of public reactions to the Becker Amendment indicated, the flow of mail reflected the strength of testimony given in the House hearings. Although initial public reaction was overwhelmingly in Becker's favour, as witnesses testified to the difficulties inherent in the proposal, public correspondence shifted away from Becker towards his opponents. The week in which most legal scholars testified saw 840 pieces of mail opposing Becker to only 80 in support. Discounting printed cards provided by organized interest groups, the Judiciary Committee received 13,000 items of mail in relation to the Becker Amendment: 8000 in favour, 5000 against, hardly the 'flood' in favour implied at the start of the hearings. Studies show that the strength of opposition testimony and detailed press coverage of the hearings led to a cooling of passions surrounding the hearings and a reassessment of the consequences of the amendment.[100] As people learnt more about the issues involved in the amendment and the complexities surrounding its potential application, a re-evaluation occurred. The figures quoted in the

1974 Gallup poll, among others, reflect the pre-Becker situation: a simple response unrelated to the complexities of the issue. A poll asking questions about the consequences of school prayer, such as excusal remedies, or the use of the Koran, Torah or other religious texts, may have generated significantly different results. Any discussion of public opinion thus requires a differentiation between informed and uninformed responses.

Although few detailed studies of compliance with *Engel* and *Schempp* were undertaken, those in existence support G. Theodore Mitau's 1967 conclusion that, 'compliance with *Engel* and *Schempp* must be assessed presently as falling far short of the court-enunciated standards of religious freedom'.[101] Such studies argued compliance occurred only when 'local adherents of the Supreme Court put their political influence on the line to make non-adherence more costly than compliance to the Court'.[102] Unwilling to cause upheaval in their communities, local officials frequently changed laws requiring prayer or Bible reading to allow decisions to be taken by individual schools or teachers: technically, communities were abiding by the law since there was no official policy; and unless complaints were received, prayer activities could continue if supported by the local community. However, an absence of state laws or local regulations banning outright the practice of prayer and Bible reading in schools does not, by itself, establish non-compliance, and few studies provided detailed evidence relating to the extent of non-compliance in the areas investigated.

An alternative approach presents a different picture of reaction to *Engel* and *Schempp*. After *Schempp*, the Supreme Court did not issue another major school prayer ruling until 1980, yet the issue remained a potent and controversial one. A consideration of the lower court rulings in such cases reveals at least part of the reason for the Supreme Court's silence: an overwhelming degree of compliance with the principles laid down in *Engel* and *Schempp*. In 1964, state supreme courts or lower federal courts heard cases in Delaware, Florida, Idaho, Massachusetts, Michigan, New Jersey, New York and Pennsylvania. Only in *Chamberlain v. Dade County Board of Public Instruction* was the Supreme Court required to intervene to uphold *Engel* and *Schempp*.[103] The cases ranged from direct opposition to the Supreme Court and deliberate attempts to avoid compliance in Delaware, Massachusetts and New Jersey to challenges to practices yet to be changed in Idaho, Michigan and New York. Although these cases provided evidence of non-compliance or opposition at local level, they also show the uniform support from lower courts for *Engel* and *Schempp* as constitutional law. As the primary interpreters of the application of the Supreme Court's rulings at state level, the state and lower federal courts played an integral part in forcing sometimes unwilling populations and school boards into compliance. Later cases reflected their success: in succeeding years cases arose increasingly from good faith attempts to comply with the Supreme Court's rulings while seeking to balance them with community demands.[104] Teachers who violated the ban on prayer and religious activities were often reprimanded or dismissed.[105] Thus, despite opposition to the ban on school mandated prayer and Bible reading, in instances where challenges reached the courts the ban was upheld repeatedly.

Courts were not the only governmental institutions upholding *Engel* and *Schempp*. In states including Maine, Massachusetts, New Jersey and Pennsylvania, state attorneys general issued reports and guidelines in support of the Court's decisions, advising how best to remain within the limits imposed. In Maine, the attorney general advised the governor and legislative leaders that public school prayer would violate the Constitution, while in Massachusetts bills allowing voluntary prayer and enforced periods of 'silent prayer or meditation' were struck down by the Governor on the advice of his attorney general. Although noting the objectives of the bill were 'well-intentioned', he argued that he could not 'in good conscience approve the measure'.[106] More significant, in symbolic if not practical terms, were the responses of the president of the United States. On 28 June 1962, President John Kennedy responded to a question about *Engel* in his press conference:

> The Supreme Court has made its judgment, and a good many people will obviously disagree with it. Others will agree with it. But I think that it is important for us if we are going to maintain our constitutional principle that we support the Supreme Court decisions even when we may not agree with them. In addition, we have in this case a very easy remedy, and that is to pray ourselves and I would think it would be a very welcome reminder to every American family that we can pray a good deal more at home and attend our churches with a good more fidelity, and we can make the true meaning of prayer much more important in the lives of all our children.[107]

Kennedy's measured response reached out to all. He recognized those who objected to the Court's ruling and did not challenge their response as unnecessary or irrational. However, his evident support for the Supreme Court and his enunciation of a feasible alternative to school prayer left no room for uncertainty about his position on this issue. Although he did not attack the Court's critics, Kennedy made clear he would not accept non-compliance. A similar response was elicited from President Jimmy Carter in response to Senator Helms's 1978 attempt to remove the Supreme Court's jurisdiction over school prayer cases. A born-again Christian who spoke publicly about the importance of his religious beliefs, Carter's religious credentials could not be doubted. Carter's position on school prayer was unequivocal. Responding to a direct question in a press conference in April 1979, he said:

> My preference is that the Congress not get involved in the question of mandating prayer in schools. I am a Christian. I happen to be a Baptist. I believe that the subject of prayer in school ought to be decided between a person individually and privately and God. And the Supreme Court has ruled on this issue and I personally don't think that the Congress ought to pass any legislation requiring or permitting prayer being required or permitted in school.[108]

Because of his religious background and his position as president, Carter's opposition to the Helms Bill, expressed after its passage in the Senate, was a significant blow to Helms and his supporters. So much of the prayer debate had been discussed in terms of 'believers' versus 'secularists' that a prominent figure with strong religious beliefs opposing school prayer was sufficiently anomalous to gain attention. That the figure was the president ensured greater exposure and significantly weakened attempts by Helms and others to overturn the Court's rulings in *Engel* and *Schempp*.

Concluding Thoughts

In 1962 and 1963 the Court struck down school-sponsored prayer and Bible reading activities in the nation's public schools on the grounds that they violated the Establishment Clause. The Court did not secularize the schools, prevent students from praying individually or in small groups or demand that any and all references to faith, belief or religion be expunged from school curricula. However, little of this was clear from the political and religious overreaction to the cases which labelled the justices as atheists and Communist sympathizers, the Court as godless and the decisions themselves as a blight on the religious heritage of the nation. The reaction shaped public perception of the cases, leading many to overlook the fact that what the Court struck down was *school*-organized or *school*-sponsored activities, instances where the school might be seen to encourage participation or support a particular belief. Beyond that the Court made no comment, except to note the limits of its rulings. *Engel* and *Schempp* were narrow and specific; the reaction to them was broad-ranging and, at times, misleading.

The vehemence of opposition and the repeated attempts to overturn *Engel* and *Schempp* by constitutional amendment have all too often led to the conclusion that non-compliance with the rulings was a widespread phenomenon. There is, however, little supporting evidence. Much public opinion regarding the Court's actions was unfavourable and, on a local level, individual teachers or school districts sought to ignore or circumvent the Court rulings. However, this does not by itself make a case for the 'widespread' nature of *actual* non-compliance. So much attention has been paid to the challenges by politicians and religious leaders to *Engel* and *Schempp* and the apparent lack of compliance with the decisions at school board and community level that it has too often been overlooked that government officials in many cases upheld the Supreme Court and did so unambiguously. Challengers such as Helms, Becker and Billy Graham were vocal and colourful and so garnered significant attention, but the number of such overt challenges was small compared to the number of towns, cities or states in the country where no challenges were laid, or where early action by government officials halted them. There may have been widespread dissatisfaction with *Engel* and *Schempp*, but there was also compliance and adherence.

Although the public and political debate that resulted from *Engel* and *Schempp* was heated and predominantly critical, it had little impact on the outcomes of the cases. Two factors account for its limited impact. First, unlike state financial aid to religious schools or allowing religious groups to meet on school grounds, both instances where the Court paid particular attention to circumstances and public opinion, prayer and Bible reading were unquestionably religious activities. Religious exercises conducted by the state or state officials was one of the evils that the Founding Fathers sought to prevent with the First Amendment and thus the outcome was clear. Whether because the state should remain strictly separate from involvement with religion, as Black argued in *Engel*, or because such activities could not feasibly be opened to all, as Clark argued in *Schempp*, school day religious activities could not be allowed on public school grounds. Second, the nature of the political debate held little relevance for the constitutional issue of Establishment Clause interpretation. From the earliest reactions to *Engel*, politicians and some religious groups portrayed the issue as being for or against God, in absolutist terms that had little to do with the Court's opinions. Symbolically, prayer was linked with broader issues of morality, values, patriotism, respect and the place of religious belief in American life outside the school environment, all highly emotive issues that could be used for political gain but which had little relevance to the Court's role of constitutional interpretation. Years of political debate about school prayer revealed little about its constitutionality but a great deal about how it could be used for political gain.

Chapter 5

School Prayer and the Reagan Era

In 1980, the Supreme Court returned to the issue of school prayer. Since Warren Burger's appointment as Chief Justice in 1969, the Court's Establishment Clause cases had been dominated by the issue of federal and state aid to religious schools, and in many ways the task facing the Burger Court on school prayer was much more difficult than that dealt with by Warren and his colleagues. In *Engel v. Vitale*, and to a lesser degree in *Abington School District v. Schempp*, the Warren Court had the luxury of dealing with school prayer as a purely legal issue: having been largely absent from political debate for decades, prayer in public schools did not initially come with a great deal of political 'baggage'. *Engel* and *Schempp*, however, returned it firmly to the political sphere. At the same time, the Court's activism firmly linked it in the public mind with the leading political issues of the day, making the law appear increasingly politicized, and making the Court itself increasingly appear as a political institution. As a result, the Court's opinions became fodder for political debate while the Court became a prime target for political attack. In the aftermath of *Engel* and *Schempp*, many had come to believe that the Court's basic approach displayed hostility towards religion, a perception reinforced by the Burger Court's refusal to countenance widespread government funding of religious schools. The school aid decisions made both separationists and accommodationists suspicious of the Court's intentions, placing an even greater burden of expectation on the Burger Court's first prayer case. A broad, sweeping opinion risked strengthening such opposition and motivating action against the Court.

The Burger Court also faced the task of 'filling in the blanks' left by the Warren Court. If *Engel* and *Schempp* established the broad principle that religious exercises in the public schools were unconstitutional and that any element of state support or sponsorship of religious practice was equally so, the Burger Court had to define what exactly constituted a religious exercise and state sponsorship or support. In effect, although the political issue remained one of whether religion should or should not be part of the public school curriculum, the legal issue had significantly changed: the decision before the Court was not whether the religious practice was constitutional, but whether the challenged exercise was a religious one. The issue was at least as controversial as that which had preceded it, if not more so. Much of the resistance to the Warren Court's prayer decisions took the form of redefining religious practices, finding secular applications for them, or removing at a superficial level the element of state support and claiming the activity was purely voluntary.[1] By undertaking a consideration of the constitutionality of such practices, the Burger Court threatened to provoke a reaction equal to or greater than that which met *Engel* and *Schempp*, while dealing with an issue of much greater technical complexity which would be far more difficult to explain to the public.

Stone v. Graham: Reigniting the Prayer Debate

Stone v. Graham was thus significant not only as the Court's first prayer ruling in seventeen years, but also as the first from the Burger Court.[2] *Stone* involved a challenge to a Kentucky statute requiring the posting of a copy of the Ten Commandments, purchased with private contributions, on the wall of each public classroom in the state. The State claimed that the posting had a valid secular purpose: as the foundation of much secular law, the Decalogue encouraged students to contemplate and meditate upon legal rights and responsibilities and the nature of American society.[3] The Court, in a *per curiam*, or unsigned, opinion, firmly rejected the claim: 'The pre-eminent purpose for posting the Ten Commandments on schoolroom walls is plainly religious in nature. The Ten Commandments are undeniably a sacred text in the Jewish and Christian faiths, and no legislative recitation of a supposed secular purpose can blind us to that fact'.[4] Thus, the Court gave warning that unless a challenged practice had a solely secular purpose and was not simply an alleged secularity to cover a blatantly religious purpose, the challenged activity would not be allowed to stand. Although neither creating new law nor exploring the boundaries of existing law, *Stone* was significant because it clearly reinforced the principles of *Engel* and *Schempp* despite the political debate of the intervening years. The Burger Court did, however, manifest a continued concern for the political and social implications of any prayer ruling much as the Warren Court had done. In particular, the Court's decision not to hear oral argument and the *per curiam* approach were pragmatic solutions to the problem posed by the case.[5] By avoiding oral argument the Court ensured that the public focus remained only on those issues it wanted to discuss, the limited issues addressed in the *per curiam* opinion. By narrowing the focus to the question of the religiosity of the Decalogue, the Court dealt as sparely as possible with the case, avoiding much of the opposition that a broader opinion may have generated.

The Court's circumspection in *Stone* was justified by succeeding events. In the summer of 1980 the Republican Party included a pro-prayer plank in their party platform and the House Judiciary Subcommittee opened hearings on the Helms Amendment that had passed the Senate the year before.[6] Both returned school prayer to a more prominent position on the political agenda than it had occupied for the previous few years. Despite the defeat of the Helms Amendment, throughout 1981 and 1982 a series of bills introduced into Congress sought to restrict or eliminate the Supreme Court's jurisdiction over a number of controversial issues, including abortion, school busing, a males-only draft and state court rulings, as well as school prayer. The Senate also took action, denying the Justice Department the ability to use federal funds to 'prevent the implementation of programs of voluntary prayer and meditation in the public schools'.[7] Although it had little practical impact since the Justice Department had almost no role in this area, its symbolic status was beyond question, portraying the Senate as being equally committed to the cause of school prayer as the House.

Support from the Reagan Administration, especially from Attorney General William French Smith, lent credibility to these activities and, by implication, to the attacks on the Court. In a 1981 speech to the Federal Legal Council, a group of leading lawyers from government departments and agencies, Smith accused the federal courts of 'constitutionally dubious and unwise intrusions upon the legislative domain', and 'weighing the balance against proper legislative action'.[8] 'We believe that the groundswell of conservatism evidenced by the 1980 election makes this an especially appropriate time to urge upon the courts more principled bases that would diminish judicial activism', said Smith, suggesting the courts had been more concerned about judicial activism and policy making than 'reasoned legal interpretation', and making clear that the Justice Department would seek to reverse this trend. Although making no specific reference to school prayer, the speech drew so heavily on the principles enshrined in the 'court-stripping' bills that it was at least implicated in the discussion, as it was when Smith stated that the Justice Department 'intends to play an active role in effecting the principles upon which Ronald Reagan campaigned'.[9] Appearing to lose the support of prominent conservative legal figures over the court bills, Smith's speech was an appeal directly to the core conservative support which had ensured Reagan's success in the 1980 election.[10]

The debates were important in highlighting a trend that would shape future church-state debates: the rise to prominence of evangelical Christian groups. Most prominent in supporting the Helms Bill, representatives from groups such as Campus Crusade for Christ, the Moral Majority and the Religious Roundtable, as well as a number of television and radio evangelists, testified to the importance of returning prayer to schools. 'The important question', William Bright, founder of Campus Crusade for Christ, said, 'is "Are we going to bring God back to our schools?"' implying, as had many before him, that the Supreme Court had barred any recognition of religion from public schools. Blaming the Court for 'the plagues' of crime, disintegration of families, racial conflict, teenage pregnancy and venereal disease and the assassinations of President Kennedy, Robert Kennedy and Martin Luther King, Bright warned that 'worse troubles lie ahead of us' if prayer was not returned to schools.[11] Reverend James Robinson, a Southern Baptist from Texas, repeated the warning, suggesting 'this nation faces the judgment of Almighty God' if lawmakers refused to return the practice of prayer to the public schools.[12] Arguably the biggest coup for Helms's supporters was the testimony of William Murray, son of Madalyn Murray O'Hair, the plaintiff in *Murray v. Curlett* seventeen years earlier, who testified that as a Christian he now believed the suit brought in 1963 had been a 'mistake'.[13] Opposing them were representatives of the forty-million member, thirty-two denomination National Council of Churches, the Baptist Joint Committee and the B'nai B'rith Anti-Defamation League. Meyer Eisenberg, the ADL representative, said the prayer bill represented 'a clear and present danger' to the constitutional protections afforded all Americans, while Reverend William Howard, president of the National Council of Churches, called prayer 'too important, too sacred, too intimate to be scheduled or administered by Government'.[14] Noting that the Court had not forbidden silent, voluntary prayers in school, Howard labelled as 'simplistic' the notion that 'putting God back into the public schools' would cure social ills. 'These may be laudable goals', he said, 'but it is a farce to suppose that they can be achieved by the recitation of a two-minute prayer at the beginning of the public-school day'.[15] The clash between Bright and Howard symbolized the increasing schism between leaders of the traditional church denominations and the mainly conservative evangelical groups which had been developing for a little over a year. The Helms Bill served as one of the first indicators of the development of the Religious Right, which further politicized the school prayer issue.[16]

The 'court-stripping' bills also brought to the Court's defence individuals and organizations who had previously remained largely outside of the school prayer debate. If the Helms Amendment had revealed the growing divide between the traditional and evangelical churches, the 'court-stripping' bills indicated differences between activist conservatives who, like Professor Charles Rice, believed they should 'teach the Supreme Court a lesson' because 'we have been unduly deferential to the Supreme Court', and 'conservative' conservatives who were concerned about the precedent such a move might set, conservatives such as Robert Bork, who referred to the bills as 'unwise and potentially unconstitutional' and a 'cure that may set a precedent more damaging than the wrong Supreme Court decisions'.[17] Ultimately it was the latter argument which proved the stronger. While liberals accused the bills' supporters of attempting to achieve *de facto* constitutional amendments without the attendant difficulty of actually achieving them, the American Bar Association (ABA) and a number of leading legal scholars sought to challenge the bills on narrower grounds. At meetings in August 1981 and January 1982, the ABA expressed concern about legislation which appeared to threaten the federal judiciary's supremacy in matters of constitutional interpretation. '[W]e are confronted at this very moment with a legislative threat to our nation that may lead to the most serious constitutional crisis since our great Civil War', argued David Brink, president of the ABA, undoubtedly overstating the issue but nevertheless dramatizing the significance of the bills.[18] The strength of the legal community's opinion was made clear to Congress during hearings in May 1981 when a number of leading scholars testified against the bills. The legal argument against the 'court-stripping' bills, as in earlier debates, drew heavily on a profound respect for the institutions of government and the Constitution.

Throughout the national debates on school prayer, the Helms Amendment and the 'court-stripping' bills, the issue continued to cause controversy at state level. Richard Dierenfield, who undertook several studies of the impact of *Engel* and *Schempp*, suggested '[p]rayer is creeping back into public schools rather sporadically ... We can't identify it exactly, but it seems to me they're trying it more and more'.[19] Likewise, Leo Pfeffer noted the issue was 'chronic, persistent, and it heats up every time it gets into the paper'.[20] Challenges were noted as far apart as Massachusetts, Minnesota, Missouri, New York, Tennessee and Texas, ranging from moment of silence laws to graduation prayers to religious groups meeting on school premises out of school hours. What the challenges also brought to light was a small number of extreme examples of flouting the Supreme Court's rulings. In

Mississippi, for example, the state Civil Liberties Union filed suit against the Rankin County school board when it discovered that prayer was being broadcast over the school loudspeaker system and a teacher called any child refusing to participate 'a devil'. More common was the case of Katherine Jolley, a history teacher in Washington for thirty-one years, who said that she used prayer to solve discipline problems in the classroom.[21] Debate about the reasons for the increasing number of challenges also existed. Reverend Edgar Koons of Sacramento argued, 'people want something done ... The great majority favor God and the pendulum has begun to swing in that direction', suggesting the greater momentum came from those wishing to encourage school prayer. This was challenged by the Texas Civil Liberties Union which suggested, 'parents were afraid to litigate because of their participation might have a negative impact ... Now people feel more threatened. There is a different, more emotional element. Now they're willing to pursue it'.[22]

The sheer variety of issues raised under the banner of 'prayer' can, in part, be traced to the limited scope of *Engel* and *Schempp* themselves. Issues that went beyond simply prayer or Bible reading were outside the scope of the Court's rulings and government officials were faced with the task of deciding how best to comply with the stated meaning of the First Amendment. Moment of silence statutes, prayer led by student volunteers, religious groups meeting before or after the school day without teacher involvement and periods of 'voluntary prayer' were among the most common practices challenged in state and lower federal courts.[23] Lack of coherence made it increasingly likely that the Supreme Court would have to revisit the subject, if only to clarify the line between permissible and impermissible activities. In this context, congressional debates about the Supreme Court's jurisdiction and prayer amendments appear as attempts to pre-empt Court action as well as overturning Court decisions. It is clear, though, that national debates did influence local action, making those discussions all the more significant. In early 1980, a Gallup poll reported that three-quarters of all Americans had 'no idea' what the First Amendment said, or meant.[24] Even if the figure was significantly lower, the poll indicated that a large number of Americans were taking their cues about the First Amendment from debates in the political arena. This made the congressional debates all the more significant in providing the terms in which the topic would be debated, while also establishing the parameters of the debate.

In this context, speeches at the August 1981 ABA meeting in New Orleans by Justices John Paul Stevens and Lewis Powell appear as attempts to deflect the political controversy over school prayer away from the Court and towards the legal interpretation of the issue. Quoting from *West Virginia State Board of Education v. Barnette* and *Engel*, Stevens said that 'symbolic gestures' of patriotism and religious faith such as saluting the flag and 'voluntary prayer and reflection' are good things 'on appropriate occasions', stressing 'the distinction between a compelled ritual and voluntary participation in a common exercise'. Asked after the speech whether he was intending to send a message to the Moral Majority and others attacking the Court's prayer rulings, Stevens replied, 'it speaks for itself'. Justice Powell reviewed 190 years of Court history in order to conclude that 'the first duty of a Justice is to remove his or her own moral, philosophical, political, and religious beliefs', refusing to be drawn on who his target was.[25] Stevens's speech appeared to engage most directly with the prayer issue but in a way which drew heavily on the Court's precedents, which effectively reinforced publicly his support for the Court's past holdings. Powell's comment could be taken either as an attempt to show that the justices based decisions on law rather than politics, or possibly as a response to the Religious Right's claim that those who opposed school prayers were 'anti-religion' by suggesting that this was an inaccurate interpretation of what the Court did. Regardless of their subtext, both speeches made pointed comments about issues on the political agenda. That they spoke at all was also significant: the relative rarity with which sitting Supreme Court justices gave speeches at the time made the timing of these speeches significant, their taking place at all as important a comment on the debates as anything actually said.

Then, on 7 May 1982, saying he wanted to foster 'faith in a Creator who alone has the power to bless America', President Reagan announced that he would propose a constitutional amendment to allow 'voluntary prayer' in public schools. Although anticipated, the announcement took the prayer debate in a new direction while there had not yet been a resolution on the 'court-stripping' issue.[26] Making the announcement to a gathering of 120 religious and conservative political leaders in the White House Rose Garden, Reagan stated:

> Today prayer is still a powerful force in America, and our faith in God is a mighty source of strength. Our pledge of allegiance states that we are one nation under God, and our currency bears the motto "In God We Trust." The morality and values such faith implies are deeply embedded in our national character. Our country embraces these principles by design, and we abandon them at our peril. Yet in recent years well-meaning

Americans, in the name of freedom have taken freedom away ... How can we hope to retain our freedom through the generations if we fail to teach our young that our liberty springs from an abiding faith in our Creator?[27]

Several things were notable about this crucial section of Reagan's speech. Suggesting that the Supreme Court rulings were brought about by 'well-meaning' people, including the justices themselves, Reagan distanced himself from the attacks on the Court which had characterized the 'court-stripping' bills, implying this amendment was not about attack but about restoring rights. His references to the Pledge and national motto were also significant since they were the symbols most frequently pointed to as next in line for challenge by critics of the Court's rulings; by mentioning them, Reagan gave credence to the idea that they could be under attack. His implication that they still retained religious significance, however, contradicted arguments made by many who sought to defend their continued use by suggesting that they were mere ceremonial references which had lost any religious meaning. Most importantly, Reagan couched his support in the language of the free exercise rights of the majority. The approach had been given legitimacy by the discussion of free exercise rights in Court opinions and various groups had used it as a defence for their pro-prayer position, but by including it in this speech Reagan forced opponents of the measure on to the defensive; they would now be forced to explain why they appeared to object to the right of the majority to pray if they so wished. It was a clever political move by Reagan, even if its legal foundations were weak at best.

Reagan's announcement initiated a familiar, well-established and, at times, highly predictable debate. 'Obviously, the purpose of the constitutional amendment is to circumvent the Supreme Court and put it out of their reach', argued Jerry Falwell, leader of the Moral Majority. 'In my opinion it will be passed because the people want it, and I doubt any Congressman or state legislator could oppose religious liberty for the children today when that's what people want them to have', he continued, echoing Reagan's use of the language of religious freedom.[28] Defending the prayer amendment in the *New York Times*, Senator Orrin Hatch (R-Utah), chairman of the Senate Judiciary Committee, challenged the 'wall of separation' metaphor and stated, 'I do see a great deal of continuing harm in maintaining a "neutrality" toward the most traditional and fundamental religious values in our nation's heritage', challenging directly the foundations of *Engel* and *Schempp* in familiar ways.[29] Those opposing the amendment also reacted in predictable language. Terming Reagan's proposal, 'antithetical to fundamental principles of civil liberty as the Supreme Court recognized twenty years ago', Norman Dorsen, president of the American Civil Liberties Union, commented: 'Apparently dissatisfied with his destructive impact on the economy, the President is now moving to destroy the Constitution', implying diversionary tactics in Reagan's agenda.[30] A familiar group of religious leaders also responded in a joint statement, arguing, as they had in the past, that the amendment violated the Constitution, would heighten religious tensions in schools, trivialize prayer, coerce participation and was unworkable since 'nondenominationalism' was impossible.[31] Arguably the biggest surprise of the debates was that the Southern Baptist Convention, long an opponent of such measures, reversed its position to support Reagan's amendment, making it the only major denomination to do so. The shift indicated the growing strength of the fundamentalist movement within the Convention. While of tremendous symbolic importance, the true impact of the move was, however, unclear, many regarding it as the beginning of a debate within the church rather than a solid verdict in favour of school prayer.[32] However, it provided an unusual twist to an otherwise familiar debate.

The Helms Amendment, related Court stripping bills and Reagan's call for a prayer amendment showed the political ends to which the school prayer issue could be employed. Even if the Helms Amendment had passed the Senate, the time restrictions made a vote in the House unlikely before the end of the session and so the issue would have to be reintroduced once the new Congress convened. Sponsors of the prayer bill demanded a recorded vote in the Senate, a measure that would provide conservatives with potent ammunition in the November elections, regardless of the reasons Senators had for opposing the bill.[33] Drawing on widespread public misperceptions that the Helms Amendment was a school prayer bill rather than a 'court-stripping' bill, misperceptions which Helms and his supporters had encouraged, they sought to force a vote on a complex issue in order to present it in a simplistic way to voters in order to gain greater support in the next Congress.

For Reagan, a school prayer amendment was an easy way to make overtures to the increasingly frustrated Religious Right, which had been critical of Reagan's failure to advance the 'social values' agenda he had campaigned so heavily on in 1980. Reagan's appointment of Sandra Day O'Connor to the Supreme Court in July 1981 over more predictably staunch conservatives and his withdrawal of approval from an Administration plan to give tax exemptions to segregated private schools led many to question Reagan's commitment to the far right of his party.[34] Following the moderate

Democratic successes of the 1982 mid-term elections, Reagan continued to use the prayer issue to attempt to placate the Religious Right. At a convention of Christian broadcast preachers in January 1983, he criticized the federal courts for 'wrong' decisions on school prayer and abortion, announced he would sign a presidential proclamation making 1983 the 'Year of the Bible' and urged the nation to 'face the future with the Bible', assuring his audience that, 'I am determined to bring that amendment back again and again and again and again, until we succeed in restoring religious freedom in the United States'.[35] He was aided by conservatives in Congress who sought in mid-1983 to return the issue of school prayer to the floor of the Senate in the form of another constitutional amendment. Problems of the past continued to haunt the attempt, however, with scheduled Senate subcommittee sessions cancelled twice when the White House and Senator Orrin Hatch (R-Utah), the Committee's chairman, could not agree on the wording of a proposal. The Committee postponed deciding the issues involved by voting to send both proposals to the Senate floor for full debate, several Senators stressing that they did not support either measure but believed that the Senate had the right to discuss them in full. The hints of deep divisions among conservatives and the problems of the language employed, combined with past failures of similar amendments, made success unlikely. Combined with Reagan's little more than tepid support for a proposal to provide tax credits to parents with children in private schools, a measure with equally small chances of success, and the decision by Attorney General Smith not to file an *amicus* brief in the case that would become *Wallace v. Jaffree*, the overall impression was that Reagan, despite his rhetoric, was more interested in scoring political points than in actually passing legislation. 'I don't see a lot of burning passion on these issues', commented Representative Trent Lott, the Republican Whip.[36] The symbolism of the prayer issue, however, was so great that, irrespective of its chances of success in Congress, Reagan's support for such a measure could be used to show his fidelity to the Religious Right.[37]

The Senate opened debate on the prayer amendments on Monday 5 March 1984.[38] Reagan had made the issue a central plank of his bid for re-election and frequently stressed the subject in campaign appearances. Howard Baker, Jr (R-Tenn), the Senate majority leader, told reporters that supporters of school prayer had their 'best chance in decades' for success in Congress.[39] Despite this, an aide to Baker noted, '[i]t's going to be a tough vote ... The sides are well drawn, and we're dealing with a handful of Senators who will make or break the outcome', an analysis which proved strikingly accurate as debate began. In a highly charged atmosphere, heavy with political undertones, Senator Strom Thurmond (R-SC) opened debate by calling the amendment 'of vital importance to the well being of our nation'. The theme was continued by Helms, who argued, '[i]t is no mere coincidence that the decline of public education parallels the banning of prayer in public schools'. In response, Lowell Weicker (R-Conn), who would become the leader of opponents of the measure, accused Reagan of using the issue for political gain and said it was brought up 'as a campaign issue' in order 'to satisfy the President's conservative supporters'.[40] The following day attempts were made to find a compromise between the two amendments which would specify that individuals or groups could choose between silent or vocal prayer in order to convince a small group of Senators to support the measure, while several hundred people joined a prayer vigil on the Capitol steps to demonstrate their support for the measure, and inside the chamber Senator Hatch argued, 'it won't kill a kid to be different from other children'.[41] As the *New York Times* noted, '[o]n neither side of the issue have the arguments changed much in two decades'.[42] The amendment was eventually defeated 56:44 – 11 votes short of a two-thirds majority – on 20 March 1984.

The activities of Reagan, Helms and the Religious Right between 1980 and 1984 inflamed debate about school prayer and further entangled it with issues unrelated to the Establishment Clause, such as public and private morality and national culture. The debates revealed little about the constitutionality of school prayer but showed how the issue was used for political ends. They also explain why the Court, although having to manage the resulting higher profile and volatility of the prayer issue, could comprehensively ignore the substance of the political debates.

Wallace v. Jaffree: Reaffirming the Warren Court

The case that would become *Wallace v. Jaffree*, the Burger Court's second and most significant prayer case, began in July 1982, right in the middle of the congressional debates about school prayer and 'court-stripping'. Alabama Governor Fob James approved a bill which allowed teachers to lead 'willing students' in prayer, stating clearly that he saw it as a vehicle for Alabama to test the Supreme Court's prayer rulings.[43] As Congress debated and his case moved through the courts, Ishmael Jaffree fought his own personal battle in his home state, facing opposition not only from the Mobile County School Board that voted to support the teachers and parents who desired prayer, but also from Governor James who, in September 1982, called on the state's teachers and students to defy a federal court injunction barring implementation of the prayer law.[44] At the same time, in New Jersey a similar debate began over the issue of moment of silence statutes. In October 1982, the state Senate passed a moment of silence bill similar to ones which had been passed in 1978 and 1981 but vetoed by the then-Governor Brendan Byrne as unconstitutional. On December 2, Governor Kean also vetoed the law, acting on advice from his counsel and a belief that the law was unnecessary since teachers could already order a moment of silence as part of ordinary disciplinary procedures: 'I prefer to leave it to the discretion of individual teachers to decide if their students need quiet time for contemplation and introspection and when their students may participate in such sessions', he said.[45] Less than two weeks later the Senate and Assembly voted by narrow majorities to override Kean's veto. The two debates ran parallel to each other; together they provided a case study of the practical application of the theories being debated at national level.

Most notable about the Alabama and New Jersey cases was the pure emotionalism of the issue and the problems faced by individuals seeking to become involved in the debates. While Senators dealt with insults, ordinary citizens often faced much worse. Testifying at the original trial, Jaffree told of the cost of his stand:

> My children have experienced all types of abuse from neighbors. Some of the children in our neighborhood, which is mostly white, have stopped playing with my children, and other children laugh at them. I have learned from others who have filed similar lawsuits that the children suffer immensely after the lawsuit is over. If it is ultimately successful, then my children will be forever stamped as the children of the father who tried to take religion out of the public classrooms. How are my children going to handle this? I don't know. I have suffered emotionally myself and it has drained me. My future here in Mobile is going to be drastically altered because of this lawsuit. I'm perceived as an outsider that is disrupting Mobile's quiet tranquility.[46]

Writing about his experiences several years later, Jaffree recalled that he received 'nasty letters and ... nasty phone calls', the local media had 'a field day' and the black community of Mobile was 'up in arms' that a black man had sought to 'take God out of the public schools'. More hurtful was the reaction of his children: 'My children started turning against me; they said it was a stupid lawsuit. They especially turned against me when Judge Hand ruled against me. They told me the judge had said what I was doing was stupid'.[47] While Jaffree sought to end the practice of organized prayer in Alabama schools, in Old Bridge, New Jersey, Thomas Cherney, a school board member, thought 'it would be nice to, you know, say a little prayer of thanks at the beginning of the school day'. Mentioning this at a school board meeting prompted 'the largest and most vocal crowd in memory to show up at the next meeting – most of them to yell at him'. Called a 'right-winger' and 'a religious nut', he was repeatedly asked if his proposal was politically motivated and if the Moral Majority was covertly supporting him; stereotyping was not all from one side.[48] The experiences of the two men illustrated the price frequently paid by those who sought to challenge the dominant views in their communities. As examples of how 'community choice' laws similar to that suggested as a compromise amendment by Reagan would work, they were damning; as examples of how national debate can influence local concerns, the experiences of Jaffree and Cherney were equally illustrative.

The moment of silence debates in Alabama and New Jersey continued throughout the congressional debates on amending the Constitution and Reagan's vocal support for doing so during 1983 and 1984. In Alabama, Federal District Judge W. Brevard Hand dismissed Jaffree's lawsuit and, calling his opinion 'a cry in the wilderness', argued that the Constitution allowed states the power to establish religion.[49] Set aside by Justice Powell until the case could be heard by the Eleventh Circuit, Jaffree's lawsuit began its way through the appeals courts. On 2 April 1984, the Supreme Court granted *certiorari*. In New Jersey, Attorney General Irwin Kimmelman, echoing the Governor's sentiments, refused to defend the state's new law on the grounds that it was 'absolutely unnecessary. If it does not have a religious purpose and was designed to allow all students a moment for reflection, the law adds nothing to the already existing authority invested in our schools'. Given this, Kimmelman concluded, '[m]andating a moment of silence is nothing more than a euphemism for required prayer'. Yet despite his certainty on the law, Kimmelman still appeared to feel the need to assert his own religiosity, most likely in the face of accusations of being 'anti-religion', explaining that his objections were 'totally on constitutional grounds' in an interview with the *New York Times*.[50] Finding an 'unconstitutional religious purpose motivated the legislature to pass the law', Federal District Court Judge Dickensen Debevoise invalidated the statute in October 1983.

Given a lack of consistency in the federal courts on moment of silence statutes as well as the continued debate surrounding school prayer, why did the Supreme Court refuse to revisit the issue for twenty-two years?[51] First, despite numerous challenges, the large majority of practices that violated

Engel and *Schempp* were struck down by courts, governors, or ultimately were not enacted at all: the Court had no need to intercede to defend its rulings because it was being done elsewhere. Second, the political controversy itself operated to keep the Court removed from the issue: several of the challenges to the Court were significant threats and the Court was unwilling to give the political branches additional ammunition with which to attack. Third, with the debate raging, the impression was that 'the people', through their representatives, had not yet decided on a course and if the Court intervened it might be seen as engaging in judicial legislation, the very thing the moderate majority of the Burger Court was trying to avoid. But as twenty-five states continued to have moment of silence statutes on their books, it seemed likely even before the Supreme Court accepted *Jaffree* that the issue would eventually have to be addressed by the Court in order to determine the constitutionality of such laws.[52]

Wallace v. Jaffree involved a challenge to the 1981 amendment of Alabama's existing moment of silence law to allow for 'meditation or voluntary prayer'.[53] The amendment was challenged by Ishmael Jaffree on behalf of his children as state support for religious activity and thus a violation of the Establishment Clause. As in *Stone*, the Court found that the state's sole purpose had been 'endorsement of prayer activities for one minute at the beginning of each school day ... characteriz[ing] prayer as a favored practice', thus violating the Establishment Clause.[54] Although the result reinforced the principles of *Engel*, *Schempp* and *Stone*, the consensus in the Court's opinions and the justices' private comments in the earlier cases had all but vanished; instead, *Jaffree* resulted in six separate opinions, including one that concurred only in result.[55] Although a majority still existed for adhering to the precedent of *Engel* and *Schempp*, the procedural divisions among the justices evident in school aid cases made the majority narrower and far less certain.

Justice Stevens's opinion for the Court was methodical, logical and narrow, relying heavily on the specific facts of the case, laying out the argument point-by-point and avoiding broad, sweeping statements of doctrine or philosophical principle. Stevens noted that prayers had been taking place in Mobile County schools in a constitutionally invalid manner irrespective of the facially valid statute. In doing so he provided the evidence of constitutional violation that Stewart had required in *Schempp* and the dissenters had demanded in *Stone*, but at the same time reinforced that *Jaffree* involved this specific statute and was not intended to be a broad statement about the constitutionality of similar laws and practices. The contrast with Black's *Engel* opinion was striking: where *Engel* spoke in broad terms, *Jaffree* was highly specific; where *Engel* skipped over precedent, *Jaffree* was firmly rooted in it. This was a function of the different circumstances in which the justices of the majority found themselves: by keeping the opinion narrow and heavily fact-specific, Stevens avoided making unnecessary *dicta* which could have alienated members of the majority and opened the Court to greater attack from critics of the ruling.

Aspects of Stevens's opinion accommodated the views of other justices to keep them within the majority. The clearest example was Stevens's use of 'endorsement' within his discussion of *Lemon*'s 'purpose' test. First proposed by O'Connor the previous year in *Lynch v. Donnelly*, it formed a significant part of her *Jaffree* concurrence.[56] Intended as a modification of the *Lemon* test, it advocated enquiring as to 'whether government's actual purpose is to endorse or disapprove of religion', and if 'the practice under review in fact conveys a message of endorsement or disapproval'.[57] Twice within the opinion Stevens made reference to endorsement as though it was a long recognized form of analysis, which was not the case. Stevens may have hoped to keep O'Connor within the majority, or at least encourage her to look favourably on the result by providing her test with an element of authority, placing it in a stronger position for future cases. That he included 'endorsement' in his opinion suggests that he and others in the majority felt it was necessary in order to ensure a strong position.

Justice Powell was the second justice whose views were accommodated by Stevens into the majority opinion. The change made was significant for the Court's reading of the 'purpose' prong of the *Lemon* test. The language of *Schempp* implied that a purely secular purpose was required to pass constitutional scrutiny since anything else might 'advance' religion, an argument supported by the *Stone per curiam* and at least implied in the early drafts of Stevens's opinion: 'As the District Court correctly recognized, no consideration of the second or third criteria [of *Lemon*] is necessary if a statute *does not have a clearly secular purpose*. At the very least, the First Amendment requires that a statute must be invalidated if it is *entirely motivated by a purpose to advance religion*'.[58] The emphasis was on the fact that anything less than a completely secular motive for legislation would be unlikely to pass constitutional scrutiny. But in response to an enquiry from Powell, Stevens wrote to the others in the majority to suggest a change to what became the final wording: 'For even though a statute that is motivated *in part* by a religious purpose may satisfy the first criteria . . . the First Amendment requires that a statute must be invalidated if it is entirely motivated by a purpose to advance religion'.[59] With this phrasing the emphasis changed: now a partly religious motivation could be acceptable depending on the circumstances of the case, a significant shift in position with regards to 'purpose' analysis. Although the change clarified some of the uncertainties of *Schempp* and *Lemon*, it also opened the Court to the possibility of new cases requiring definition of a religious, yet still sufficiently secular, motivation.

This change, as with the inclusion of 'endorsement', served no other purpose than to gain the support of wavering justices. Its significance was evident from communication among the justices regarding *Jaffree* during the period of opinion writing. A memorandum from Burger to Stevens in February 1985 suggested that Stevens did not have a majority.[60] Stevens's letter to the others in the majority regarding Powell's suggested change was sent to Justices William Brennan, Thurgood Marshall and Harry Blackmun, with no mention of O'Connor, suggesting agreement among only four justices: without either Powell or O'Connor the opinion would only be a plurality of the Court and would not be binding precedent.[61] Stevens's suggested alteration might allow Powell to 'change' his vote, suggesting that he had originally voted with the dissenters, further weakening Stevens's majority position.[62] The importance of Powell and O'Connor's concurrences to the eventual majority opinion was indicated by the difficulty of finding a way for the two to agree. While O'Connor advocated altering *Lemon*, Powell issued a passionate defence of the test, the disagreement resting not on a fundamental difference about the place of religious exercises in public schools, but on the method for determining constitutionality: a procedural rather than a substantive disagreement. That Stevens found a way to reconcile the Powell and O'Connor positions given the centrality of the 'purpose' test to the case, even if only convincing the two to file concurrences rather than join the majority, was a significant achievement, and one which turned a potential plurality opinion into a majority decision with far greater weight. Thus the majority, barely, managed successfully with the prayer issue to negotiate through the problems and divisions causing so much trouble in other areas of Establishment Clause jurisprudence.

The debate over *Lemon* in *Jaffree* revealed the divisions among the justices over procedural issues that had been increasingly evident in school aid cases. Stevens's majority opinion was clearly a defence of the beleaguered test: he made very clear that the majority was using *Lemon* and that while only the first part of it was being used, the majority still adhered to the rest of *Lemon*, effectively providing a vote of confidence in the test.[63] Yet it was Powell's concurrence which responded directly to criticisms of *Lemon* and provided a passionate defence of it, answering O'Connor and encouraging the majority to be more forceful. 'It is the only coherent test a majority of the Court has ever adopted,' asserted Powell, continuing, '*Lemon* has not been overruled or its test modified . . . [it] has been applied consistently in Establishment Clause cases since it was adopted in 1971. In a word, it has been the law. Respect for *stare decisis* should require us to follow *Lemon*'.[64] Combined, the majority opinion and Powell's concurrence provided a defence of *Lemon* that was both theoretical and practical. The debate, however, revealed more clearly the growing divisions among the justices and the controversy over the 'proper' test to be used for judging Establishment Clause violations. Although not influencing the result in *Jaffree*, the divisions suggested difficulties for future cases.

Rehnquist's dissent revealed additional issues for consideration in future cases. A personable, highly intelligent man who was described as 'today's equivalent of Hugo Black – only at the other end of the judicial spectrum', Rehnquist brought a highly developed conservative philosophy to the Court, a technical mastery of the law and a forceful writing style 'which at times employs colorful, emotionally charged imagery to underscore distaste for the positions of his liberal colleagues'.[65] Unlike many on the Burger Court, Rehnquist was willing to return to first premises in his opinions and rethink doctrines in terms of his personal constitutional philosophy. In *Jaffree* he did so by challenging Brennan's interpretation of the history of church-state relations from *Schempp*, suggesting, '[i]t is impossible to build sound constitutional doctrine upon a mistaken understanding of constitutional history, but unfortunately the Establishment Clause has been expressly freighted with Jefferson's misleading metaphor for nearly 40 years'.[66] Reconsidering the history of the framing, ratification and the actions of the First Congress, Rehnquist produced a concise accommodationist interpretation of the period, concluding, '[t]here is simply no historical foundation for the proposition that the Framers intended to build the "wall of separation" that was constitutionalized in *Everson*'.[67] Rehnquist's historical interpretation has been widely criticized – indeed, Marshall's opinion was unambiguously scribbled on the front of his copy of Rehnquist's first draft – but his willingness to address the issue at all indicated his far greater activism when compared with the Court's majority.[68] What was most significant about Rehnquist's dissent was that it staked out a position quite different from that of the centre or the liberals of the Court and signalled his future intentions, suggesting the beginning of a battle that would shape the Court's jurisprudence.

Equally significant for future Establishment Clause cases was O'Connor's concurrence. In her first few years on the Court, O'Connor was seen as a close ally of Justice Rehnquist, frequently voting with him and joining his opinions, and so placing herself on the political right of the Court. By the time *Jaffree* was heard, however, it appeared O'Connor was moving away from Rehnquist; while remaining slightly right of centre, she increasingly found herself as the pivotal justice in close cases. Her *Jaffree* concurrence was symbolic of that position: while she concurred in result, she refused to join any part of the majority's reasoning, staking out a clearly defined position of her own. In addition to her endorsement test O'Connor also drew heavily on Free Exercise concerns: 'It is obvious that either of the two Religion Clauses, if expanded to a logical extreme, would tend to clash with the other', stated O'Connor, echoing an argument made by many legal scholars and some justices, although one that was not widely accepted.[69] For O'Connor, the Court's traditional reliance on the language of neutrality threatened the continued vitality of accommodation of the religious beliefs of minorities under the Free Exercise Clause, and thus of the Free Exercise Clause itself. Her development of an 'endorsement' analysis was a symptom of this concern: it modified the *Lemon* test to an extent sufficient to avoid a conflict between the clauses without rejecting the test outright. The problem with such an approach, at least with respect to O'Connor's position, was that the need for a unified test was not widely accepted since the issue of the 'clash' between the Religion Clauses was not widely accepted, and remains controversial. However, as the most likely swing vote in Religion Clause cases, O'Connor's position was central to the Court's vote.

In its two major prayer rulings, *Stone* and *Jaffree*, the Burger Court thus continued the legacy of the Warren Court. Both rejected the possibility of religious practices in the public schools; once it had been decided that the practices were religious, there was no doubt about the result. The controversy that surrounded *Engel* and *Schempp* and the increasing politicization of the issue of school prayer did not divert the Burger Court from the course laid out by the Warren Court: the ultimate principle of separation of schools and religious exercises remained intact. Equally, the Court remained attuned to the potential controversy resulting from the cases, and, similarly to the *Schempp* majority, took steps to reassure the public of the central place of religion in American life and to make explicitly clear the ruling of the Court. However, both cases were also examples of the dominant feature of Burger Court jurisprudence: the control of the centre. Richard Nixon campaigned for president in 1968 by attacking the activism of the Warren Court and claiming that for any future nominees he would insist on two standards: that they be among the best lawyers in the country and that they be judicial conservatives who would 'not twist or bend the Constitution in order to perpetuate his personal, political, and social values'.[70] With four appointments in his first term, Nixon had ample opportunity to turn his promise into reality. The influence of the liberal majority of *Schempp* and the later Warren Court was already waning by the time of Warren's retirement in 1969, but the loss of Warren along with the retirements of Hugo Black in 1971 and William Douglas in 1975 further reduced the liberal wing. By *Stone*, the only justices of the *Schempp* majority remaining on the Court were William Brennan and Byron White.[71] Harry Blackmun joined the Court in 1970 to replace Abe Fortas, and in 1972 Rehnquist was appointed by President Nixon to replace John Marshall Harlan. The overall impact of the personnel change was a significant weakening of the liberal wing and an increase in the number of conservatives on the Court. However, despite the fears of Warren's supporters, this did not make the Burger Court a conservative Court, but rather a moderate, pragmatic one.

Three factors account for the pragmatism of the Burger Court. First, the backlash against the liberal activism of the 1960s appeared to be less a reaction against the liberalism than a reaction against the activism itself. As such, in the decade following Warren's retirement, conservative activism by the Court was unthinkable; the social and jurisprudential upheaval implicit in an overturning of Warren Court precedents would be as unwelcome as a rapid expansion of them. Second, the divisions among some of the justices as to the 'proper' test to be used in analysing Establishment violations worked to restrict the scope of any opinion. The variety of views held by the justices of the Burger Court, revealed most clearly in the school aid cases, required decisions based on the narrowest grounds to ensure a workable majority. No procedural or philosophical approach commanded a majority of the Court and thus decisions remained moderate and pragmatic and closely tied to the specific facts of a case. Third, the men appointed to the Court by Presidents Nixon and Ford showed no interest in radical action. Coming after two embarrassing failed nominations, Nixon appointed Blackmun believing his judicial philosophy advocated judicial restraint and strict construction of the Constitution.[72] Although initially allying with Burger on the right, Blackmun shifted toward the centre of the Court and closer to the positions of Brennan and Marshall.[73] Powell, appointed to the Court to replace Black, is widely considered to have been a crucial part of the centre dominating the Burger Court.[74] John Paul Stevens was appointed as Douglas's successor by President Ford with the expectation that he would take a moderate conservative position on the Court, similar to that of Ford himself. With White and Stewart, these men combined to form the major controlling influence on the Burger Court. Although appointed by conservative presidents, their individual tendencies were towards moderation and pragmatism, a trend clearly present in the Burger Court's prayer jurisprudence.

In *Jaffree*, the most striking evidence of this was Justice Stevens's authorship of the majority opinion despite the presence of renowned liberals Brennan, Marshall and, by this time, Blackmun. Balanced, taking logical steps towards its conclusion, making no sweeping doctrinal pronouncements and strictly confined to the facts of the case, Stevens's opinion reflected the approach of the centre bloc. His willingness to make accommodations to the concerns of other justices illustrated the difficulty of a pragmatic approach to judging: different people will attach different weight to certain facts and approaches. The narrowness of the case was emphasized by both Powell and O'Connor, who used their concurrences to show why moment of silence statutes generally might be constitutional and why Alabama's was not, simultaneously reassuring the public that this was not an assault on the practice in general and ensuring that it was not by providing limits to the majority opinion.[75] Even the dissents of Burger and White avoided sweeping philosophical or doctrinal statements with regards to prayer. Both opinions took a balanced, limited approach, confining themselves to the facts of the case. Thus, despite higher levels of disagreement among the justices than in earlier cases, the moderate, pragmatic approach of the centre found sufficient common ground in the result in *Jaffree* to formulate a workable majority.

'The Burger Court's activism . . . has been generated as well as moderated by the pragmatic men of the center . . . in the hands of the Burger Court judicial activism has become a centrist philosophy – dominant, transcending most ideological divisions, but essentially pragmatic in nature, lacking a central theme or an agenda'.[76] Vincent Blasi's 1983 assessment of the Burger Court aptly described the results of the prayer cases of the era, even *Jaffree*, which was decided two years after he wrote. Blasi termed the actions of the Burger Court 'rootless activism' in that they were based not on any overriding philosophy but on a need to make reasoned, balanced and logical decisions. The result, he asserted, was an increasingly fact-based analysis and result in Supreme Court jurisprudence, where a minor difference in the facts of a case could mean the difference between a reversal and an affirmance. This led to criticism of the Court for a lack of coherence. It is, however, an unfair analysis of the prayer cases, although aspects of it could be seen in the justices' increasing reliance on factual specifics and procedural disputes. The Court may have been more divided on the issue than its predecessor, but the majority of the justices made no attempt to overturn the precedent established by *Engel* and *Schempp*: despite significant political pressure to do so, they strengthened it with their rulings.

Passions Calmed: The Aftermath of *Jaffree*

Reaction to *Jaffree*, handed down on 4 June 1985, was muted. While, predictably, liberals claimed it preserved the freedoms of the Bill of Rights and conservatives denounced it as a rejection of religion, the passion that had been so clear at earlier times and surrounding the recent congressional debates was almost entirely absent. In part, it was because for many the result was unsurprising: when granting *certiorari* the Court additionally struck down organized prayer in Alabama schools and reaffirmed its decisions in *Engel* and *Schempp*, indicating that a defence of the laws would not be an easy task. Equally, however, both sides could claim a victory of sorts. For those who objected to moments of silence as 'smokescreens' for school prayer, the Supreme Court's recognition of an unconstitutional motive on the part of the legislature appeared to recognize their concerns and act upon them. For those who supported moment of silence legislation, the narrowness of the Court's holding and the obvious implication in the concurrences by Powell and O'Connor that a majority existed to uphold some such laws offered hope that this was not the end of their campaign. Ishmael Jaffree offered the most telling conclusion on the situation upon hearing of the Court's ruling: 'For me the battle is over', he said. 'But prayer will go on in the schools. It just won't go on in any of my children's classes'.[77]

For those who had been watching the Court closely, there was an element of the surprising in the *Jaffree* result. On 5 March 1984, the same day that the Senate began its debates on the prayer amendments, the Court handed down its opinion in *Lynch v. Donnelly*. Arising from a challenge in Rhode Island to the inclusion of a nativity scene as part of a Christmas display erected by the town council, the case was another in a series of challenges to the 'silent symbols' of religion in American life to which *Jaffree* also belonged. However, noting that the crèche was only part of the display, a bare majority of the justices ruled that Pawtucket did not unconstitutionally favour or advance religion but simply recognized that, for some, the holiday season was also a religious celebration. Although the opinion made clear that the Court was not inclined to reconsider *Engel* and *Schempp*, many believed the opinions in *Lynch* symbolized a significant shift away from separation towards a greater accommodationist position. This apparent shift in emphasis came at the same time that commentators were beginning to note the increasing strength of the Court's conservatives, while simultaneously the Court appeared to be reaching out for religion cases. Establishment cases had been a regular feature on the Court's docket since the 1960s, but in early 1984 the Court accepted an unprecedented number of cases for review. The sudden activity led some to wonder uncomfortably if the newly influential conservative bloc was attempting to overrule, or narrow, the Court's unpopular past rulings.[78] In the *New York Times*, Linda Greenhouse called the Court's *Jaffree* decision, 'an unprecedented about-face in its approach to the relationship between church and state'.[79] Although this was rather overstating the case it revealed the concern *Lynch* had stimulated about the Court's position on church-state relations. With regards to prayer, *Jaffree* appeared to calm such fears, and, with the Senate's rejection of yet another Helms-sponsored bill to prevent federal court challenges to organized prayer in schools in September 1985, the issue appeared to have dissipated for the time being.

Between the handing down of *Jaffree* and the Court's acceptance of *Lee v. Weisman* for oral argument in March 1991, the issue of school prayer and all its attendant debates moved into the background of US politics. However, in a reprise of the 1981 debates over 'court-stripping', attention turned to divisions over the proper role of the court and judges in the American constitutional system. In a speech to the ABA in July 1985, Attorney General Edwin Meese criticized the Supreme Court and the justices for their apparent activism: 'Far too many of the Court's opinions on the whole, have been more policy choices than articulations of long-term constitutional principles', he asserted.[80] The criticism was not new: it had been levelled at the Warren Court, the New Deal Court of the 1930s and others before that, mainly by those who disliked the results being handed down Neither was Meese's solution original to the debate: the Reagan Administration, he argued, would urge the Court to follow 'a jurisprudence of original intention', seeking to 'resurrect the original meaning of constitutional provisions'.[81] Meese's speech indicated no major policy change on behalf of the Administration: conservatives had urged the adoption of 'original intent' as an interpretative method and chosen judicial nominees based on this from the beginning of Reagan's term in office. But the argument had a longer history than that: Brennan had addressed the issue in his *Schempp* concurrence in 1963.[82] Meese's speech, then, seemed little more than another attempt to challenge the Court about its rulings, in religion cases and others, without specifically challenging the institution or raising the issue of school prayer.

Although criticism that the Supreme Court was ignoring the intent of the Founding Fathers and being 'too activist' was not new, what made this debate unusual was that the Court, or the justices, responded to the challenge publicly. In a speech at a seminar at Georgetown University in October 1985, Justice Brennan challenged the idea that original intent could prove useful to the Court in an argument with distinct echoes of his 1963 *Schempp* opinion. The speech was notable as the first by a member of the Court that appeared to take issue with the Reagan Administration's approach to constitutional law; although Brennan mentioned neither the Administration nor the Attorney General by name, his pointed comments were clearly directed at both. Original intent, he argued, 'is a view that feigns self-effacing deference to the specific judgments of those who forged our original social compact. But in truth it is little more than arrogance cloaked as humility. It is arrogant to pretend that from our vantage we can gauge accurately the intent of the Framers on application of principle to specific, contemporary questions'.[83] Less than two weeks later, Justice Stevens joined the debate with a speech that offered a point-by-point rebuttal of Meese's views on some major constitutional issues. If Brennan's speech had been significant, Stevens's was a greater challenge to the Administration: first, he challenged Meese by name; second, as a moderate on the Court his views could not be dismissed by staunch conservatives as misguided liberal philosophy. Making arguments that differed little from those offered by Brennan, Stevens suggested that Meese's argument was 'somewhat incomplete . . . because its concentration on the original intention of the Framers of the Bill of Rights overlooks the importance of subsequent events in the development of our law'.[84] But in many ways the content of the speeches was less important than that the justices gave them. The Court had remained silent during the repeated attacks upon it throughout the first half of the decade; this new willingness to address certain issues reflected a new political reality. The power of the Administration to attack the Court had been weakened by the repeated failures of legislation designed to do just that, undermining the sense of threat to the institution and allowing the justices freedom to respond to any perceived attack.

The political situation for Reagan and his supporters had changed in other ways too by the middle of his second term in office. The aftermath of the Iran-Contra affair and the return of the Senate to Democratic control in the 1986 mid-term elections served to weaken his political influence more generally. In addition, despite his attempts to reshape the federal judiciary by appointing only judicial conservatives, in Reagan's words, 'judges of the highest intellectual standing who harbor the deepest regard for the Constitution and its traditions – one of which is judicial restraint', commentators were beginning to note the emergence of conservatives as the new judicial activists.[85] Although this may have been Reagan's intention all along, it contradicted his publicly stated objectives and thus appeared as another fundamental weakness in his programme. The defeat of Robert

Bork (Reagan's nominee to replace the newly retired Justice Powell) in October 1987 simply underscored Reagan's weakened position, both politically and with regards to his 'social values' agenda. Aware that the Court was ideologically divided and finely balanced, the Senate was unwilling to replace the moderate, pragmatic Powell with someone viewed as an arch conservative and too far from the political mainstream. The threat to the Court, so strong in the early 1980s, had thus dissipated.

Concluding Thoughts

The 1980s saw a re-emergence of school prayer as a major political issue for the first time since the mid-1960s. The growing conservatism of the electorate brought to power politicians who looked to use their new-found influence to challenge some of the remaining pillars of 1960s liberalism. *Engel* and *Schempp* specifically, and the prayer issue more generally, became symbols of a broader debate about the nation and its future direction. Whereas the Warren Court's decisions had sparked the broader political debate in the 1960s, two decades later the Court found itself at the centre of the debate despite the absence of rulings in this area. The school prayer debates of the 1980s were fuelled by the politics of the era rather than by the Court; in fact, the Court found itself required to negotiate a potentially dangerous situation, in which threats to limit its jurisdiction were taken seriously, in order to address cases raising only indirectly the prayer issue.

However, as with the situation faced by the Warren Court, the political debates had little impact on the Court's rulings. To an even greater extent than before, the political debates diverged from the constitutional issues addressed by the Court. Despite growing differences among the justices as to the proper approach to Establishment Clause cases, the principles established in *Engel* and *Schempp* remained controlling in *Stone* and *Jaffree*: school-sponsored religious activities were not permitted on public school grounds. If the practice was religious, it was struck down. Thus the Court's concern was not if such exercises were permitted but whether the challenged practice was religious. The political debate, however, remained focused on the former issue with proponents of constitutional amendment decrying the damage done to the nation's children by the secularization of public schools. The debate reflected not the constitutional issue but the political debate about the place of faith in American society. Equally, participants in the debate continued to link school prayer with issues of morality, patriotism and national values, which further removed it from constitutional debates.

Outside of law reviews and court opinions, prayer in schools became important not for what it was but for what it symbolized. Politicians who wanted to portray themselves as defenders of traditional values, or their opponents as lacking a personal moral code, drew on school prayer as a campaign issue. Challenges were brought by politicians, school officials and, in rare cases, judges, who claimed they wanted to challenge the Supreme Court, return God to the schools, encourage moral behaviour in students, or just return the US to the God-fearing, religious nation it had been in some glorified past age. Even President Reagan submitted to the temptation when he was facing harshest criticism from the Religious Right. But, as with earlier debates, political debates about school prayer in the Reagan era added little to the constitutional debates while increasing public sensitivity to prayer and related issues.

Hints of divisions within the Court suggested, however, that future cases might result in a different outcome. Divisions over the place of the *Lemon* test in Establishment Clause jurisprudence that had been increasingly evident in school aid cases shaped the variety of opinions offered in *Jaffree*. Rehnquist's willingness to challenge precedent and O'Connor's emphasis on endorsement as a means of analysis suggested that future cases might be decided on different grounds that could open up the opportunity to at least narrow the scope of *Engel* and *Schempp*. As the political debates faded with the defeat of prayer amendments and Court stripping bills, evidence from within the Court hinted that some degree of change might still be possible.

Chapter 6

All Change? The Rehnquist Court

The late 1980s and early 1990s saw a reassessment of attitudes and reactions to the Supreme Court's prayer rulings. With the defeat of constitutional amendments in Congress, the weaker influence on national politics of the Religious Right and the affirmation of precedent by the Supreme Court, the political atmosphere was more conducive to a reasoned, rational discussion about whether school officials had gone too far in trying to avoid breaches of the Constitution and, if so, how that should be remedied to create true 'neutrality' towards religion. Despite also being a reaction to conservative evangelical groups who asserted that the Supreme Court's rulings had led to the endorsement of 'secular humanism', the moves attracted significant bipartisan support. With echoes of the 1950s, one such development was a reassessment of the way schools dealt with religion in their curricula. In July 1987, a report commissioned by the non-partisan professional Association for Supervision and Curriculum Development deplored the 'benign neglect' of the role of religion in shaping American and world history. It criticized 'bland' textbooks that it said 'virtually ignore religion' and asserted that educators must move beyond the mistaken notion 'that matters of religion are simply too hot to handle in public schools'.[1] This followed reports issued by People for the American Way, a liberal lobby group, as well as Americans United for the Separation of Church and State, suggesting large numbers of textbooks slighted religion, either by ignoring it entirely or by misrepresenting its role. Following such criticisms, attempts were made to remedy the situation. In October 1988, the Williamsburg Charter Foundation, a newly formed group of scholars and educators, announced the development of a curriculum which, they argued, taught religion without promoting a faith. In August of the same year, the Arizona Board of Education adopted an outline of 'social studies essential skills' for its elementary and secondary schools that required teaching the religious roots of ethical convictions and religious differences; and in January 1989, the North Carolina Board of Education ordered that the state's outline of social studies courses be revised to include religious topics in history, government, economics, world cultures and other subjects.[2] The beginning of attempts to implement what had, after all, been explicitly mentioned as acceptable in *Engel* and *Schempp* reflected the declining volatility of the issue of religion in schools.

The moderate, pragmatic approach of the Court's centre, which had been a feature of the Burger Court, remained dominant on the Court in the early years of William Rehnquist's chief justiceship.[3] In January 1987, the justices granted *certiorari* in a case challenging New Jersey's moment of silence law, the law that had been debated at the same time Ishmael Jaffree was beginning his challenge in Alabama. The case, which might have been used by the conservatives on the Court to make explicit what had been implied in *Jaffree* – that moment of silence laws did not violate the Constitution – was eventually decided on a procedural issue by a unanimous Court.[4] The effect of the case was to end attempts to reinstate the New Jersey law, which did not mention prayer but had been struck down by the lower courts on findings of unconstitutional legislative purpose, without the Court needing to express any view about whether those decisions had been correct. The ruling was a careful one by the Court; without revisiting in detail the arguments in *Jaffree*, the Court implicitly reiterated support for the ruling by allowing the lower court decision, which had rested on foundations very similar to the 1985 case, to stand. The procedural foundation of the opinion also served to mute reaction to the ruling: since the opinion made no mention of the constitutionality of moment of silence laws, critics could hardly argue that it was a rejection of religion. Such an approach prevented a resurgence of debate about prayer in public schools.

Attempts to define the boundary between churches and the state, or more blatant challenges to the Supreme Court's rulings, also continued, although not with the frequency of earlier periods. In Benicia, California, for example, 'a virulent and protracted clash between fundamentalist Christians and their more liberal neighbors' occurred when the town's mayor refused to proclaim 1990 the 'international year of Bible reading', a measure supported by President George Bush and Congress and the governors of thirty-six states, including California.[5] In Hartford, Connecticut, some members of the faculty at Trinity College, founded by the Episcopal Church in 1823, asked for an end to the tradition of reciting prayers at campus ceremonies, arguing that they had become 'a symbol of division and exclusion' in a time of greater religious pluralism, and in a Dallas suburb the American Civil Liberties Union challenged a twenty-year practice of having a girls' basketball team kneel and recite the Lord's Prayer at the end of a game.[6] Sporting events were also the focus for a debate in Atlanta, Georgia, when the ACLU brought a challenge on behalf of an agnostic student to the reciting of prayer before high school football games. In a massive example of resistance, towns in Alabama and Georgia continued the practice in direct violation of the ruling by the Eleventh Circuit. In Montgomery, Alabama, leading officials marched to the fifty-yard line and led a prayer before the first game of the season; in some communities, ministers stood and led prayers from seats in the audience. 'There is a subculture that surrounds football – it's almost a cult unto itself', said Reverend Jamie Jenkins, Methodist minister in the Atlanta suburb at the centre of the controversy, attempting to explain the emotional reaction to the case. 'When you mix that with the religious history of the Deep South, you have an exercise that is very important to the community'.[7] Such controversies revealed that in some places, and under certain circumstances, school prayer and related issues maintained the ability to divide the public and inspire political controversy. The issue of prayer in the schools continued to invite comment, criticism and exploration, especially in areas outside the traditional classroom environment discussed in the Supreme Court's opinions, where precedents were few and those which did exist were contradictory. Then, in March 1991, the Supreme Court granted *certiorari* in a case involving one of these 'grey' areas: graduation prayers.

Lee v. Weisman

Until *Lee v. Weisman* there had been very little litigation surrounding prayer at graduation ceremonies. In the few cases that had reached the courts, the judiciary was more receptive than to schoolday prayer activities. As infrequent activities containing no instructional element, graduation exercises did not raise the same concerns considered in *Engel* and *Schempp*.[8] However, such positions conflicted with principles announced in other Establishment Clause cases. The voluntariness of participation, rejected as a basis for justification in *Engel* and *Schempp*, was significant in defending graduation exercises. Equally, in disallowing student religious groups from meeting in public school facilities, courts had held that even the 'hint' of state approval of sectarian activities violated the Establishment Clause: prayers at school-organized graduation ceremonies implied more than a hint.[9] Such untested arguments made it increasingly likely that the Court would intervene, although it was unclear whether it would simply decide the issue or address the procedural confusion which had led to the different rulings; in other words, whether it would clarify the status of *Lemon*. It was possible that the Court might be encouraged to revoke the *Lemon* test entirely by the 1991 Term, despite the majority's assertions in *Jaffree* that it remained good law: between the two cases, four justices had retired from the bench, three of whom had been part of the *Jaffree* majority.[10] The personnel change gave *Lee* added significance: it would be the first major ruling on the prayer issue from a Court that, while considered more politically conservative than its predecessor, was comprised of justices whose position on the Establishment Clause was relatively unknown. While it seemed likely that the Court's conservative bloc of Chief Justice Rehnquist and Justices Antonin Scalia and Clarence Thomas would vote together, joined by Justice Byron White, most likely in favour of graduation prayer, and Justices Harry Blackmun and John Paul Stevens would be likely, based on past opinions, to vote against, the balance of the Court was held by Sandra Day O'Connor and two of the Court's most junior members, Justices Anthony Kennedy and David Souter, who had little record in the area.

It was to Kennedy and Souter that much of the case was addressed. In *County of Allegheny v. ACLU* in 1989, Kennedy, joined by Rehnquist, White and Scalia, had dissented from the majority's holding that a nativity scene displayed in a Pittsburgh courthouse violated the Establishment Clause. His forceful dissent, combined with his alliance with the Court's conservatives, suggested he would provide a guaranteed vote to overturn the beleaguered *Lemon* test, and possibly to overturn *Engel*, *Schempp* and *Jaffree*. Souter's record was entirely void of any indication of his position on church-state issues. Asked at his confirmation hearings about the Court's approach to such cases, Souter's answer indicated his awareness of the debate on the Court and some sympathy for the criticism of *Lemon*.[11] Lawyers for the Bush Administration were searching for a case which might attract Souter into Kennedy's camp before he had the chance to cast a vote in a religion case which might put him on record as favouring the continued validity of a precedent.[12] A forceful *amicus* brief filed by Solicitor General Kenneth Starr made it more likely that the Court would hear the case, if only by raising its profile. For the Bush Administration and many pro-prayer advocates, *Lee* presented the possibility of success in challenging both the existence of the *Lemon* test and the unpopular school prayer decisions.[13]

Lee v. Weisman arose from a challenge by Daniel Weisman to the inclusion of an invocation and benediction at his daughter, Deborah's, middle school graduation ceremony. School principals in Providence, Rhode Island, were permitted to invite clergymen to offer such prayers on these occasions, although it was not required and many did not do so. In response to an earlier challenge by Weisman to graduation prayers, Robert E. Lee, the school principal, invited Rabbi Leslie Gutterman to deliver the prayers. Having accepted, Gutterman agreed with Lee that the invocation and benediction should be 'non-sectarian' and should conform to the 'Guidelines for Civic Occasions' prepared by the National Conference of Christians and Jews. The case rested on several key issues. First, whether this was a religious exercise as envisioned under the Establishment Clause, and if it was, to what extent the state was involved. Second was the issue of coercion that had caused such confusion in earlier cases: did the nature of the graduation ceremony coerce either attendance or participation in the prayer activity and, if it did, was that sufficient to declare the practice invalid. Finally, the Court was required to decide what relevance, if any, its decision in *Marsh v. Chambers* held.[14] For defenders of the prayers the activity was an attempt to solemnify an important rite of passage, conformed to the desire of a majority of the community for such exercises, coerced no-one to participate since attendance was voluntary, and was a practice with such long standing and historical support that there could be no Establishment Clause violation. No religion was 'established' by the exercises. For the Weismans and their supporters, however, the prayers were state-sponsored religious exercises at a ceremony that, to all intents and purposes, was compulsory for their daughter to attend. The state 'endorsed' religion when the principal invited clergymen to recite prayers at the ceremony and required attendees to participate by virtue of their attendance, the very basis of 'establishment'. The Court agreed, in an opinion written unexpectedly by Justice Kennedy. Writing for a bare majority, Kennedy quoted from *Engel* that, 'it is no part of the business of government to compose official prayers for any group of the American people to recite as part of a religious program carried on by government', and held, 'that is what the school officials attempted to do'.[15] 'The Constitution', wrote Kennedy, 'forbids the State to exact religious conformity from a student as the price of attending her own high school graduation. This is the calculus the Constitution commands'.[16]

The tone and structure of the Court's opinion in *Lee* were the result of the unusual way in which the case was decided. In November 1991, shortly after the Court announced that it would accept *Lee* for oral argument, the *National Law Journal* speculated that it had done so in order to reverse the First Circuit's ruling that graduation prayer violated the Establishment Clause.[17] The Supreme Court's acceptance of the case for full argument when both the trial court and the appeal court had agreed that the prayer violated the *Lemon* test, and thus the Establishment Clause, gave credence to the speculation: had the justices intended to uphold the result they might have refused the appeal or affirmed the lower court decision without oral argument. Initial voting in conference confirmed strict separationists' worst fears: a bare majority supported reversing the Court of Appeals and holding graduation prayers did not violate the Constitution. Kennedy was assigned to write the opinion. However, in late March 1992, Kennedy wrote to Blackmun, the most senior justice in the minority, that 'my draft looked quite wrong', informing Blackmun that he had now written an opinion upholding the lower court.[18] Kennedy's switch altered the outcome of the case; however, it also raised a number of problems, as he noted to Blackmun: 'After the barbs in *Lynch v. Donnelly*, many between the two of us, I thought it most important to write something that you and I and the others who voted this way can join'.[19] Given the narrowness of the majority and the divisions on the Court, avoiding sweeping philosophical and doctrinal statements and including explicit links to accepted, established precedent was the safest course to ensure the majority held. The need to secure agreement between five justices with quite different approaches to prayer cases meant writing on the narrowest possible grounds.

Kennedy sought to maintain his tenuous majority by appealing to the Court's first principles in Establishment cases and drawing directly on the principles established in *Engel* and *Schempp*. For the majority, the invocation and benediction at this graduation ceremony was a religious exercise supported by the state: the principal decided that the prayers should be given, provided the rabbi with guidelines as to the nature and scope of the prayers, and the school provided the forum for their expression. This was sufficiently close to the prayer in *Engel*, even to the point of being 'non-sectarian', to bring *Lee* under its auspices and invalidate the practice. Kennedy's concern for issues of the school environment, school culture, social pressure and the combination of coercion and free exercise issues also echoed *Engel* and *Schempp*. The importance of graduation as a rite of passage, the very reason supporters advocated prayers in the first place, was, for the Court, the exact reason why prayers must be excluded: the practice forced Deborah Weisman to choose between her religious belief and attending the ceremony, a choice the Court had consistently held invalid.[20]

Kennedy's attention to voluntary attendance, however, reflected more than concern for fidelity to precedent; it addressed the existence of so-called 'equal access' cases in which questions of speech and free exercise were more central concerns. Kennedy needed, in Establishment Clause terms, to distinguish the graduation ceremony in *Lee* from the meetings of religious groups on school property in order to justify his use of the Court's traditional prayer case analysis, and the issue of 'voluntary attendance' was the clearest way to do so. Although in comparison to the compelled flag salute of *West Virginia State Board of Education v. Barnette*, or the required prayer recitation in *Engel*, the graduation prayers appeared to involve little coercion; when compared to weekly student group meetings on campus the greater symbolic nature of graduation and the indirect pressure to attend as a result reinforced Kennedy's point about coercion to attend. The distinction was important to protect the viability of 'equal access' analysis. Since the Court had recognized previously that schools must make certain accommodations to religion and the beliefs of religious students, Kennedy needed to show that graduation prayer was significantly different in nature: the atmosphere of the graduation ceremony was the clearest way to do this. Repeated references to, and echoes of, *Engel* and *Schempp* also ensured the majority opinion could make clear that the decision was based firmly on Establishment grounds and in no way undermined the validity of equal access cases. Thus, by avoiding the most contentious issues in the Court's Establishment Clause jurisprudence, writing on the narrowest grounds and drawing on the Court's first prayer cases, Kennedy managed to hold his new majority.

Kennedy also sought to maintain his narrow majority by avoiding the issue that had caused most division on the Court: the *Lemon* test. Although noting that the District Court had used the *Lemon* test in its analysis and rejecting the numerous invitations in petitioners' and *amici* briefs to reconsider the use of the test, Kennedy practically ignored its existence throughout the rest of the opinion. 'We can decide the case without reconsidering the general constitutional framework by which public schools' efforts to accommodate religion are measured. Thus we do not accept the invitation of petitioners and *amicus* the United States to reconsider our decision in *Lemon* . . .', he argued.[21] While the Court thus refused to overturn *Lemon* and repudiate the test, any support was promptly undermined when Kennedy asserted that the case was not sufficiently nuanced to implicate *Lemon*: 'The government involvement with religious activity in this case is pervasive, to the point of creating a state-sponsored and state-directed religious exercise in a public school. Conducting this formal religious observance conflicts with settled rules pertaining to prayer exercises for students, and that suffices to determine the question before us.'[22] Overlooking *Lemon* avoided the danger of getting caught in the same kind of procedural debate that had so dominated *Jaffree* and which increasingly threatened to divide the justices in school aid cases.[23] Combined with the references to *Engel* and *Schempp*, Kennedy's opinion sought as its foundation the areas of least controversy in order to avoid further dividing the Court.

'It must not be forgotten, then, that while concern must be given to define the protection granted to an objector or a dissenting nonbeliever, these same Clauses exist to protect religion from government interference'.[24] The sentiment was also similar to that of *Engel* and *Schempp*, the idea that the Establishment Clause was not just about protecting the individual but about protecting religion. Kennedy went so far as to note that accommodation may make the danger to religion worse, echoing Brennan's earlier concerns about a 'common core' religion that was devoid of true religious sentiment.[25] But the manner in which the argument was made was noticeably different from that of the Warren Court cases. In *Engel* and *Schempp*, the justices had argued that the Establishment Clause was designed to protect religion as a way to defend themselves and the Court against attacks that suggested they were Communists and atheists intent on secularizing and destroying American society. In *Lee*, Kennedy's point was that the case involved more than simply damage to a single family, that it involved protecting the fundamental strength of religion as a whole, and as such was making a positive rather than a defensive statement. In *Lee*, the Court did not attempt to reassure the public about the central place of religion in American life in the same way the justices believed it necessary to do in *Engel* and *Schempp*; the Court appeared to assume that the public would understand this decision and that further explanation was unnecessary.

The concurrences filed in *Lee*, by Blackmun and Souter, both joined by Stevens and O'Connor, added little to the debate. Blackmun's opinion appeared to do little more than reinforce the argument made by the majority. He placed more emphasis on the role of endorsement, noted that the separation of church and state was intended to be beneficial to both religion and government and provided a slightly more detailed defence of *Lemon*, although without making explicit use of it in his opinion.[26] Souter's opinion was significant, less for what it contained than for what it said implicitly about the justice himself. Nothing in his previous career as New Hampshire's attorney general or state Supreme Court judge suggested that he was an ideological crusader. 'In fact, his testimony at his confirmation hearings and his admiration for the late Justice John M. Harlan ... suggested the opposite'.[27] But by the summer of 1992, based in part on his opinion in *Lee*, commentators were beginning to see Souter as active in the search for the Court's 'lost' centre.[28] His *Lee* concurrence showed evidence of judicial caution, although combined with a willingness to take on the more ideological members of the Court on their own ground. Souter's overall conclusion was that nothing in this case provided sufficient evidence or merit to justify overturning the Court's established precedent.

Challenging Rehnquist's reading of history in *Jaffree*, Souter concluded that a 'more powerful argument supporting the Court's jurisprudence' could be found in the long history of requiring adherence to a position of neutrality, reinforcing, in the process, the majority's argument that a prayer is a prayer, regardless of whether it is non-denominational or sectarian.[29] In methodically reiterating points that were not new to the Court's Establishment Clause jurisprudence and simply applying them to the situation in *Lee*, Souter reinforced those arguments. While not adding anything new to the debate, Souter's opinion indicated his views on the issue and served notice to others on the Court that his was a position which must be taken into consideration in future cases.[30]

In contrast to Souter's concurrence was the sharp, sarcastic dissent from Justice Antonin Scalia. Well known for his harsh, biting language, Scalia accused the majority of ignoring history, tradition and the Court's past reliance on both, 'lay[ing] waste [to] a tradition that is as old as public school graduation ceremonies themselves, and that is a component of an even more longstanding American tradition of nonsectarian prayer to God at public celebrations generally'.[31] His most significant attack was on the Court's use of coercion analysis which, arguably, had been part of the Court's Establishment Clause jurisprudence since *Everson* in 1947, and which was so crucial to the majority's holding. 'As its instrument of destruction, the bulldozer of its social engineering, the Court invents a boundless, and boundlessly manipulable, test of psychological coercion', claimed Scalia, continuing:

> I find it a sufficient embarrassment that our Establishment Clause jurisprudence regarding holiday displays . . . has come to 'require[] scrutiny more commonly associated with interior decorators than with the judiciary' . . . But interior decorating is a rock-hard science when compared with psychology practiced by amateurs. A few citations of '[r]esearch in psychology' that have no particular bearing on the precise issue here . . . cannot disguise the fact that the Court has gone beyond the realm where judges know what they are doing.[32]

For Scalia, and Rehnquist, White and Thomas who joined him, nothing could justify the striking down of a practice which had the support of history and common sense. The virtue of maintaining respect for the beliefs of others and the role of prayer as a social unifier were too important for the dissenters to be sundered on as seemingly inconsequential a foundation as 'coercion'. The argument reflected both Scalia's deep personal religious convictions and his political conservatism that saw nothing wrong in educating America's children in the moral and religious values of society, especially when no-one could possibly be coerced into participating. The dissenters' additional criticisms, that the ruling did not comport with history, that there was no meaningful state intervention or involvement and that *Lemon* should be abandoned, were little more than repetition of arguments made in other cases, albeit in Scalia's distinctive style. What marked the dissent out was its tone and the biting sarcasm, clearly indicating the depths of the divisions among the justices and indicating to anyone watching that a majority-in-waiting existed to hand down a different result if the facts of the case were amenable to one or more of the centrist justices. The narrowness of Kennedy's opinion reinforced this perception and made it seem likely that the prayer issue would return to the Court.[33]

Prayer and Politics

In the fifteen months between granting *certiorari* and issuing an opinion in *Lee*, the Court had postponed action on every new appeal which raised the issue of interpreting the Establishment Clause. The cases involved issues ranging from the display of a privately owned Hannukah menorah in a city park, the designation of Good Friday as a public holiday, a judge's personal religious invocation at the start of each court session and the use of religious imagery on town seals. The narrowness of the opinion in *Lee* suggested that the Court might be willing to turn to many of these issues to review them with the same fact-based analysis. However, five days after *Lee*, the Court turned down a dozen appeals in such cases, indicating that, for now, the justices had said all they intended to on the issue.[34] But the combination of discussions about *Lee* and the increasing political success of conservative Republicans in a backlash against the first year of the Clinton Administration served to stimulate another round of challenges to the school prayer ban. In a misleading article in the *New York Times* in November 1994, Peter Applebome declared, 'Prayer in Public Schools? It's Nothing New For Many'.[35] The headline suggested a large-scale flouting of the prayer ban, playing on the fears of many strict separationists. A closer reading of the article, however, indicated that '[m]uch of the activity is private and voluntary and within constitutional guidelines', such as moments of silence or student-initiated lunchtime or after-school activities which did not involve school officials. After a relatively quiet few years, there were a number of high-profile debates about school prayer in some states, but, as with earlier periods, the most frequent reaction was compliance.[36]

In 1994, President Bill Clinton's actions showed that the school prayer issue had lost none of its political symbolism. Politically weakened by Waco, Whitewater, healthcare and the failure of middle-class tax cuts and reform of military policy regarding homosexual personnel, Clinton faced a re-energized and organized Republican opposition that, for the first time since 1952, captured both houses of Congress. Although the priority was the 'Contract With America', expounded during the election campaign, Speaker of the House Newt Gingrich (R-Ga), the most prominent of the new Republican leaders, also commented in late November, 'I would like to see this Congress take an up-or-down vote on school prayer. I think that's an issue that deserves to be addressed'.[37] In a typical election year tactic, Congress had already begun to discuss school prayer again in February 1994, in terms that would have little practical impact but would send a symbolic message, many hoped, to the electorate.[38] Fairly low key and unemotional, what was almost certainly unexpected by Republicans and Democrats alike was that shortly after the election President Clinton hinted at his willingness to work with Congress to pass a constitutional amendment guaranteeing a right to prayer in public schools. Saying he did not want issues such as school prayer to become the subject of partisan wrangling, he observed, 'I want to see what the details are . . . I certainly wouldn't rule it out'.[39] Thus began a bizarre, week-long series of statements, retractions, assertions and denials, which left the issue more confused than it had been before. In the absence of any comment from Clinton himself, it remained unclear exactly what Clinton's position was on a school prayer amendment and what consequence, if any, it would have for future debates. While reporters, congressmen and even the White House sought to uncover Clinton's meaning, a wide range of groups on both the left and right of the political spectrum offered vocal criticism of the president and of Republican attempts to require a vote in Congress on the prayer issue. No consensus seemed to exist, except for concern that the manner in which the issue had been raised was rather dubious. Clinton finally addressed the issue again on 22 November, saying his earlier remarks had been 'over-read'. 'I do not believe that we should have a constitutional amendment to carve out and legalize teacher- or student-led prayer in the classroom', stated Clinton, going on to oppose the leading prayer amendment offered by House Republicans.[40]

Clinton's remarks appeared to clarify his position on a school prayer amendment definitively after a week of rather confused debate, although attempts to cover up his reversal of position were almost farcical.[41] The episode showed that school prayer continued to have a powerful influence as a symbolic issue that individuals could use to make broader points about their personal beliefs and political positions. Clinton had always been outspoken about his faith, more than many Democratic leaders, and in a vein similar to Carter he sprinkled his speeches with biblical references and openly discussed his frequent reading of the Bible, a characteristic that certainly did not harm his attempts to break the dominance of conservative Christians over religious discourse in politics. Clinton had also espoused the idea of bipartisanship in politics and the prayer issue provided a powerful opportunity to continue the two. Believing that school prayer could be used to symbolize his commitment to social values, to avoid being outflanked by what Clinton himself called, 'this whole values debate' which he predicted would 'intensify in the next year', Clinton adhered to a common view that the majority of the American people perceived it as a moral issue, a view rarely challenged and even more infrequently investigated.[42] When, however, it became clear that the move was not popular with a wide variety of groups with a long history of defending social and moral values, Clinton shifted his position, suggesting it was the symbolism of the amendment rather than the amendment itself to which he was dedicated.[43]

Attempts to pass a constitutional amendment on school prayer began again in June 1995 and continued until 1998 when a 224 to 203 vote in the House, 61 votes short of the required two-thirds majority, signalled the end of the debate on school prayer for the 105th Congress. There had been nothing remarkable about any of the debates which echoed those of earlier congresses. Whether, like Clinton, the Republicans who pushed for the measure were more interested in making political points with the debates rather than actually achieving passage of the amendment was unclear from the debates themselves, but the former seemed more likely in light of events of 1995. In July, President Clinton sought to end debates about religious exercises in public schools, to clarify the misunderstandings and misperceptions that surrounded the school prayer issue and to find a way to ensure balance between the rights of students to express their religious beliefs while in school and the need to abide by the provisions of the Constitution. Critics of the prayer decisions had, for at least two decades, argued that overreaction by school officials to the Supreme Court's rulings and oversensitivity to the possibility of lawsuits had led to situations in which the rights of children to hold and express religious beliefs in school had been denied. Attempts in the late 1980s to restore to schools the teaching of the role of religion in history and society had been a tacit recognition of exactly this problem, and any number of examples of individual cases could be recited by those who challenged the rulings.[44] Clinton argued that the guidelines, drawn up by Attorney General Janet Reno and Education Secretary Richard Riley, clarified the situation regarding religious expression and activity in the public schools to restore educators' confidence in their own ability to judge what activities were permissible within their schools.[45]

'I share the concern and the frustration that many Americans feel about situations where the protections afforded by the First Amendment are not recognised or understood', said Clinton, announcing his effort. 'This problem has manifested itself in our nation's public schools ... As our courts have reaffirmed, however, nothing in the First Amendment converts our public schools into religion-free zones or requires all religious expression to be left behind at the schoolhouse door'.[46] The guidelines were comprehensive and put forward in a clear, dispassionate manner, something which had been lacking outside of Supreme Court opinions for several decades. The guidelines drew support from both left and right, as well as neutral organizations of educators. Representatives from the ACLU said they were 'heartened' and 'guardedly optimistic' about them, while some Republicans and conservative religious groups praised the Administration for recognizing discrimination against students, with chief counsel for the American Center for Law and Justice, Jay Sekulow, commenting, 'it's a clear signal that what we have been talking about has not been issues that we've made up'.[47] Criticism was also bipartisan. Reverend Lou Sheldon, chairman of the church-lobbying organization, the Traditional Values Coalition, called Clinton's statements 'too little, too late', while a number of secular lobby groups expressed concern that the guidelines would be insufficient to prevent continued abuses of the Establishment Clause.

Additional criticism came from those who accused Clinton of using the guidelines as a tool for electioneering. 'For purposes of his re-election, Mr. Clinton needs to reassure swing voters that he endorses traditional religious values and practices', commented the *New York Times*, implying that Clinton was using this in the same way he had the prayer amendment issue in late 1994.[48] 'I think it's a very smart move on Clinton's part', said Robert Boston, representative of Americans United for the Separation of Church and State, commenting on the political advantages for Clinton from the measure. 'It has cut the religious right off at the knees and put them on the defensive. For years they have been saying the public schools are religious-free zones. Now, along comes a President who says they are not'.[49] In light of the amendment fiasco the previous year, the criticism was not entirely without foundation, although Clinton's aides made no attempt to disguise the fact that the guidelines and the speeches Clinton gave on the subject were part of an effort to portray Clinton's ideas as a moderate alternative to more extreme positions on the issue. Clinton himself recalled the speech he gave announcing the guidelines and his reasons for issuing them in his memoirs, published in 2004. Setting out his views on church-state relations, he wrote:

> I believe strongly in the separation of church and state, but I also believe that both make indisputable contributions to the strength of our nation, and that on occasion they can work together for the common good without violating the Constitution. Government is, by definition, imperfect and experimental, always a work in progress. Faith speaks to the inner life, to the search for the truth and the spirit's capacity for profound change and growth. Government programs don't work as well in a culture that devalues family, work, and mutual respect.[50]

Belief in the importance of religion and respect for church-state separation were evident in Clinton's attempt to clarify church-state relations in the United States, but Clinton also knew that certain political advantages would come from this move. Critics suggested this weakened the guidelines, made them suspect, a conclusion which was remarkably unfair. Clinton's Memorandum was the first attempt by any federal government official to issue detailed guidelines as to what kinds of religious activities public schools could allow under the current law.[51] In an area that had become so confused, emotional and dependent on minor differences in fact, any attempt to clarify the situation was laudable. That Clinton may have had ulterior motives for doing so should not serve to negate the importance of the action itself.[52] For the first time a clear, unambiguous statement of permissible and impermissible activities existed that could be accessed by all interested individuals summarizing the current position of constitutional law. After decades of uncertainty and political game-playing, the Memorandum sought to remove both from school prayer debates. Regardless of its success, the attempt showed willingness to bring political debate closer to that of the Supreme Court.

Concluding Thoughts

'We are a religious people . . .', stated Justice Douglas in *Zorach v. Clauson* in 1952, acknowledging the important place of faith in the lives of many Americans. The school prayer debates of the second half of the twentieth century reflected attempts to reconcile this faith with the constitutional proscription against religious establishments. The role of the Supreme Court was crucial: as chief interpreter of the Constitution, the Court was required to find the balance between these two aspects of American life. Most important in understanding the Court's role is its consistency: since *Engel* and *Schempp* the Court has refused to allow religious activities of any kind to occur on public school grounds where any suggestion exists of coercion or state or school involvement.[53] Despite personnel changes, a highly vocal opposition, political attacks on the Court and attempts at amending the Constitution, the Court has remained committed to the principles laid down by the Warren Court in 1962 and 1963. The continued adherence to these principles by the Rehnquist Court was all the more surprising in light of the majority's shift towards greater accommodation in school aid and equal access cases. However, the results in *Lee* and *Santa Fe Independent School District v. Doe* (2000) are testament to the strength of the ideas laid out by the Warren Court in 1962 and 1963. In particular, Kennedy's switch in *Lee* revealed just how dominant these ideas remained. Despite innumerable challenges, both from inside and outside the Court, the basic principle that public schools and their staff may not support, endorse, or encourage religious exercises or practices during the school day or at other school events has endured.

Table 2 School Prayer Cases: Dates, Rulings, Authors

Year	Case	Court Holding	Vote	Author	Concurrences (Author in Bold)	Dissenters (Author in bold)
1962	*Engel v. Vitale* 370 US 421	Struck down a twenty-two word non-denominational prayer written for daily use in New York public schools. The Court held that school-sponsored prayers violated the Establishment Clause. (Justices Frankfurter and White did not participate in the case). (Overturned New York Court of Appeals' ruling that, so long as no student was required to participate, the use of the prayer did not violate the Constitution).	6:1	Black	**Douglas**	**Stewart**
1963	*Abington School District v. Schempp* (including *Murray v. Curlett*) 374 US 203	School-sponsored Bible reading and recitation of the Lord's Prayer in public schools held unconstitutional. (Affirmed District Court ruling in *Schempp*; in *Murray*, overturned Maryland Court of Appeals, which held no constitutional violation occurred).	8:1	Clark	**Douglas** **Brennan** **Gold berg** with Harlan	**Stewart**

All Change? The Rehnquist Court

1980	*Stone v. Graham* 449 US 39	Kentucky law requiring posting of the Ten Commandments in public classrooms held unconstitutional. (Dissents filed on procedural grounds, not addressing the substantive issues). (Overturned Kentucky Supreme Court ruling that posting was secular and therefore did not violate the Constitution).	5:4	*Per curiam*	**Burger** with Blackmun **Stewart Rehnquist**
1985	*Wallace v. Jaffree* 472 US 38	Alabama's moment-of-silence statute ruled unconstitutional. (District Court held law did not violate the Establishment Clause since the Clause permitted states to establish religion. Eleventh Circuit overruled and Supreme Court affirmed).	6:3	Stevens	Powell O'Connor (in judgement only)	**Burger** White **Rehnquist**
1992	*Lee v. Weisman* 505 US 577	School-sponsored prayers at graduation ceremonies held unconstitutional. (Affirmed First Circuit's finding of unconstitutionality).	5:4	Kennedy	**Blackmun** with Stevens and O'Connor **Souter** with Stevens and O'Connor	**Scalia** with Rehnquist, Thomas and White

Part Three

Equal Access

Introduction

A group of high school students from similar religious backgrounds wish to meet on a regular basis to share and practise their faith. The most convenient place for them to do so is in the school building that they attend every day. Should the school allow the group to meet before or after the school day or during the lunch break? A public school rents out its hall to local groups for meetings and discussion. A religious group wishes to hire the hall for prayer, discussions of faith and religious services. May the school permit the group access to its facilities? These and similar questions are raised by the series of cases referred to as 'equal access' cases.

Such issues arose in the aftermath of the Court's school prayer decisions, *Engel v. Vitale* (1962) *and Abington School District v. Schempp* (1963). A close reading of those opinions reveals that the Justices did not comment on the use of school facilities outside of the formal school day. The Court did, however, take pains to ensure that its opinions were directed to activities organized or sponsored by school authorities and made clear that truly voluntary student activity was not restricted as a result of these cases. As such, student groups were not prevented from meeting, at least under the *Engel* and *Schempp* rulings, and schools were neither required to, nor forbidden from, hiring out their facilities to religious groups outside of school hours. The nature of the public and political debate which followed *Engel* and *Schempp*, however, made this less clear. As politicians and religious leaders declared that the Court had 'removed God' from the nation's public schools, the message to the public was that schools were now secular institutions where religion in any form was no longer permitted. The debate also sensitized many to the issue, often resulting in conflict over practices which had previously been uncontroversial. For fear of litigation, school boards often turned the fears of religious leaders into reality, barring religion from school campuses in an effort to prevent lawsuits and avoid causing local controversy.

Such actions, while outraging individuals of faith, also conflicted with other protections embedded in the First Amendment. In addition to the Establishment Clause, the First Amendment also protects the free exercise of religion, freedom of speech and of the press and the right to freedom of assembly. The 'secularization' thesis as an interpretation of *Engel* and *Schempp*, as well as actions by school boards and educators which turned it into reality, undermined such principles. If the lunch break was not scheduled class time, why did the school have the right to prevent like-minded students from meeting voluntarily to share their faith and beliefs? Since the Court had already held in cases such as *West Virginia State Board of Education v. Barnette* (1943) and *Tinker v. Des Moines* (1969) that students did not shed their constitutional rights at the schoolhouse door, how could a student be reprimanded for reading a Bible in a free period or saying grace before a meal? The confusion wrought by the school prayer debates of the mid-1960s threatened to undermine the rights of individual students. In 1984, Congress passed and President Reagan signed the Equal Access Act, an attempt to provide guidance to school boards about correct and acceptable practices, and to prevent what many saw as infringements of students' rights perpetuated by misunderstandings of *Engel* and *Schempp*. Although the Act did not end the debate over what constituted equal access, it did go some way to correcting the perception that schools were to be entirely free from religion.

With the principles of equal access enshrined in federal legislation and a noticeable lack of controversy surrounding the issue, especially when compared with the reaction to school prayer and school aid cases, questions surround the significance of the Supreme Court's equal access jurisprudence. The Court established the principle in *Widmar v. Vincent* (1981), a case dealing with university students, and upheld the constitutionality of the Equal Access Act as it applied to high school students in *Board of Education of the Westside Community Schools v. Mergens* (1990): at first glance, this is the extent of the significance of equal access jurisprudence. However, familiar divisions on the Court appeared behind the apparent consensus. The interplay of free speech and Establishment concerns in equal access cases also reveals significant aspects of the Justices' approach to Establishment issues, and these cases reveal much about the internal divisions in the Court which shaped the Court's jurisprudence.

Chapter 7

The Issue Emerges: *Widmar* and the Equal Access Act

The First Case: *Widmar v. Vincent*

In October 1981, the Supreme Court heard oral arguments in *Widmar v. Vincent*, a challenge to the University of Missouri at Kansas City's regulation prohibiting the use of university buildings or grounds 'for purposes of religious worship or religious teaching'. Between 1973 and 1977, Cornerstone, an organization of evangelical Christian students from various denominational backgrounds, had been granted permission to meet in university buildings, as had more than 100 other political, philosophical and non-religious student groups. In 1977, however, their request was denied, the university administration asserting that the requirements of the Establishment Clause mandated the refusal.[1] Eleven members of Cornerstone challenged the restriction claiming that it violated their rights to equal protection under the Fourteenth Amendment and equally their rights to free exercise of religion and freedom of speech under the First Amendment. The Court, in an 8:1 opinion, agreed, holding, 'we are unable to recognise the State's interest as sufficiently "compelling" to justify content-based discrimination against respondents' religious speech'.[2]

At first glance, *Widmar* raised the difficult issue of how to resolve a clash between competing constitutional rights: the free speech and free exercise of students versus the Establishment Clause prohibition of state involvement with religion. Justice Lewis Powell's majority opinion ducked the issue entirely, deciding the case on free speech grounds and noting, '[n]either do we reach the questions that would arise if state accommodation of free exercise and free speech rights should, in a particular case, conflict with the prohibitions of the Establishment Clause'.[3] The intent to treat *Widmar* as a free speech case was evident early in the opinion: Justice Powell's first argument after establishing the case's history was that the university had created a 'forum generally open for use by student groups', and that having done so, 'the University has assumed an obligation to justify its discriminations and exclusions under applicable constitutional norms'.[4] Drawing on the Court's cases protecting the free speech rights of students on the grounds of public educational facilities, the State was required to show that the regulation served a compelling state interest and was narrowly drawn to achieve that end.[5] By beginning in such a way, Powell ensured that his subsequent argument fell within the framework of free speech analysis, significant in light of the university's Establishment Clause defence in ensuring that the case avoided establishing one constitutional protection as being more dominant than others.[6]

Despite its free speech foundations, *Widmar* proved significant for Establishment Clause jurisprudence too. 'It does not follow', wrote Powell, addressing the university's defence of its actions, '. . . that an "equal access" policy would be incompatible with this Court's Establishment Clause cases'.[7] Drawing on the three-part *Lemon* test, the majority held that since the university neither endorsed nor promoted any group, religious or secular, or the ideas they expressed in the forum, there was no unconstitutional purpose behind the policy. The Court also agreed with the Eighth Circuit that simply allowing a religious group access to a broad forum did not entangle the state with religion. Significantly, it asserted that the university would risk greater entanglement by trying to exclude religion since such exclusion would require a definition of the 'religion' to be excluded.[8] Having expressly denied to the state the right to make such judgements about what constituted 'religion', most frequently in conscientious-objector cases, forbidding the University of Missouri at Kansas City (UMKC) the right, in this instance, maintained consistency across the Court's jurisprudence.[9] However, it was in the discussion of the effects test that the Court provided most guidance for Establishment Clause analysis of equal access policies. 'We are satisfied', Powell wrote, 'that any religious benefits of an open forum at UMKC would be "incidental" within the meaning of our cases'.[10] First, the university had created a truly open forum and disassociated itself from any views, aims, policies or ideas expressed there. Second, because the forum was available to a broad range of religious and nonreligious groups, the involvement of the former could not be taken to be a primary benefit to religion and thus did not violate the second prong of the *Lemon* test.[11] As with the Court's school aid cases, the majority was willing to allow incidental benefits to religion, here the right to participation in a public forum, so long as such benefits were the result of a neutral programme involving a broad range of actors. Although structured as a denial of UMKC's claim that the Establishment Clause provided a compelling interest to justify content-based discrimination in its limited forum, Powell's opinion for the Court in *Widmar* provided a strong case for the constitutionality of equal access programmes so long as they met the criteria discussed.

In December 1981 when the Court handed down *Widmar*, it was a relatively uncontroversial and unremarkable case: under the Free Speech and Free Exercise Clauses, the Court had protected the rights of religious groups and individuals before, and *Widmar* seemed little different.[12] No one, even the staunchest defenders of strict separation, disputed the right of religious groups and individuals to freedom of speech. Equally, *Widmar* involved university students, who, as adults, the Court had previously recognized were in need of less protection from state coercion or endorsement of religious beliefs than students of a younger age.[13] However, several factors about *Widmar* should be noted. Significantly, the case revealed a high degree of consensus among the justices. In the Court's most recent school aid case, *Wolman v. Walter* in 1977, the Court had fractured, while in *Stone v. Graham*, the Ten Commandments case heard the year before *Widmar*, the Court had split 5:4. Yet in *Widmar*, Powell commanded a majority of seven with an additional concurrence from Justice John Paul Stevens and the lone dissent from Justice Byron White. In conference, at least five justices had agreed that the case involved freedom of speech and at least three held that the Establishment Clause was of little, or less, relevance to the case.[14] Only White argued that the case raised a conflict between the Religion Clauses of the First Amendment and that the state's concern to comply with the Establishment Clause might justify the restrictions imposed on Cornerstone by the University of Missouri, and even he noted in conference that he was 'out of line in the Religion cases'.[15]

Despite such consensus, however, the majority opinion was narrow, announced no sweeping principles and stuck closely to the specific situation present at UMKC. Powell was forced to accommodate changes to his opinion from Justices Harry Blackmun, William Brennan, Sandra Day O'Connor and William Rehnquist, dealing with issues from style and structure to the use of the Free Exercise Clause, in order to secure his majority.[16] Although not unusual, the nature of the changes and the tone of the memos suggest that the majority's consensus on the results did not extend to the method for deciding the case. While minor disagreements in *Widmar* were accommodated by a willing Powell, their existence suggests that the narrowness of the opinion was not simply Powell's preference but a necessity to hold the majority. Twice Powell explicitly noted the limited scope of the opinion, reinforced by the majority's refusal to address a potential constitutional clash and the possible applicability to public schools.[17] Nothing in the opinion was intended to address situations other than that at issue in *Widmar*: the justices neither saw nor intended this case to be a new area of jurisprudence. Within two years, however, circumstances conspired to turn *Widmar* into the founding statement of equal access principles.

Congress and the Equal Access Act

In 1982, President Ronald Reagan announced his support for a renewed attempt to overturn the Supreme Court's school prayer rulings by constitutional amendment. Hearings in Congress and debates outside it throughout 1982 and 1983 divided politicians, religious groups and civil liberties organizations over a range of related issues, including the rights of students to voluntarily assemble for religious purposes. In February 1983, Senator Jeremiah Denton (R-Ala) proposed 'a new approach to the school prayer issue that recognises the reservations that several of my colleagues voiced during the last Congress', when he introduced an equal access bill into the Senate.[18] Denton's bill proposed to make it unlawful for schools or school boards to deny student religious groups access to their facilities if those facilities were already available to secular student groups, effectively extending the *Widmar* principle to high school students. By concentrating on groups meeting voluntarily during non-curricular hours, Denton's bill sought to address the two major concerns of school prayer opponents: that the machinery of the school would be used to require participation and that the schools would be perceived as endorsing the religious practice concerned. A second, similar bill was introduced in March 1983 by Senator Mark Hatfield (R-Ore), a long-time opponent of the school prayer amendment, all but ensuring committee hearings. The following month, Representative Trent Lott (R-Miss) introduced HR.2732 to the House, a bill with similar provisions to those of the two Senate bills, and exhorted the House: 'The religious liberties of our children are too important to be neglected by this Congress'.[19] Despite House and Senate hearings between April and October 1983, the Senate took no immediate action on the bills and the House defeated the equal acccss proposal before it on 15 May 1984.[20] However, on 27 June 1984, the Senate debated and approved an equal access amendment to a bill to improve the quality of science and maths teaching in public schools. Similar in structure to earlier bills, the wording of the Denton-Hatfield Amendment nevertheless reflected concerns raised in both House and Senate hearings and debates.[21] The specific wording, however, was never explained, nor was the writing process ever publicly discussed. As Senator Hatfield noted, the bill was a compromise among the various interested groups and individuals, 'some kind of coalition' to obtain the most effective bill to remedy 'the situation now of having the rights of students violated'.[22] Passed 88:11 by the Senate, the provision was approved by the House 337:77 on 25 July and signed into law by Reagan the following month.

The irony of the equal access debate was that legislation should have been unnecessary. Truly voluntary student meetings for religious purposes had never been limited by the Supreme Court. In both *Engel v. Vitale* and *Abington School District v. Schempp*, the majority had stated that the opinions related to school-*sponsored* or school-*organized* prayer and Bible reading activities but that students' right to pray individually or in small groups, whether before school or in a lunch break, was not affected.[23] Neither did the Court address the use of school facilities outside of the regular school day and thus had not restricted them. Yet the loudest outcry after *Engel* and *Schempp* had implied that the Court had secularized the schools completely and made any mention of God inside the classroom unconstitutional. As the most common message provided by politicians, religious leaders and the media, it was unsurprising that school officials and, equally importantly, parents who might bring expensive lawsuits, should be persuaded that any religious activity on school grounds was constitutionally suspect. Since the Court had not specifically addressed equal access in high schools, lower courts appeared to stand on weak precedent when trying to uphold such policies, particularly in the light of the *Lemon* test and its concern about church-state entanglement. In this respect the problems that equal access supporters claimed the legislation was needed to correct were, in part, caused by the misinformed overreaction of some of the same groups and individuals in 1962 and 1963. As Dr James Dunn of the Baptist Joint Committee on Public Affairs testified in March 1984:

> Religious leaders have failed to educate their people regarding the Court decisions and have failed to do their homework as to the positive, constructive opportunities for religious expression within the law. Reporters have flunked Journalism I by continuing to report that prayer has been banned, as if that were possible. Some politicians have played games with the most sacred aspects of public and private life for gain at the ballot box. Public school officials have been left in a most unfair and untenable position regarding the role of religion in public education.[24]

In this context, however, congressional debates over equal access provide an insight into the motives of those involved and explain, albeit indirectly, many of the provisions of the Equal Access Act. The debates also reveal both the similarities between equal access and school prayer issues in particular, and some of the important differences that ultimately resulted in greater legislative success.

Despite a rather complex legislative history, congressional hearings and debates on the various bills that preceded the Equal Access Act provide a valuable insight into the motives of those involved and the reasons for their particular positions. Debates over equal access legislation in the House and Senate committees in 1983 and 1984 revealed many similarities to the debates over school prayer: conservative religious groups, especially those associated with the Religious Right, and individuals sympathetic to their position, supported the legislation; liberal religious groups and secular organizations, such as the American Civil Liberties Union, opposed it. Advocates asserted the rights of the majority, opponents responded with the danger to dissenting individuals. For many of the former there was little difference between the two issues. The National Association of Evangelicals, Campus Crusade for Christ, Rutherford Institute and the Freedom Council, among others, were groups testifying in favour of equal access which had also supported school prayer. It is 'a just and creative approach to the school prayer issue', testified Ted Pantaleo for the Freedom Council before raising the spectre of 'spiritually hungry students' being denied their views by 'a ruthless clawing and deep-seated anti-God conviction ... perpetrated by humanists'.[25] Carl Perkins (D-Ky), Chair of the House subcommittee, opened his comments by relating his school experience of prayer, concluding, 'it's a mighty good habit to open the classroom with a prayer in my view. So I see nothing wrong with it'.[26] Senator Denton (R-Ala), sponsor of S.1059, frequently implied that God had been banished from schoolrooms, and Patrick Monaghan of the Catholic League for Religious and Civil Rights harangued the Supreme Court for every poor decision it had made from *Plessy v. Ferguson* in 1896 and *Lochner v. New York* in 1905 to the prayer decisions of 1962 and 1963.[27] Thus, for some, equal access was exactly what opponents such as Representative William Lehman (D-Fl.) feared: 'voluntary prayer in public schools by another name'.[28]

Such statements, combined with the rhetoric of the school prayer amendment hearings of 1982 and 1983, gave credence to opponents' fears that equal access might provide the legislative foundation to circumvent *Engel* and *Schempp* that critics of the decisions had previously lacked. The American Civil Liberties Union, People for the American Way, Americans United for the Separation of Church and State (Americans United), the National Education Association, American Jewish Congress, Anti-Defamation League and the Unitarian Universalist Association of Churches, all of whom had actively opposed the prayer amendment, challenged the philosophy and practicality of equal access. The biggest fear among them was that this policy was an attempt to circumvent the Constitution by majority vote, that it would ultimately lead to religious exercises in public schools under the guise of neutrality. 'In almost every instance in which the courts have examined so-called "neutral" extra-curricular use policies', testified Jack Novick, associate director of the ACLU, 'they have been rejected precisely because the courts found they were adopted for the purpose and had the effect of advancing religious, sectarian ends'.[29] There was a foundation for their concern. The rhetoric of the school prayer amendment hearings of 1982 and 1983 revealed that there were individuals and groups who were ready to use any available means to circumvent *Engel* and *Schempp*. Attempts had been made throughout the 1960s and 1970s with only limited success, but the language of the proposed equal access bills might easily provide the legislative foundation lacking in earlier eras. Early versions of the bill protected activities 'that involve prayer, religious discussion, or silent meditation' and prevented discrimination 'against any meeting of students on the basis of the religious content of the speech'.[30] Although couched in negative language, opponents feared it could be used as a positive demand for religion on public school grounds. Although overstated, Representative Don Edwards's (D-Cal) statement that, 'This bill licences, authorizes, encourages, religious services, prayer meetings, revival meetings in high school classrooms', contained a sentiment shared by many of the bill's opponents.[31] Having fought to ensure that no student was coerced, required or intimidated into participating in religious exercises during the school day, often against harsh and unfair criticism, school prayer opponents feared equal access legislation could remove all existing safeguards and undermine progress made since 1962. The parallels between equal access and school prayer debates were thus made explicit by those on both sides of the issue.

A further similarity came with opponents' claims of the danger posed to religion, and particularly to students of minority faiths, by equal access legislation. 'As Jews, we . . . know that although the divisiveness which inevitably results when sectarianism enters the public school system, in whatever fashion, adversely affects all children, it is the children of minority faiths . . . who are injured most severely', testified Marc Pearl for the American Jewish Congress before the House subcommittee.[32] One of the most compelling arguments made against school prayer had been that it could not include all; non-denominational prayers offended those with strong faith as watering down their communion with God, while rotating systems of prayers or readings from different religious texts often overlooked those of minority faiths. Equal access raised the problem of schools with limited resources allowing groups with larger numbers to meet, thus favouring the dominant religious groups in a community to the detriment of others. This would not be equal access but distinctly 'unequal access' based on majority status.[33] This danger was reinforced by a discussion in the House hearings about what schools could do in instances of limited resources that implied schools might be allowed to set minimum numbers of students to qualify a group to use the school facilities.[34] While a sensible, pragmatic idea in theory, in practice it might lead to the exclusion of minority faiths. Equally, argued Senator Howard Metzenbaum (D-Ohio), 'religious activities at schools would encourage some students to tease and ridicule others who do not attend religious meetings before or after school . . . Let us remember that our children are susceptible to peer pressure'.[35] This presented a danger to all students, but particularly those of minority faiths who might be made to feel embarrassed or ashamed of their faith, something the First Amendment was clearly intended to prevent. Just as prayer and Bible reading involved the danger of deliberate or inadvertent favouring of the majority faith in a community, so too might equal access policies in their practical form, argued opponents.

Decisions about constitutionality, opponents also asserted, were better left to courts that were in a much better position than Congress to make judgements in specific cases: 'constitutionality . . . depends upon the total factual setting of that use, including the factual circumstances surrounding the adoption and implementation of that policy. Such sensitive and individual judgments do not lend themselves to broad, vague federal legislation'.[36] Such factual differences, argued Jack Novick for the ACLU, accounted for different rulings at state level, circumstances for which no sweeping federal legislation could hope to account.[37] The Supreme Court's Establishment Clause jurisprudence, especially in school aid cases, relied heavily on analysis of such factual circumstances when deciding constitutionality, and thus Novick's claim for similar consideration in equal access cases made logical sense. Instead, 'the more appropriate process would be to permit the courts to develop the law on the basis of specific facts, testing them against the First Amendment principles', argued Americans United executive director, W. Melvin Adams.[38] The argument held the benefit of flexibility to local circumstances, maintained local control over educational decisions and avoided the potential problems of a formal equal access policy.

However, coming just after a sustained, if unsuccessful, campaign to strip the Supreme Court of power in prayer and abortion cases, allowing courts discretion in this area was unlikely to convince those equal access supporters suspicious and critical of the Supreme Court. Also, little in this argument addressed the concerns of equal access advocates that school boards and courts were getting the decisions wrong. While they might accept that cases such as *Lubbock Independent School District v. Lubbock Civil Liberties Union* and *Brandon v. Board of Education* were ultimately correctly decided when considered in detail, the argument did not solve the problem of the student reprimanded for praying before a meal, or of the students told that they could not discuss religious issues informally while at school. While logically and practically the argument made a great deal of sense, it could not address the fundamental concerns that had brought equal access before Congress.

Yet vocal as the Religious Right and their supporters were, alone they could not force congressional action on legislation in their favour: the school prayer debates had illustrated that. Successful passage of the Equal Access Act required more than just the support of those dedicated to returning organized prayer to public schools: advocates would need allies among those who had opposed them in earlier debates. Significantly, equal access involved principles on which groups such as the National Council of Churches and individuals – including Senator Hatfield, who had actively opposed Reagan's school prayer amendment – could agree with school prayer advocates. Whereas the prayer amendment had involved potential coercion and school officials' participation, a true equal access policy, they argued, would do little more than protect the religious rights of students as guaranteed by the Free Exercise Clause of the First Amendment by allowing religious groups organized and run by students the same access to facilities as schools provided for secular, non-religious groups. Recognizing and accommodating students' wishes to discuss religion and pray together outside of class hours and without school participation did not support or advance religion so much as protect the rights of religious students to express their beliefs.[39] 'We can act in a manner that will adequately protect the right of our people from having an alien religious practice forced upon their children by governmental action', argued Hatfield, 'but at the same time allow them to freely exercise their own religion without government hostility'.[40] Hatfield's statement echoed sentiments expressed by Forest Montgomery of the National Association of Evangelicals: 'The enactment of this important measure would send a much needed message to the American people – that our public schools need not be a sterile, secular environment but can accommodate student-initiated and student-run meetings of a religious character'.[41] If properly adhered to, equal access thus would not violate the Constitution: an argument with which those on both sides of the prayer debate could agree.

Other significant differences separated the equal access debates from those over school prayer. Rhetoric was less fiery, the views of Perkins and Denton were clearly in the minority, and among many participants was a clear concern about the perceived overreaching attempts by schools to abide by *Engel* and *Schempp* that ultimately violated the Free Exercise Clause. Before the Senate Judiciary Committee seven students testified to their personal experiences of school administrators' actions with regard to student religious groups.[42] Stuart Kennedy, a ninth-grade student from College Park, Georgia, discussed how a mini-concert by a performer who told jokes, played instruments and sang songs, including religious songs, was barred by the school after a challenge by the ACLU, and how after eleven years the Youth for Christ club had been stopped from meeting on school premises after hours.[43] Other instances raised in testimony included: a fourth-grade student in Minnesota reprimanded for lowering her head in prayer before a meal; a Boulder policy that two or more students may not sit together for purposes of religious or spiritual discussion; an Indianapolis policy that students may not be picked up at the end of the day by a youth worker or youth pastor; students in Philadelphia reprimanded for sharing a booklet of Bible verses with other students; a Minnesota student told he could not write a research article on the resurrection of Christ and the refusal of a school newspaper to print a letter from a Christian student challenging the paper's coverage of church-state issues as one-sided.[44] None of these activities, advocates argued, violated the Supreme Court's rulings in *Engel* and *Schempp* since there was no school involvement and all were student-initiated. 'School authorities', Representative Robert D. McEwen (R-Ohio) argued, 'seem to have confused student-initiated, student-run religious meetings with the landmark Supreme Court decisions of the early 1960s which invalidated state prescribed prayers in the classroom'.[45] The frequency with which these and other examples were raised, and the tone and manner in which they were discussed, made clear that participants' concern was neither entirely about the political benefit they could gain from passage of equal access legislation nor about political point-scoring by embarrassing their opponents, but reflected a genuine concern that the religious rights of students were being abridged.

Evidence that students wished to pray and be involved in Bible clubs or other religious groups was provided by testimony from several students in both House and Senate hearings.[46] Quoted most frequently was the testimony of Bonnie Bailey, a graduate of Monterey High School in Lubbock, Texas, and one of the students involved in *Lubbock Independent School District v. Lubbock Civil Liberties Union*, an equal access case from the Fifth Circuit widely criticized throughout the testimony: 'I can decide if I want an abortion, or if I want to use contraceptives', she argued, 'but I can't decide if I want to come to a meeting to talk about religious matters before or after school'.[47] Although taken by conservative Christians as evidence of the lack of morality in public schools and used by politicians decrying religious discrimination, what Bailey's comment most clearly revealed was the difficulty of the claim that high school students were not sufficiently mature to withstand the pressure that might come with allowing religious groups on campus: students made fundamental decisions about other aspects of their lives and were granted the right to do so, they argued, so why not allow them the choice to attend prayer or Bible clubs outside of school hours so long as no school advocacy or involvement was present? The State must abide by the Establishment Clause and schools and teachers should not dictate or demand a particular belief or practice but, Bailey's statement suggested, concern to avoid this had arguably gone so far as to exclude voluntary student religious activity.[48]

One major reason for such activities by school boards became clear during House and Senate hearings. High school principals C. Luke Thornton and Richard Ocker both noted that they had taken action with regard to student religious clubs without full certainty as to the scope of the law, while several students recalled being told by school officials that while they were sympathetic to the students' wishes, uncertainty as to the law and the potential for lawsuits led to the rejection of their applications to meet on campus.[49] 'While there are undoubtedly some persons who merely seek loopholes through which they may reassert school-sponsored religious activities, the vast majority of school officials wish to comply with the law but are uncertain as to its current scope of protection of student religious speech', commented one witness before the Senate committee.[50] Such claims deserve a degree of scepticism. Suggesting a lack of clarity in the law enables those who are unhappy with a court decision to argue that the issue needs revisiting in the hope that a new case before a new court might result in a different outcome. Such an approach had been employed in the South as a challenge to the Civil Rights Movement and sympathetic court rulings. Yet the situation revealed strong support for claims of lack of guidance. Shortly before congressional hearings had begun, equal access policies had been rejected as unconstitutional in *Brandon v. Board of Education* and

Lubbock Independent School District v. Lubbock Civil Liberties Union, but upheld in *Bender v. Williamsport Area School District*.[51] The Supreme Court provided no answer either: equal access had not been addressed in either *Engel* or *Schempp*, and in *Widmar*, the majority had specifically reserved the question of applicability to high schools and elementary schools. The Court's refusal to accept *certiorari* in *Lubbock*, despite the urging of 24 US Senators as *amici*, left school officials in a perceived grey area of law.[52] 'The courts are telling us what we are supposed to do or not supposed to do', argued Representative William Goodling (R-Penn) before the House subcommittee. 'Each court decision is telling us something differently. And this has been going on now since the prayer decision and for the life of me I can't find six people who will say what exactly that means and say the same thing'.[53] In passing equal access legislation, Congress could provide the guidance and legal foundation required by school officials, administrators and lawyers, and ensure that the rights of religious students were protected.

A further significant difference from the prayer hearings was a tendency among many participants in the equal access debates to avoid absolute statements and a willingness to discuss the potential consequences of equal access legislation. Testimony from groups such as the National Council of Churches and the American Lutheran Council not only criticized the proposed legislation, but suggested ways in which it might be altered to accommodate their concerns.[54] Before the House subcommittee, Senator Denton described changes that had been made to his bill, S.1059, in response to challenges raised before the Senate Judiciary Committee, indicating such concerns were being taken seriously by those responsible for the legislation. The general support for genuine equal access meant there was room for discussion and compromise. For example, the American Civil Liberties Union, the American Jewish Congress and Americans United forcefully challenged the suggestion that the principles of *Widmar* should simply be extended to younger students. The broad range of political and philosophical groups meeting on the campus of the University of Missouri at Kansas City was, they argued, a far different situation from that of high schools or elementary schools where clubs were most frequently related to academic or curricular pursuits, were faculty-initiated not student-initiated, often required a staff sponsor, advisor or monitor and rarely involved the kinds of subject matter a religious group might discuss.[55] Although lengthy discussions of these issues did not fully resolve all of the problems, the original proposals were modified to ensure that the Equal Access Act applied only to high schools, excluding the very youngest students, and statements from participants suggested that schools must be careful about the way their extra-curricular activities programmes operated if religious groups were allowed to meet.[56] A second major change made as a result of congressional hearings involved a provision protecting the 'religious content' of speech or 'prayer, religious discussion, or silent meditation'. Such language, opponents argued, might give religion a preferred status in a way that violated the Establishment Clause.[57] In *Widmar*, the Supreme Court had ruled the student group should be allowed to meet because other political and philosophical groups were also present in the forum. Excluding or overlooking this kind of speech might lead school officials to discriminate on grounds other than religion, which should be equally forbidden. The Equal Access Act prohibits discrimination on the grounds of 'religious, political, philosophical, or other content' of speech.

These discussions and others – including what groups constituted school-related activities and which were extracurricular, how many extracurricular groups were necessary for equal access to become applicable, what kinds of controls schools would maintain over use of their own property, what schools with limited resources could do to avoid violating any equal access legislation, how schools might establish neutral criteria for use of facilities when those resources were limited and whether equal access would allow outside speakers to address student groups – showed a willingness to discuss these broader issues that had often been lacking in the prayer amendment hearings. A greater open-mindedness about equal access legislation permeated the hearings in a way that suggested, for most advocates, that this was not a back-door attempt to force religion into schools but a genuine desire to right perceived wrongs committed against some students due to misunderstandings or insufficient information.[58] Committee members were willing to listen to and address the concerns of equal access opponents to ensure that such protection was not granted at the expense of religious minorities, the non-religious and others. In doing so, they ensured a broad base of support that resulted in legislative success.

The Equal Access Act, as signed into law by President Reagan in August 1984, was not extensively discussed by Congress, either in committee or by the House or Senate. Two interpretations of this relative silence are possible. First, politicians and religious groups had already gained the necessary political capital from the issue as a result of the committee hearings; further debate brought no additional political advantage. Some politicians, Denton for example, used the hearings as a platform to express views they had long held and were mindful of the broader audience they were addressing. But, compared to the prayer hearings, equal access garnered less extensive and less detailed press coverage that might benefit the politicians. The electorate, the broader audience, were thus less likely to be aware of who took which position; those reading the publications by groups or organizations involved in the debate which might contain such detailed information, were, most likely, already sympathetic to the position taken by the group and its supporters.[59] Political grandstanding in equal access hearings brought far less reward than it might have done in prayer hearings. Instead the compromise should be regarded as a desire on the part of interested groups and individuals to find a remedy for the situation discussed before the committees: advocates ensured protection for the right of students to express religious views and participate in religious activities and opponents ensured that the correct safeguards were in place to protect minority groups, that activities remained voluntary and limited the involvement of school officials. Comparison of the wording of the Act to the concerns raised in committee suggests that the former was significantly influenced by the latter. The compromise engineered by Hatfield and Denton thus brought concrete results for all involved in the debate, results far more politically beneficial than simple speech-making. While for a limited few equal access was about political point-scoring in the same manner as school prayer, the significant differences in tone, rhetoric levels and detailed discussion before the committees revealed a genuine concern for the rights of students and a perceived need for greater clarity about the scope and application of *Engel* and *Schempp*. Agreement on these issues allowed for the assembling of a broad coalition of groups and individuals, which resulted in the legislative success denied to the smaller, more divisive group advocating school prayer.

Concluding Thoughts

Widmar v. Vincent and congressional debates about equal access policies reveal a great deal about the impact of the public debate which followed *Engel* and *Schempp*. In House and Senate hearings a litany of examples from across the country revealed the continued controversy that school prayer-related issues could cause and the extent to which heightened sensitivity to such issues had resulted in reactions that had not been intended by the justices in their 1962 and 1963 opinions. Local controversies, such as those testified to by Bonnie Bailey and Stuart Kennedy, also suggested that no broad consensus had been reached about the place of religion in the nation's public schools. While this undoubtedly reflected the difficulty of balancing the rights of majority and minority faiths, the general misunderstanding about the meaning of *Engel* and *Schempp* also clearly limited the ability of participants to reach a workable compromise.

The Court's approach to *Widmar* made the legal and constitutional foundations of equal access far easier than those of school prayer or school aid. By 1981 the Court had a long history of protecting the free exercise and free speech rights of religious and secular minority groups and had recognized that students did not give up all of those rights as they entered schools. Dealing with adults in *Widmar* made the case less controversial than it might have been had students under the age of eighteen been involved, but few disputed the right of university students to believe and speak as they wished. Resting the case more heavily on free speech rather than Establishment grounds would, however, have significant consequences in later cases.

Passage of the Equal Access Act presented the Court with an additional factor to consider in future equal access cases. The Act held that high schools which allowed student groups to meet in non-class hours could not refuse permission to student religious groups to meet under the same conditions as secular groups. Despite the fears of school prayer opponents that equal access would become little more than school prayer in a different form, hearings on equal access legislation revealed a much broader base of support. While congressional hearings allowed school prayer advocates to repeat their long-held criticisms of the Supreme Court, the general atmosphere of the hearings revealed a wider concern that overreaction to the Court's rulings was infringing students' constitutional rights. The Equal Access Act aimed to provide clearer guidelines as to acceptable practices within schools with regards to students' non-class activities than had been available from the Court's opinions. However, ambiguities about the Act's application and operation remained – ambiguities that, it seemed likely, the Court would be asked to address.

Chapter 8

The Court United and Divided: The Path to *Rosenberger*

By 1985, issues relating to school prayer and equal access appeared more settled than they had been for some time. The defeat in September 1985 of Senator Jesse Helms's (R-NC) bill to restrict the Supreme Court's jurisdiction over school prayer cases saw Congress withdraw from the issue after heated debates. The passage of the Equal Access Act in August the previous year offered the possibility that with clearer guidelines as to what practices and activities were permitted in schools, and under what circumstances, controversy surrounding the broader issue of religion in public schools would also subside. However, although Congress had extended students' right of equal access to school facilities, the practical consequences of that decision had not been fully discussed. For example, in the 12 states of the Second, Third, Fifth and Eleventh Circuits, school districts ran the risk of violating court orders if they attempted to implement the Act.[1] The relative lack of specific discussion in the House and Senate hearings left unanswered questions about how the Equal Access Act should be applied, questions made more forceful by the fact that the Act's legislative history meant congressional hearings were not specifically about the Act as enacted. Contradictory decisions from state courts and the limited discussion of the specifics of the Equal Access Act made it likely that the issue would, in some form, return to the courts for clarification.

The Court United and Divided

In January 1990, the Supreme Court heard oral arguments in *Board of Education of the Westside Community Schools v. Mergens*, a challenge to the constitutionality of the Equal Access Act and its applicability to Westside High School.[2] In January 1985, Bridget Mergens had requested permission from her high school principal to form a Christian club for students to read and discuss the Bible, have fellowship and pray together. Membership would be voluntary and open to all students regardless of religious affiliation. The principal and the school superintendent denied the request on the grounds that it would violate the Establishment Clause. In response to Mergens's claim that the denial violated the Equal Access Act, school officials held that it did not apply to Westside High School because it did not operate a limited open forum as defined by the Act. They further asserted that even if the school did operate such a forum, the Equal Access Act violated the Establishment Clause and thus any action in compliance with it would be similarly violative. The case thus raised two key questions: whether the Equal Access Act was, in fact, constitutional, and what exactly was meant by a limited public forum.

Mergens revealed that the divisions on the Court over school aid were also present in other areas of Establishment Clause jurisprudence. Eight justices agreed that the Equal Access Act applied to Westside High School, but only six agreed that the Act did not violate the Establishment Clause.[3] Of the six, Justices Anthony Kennedy and Antonin Scalia objected to Justice Sandra Day O'Connor's use of the *Lemon* and endorsement tests in her opinion for the Court and offered their own reasoning for constitutionality, leaving O'Connor to speak for a plurality of four. Justices Thurgood Marshall and William Brennan concluded that while the Act as applied to Westside *could* withstand Establishment Clause scrutiny, it would depend on the totality of the circumstances, while Justice John Paul Stevens in dissent argued that it was unnecessary to address the issue of constitutionality at all since, in his view, Westside had not created a limited open forum and so the Act did not apply. Consequently, although the result in *Mergens* affirmed the constitutionality of the Equal Access Act and allowed Mergens and others to establish their religious club, it did so on very narrow grounds and without a clear foundation.[4] Although the agreement on the result reflected a continuation of the consensus in *Widmar*, the divisions seen in other Establishment cases as to the reasoning and tests were far more visible.

In assessing the constitutionality of the Equal Access Act, O'Connor drew heavily on the *Lemon* test. 'We think the logic of *Widmar* applies with equal force to the Equal Access Act', she wrote, 'the Act's prohibition of discrimination on the basis of "political, philosophical, or other" speech as well as religious speech is a sufficient basis for meeting the secular purpose prong of the *Lemon* test'.[5] Although her finding of a secular purpose was relatively uncontroversial, O'Connor's interpretation of 'effect' divided the Court. 'We think that secondary school students are mature enough and likely to understand that a school does not *endorse or support* student speech that it merely permits on a non-discriminatory basis', she argued.[6] The principle made sense, but in approaching the issue in this way, O'Connor substituted her preferred 'endorsement' test for the more traditional effects analysis, which garnered a sharp response from Kennedy and Scalia. 'The word endorsement', Kennedy wrote, 'has insufficient content to be dispositive . . . [and] its literal application may result in neutrality in name but hostility in fact when the question is the government's proper relation to those who express some religious preference'.[7] The better test would be whether the benefit provided was direct or indirect and whether there was present any element of coercion to participate, Kennedy asserted. In using these criteria, Kennedy avoided explicit use of the *Lemon* test of which he had previously been so critical, but drew on the criteria that had developed in the school aid cases: since the Equal Access Act coerced no one into participating in religious activities and any benefit to religion was incidental, Kennedy agreed with O'Connor that it did not violate the Establishment Clause. This division between the plurality and Kennedy and Scalia over the proper way to analyse the effect of a challenged programme added further confusion to the debate over the *Lemon* test and limited the guidance that *Mergens* provided to those in similar situations. Equally, the division further underscored what was becoming clear in the school aid cases: the battle on the Court was not simply between the separationists and those favouring accommodation but was also a battle over the correct way to analyse attempts at accommodation.

Justice Marshall's opinion, concurring in judgement, also revealed the limits to the consensus on equal access that had been present in *Widmar v. Vincent*. Both Marshall and Brennan, who joined the opinion, had been long-standing defenders of the separationist position on the Court, a position that was clear in the pages of Marshall's *Mergens* opinion. 'The Act's low threshold for triggering equal access . . . raises serious Establishment Clause concerns where secondary schools with fora that differ substantially from the forum in *Widmar* are required to grant access to student religious groups', wrote Marshall, echoing the views of many who had spoken against equal access legislation before congressional committees.[8] Marshall's concern, similar to Stevens in dissent, was that when a school has a religious club but no other political or ideological organizations, students may be led to believe that the school endorses the group and its views, especially if other student groups are supported by the school. In *Widmar*, the presence of a broad range of political and ideological organizations made it unlikely that any implication of support for a single group would be perceived; in a school where the religious group is the only such group, that may not be the case.[9] 'Westside must redefine its relationship to its club program', argued Marshall, to ensure that the school did not inadvertently imply support for the religious group the Equal Access Act allowed to meet.[10] Marshall's opinion reflected his position on church-state issues: genuine equal access did not support or hinder religion and religious groups but it should not be used as a cover for allowing religion in public schools or other unconstitutional benefits. If such aid was provided, the activity would be unconstitutional. With no clear majority for any approach to Establishment Clause analysis of the Equal Access Act, Marshall's opinion provided an additional perspective to consider, one far narrower than that of either the plurality or Kennedy's concurrence.

The second issue raised in *Mergens*, the applicability of the Act to Westside High School, illustrated the accommodationists' growing influence on the Court. Outlining the provisions of the Act, O'Connor noted that the key phrase in assessing applicability was 'noncurriculum related student group' and its meaning. 'The difficult question', she wrote, 'is the degree of "unrelatedness to the curriculum" required for the group to be considered "noncurriculum related"'.[11] The ambiguity of the phrase itself and the lack of specific guidance provided by congressional debate made the task more difficult. However, analysis of congressional discussion revealed for O'Connor that 'the Act was intended to address perceived widespread discrimination against religious speech in public schools'.[12] The breadth of this aim, combined with Congress's 'intent to provide a low threshold for triggering the Act's requirements', led the majority to conclude that the term 'noncurriculum related student group' 'is best interpreted broadly to mean any student group that does not *directly* relate to the body of courses offered by the school'.[13] In conference and in dissent, Justice Stevens offered an alternative definition. Stevens's main concern was that the implication of the majority's definition might force schools to open to religious clubs simply because they allowed a chess club or a scuba diving club, groups 'no more controversial than a grilled cheese sandwich'.[14] Advocacy groups, whether religious, political or philosophical, he suggested, were substantially different from activities groups most commonly found in the nation's high schools: to suggest that the presence of such non-controversial groups would require that schools automatically allow similar access to more controversial groups not only removed the traditional authority of schools to manage their own facilities, but also was blatantly absurd. A better understanding of the phrase, he argued, would be if a group 'has as its purpose (or part of its purpose) the advocacy of partisan theological, political, or ethical views', understanding 'noncurriculum' to mean 'either subjects that are "not a part of the current curriculum" or the subjects "that cannot properly be included in a public school curriculum"'.[15] For Stevens, the category of organizations about which the Court was concerned was far narrower than for the majority.

The Court opinion and Stevens's dissent proposed alternative definitions of the Equal Access Act: a broad interpretation which followed legislative intent or a narrower version concerned more with the pragmatic implications of the language used.[16] In following the latter, Stevens returned to the concerns about schools' control over their own property that he had expressed in *Widmar* nearly a decade earlier.[17] In following the former, O'Connor and the majority deferred to legislative intent and took a position more compatible with other Establishment Clause cases than that of Stevens. In *Witters v. Washington Department of Services for the Blind* in 1986, the majority had allowed a disabled student to use federal disability grants to attend a seminary because the aid was neutral and not provided on the basis of religious criteria, a trend continued in *Zobrest v. Catalina Hills Independent School District* in 1993 when permitting the presence of a sign language interpreter paid for by the state in a religious school, three years after *Mergens*. In *Mergens*, O'Connor's broader definition of 'noncurriculum related' remained facially neutral and avoided religious criteria while ensuring that the law applied broadly, as Congress had intended. By standing in contrast, Stevens's dissent more clearly highlighted the majority's position of accommodating religion and religious belief so long as it could be done on a neutral basis without unconstitutionally favouring the religious over the non-religious.[18] The result in *Mergens* was that because the school allowed, among others, a chess club and a scuba diving club to meet on campus, they had created a limited public forum and therefore could not, according to the majority, deny access to a religious group. However, while the result in *Mergens* was clear, the route to that result remained debatable.

Similar divisions wracked the Court two years later in *Lamb's Chapel v. Center Moriches Union Free School District*.[19] Lamb's Chapel, an evangelical church, applied twice to the school district for permission to show a six-part film dealing with family and child-rearing issues from a religious perspective. In both instances permission was denied on the grounds that the film 'appear[s] to be church related'.[20] The Court found little difficulty in holding that the denial violated the free speech rights of Lamb's Chapel. Finding no 'indication in the record before us that the application to exhibit the particular film series involved here was, or would have been, denied for any reason other than the fact that the presentation would have been from a religious perspective', Justice Byron White for the Court held this was viewpoint discrimination in a vein similar to that in *Widmar*. The Court agreed that the school district could maintain control over the way in which its property was used but only if 'the distinctions drawn are reasonable in light of the purpose served by the forum and are viewpoint neutral'.[21] Since the school's facilities had been used in the past for discussions of family and child-rearing issues, the only ground for the denial was the religious nature of the film, which amounted to unacceptable viewpoint discrimination – an argument concurred in by all nine justices. The Court's decision was extremely narrow and intended to apply only to the specific factual circumstances in Center Moriches: the opinion had little value as a guide for other equal access cases. However, the significance of *Lamb's Chapel* lay less in its result than in what the opinions revealed about the battle within the Court over the proper grounds for deciding Establishment Clause cases.[22]

The division occurred over two different but related issues. The first was the *Lemon* test. White mentioned *Lemon* only briefly near the end of his opinion when discussing why allowing the film showing of Lamb's Chapel did not violate the Establishment Clause. There was no lengthy discussion of the test or its specific application to the case under discussion. However, even this brief reference was enough to upset Justices Scalia and Thomas, both of whom had called for the abandonment of the test. In characteristically sharp language, Scalia commented:

> Like some ghoul in a late night horror movie that repeatedly sits up in its grave and shuffles abroad, after being repeatedly killed and buried, *Lemon* stalks our Establishment Clause jurisprudence once again, frightening the little children and school attorneys of Center Moriches Union Free School District . . . The secret of the *Lemon* test's survival, I think, is that it is so easy to kill. It is there to scare us (and our audience) when we wish it to do so, but we can command it to return to the tomb at will . . . Such a docile and useful monster is worth keeping around, at least in a somnolent state; one never knows when one might need him.[23]

Scalia's comments, and the response they engendered from White, were simply a new exchange in a long battle. For several years the *Lemon* test had withstood increasing criticism from legal scholars and Supreme Court justices, including Kennedy, O'Connor, Rehnquist, Scalia and Thomas.

The year before *Lamb's Chapel* in *Lee v. Weisman*, Kennedy had completely ignored the *Lemon* test when holding prayers at high school graduation ceremonies unconstitutional, leading many to proclaim the final demise of the test. White's passing mention of *Lemon* and Scalia's response showed that the debate over the three-part test was not settled but remained a central part of the Court's jurisprudence and that *Lemon* remained a valid, but controversial, precedent.

The second debate concerned Justice Scalia's assertion that the Establishment Clause prevents only government favouritism of a single group or denomination, not government favouritism of religion more broadly. For the majority, Justice White commented: 'Under these circumstances, as in *Widmar*, there would have been no realistic danger that the community would think that the District was endorsing religion or any particular creed, and any benefit to religion or the Church would have been no more than incidental'.[24] The implication of this statement was that to pass constitutional muster, a statute must neither provide direct benefits to religion nor involve government endorsement of religion, both with precedent in the Court's earlier Establishment cases. This position limited more strictly the kinds of relationship between church and state that could be deemed constitutional than Scalia's accommodationist stance, with which Thomas and Kennedy were both broadly sympathetic. In the concurrences filed, both Kennedy and Scalia noted their disagreement with the Court with brief discussions of their reasoning. Their brevity, however, concealed a much deeper disagreement which had sparked a sharp exchange between Justices Scalia and Stevens during opinion writing.[25] The division was crucial to Establishment Clause interpretation. White's analysis recognized, as the Court had before, that church and state were likely to interact, and sought to ensure that such contact was within acceptable limits; Scalia's position suggested that the only limitation on the relationship should be the favouring of one religious group over another. White's approach reflected the balancing of concerns seen in earlier cases; Scalia's approach suggested that if at some future point he found a sympathetic majority, then the Court's Establishment Clause jurisprudence would become far more accommodationist. This debate over what Kennedy referred to as 'a subsidiary point', in the context of *Lamb's Chapel*, as well as the more public discussion about *Lemon*, suggested that White's opinion was drawn narrowly to avoid exactly this disagreement, not simply to avoid making sweeping statements on equal access. Equally, this disagreement on method clashed with the broad consensus on the result in the case, unlike the school aid cases in which the justices were divided over both. In school aid cases, these divisions had been apparent for some time; in equal access cases, however, the disagreement had more often been obscured by the consensus on the result and by the Court's tendency to address equal access cases on free speech rather than Establishment grounds. The consensus on results was thus built on tenuous foundations. A case that raised a clearer conflict between the guarantees of the First Amendment might shatter the Court so that no single view could command a majority, as seen in the school aid cases of the early Burger Court.

A Clash of Principles? Speech or Money

Such a case reached the Court in its 1994 Term. The University of Virginia operated a Student Activities Fund paid into by all students through a mandatory $14 per semester fee which could be accessed by a variety of student groups to fund their activities. Wide Awake Productions, a Christian group operating at the university, applied to the Student Activities Fund for funds to pay an outside printer for the cost of printing their newspaper, *Wide Awake: A Christian Perspective at the University of Virginia*. Their application was refused on the ground that the newspaper 'primarily promotes or manifests a particular belief in or about a deity or ultimate reality' as prohibited by the Student Activities Fund guidelines. Wide Awake Productions challenged the refusal of funds as a denial of their right to free speech, contending that, as other student newspapers were funded, denying similar resources to *Wide Awake* discriminated against them based solely on their point of view. The University of Virginia contended that funding such a religious newspaper was forbidden by their existing guidelines and by the requirements of the Establishment Clause. Although the District Court and the Fourth Circuit disagreed over the presence of viewpoint discrimination, both agreed that the Establishment Clause provided a reasonable foundation for the university's denial of funds for the printing of *Wide Awake*.[26] In *Rosenberger v. the Rector and Visitors of the University of Virginia*, the Supreme Court, in a 5:4 decision, disagreed. In an opinion based heavily on freedom of speech rather than Establishment grounds, Justice Anthony Kennedy for the Court held, 'it was not necessary for the University to deny eligibility to student publications because of their viewpoint. The neutrality commanded of the State by the separate clauses of the 1st Amendment was compromised by the University's course of action'.[27]

Rosenberger represents a microcosm of the Establishment Clause debate as it stood in the mid-1990s, revealing both the philosophical divide among the justices and their consequent differences in approach. The case presented the Court with a dilemma similar to that sidestepped in *Widmar* 14 years earlier: the clash of rights enumerated in the First Amendment. Free speech analysis places the burden of proof on those wishing to restrict the speech while Establishment analysis places that burden on those wishing to speak or receive funds: one is arguably more permissive, the other more restrictive and, in the context of *Rosenberger*, represented opposite approaches.[28] The approaches taken by the majority and the dissent revealed the growing accommodationist-separationist divide on the Rehnquist Court that had been increasingly evident in school aid cases: Chief Justice Rehnquist and Justices Kennedy, Scalia and Clarence Thomas in the former, and Justices Stephen Breyer, Ruth Bader Ginsburg, Stevens and David Souter in the latter, with O'Connor at the centre.

Kennedy's opinion for the majority took a clearly accommodationist approach. By concentrating on the free speech approach of earlier equal access cases despite the clear involvement of a financial issue, Kennedy chose the more permissive standard of review, placing the burden of proof on the University of Virginia to show why Wide Awake Productions should be excluded from access to the Student Activities Fund. While the university, or any forum moderator, could legitimately restrict the topics of acceptable discussion within the forum to maintain its intent and scope, the university could not prevent an individual or group discussing a permitted topic from a particular perspective. Because the university did not restrict religion as a subject matter, it could not prevent discussion of other topics from a religious perspective.[29] Ignoring the dissent's claim that *Wide Awake* did not teach about religion so much as teach religious precepts, Kennedy made one of the most sweeping claims found in the Court's Establishment Clause jurisprudence: 'Vital First Amendment speech principles are at stake here', he argued, suggesting that the university's actions amounted to government censorship of speech with a 'chilling effect' on individual thought and expression. Such an approach, he suggested, would lead to the exclusion of articles by hypothetical student contributors Plato, Spinoza, Descartes, Marx, Bertrand Russell and Sartre.[30] Overstating the case, Kennedy's opinion sought to make the University of Virginia's decision seem like an overreaction based on misunderstood principles and the Court's approach appear as a reasonable reaction to the facts of the case. As Black in *Everson v. Board of Education* sought to distinguish the New Jersey bus statute from eighteenth-century meanings of establishment, Kennedy sought to distinguish the protection of *Wide Awake*'s speech from Establishment Clause issues. Such obvious overstatement served only to weaken the impact of the argument and detract from the briefer Establishment Clause arguments put forwards later in the opinion.

Central to the Court's rejection of the university's position was the breadth of the programme and the intent behind it, arguments familiar from *Witters* and *Zobrest*. 'The governmental program here is neutral toward religion', wrote Kennedy. 'There is no suggestion that the University created it to advance religion or adopted some ingenious device with the purpose of aiding a religious cause'.[31] Since a wide spectrum of groups used the university's facilities, including the Student Activities Fund, the university could not be considered to favour *Wide Awake* by granting it funds on the same basis as others.[32] Equally important to the analysis was the similarly familiar argument that Wide Awake Productions received an indirect benefit and a non-financial one. Since funds went directly to the printer and not Wide Awake Productions, the majority claimed, the net effect was no different to allowing the group to use the university's printers to produce the newspaper themselves. Thus, the Student Activities Fund was no different in principle to the school hall at issue in *Lamb's Chapel*.[33] Derided by the dissenters, the majority's focus on indirect benefits and facially neutral eligibility criteria restated the themes dominant in the Court's school aid analysis that two years after *Rosenberger* would result in *Agostini v. Felton*.

Why did Kennedy choose to emphasize the speech elements if the Establishment arguments alone were sufficient to defend the majority's decision? First, it drew attention away from the financial issue, the fact that the forum concerned was not a hall, street or park, but a fund to which contribution was mandatory. The Student Activities Fund issue placed the benefit far closer to that ruled unconstitutional by the Court in school aid cases and made the Establishment argument more complicated than it had been in equal access cases; Kennedy's approach simply ignored the issue and thus sidestepped the problem.[34] Second, because of the speech element implicit in equal access analysis, the burden of proof had always rested more heavily on those denying the aid or use of facilities, providing greater opportunity for religious groups. This made it easier to achieve a more accommodationist result without dealing directly with the implications for school aid cases, something, given O'Connor's status as a swing vote, Kennedy may not have had five votes to achieve.

This, however, did not stop the dissenters discussing the implications in an opinion, written by Justice David Souter, firmly rooted in separationist principles that would have been familiar to the *Everson* dissenters in 1947. For Souter, Stevens, Ginsburg and Breyer, this was clearly an Establishment case: it involved the transfer of money to a religious group espousing a clearly religious message:

> The subject is not the discourse of the scholar's study or the seminar room, but of the evangelist's mission station and the pulpit. It is nothing other than the preaching of the word, which (along with the sacraments) is what most branches of Christianity offer those called to the religious life. Using public funds for the direct subsidization of preaching the word is categorically forbidden under the Establishment Clause, and if the Clause was meant to accomplish nothing else, it was meant to bar this use of public money.[35]

Wide Awake was a religious magazine, the Student Activities Fund constituted public money controlled by the University, thus under the Court's Establishment Clause jurisprudence, the University of Virginia's decision not to fund *Wide Awake* was legitimate.[36] The facial validity of the regulations governing the Student Activities Fund was irrelevant, argued the dissenters, since neutrality was a necessary condition, but not a dispositive one. Funding all religious groups would be as unacceptable as only funding *Wide Awake*, therefore other issues needed to be addressed. The more important principle established in prior cases was that any benefit to religion must be indirect and incidental, and in this instance, 'there is no third-party standing between the government and the ultimate religious beneficiary to break down the circuit'.[37] Although arguing this was the controlling principle in all the Court's prior cases, the dissenters' need to make their case so forcefully suggested that in fact *Witters* and *Zobrest* had changed the emphasis in the Court's school aid cases and that facially neutral eligibility criteria had become the Court's main focus. The dissenters' arguments suggested that they were attempting to reassert the principles of cases such as *Everson*, *Lemon* and *Aguilar* and their concern with the relationship between the provider and beneficiary of the aid or benefit.[38] The *Rosenberger* dissent thus showed that while a bare majority of the Court may have moved to a more accommodationist position on church-state issues, the separationist argument continued to have its supporters on the bench.

The (Non) Reaction to Equal Access

Equal access is an unusual element of the Supreme Court's Establishment Clause jurisprudence. Although the justices divided over the tests to be used and the principles to be applied, until *Rosenberger* introduced a financial element into the debate, the justices remained broadly unified in supporting the idea of equal access. The principle that religious individuals or groups should not be discriminated against in their use of public spaces and facilities simply because they hold or espouse religious beliefs is difficult to dispute in a nation that protects 'free exercise' at the same time as preventing an 'establishment' of religion. It is, perhaps, the widespread agreement on this principle that accounts for the relative lack of public controversy that has surrounded the Court's equal access jurisprudence. Unlike *Engel, Schempp, Aguilar* or others, the Court's decisions in *Widmar, Mergens, Lamb's Chapel* and, to a lesser extent, *Rosenberger*, did not spur public demonstrations, rebukes from politicians or letter-writing campaigns on a massive scale.[39] The kind of anti-Court sentiment expressed after most school prayer and several school aid decisions was notable by its absence after equal access cases.[40] Although a lack of evidence for these non-occurrences makes it difficult to definitively account for the lack of public and political reaction in equal access cases, three factors seem likely to have had an influence.

First, the Court upheld the principle of equal access in the cases before it, unlike the prayer cases and several school aid practices. Those who had been most critical of the Court's holdings in the latter cases had nothing to oppose: the Court had handed down the result they advocated. Groups from the Religious Right and others who advocated accommodation of religion under the Establishment Clause had no foundation upon which to challenge the Court: the only criticism came from some who believed the Court had not gone far enough.[41] On the other side of the debate, groups who had traditionally taken a strong separationist stand did not challenge the principle of genuine equal access for religious groups. The ACLU did not oppose the Equal Access Act for this reason and in 1993 filed an *amicus* brief in favour of the right of Lamb's Chapel to use public facilities to show its film. Thus, the ACLU and others only challenged practices that occurred under the auspices of equal access, as they did in *Mergens* and *Rosenberger*, when they perceived that the activities went beyond the limits of equal access into the realm of aid or benefit. Support for the general principle but opposition to specific instances of its application limited the scope of opponents' challenges: their dislike of the situation in *Mergens*, for example, did not necessarily threaten other equal access policies. The scope of any dispute was thus restricted, unlike school prayer and school aid challenges. Second, the actions of the Supreme Court also ensured that debates and conflict would be limited. In each of the four equal access cases, the Court's opinions were narrowly written and tailored to the specific facts of the case. They provided only limited guidance on equal access generally, deciding only the controversy before the Court. As such, the Court's acceptance of one particular practice did not imply acceptance of them all, just as a rejection did not suggest abandonment of the principle generally. The narrowness of the opinions further restricted debate to individual cases and thus limited the nature of public reaction. Finally, the terms of the Equal Access Act itself limits its application. The Act applies only to schools with a limited open forum; if the school does not operate such a forum, the Act does not apply. As with the Court's decisions, the specific circumstances are crucial: one school's violation of the terms of the Act does not imply that all with equal access policies do so. In combination, all these factors have served to restrict public, political and legal debate to specific instances and practices, thus ensuring that the broad, divisive debates over school prayer and school aid were not replicated.

Concluding Thoughts

Equal access cases have more in common with the Supreme Court's freedom of speech cases than with Establishment Clause cases. The question of whether groups or individuals should have the right to speak or meet seems far removed from the Establishment debates of school prayer and school aid, and the Court's predominant use of free speech principles in such cases strengthens this impression. However, the questions raised by school aid, in particular about the 'proper' relationship between church and state, apply equally when the question is whether religious groups and individuals should be allowed to make use of space or property that belongs to the state. It was this situation that the Court faced in *Widmar v. Vincent* in 1981 and has sought to negotiate since. The Court's approach since *Widmar*, relying heavily on free speech principles, does not, however, reduce their importance for understanding the Court's Establishment Clause jurisprudence.

The greatest value of equal access cases to an understanding of the Court's Establishment Clause jurisprudence is that they revealed the deepening divisions between the Justices. In school aid cases, philosophical differences have often been obscured by disagreement on the results of a case.[42] In equal access cases, the greater consensus on the results brings into sharp focus these deeper disagreements. The single exception, *Rosenberger*, reinforced this perception: the difference in the findings of the majority and dissent lay in a fundamental difference of approach to the issues raised. In allowing student religious groups to meet in *Widmar* and *Mergens*, the Court reinforced its long-held position that a complete separation of the church and the state is neither necessary nor desirable. Similar sentiments were expressed in *Everson*, *Allen*, *Nyquist* and other school aid cases, as well as in *Engel* and *Schempp*. However, the elements brought in to Establishment Clause jurisprudence by the free speech implications of equal access, particularly neutral eligibility criteria and the greater burden of proof placed on those wishing to restrict speech, have spread into other areas of Establishment Clause analysis. The majority's approach in *Rosenberger* prefigured the same majority's approach in *Agostini* three years later in its emphasis on neutral eligibility criteria. However, the public and private debates in *Lamb's Chapel* and *Rosenberger* showed divisions between the justices who saw government accommodation as limited to instances where the benefits provided are no greater than those available to secular groups and others, particularly Scalia and Thomas, who consider accommodation to prevent government favouritism of particular groups or denominations but not government preference of religion. The divisions between these groups, combined with the more separationist views of Breyer, Ginsburg, Souter and Stevens, suggest a clear definition of the meaning of the Establishment Clause, with regards to equal access, remained as elusive and controversial at the end of the twentieth century as it had been in 1947.

Disagreement among the nine justices of the Supreme Court on equal access issues appears broadly reflective of disagreements in American society about the place of religion in the nation's schools and the role it should play there. The Equal Access Act itself operates in such a way as to allow decisions to be made by individual students, school boards and communities to reflect the particular circumstances and points of view present in each case. Ironically, such a case-by-case analysis echoes the Burger Court's approach to school aid issues which has been so heavily criticized. But such an approach also seems to reflect an understanding that there is no broad consensus about religion in public schools in this context. The debates over school prayer and school aid, while different in focus, clearly reveal the breadth and depth of opinion in this field and the controversy that can emerge when a nationwide solution is attempted. The Equal Access Act arguably takes the least controversial path: protecting the foundations of students' rights and establishing the parameters while allowing individual states or school boards to work out their own solutions within the established framework.

Table 3 Equal Access Cases: Dates, Rulings, Authors

Year	Case	Court Holding	Vote	Author	Concurrences (Author in Bold)	Dissenters (Author in Bold)
1981	*Widmar v. Vincent* 454 US 264	Religious student group permitted to use public university facilities to hold religious meetings and discussions. (Affirmed Eighth Circuit ruling that equal access does not violate Constitution and that denial of access to facilities was content-based discrimination).	8:1	Powell	**Stevens** (in judgement only)	**White**
1990	*Board of Education of the Westside Community Schools v. Mergens* 496 US 226	Religious student group allowed to use public school facilities to hold meetings during lunch-breaks and after school hours. Equal Access Act held constitutional. (Affirmed Eighth Circuit ruling on similar grounds).	8:1	O'Connor	**Kennedy** with Scalia **Marshall** with Brennan (in judgement only)	**Stevens**
1993	*Lamb's Chapel v. Center Moriches Union FreeSchool District* 508 US 384	Public schools that provide after-hours access to secular groups may not deny similar access to religious groups. (Overturned Second Circuit ruling that school did not operate an open forum and thus could deny access to facilities since reason for denial was reasonable and viewpoint neutral.)	9:0	White	**Kennedy** **Scalia** with Thomas	
1995	*Rosenberger v. the Rector and Visitors of the University of Virginia* 515 US 819	University of Virginia's policy of denying religious student groups access to activities funds denied groups' freedom of speech; provision of funds to religious groups in these circumstances did not violate the Establishment Clause. (Agreed with Fourth Circuit that denial of funds was viewpoint discrimination but overturned ruling that the Establishment Clause justified the denial).	5:4	Kennedy	**O'Connor** **Thomas**	**Souter** with Stevens, Ginsburg and Breyer

Conclusion

Relijon is a quare thing. Be itself it's all right. But sprinkle a little pollyticks into it an' dinnymit is bran flour compared with it. Alone it prepares man f'r a better life. Combined with pollyticks it hurries him to it.[1]

The aim of this book has been twofold. First, to introduce anyone with an interest in church-state issues to the crucial role played by the Supreme Court. The Court has both shaped and reflected public attitudes and, in interpreting the Constitution, provides the framework within which almost all the church-state debates take place. Without an understanding of the Court's decisions in Establishment Clause cases the broader picture of church-state relations in the post-World War Two United States is incomplete. The second aim of the book, however, has been to show that an understanding of the Court, in and of itself, is not sufficient for understanding the church-state debate either. The conflicts and debates discussed here were influenced not just by the Court, but by state governments, politicians, political and policy debates, religious leaders, religious beliefs, community pressure, economic circumstances and educational developments. The Court's cases and the debates which surround them cannot be fully understood without an appreciation of the role played by non-legal factors. Too often, lawyers overlook the history and historians fail to engage with the law; understanding the relationship between institutions of the church and those of the state in the second half of the twentieth century requires knowledge of both.

In 1947 when the Supreme Court heard oral argument in *Everson v. Board of Education* it is unlikely that the justices knew or realized the scope and nature of the debate they had begun. By holding the Establishment Clause applicable to the states as well as the federal government the Court became an arbiter of the line which governs church-state relations in the United States. Unwittingly or not, in *Everson* the Court accepted the task of defining the boundaries of the relationship between the institutions of church and state, a task that has continued and expanded for over sixty years. Several factors complicated this task. The increasing size, scope and responsibilities undertaken by the federal and state governments brought the institutions of church and state into closer proximity in the second half of the twentieth century than at any other time. Equally, religious groups, both old and new, became more active and more politically orientated in the twentieth century. The rise of the Religious Right in the late 1970s and the response of liberal religious groups and secular civil liberties groups in opposition, when coupled with government's expanded role, brought religion and politics together in ways not seen for generations. However, the Court also helped move religion into the political sphere. The Court is a legal institution but it is also a political one; constitutional decisions have political consequences, and the Court's Establishment Clause decisions were no different. More than any other decisions, the Court's prayer cases, *Engel v. Vitale* and *Abington School District v. Schempp*, brought Establishment issues into the political realm; the growing sense of judicial activism by the Warren Court throughout the 1960s ensured that they would stay there long after members of the Warren Court had left the bench. In addition, the Court's incorporation of the Free Exercise Clause and the Establishment Clause separately implied that they were separate provisions which might, in certain circumstances, conflict with each other: challenges to one might be brought by relying on the other. After incorporating the Establishment Clause, however, the Court became responsible for drawing the line between the permissible and the unconstitutional in church-state relations. How, and how well it has done so, remains open for debate.

The Theories

The Court has consistently refused to adhere to any of the three theories of Establishment Clause interpretation. Strict separation, neutrality and accommodation echoed in many of the opinions from the Court and individual justices but at no point did the Court endorse broad acceptance of one approach over others. The justices recognized the existence of the three theories and their academic and scholarly value in interpreting the meaning of the Establishment Clause. However, the Court also recognized that adherence to any individual theory was not practical when addressing real life cases. The facts of the cases heard by the Court did not lend themselves to a single philosophical approach even if the justices had favoured one over the others. Separationism, neutrality and accommodationism are thus useful tools in understanding the debates surrounding the Establishment Clause, but they cannot alone explain the Court's jurisprudence.

If the traditional legal approach, with its emphasis on the legal theories of separation, accommodation and neutrality, cannot fully explain the Court's behaviour in Establishment Clause cases, the models of political science theory offer alternative approaches with a broader understanding of the Court. *Stare decisis* and the role of precedent, as advocated by the Legal Model, influenced individual justices in particular cases and has particular relevance for the Court's prayer cases. The enduring nature of the principles established in *Engel* and *Schempp* is most clearly revealed in Justice Anthony Kennedy's switch in *Lee v. Weisman*, an opinion that is at odds with Kennedy's more accommodationist position in school aid and equal access cases. The Attitudinal Model, with its emphasis on the significance of justices' personal preferences, is particularly useful in understanding the emergence of blocs on the Court. Justices Wiley Rutledge and Robert Jackson in dissent in *Everson* clearly favoured strict separation, as did Justices William Brennan and Thurgood Marshall throughout their careers on the Court. The liberal bloc on the Rehnquist Court, Justices Stephen Breyer, Ruth Bader Ginsburg, David Souter and John Paul Stevens, continued to espouse separationist sentiments in opposition to a majority more favourable to accommodation, espoused particularly by Chief Justice William Rehnquist and Justices Antonin Scalia and Clarence Thomas. The justices forming these blocs, their responses to cases and the positions they took epitomized the justice of the Attitudinal Model. Yet while these blocs arguably account for the outcome in *Rosenberger v. the Rector and Visitors of the University of Virginia*, for most of the period 1947–1997 no group dominated the Court and the Court's opinions reflected both compromise between those of differing philosophical positions and the influence of the pragmatists on the Court who frequently held the balance between opposing groups. The negotiation and compromise among justices posited by the internal Rational Choice Model is seen most clearly in the influence of the centre on the Burger Court. The influence of Justices Harry Blackmun, Lewis Powell and Potter Stewart in forming majorities and shaping opinions is crucial for understanding the Burger Court. Justice O'Connor played a similar role on the Rehnquist Court. Their approach to cases, concern for the practical implications of challenged policies, consideration of the political and social context, including government positions, and a familiarity with precedent without unquestioning reliance upon it, echo concerns posited by the external Rational Choice Model. Thus all three Models help broaden our understanding of the Court's Establishment Clause jurisprudence. Although no single theory fully accounts for the behaviour of all the justices or for the Court as a whole during the period 1947–1997, in combination they reveal different aspects of justices' and Court behaviour that gives a fuller, deeper understanding of the Court and its jurisprudence than that provided by traditional legal theories.

The Court

The Supreme Court's Establishment Clause jurisprudence can be understood as three distinct periods. The Court's earliest decisions – *Everson, McCollum v. Board of Education, Zorach v. Clauson, Engel, Schempp* and *Board of Education v. Allen* – showed the justices working out approaches to and the requirements of Establishment Clause cases. Although some justices favoured certain results or approaches, the *Everson* dissenters' strict separationist argument or Justice William Douglas's position on funds for religious activities in public schools for example, the Court itself did not settle on the questions to be asked or the issues raised when assessing constitutionality. The variations in the approaches seen in these early cases (also seen in the Court's conference discussions) reflected the sense of the Court finding its way in this infrequently addressed area of constitutional jurisprudence.[2] Several general principles, however, emerged from these cases. Most significant was the Court's unwillingness to accept strict separation as an approach to Establishment Clause interpretation. In *Everson, Zorach, Schempp* and *Allen* the Court refused to invalidate all interactions between the spheres of church and state without further investigation. However, in *Engel* and *Schempp* the Court also made clear that overtly religious exercises initiated, sponsored or conducted by schools and their staff were not acceptable under any interpretation of the Establishment Clause. Where activities fell short of state direction or encouragement of religious activities, the Court considered the broader context of the case, including similar activities in other states and the actions of lower courts, in addition to the operation of the challenged programme before assessing constitutionality.[3] The Court enshrined this approach in the two-part test expounded in *Schempp*: 'there must be a secular legislative purpose and a primary effect that neither advances nor inhibits religion'.[4] This test showed the justices beginning to agree on the grounds for assessing Establishment Clause violations and codifying those principles in order to provide some guidance to lower courts.

The end of this first period of Establishment Clause interpretation, which began with *Everson*, came with Earl Warren's retirement, the appointment of Warren Burger as Chief Justice and a number of additional personnel changes. The Burger Court faced a different situation to that of the Vinson and Warren Courts. The Court had laid down precedent in Establishment cases and although no strong agreement on all the key factors for judging constitutionality in Establishment cases had been reached by earlier Courts, the cases themselves established certain principles and Justice Tom Clark's *Schempp* test provided fixed elements that would need to be applied. Also, the Warren Court was known as an activist Court in this area. The Warren Court's landmark decisions in areas as diverse as race, due process and defendants' rights, election practices and free speech had broad social and political consequences; the Court's activities became fodder for political debate to an unprecedented extent and any constitutional decision in such areas met extensive political scrutiny.[5] Combined with the hostility that had developed in the aftermath of the school prayer decisions, the Burger Court faced a far different political landscape to that of the early Warren Court.

Pragmatism dominated the Burger Court's Establishment Clause jurisprudence from *Lemon v. Kurtzman* in 1971 to *Witters v. Washington Department of Services for the Blind* in 1986. While partly a recognition of the political context in which the Court was operating, the Court's approach was fundamentally influenced by new personnel. Of central importance were Justices Blackmun, Powell and Stewart. Less sympathetic than their colleagues to particular philosophies of Establishment Clause interpretation, these three justices sought the most appropriate result in each case based on the particular factual circumstances.[6] They influenced all aspects of the Court's Establishment Clause jurisprudence. As with the Vinson and Warren Courts, no single philosophy of Establishment Clause jurisprudence attracted a majority of justices; however, while during Warren's tenure the resulting pragmatism was a result of the Court trying to find its way, under Burger pragmatism was a deliberate consequence of the balance of power held by the justices of the centre bloc.

This control of the centre and the pragmatic approach to cases that followed influenced the Court's Establishment Clause jurisprudence in several key ways. First, the factual circumstances of each case became particularly significant; the constitutionality of an activity rested on the context specific to each case. Although important in *all* Court cases, the frequency of the Court's concentration on factual similarities and differences between cases, especially school aid cases, revealed their particular importance. When the activity concerned was not overtly religious, the justices were willing to consider the cumulative impact of the situation addressed. This led the Court into detailed analysis of schools, aid programmes, communities, local history and the social and political context of the case.[7] Second, in order to analyse these factors, the Court developed a series of informal, flexible concerns that were loosely codified by Burger in *Lemon* in 1971 and became central to the Court's Establishment Clause analysis: on-campus or off-campus aid, financial or non-financial benefits, the direct or indirect nature of the benefit, the breadth of the programme and facial neutrality of statutes or policy guidelines were all regularly addressed by the justices.[8] These questions were considered as often in dissent as by the majority, revealing a broad consensus on the issues to be addressed despite the frequent lack of consensus about which issues were raised by particular cases. The third key influence of the control of the centre was more divided Courts and an increased number of concurrences and dissents. Despite agreement on the questions to be asked, the justices frequently disagreed on their relative importance in a particular case and on the factors involved in the implementation and operation of a programme or policy. Such disagreement was the result of the pragmatic approach of the Court's centrists and their rejection of a 'one size fits all' philosophy of Establishment Clause interpretation.

The Court's approach to Establishment Clause cases changed in the early years of the Rehnquist Court, beginning a third period of Establishment Clause interpretation. With the exception of *Lee v. Weisman*, the 1992 school prayer case, the Court after 1986 showed itself increasingly willing to accept greater interaction between church and state. The change was, once again, partly a function of the change of personnel on the Court. Most significant was Justice Kennedy's appointment in 1988 and his alliance with Justice Sandra Day O'Connor at the Court's centre on Establishment issues. Kennedy and O'Connor, despite forming the balance between the Court's liberals and conservatives, were willing to allow greater church-state interaction than the centre justices of the Burger Court but would not allow as much interaction as the Court's conservatives advocated. The principles employed in equal access cases provided the foundation for a more accommodationist approach to church-state relations in aid cases while, in addition, the justices placed greater emphasis on neutral eligibility criteria. The effect of these changes, although evident in limited form in *Zobrest v. Catalina Hills School District* and *Lamb's Chapel v. Center Moriches Union Free School District*, became clearer in *Rosenberger* and *Agostini v. Felton*.[9] These were significant changes in the Court's approach to Establishment Clause issues and this was reflected in the Court's rulings: the Rehnquist Court moved the Court closer to accepting full accommodationism than at any time in the Court's history.

The Rehnquist Court's acceptance of accommodationism was not, however, total. Two factors prevented its acceptance in full. The first was Justice Kennedy's switch in *Lee*. His assertion that his original opinion 'looked quite wrong' was, however, testament to the strength of the principles established in *Engel* and *Schempp*.[10] More than any other area of Establishment Clause jurisprudence the prayer cases, and *Lee* in particular, illustrate the importance of *stare decisis*: the principles laid down in 1962 and 1963 of no school-sponsored religious activity on public school grounds have endured despite the philosophical changes wrought by personnel changes in the intervening years. Second, the growing philosophical divisions on the Court worked to restrict the scope of the accommodationists. Rehnquist, Scalia and Thomas were more than ably opposed by Justices Breyer, Ginsburg, Souter and Stevens, all four committed to a separationist approach. Equally, although Kennedy and O'Connor as swing votes were more disposed towards accommodation than the centrist justices of the Burger Court, they did not accept it unquestioningly: Kennedy and O'Connor were key votes who could be won to *either* side if the argument was strong and the circumstances right. Aware of needing *both* swing votes for a majority, Rehnquist, Scalia and Thomas were forced to temper the breadth and tone of their opinions to hold a majority.[11] This became increasingly important as the philosophical divisions resulted, for the first time, in disagreements over the proper way to approach Establishment Clause cases. The increasingly harsh criticism of the *Lemon* test under Rehnquist revealed divisions over these basic principles that reflected the broader philosophical disagreements. Compromise became more difficult, requiring more concentration on the few areas of agreement between the justices seeking a majority. The Rehnquist Court gave a very different interpretation to the Establishment Clause, and the limitations on aid to religion were substantially reduced. However, the relationship between church and state was not completely unrestricted and limitations remained in place, reinforced in particular by Justice O'Connor; the relationship was freer but it was not free.

The Issues

As important to Establishment Clause jurisprudence as the justices, their philosophical differences and their approaches to interpreting church-state relations were the different kinds of activity challenged: school aid, school prayer and equal access involve different kinds of activity and, despite similarities in approach, the Court treated the three types of cases quite differently. In school prayer cases the single fundamental principle established by *Engel* and *Schempp* dominated the Court's jurisprudence: no school-sponsored religious exercises were permitted on school grounds during school hours; if a practice or activity was religious in nature and operated with any element of school support then it was constitutionally invalid. The only question to be asked was whether a challenged practice or activity was religious; if the answer was yes, then the activity was struck down – the context of the activity was irrelevant to the question of constitutionality, the only concern was the nature of the challenged activity itself. By contrast, context was crucial to the Court's analysis of equal access cases. Although striking down *school*-sponsored religious activities, the Court's prayer cases did not address the question of *student*-initiated religious exercises and activities on school grounds, or the use of school facilities outside school hours. Without a clearly unconstitutional benefit accruing to religious groups as a result of being allowed to meet, the Court held, there was no compelling reason to exclude religious groups simply because they were religious. The only way to tell if religion had unconstitutionally benefited was to consider the context in which the group was allowed to meet. In applying the 1984 Equal Access Act, the Court showed particular concern with the school environment and the context of the requested meetings in *Mergens* and *Lamb's Chapel*. Even in *Rosenberger*, both the majority and the dissent considered the context in detail to construct their arguments. The nature of equal access and the questions it raised thus required a different approach to that employed in prayer cases.

The Court's approach to school aid cases was similar to equal access cases in its focus on the context of the challenged programme, although without the free speech implications. In allowing reimbursement to parents of the cost of transporting their children to religious schools in *Everson* and the loan of secular textbooks to religious school students in *Allen*, the Court rejected strict separation and allowed benefits to flow to students attending religious schools which indirectly benefited the schools themselves. The child benefit rationale and indirect benefit test relied on in these cases were codified with a series of other concerns, including on-campus/off-campus aid and financial/non-financial benefits, by Chief Justice Burger in *Lemon v. Kurtzman* in 1971. The *Lemon* test – that aid must have a secular purpose, an effect that neither advances nor inhibits religion and must not result in excessive entanglement between church and state – is crucial for understanding the Court's school aid cases. It is essentially a balancing test, concerned with ensuring that there is no establishment of religion while at the same time protecting religious individuals and groups from discrimination based on their religious status. Unlike the clear pronouncement of principle in the prayer cases, the Court's approach to school aid challenges required careful analysis of the specific facts of the situation and the rulings became heavily context-dependent. Although the Court employed uncodified guidelines in analysing these cases, the manner in which they were employed and their relative importance varied. As personnel changed on the Court, school aid cases became increasingly dominated by debates among the justices over these guidelines and the proper way to analyse Establishment Clause violations. As the majority on the Court shifted away from the pragmatic balancing of interests espoused by the centre of the Burger Court towards the accommodationists on the Rehnquist Court, the Court's jurisprudence was shaped significantly by the different priorities placed on particular facts and tests by the various groups. The clash of traditional school aid issues with equal access principles in *Rosenberger* showed the significance of different types of cases to the Court's approach: the majority relied heavily on equal access and the dissent on school aid, each representing fundamentally different interpretations of the case. In addition, the Court's continued objection to school-sponsored religious exercises on public school grounds at the same time as developing more lenient standards of review in school aid cases arises because they raise different issues: the cases are not contradictory because they require a different analysis. Thus, recognition of the differences between the school aid, school prayer and equal access issues that influenced the Court's analysis and decisions allows a clearer understanding of the Court's Establishment Clause jurisprudence.

School aid cases have been the focus of much of the criticism of the Court's Establishment Clause jurisprudence that claims the Court has been inconsistent in its application of the Clause. Critics point particularly to the cases of the Burger Court to support such claims. Upholding textbook loans but striking down the loans of other instructional equipment, allowing tax deductions for school expenses but not reimbursement for the same costs and upholding diagnostic services but not the therapeutic services resulting from them appears, at first glance, to be entirely inconsistent. Yet such focus on the results overlooks the key interest of the Court: the operation of each individual programme. Focusing on the results does not allow consideration of to whom the instructional materials were loaned, who was entitled to receive the reimbursement of school costs and claim tax deductions and where the auxiliary services took place. Without this context the Court's opinions appear inconsistent; within that context they reflect the Court's approach to school aid issues. Understanding the Court's Establishment Clause jurisprudence thus requires consideration not just of the results in cases, but the context from which they developed and against which they were decided. This is not, however, to claim that the Burger Court was entirely consistent. Rehnquist's opinion for the Court in *Mueller*, upholding tax deductions for parents, was thinly disguised accommodationism that only barely managed to justify a result different to that in *Nyquist*. Although the Court provided some explanation for the differences between textbook loans and loans of other instructional equipment, without close examination the foundation was weak and, from a commonsense perspective, practically inexplicable. However, these problems were neither as widespread nor as pervasive as critics have claimed. Critics have also pointed to the Court's overturning of precedent in *Agostini* to claim inconsistency by the Rehnquist Court. This argument has a stronger foundation. *Rosenberger* and *Agostini*, in particular, represented a significant shift in the Court's jurisprudence from the pragmatism of the Burger era towards greater accommodationism. However, while the Court has not been entirely consistent in its cases, claims of inconsistency need to be made after consideration of more than simply the results in particular cases.

As Justice Lewis Powell noted in 1977, the Court's decisions, 'have sought to establish principles that preserve the cherished safeguard of the Establishment Clause without resort to blind absolutism. If this endeavor means a loss of some analytical tidiness then that ... is entirely tolerable'.[12] The Court's jurisprudence between *Everson* and *Agostini* is best understood as creating neither an inflexible wall nor a 'blurred, indistinct, and variable barrier' between the activities of church and state but as a series of pragmatic decisions based on all the circumstances of each individual case.[13] Given this, traditional scholarship which aims to understand the Court's jurisprudence by considering only the results in cases is severely limited. Claims of inconsistency by the Court based only on the results in cases fail to understand what the Court was seeking to do. Consistency in *results* was not a concern of the Court; consistency in *approach* was. Understanding the Court's Establishment Clause jurisprudence requires understanding the Court's methodology, the questions asked, the issues considered most important, the operation and use of the *Lemon* test and the alliances and disagreements among the justices. Understanding how the Court's key principles developed after 1947 and how, in the latter part of the period here discussed, these principles were challenged and criticized, explains the Court's jurisprudence over fifty years. Placing cases in their legal, social and political context is crucial, since such context was central to the Court's analysis. Viewed from this perspective, far from being an inconsistent, incoherent jurisprudence that needs to be corrected, the Supreme Court's Establishment Clause jurisprudence is instead one consistently concerned with method, context and a fair application of existing principles to specific circumstances raised in particular cases that has upheld the Establishment Clause and adapted it to modern circumstances, thus ensuring its continued relevance.

The Context

Close analysis of the Court, the justices and the resulting Establishment Clause jurisprudence provides a clearer understanding of the Court and its cases. However, for the church-state debate, the Court and its jurisprudence provide only part of the picture. The cases discussed here developed and were debated, argued and decided against a broader backdrop of local and national political concerns and debates, economic and policy crises, religious and secular advocacy and social change. Without consideration of these factors a full understanding of the issues, and the significance of the cases within them, is virtually impossible.

The school prayer cases, particularly *Engel* and *Schempp*, resulted in the most vocal and sustained opposition to any of the Court's Establishment Clause rulings. Several attempts were made to overturn the Court's rulings, the most prominent in the 1960s and again in the 1980s, although without success. Politicians and some religious leaders lambasted the Court for being anti-God and hastening the progress of secularization in the United States. While the timing of the reaction is explained by the cases, the vehemence of the reaction is surprising until viewed against the backdrop of the Cold War, the fight against Communism and the place of schoolday religious activities in related domestic policies. Likewise, *Schempp* appears an unremarkable case if viewed solely in the context of *Engel*: the principles of the earlier cases were followed and expanded. Yet this overlooks the tremendous pressure placed on the Court by the breadth and depth of the opposition that emerged following *Engel* which had not subsided by the time the justices decided *Schempp*. And that opposition itself reflected a general misunderstanding of the ruling in *Engel*, a misunderstanding fuelled by politicians and some religious leaders for political, policy or electoral purposes. Such manipulation of the school prayer issue continued long after the initial furore had died down, providing a template that conservative Republicans used again in the 1980s. While it may be possible to understand the school prayer *cases* without consideration of such factors, understanding the school prayer *issue* demands that this context be considered alongside the cases.

The political debate surrounding school prayer does, however, permit a clearer understanding of some elements of the Court's prayer cases. While the Court did not directly address the critics, it did respond in more subtle ways. In *Schempp*, Justice Clark was assigned to write the majority opinion. Publicly identified as a conservative on the Court, in contrast to Black who wrote for the Court in *Engel*, Clark also avoided the rigidity of constitutional absolutes that characterized Black's jurisprudence. Although upholding the principles established in *Engel*, Clark was a less controversial figure, suggesting the justices hoped to make *Schempp* less inflammatory. Also seeking to avoid, or at least limit, controversy, the Court eschewed oral argument and offered a *per curiam* opinion in *Stone v. Graham* in 1980. This approach limited the discussion of the case to those issues the Court dealt with directly in its opinion, thus restricting the number of issues available for potentially divisive political debate. In addition, frequent comments about the importance of religion in American life and the Court's respect for the place of faith in people's lives held little relevance for the Court's legal reasoning. In light of criticisms directed at the Court after *Engel*, they should be viewed as challenges to the claims that the Court was godless and anti-religion and that *Engel* and *Schempp* were threats to religious faith. Although indirect evidence, these actions are nevertheless evidence that the Court's opinions in prayer cases were, in part, shaped by the political reaction to them.

However, if the Court accommodated the political situation in terms of the tone and structure of opinions, its rulings were not so influenced. The nature of the political debate itself made the Court's steadfastness easy. Almost all the political debates involving school prayer, both in the 1960s and again in the 1980s, were fuelled by misinformed overreaction, deliberately skewed presentation of the Court's rulings and other 'facts' of school prayer, or by politicians pandering to their perception of the demands of the electorate. In the 1960s the idea that the Court had made schools religion-free zones was challenged by the opinions themselves and by testimony given during the Becker hearings. In the 1980s, while Reagan and Congress debated whether religious exercises should be 'returned' to public schools by constitutional amendment, the Court was considering what religious exercises beyond prayer and Bible reading should also be excluded: the legal debate had moved on; the political debate had not. The debates revealed a pattern of activity used by conservatives over more than twenty years as political theatre: school prayer became a substitute or shorthand for other issues. Public and private morality, the 'decline' of moral standards in modern society, the power of the Supreme Court and the intrusion of federal government into the lives of the people all resonated in the school prayer debates. Cardinal Spellman, the Religious Right, President Reagan and a range of other religious and secular groups actively encouraged, or at least perpetuated, this practice. The continued failure of Congress to pass a prayer amendment and the lack of any real activity by politicians on behalf of the campaign to 'restore religion to America' beyond symbolism and rhetoric suggested that for many, although not all, the debate about religion in American life was about politics and symbolism rather than genuine concern for faith.

While the substance of such debates had little bearing on the issue of the constitutionality of school prayer and played little role in the Court's decisions, they had far-reaching consequences for the place of religion in the nation's public schools. The emergence of equal access as an issue in the early 1980s can only fully be explained as a reaction to actions taken by school boards, educators and parents in light of the general perception of the meaning of *Engel* and *Schempp*. Crucially, it was an interpretation of the cases based on the message created by the political debate, not the actual meaning of *Engel* and *Schempp*, that was frequently employed. The equal access debates of the 1980s revealed that increased sensitivity to church-state issues in schools as a result of the debates of the 1960s had led, in some cases, to exactly the kind of discrimination against those of faith that critics had accused the Court of creating. While for some equal access was clearly an attempt to find a back door to prayer in schools, the broader context of the earlier school prayer debates helps to explain why equal access became an issue and why many who had opposed school prayer supported equal access legislation.

Two factors in particular are important when considering the context of school aid debates in the second half of the twentieth century: religious divisions and their decline from the early 1960s onwards, and the economy. The bitterness caused by the Protestant-Catholic divides during the school aid debates of the 1940s and 1950s goes some way to explain the difficulty of passing needed federal aid legislation until the 1960s. Opposition to federal aid to education was considered by many Catholics and supporters of federal intervention to be motivated by anti-Catholic bias, while opponents portrayed the move for federal aid as an attempt by the Catholic Church to gain control of increasing numbers of students. In *Everson*, Black and Rutledge's approaches and arguments suggest both were sensitive to the religious divisions that might be fuelled by the case. Both undertook changes in structure and wording that ensured their opinions could not be associated with one denomination or religious group. By the time the

Burger Court addressed school aid, religious division had become a less prominent issue. Vatican II had opened up the Catholic Church, a Catholic had been president of the United States, the Cold War had encouraged all of faith to unite against a common enemy and the 1965 Elementary and Secondary Education Act allowed limited forms of federal aid to flow to religious school students. All helped calm the fractiousness of the previous twenty years. In the same way that religious tensions help explain the circumstances of *Everson*, their absence helps explain the different focus of the Burger Court's cases.

The bulk of the Court's school aid cases were heard in the 1970s. Consideration of the cases alone suggests an increased trend within states to challenge or circumvent the Court's rulings and to break down the metaphorical wall between church and state. Consideration of the context of those cases, however, reveals the interplay of economic and pedagogical debates which led to them. The severe financial difficulties of the 1970s combined with a growing sense of failure in the urban public schools to move the focus to the educational role of religious schools, which reportedly had better discipline and educated students at a lower per pupil cost. A number of states, including New York, Pennsylvania and Rhode Island, sought to provide benefits to religious school students or initiated programmes to aid the secular functions of religious schools in an attempt to ease the burden of both schools and parents. In most cases, although not all, the motivating factor for the school aid programme was the need to cut budgets while maintaining the same level of educational provision. As studies claimed to show that in the inner cities religious schools were providing better educational opportunities than many public schools, and doing so at little or no cost to the state, it is perhaps unsurprising that attention turned to them as potential solutions to the two key difficulties. The Court itself appeared to recognize these cases as responses to changing circumstances rather than attempts to undermine the Court's jurisprudence. The Court's unwillingness to strike down all aid programmes intended to address the educational and financial problems faced by schools without examining the specifics of each programme showed not only the influence of the Court's pragmatists, but also suggested deference to legislative decision-making regarding issues outside the Court's expertise.[14] Chief Justice Burger's acknowledgement of the financial crisis as an influence on him in *Lemon* reinforces the sense of a Court aware of the context of its cases. The educational and financial issues of the 1970s are thus crucial for any analysis of the school aid issue in this period. They shed light on why so many cases reached the Court in this period, help understand at least some of the reasons for the implementation of school aid policies and reveal further influences on the Court's decision-making.

Concluding Thoughts

If context, both historical and contemporary, is so crucial for understanding legal cases and, in turn, if the rulings in those cases are important for understanding debates about the issues they involve, why have historians so often downplayed the law and legal scholars overlooked the context? Legal cases, especially those involving constitutional law, are complex, involving close scrutiny of the minutiae of language, and frequently employ a language of their own which can seem impenetrable to the non-legal scholar. Endless debates about this phrasing or that wording can also appear dull and uninspiring while the technicalities and structures of legal opinions often obscure the drama of the debates contained within them. In turn, for lawyers the context of a case is frequently less important than the final ruling. It is the decision and analysis leading to it which establishes the precedent which governs future cases. Internal divisions among the justices might suggest an opening for a future challenge but the economic circumstances which led to the case have little or no immediate significance. For the practice of the law, such history is often of little help.

The job of the historian, however, is not that of the lawyer, and thus the context remains important. For an understanding of how Establishment Clause debates since the 1940s have shaped, developed and prompted discussions of the church-state relationship in the modern United States, both the law and the history are important. The school aid cases of the Burger Court, for example, were shaped by the influence of the centrist justices, the structure that had developed for analysing such cases and the economic circumstances which initiated the policies they considered. Likewise, Justice Kennedy's switch in *Lee* encompassed the Court's precedent, the history of school prayer debates and the liberal-conservative balance on the Court. Equal access cases, from a legal perspective, involve a balancing of provisions contained within the First Amendment. Taken in the context of school prayer debates a broader picture of political motivations and school actions becomes apparent. The law can be understood on its own terms, the history understood without in-depth knowledge of the law, but combining both creates a fuller, richer understanding of the issues and debates involved.

Despite significant criticism, the Supreme Court's Establishment Clause jurisprudence as applied to schools has had positive results. As a result of the Court's rulings no student is required to participate in any religious activity conducted during school hours, and schools and their staff are forbidden from conducting such exercises. If such events occur, students have access to the courts, a legal remedy and a mandate from the Supreme Court as to what is and is not acceptable. Students of minority faiths should no longer be made to feel religious outsiders within the school environment. As the United States becomes ever more religiously diverse, the Court is committed to ensuring that students of all faiths are accepted. Students are, however, allowed to meet voluntarily on school premises for religious meetings, either before or after the school day or during free time if the school allows other groups to meet. This is not an absolute right: its existence depends on a variety of circumstances – including the school, the age of the students, the type of clubs allowed to meet and any history of conflict over religious issues, among others – to ensure that students' right to free exercise of religion and protection against forced religious observance are maintained. Students have legal recourse to the courts under Supreme Court precedent and the Equal Access Act. Although the rights of students are given greater weight, schools have been able to defend their actions in court with success.[15] Equal access, if fairly applied, helps to secure the rights of students damaged by some of the misrepresentations of *Engel* and *Schempp* while maintaining schools' control over their facilities. Although open to abuse, equal access is a reasonable balance between the need to avoid school sponsorship of religious activities and the desire of religious students to communally practise their faith during non-school hours. In school aid cases, the strength of the *Lemon* test lies in its ability to allow flexibility to local circumstances. Burger established a test for constitutionality that laid out the guidelines to be followed, not the absolute result. Combined with the pragmatic approach to aid cases taken by the dominant centre bloc of justices, the consequence was decisions that applied only to particular factual situations, leaving open the possibility of flexibility to local circumstances. This is reinforced by the Court's view that federal school aid decisions do not supersede state Blaine Amendments that are more restrictive of the church-state relationship: the Court's decisions established the boundaries of the church-state relationship, not the absolute requirements. The Court's concern to consider all the circumstances of a particular relationship allows states to find their own approach to school aid issues while ensuring that the principles of the Establishment Clause are not violated.

Notes

Introduction

[1] US Constitution, First Amendment.
[2] *Board of Education v. Barnette* 319 US 624 (1943); *Sherbert v. Verner* 374 US 398 (1963); *Wisconsin v. Yoder* 406 US 205 (1972); *Douglas v. City of Jeanette* 319 US 157 (1943); *Martin v. Struthers* 319 US 141 (1943).
[3] *Cantwell v. Connecticut* 310 US 296, 303–4 (1940) (*per* Justice Roberts).
[4] *McGowan v. Maryland* 366 US 420 (1961); *Braunfield v. Brown* 366 US 599 (1961); *Garber v. Kansas* 389 US 51 (1967); *Bowen v. Roy* 476 US 693 (1986); *Lyng v. Northwest Indian Cemetary Protective Association* 485 US 439 (1988).
[5] Massachusetts was the last state to abandon such arrangements in 1833. Levy, L., *The Establishment Clause: Religion and the First Amendment* (London and Chapel Hill: University of North Carolina Press, 2nd edn, revised, 1994), pp. 1–95.
[6] In *Pierce v. Society of Sisters* 268 US 510 (1925) the Court guaranteed the right of parents to send their children to religious schools, and thus the right of such schools to exist, when overturning an Oregon law requiring all children to be educated at public schools. However, the result rested on parents' right to determine the kind of education received by their children and did not implicate the Establishment Clause.
[7] *Barron v. Baltimore* 7 Pet. (32 US) 243, 250 (1833).
[8] There were two exceptions: *Missouri Pacific Railway Co. v. Nebraska* 164 US 403 (1896) and *Chicago, Burlington, and Quincy Railway Co. v. Chicago* 166 US 226 (1897). Both involved the Fifth Amendment prohibition against the taking of private property for public use without just compensation. O'Brien, D., *Constitutional Law and Politics, Volume Two: Civil Rights and Liberties* (New York: W.W. Norton & Company, 3rd edn, 1991), pp. 294, 296.
[9] *Gitlow v. New York* 268 US 652, 666 (1925).
[10] *Everson v. Board of Education* 330 US 1 (1947) (holding New Jersey could reimburse parents for the cost of transporting their children to religious schools on public transport).
[11] For debates over the uses and value of these sources, see Crosskey, W., *Politics and The Constitution in the History of the United States* (Chicago: University of Chicago Press, 2 vols., 1953); Hutson, J., 'The Creation of the Constitution: The Integrity of the Documentary Record', 65 *Texas Law Review* 1 (1986); Levy, L., *The Establishment Clause: Religion and the First Amendment*; Wofford, J., 'The Blinding Light: The Uses of History in Constitutional Interpretation', 31 *University of Chicago Law Review* 502, 503–6 (1964).

[12] 'In the religiously divided tribal United States, nothing could kill the proposal quicker than to take a stand on religion so the Framers said as little as possible about the subject.' Marsden, G., *Religion and American Culture* (Harcourt Brace Jovanovich, Inc., 1990), p. 46.

[13] Hutson, J., p. 39 (at n.12).

[14] Justice Frankfurter quoted in Tussman, J., 'Preface to the 1962 Edition,' in Alley, R. (ed.), *The Supreme Court on Church And State* (New York and Oxford: Oxford University Press, 1988), p. *ix*. Also, see Wofford, J., 'The Blinding Light,' especially pp. 521–533.

[15] This is the essence of the argument for judicial legislation. Often advocated in direct opposition to the 'original intent' approach, it holds that in interpreting the meaning of the Constitution judges and justices bring new meaning to existing principles as they are applied to new circumstances. For example, free speech, pornography and obscenity, symbolic speech, right to privacy and 'cruel and unusual punishment'. 'Oliver Wendell Holmes said, "historical continuity with the past is not a duty, it is only a necessity." That delphic statement can be construed to mean that we cannot escape history because it has shaped us and guides our politics, but we are not obliged to remain static'. Levy, L., *The Establishment Clause*, p. 239 (footnote omitted).

[16] Paul Freund's 1969 response to the Court's first textbook loan case, *Board of Education v. Allen*, is a moderate, thoughtful introduction to this position. Freund, P., 'Public Aid to Parochial Schools', 82 *Harvard Law Review* 1680 (1969). See also Kramnick, I. and R. L. Moore, *The Godless Constitution, The Case Against Religious Correctness* (New York and London: W.W. Norton & Co., 1996); Feldman, S., *Please Don't Wish Me A Merry Christmas: A Critical History of the Separation of Church and State* (New York and London: New York University Press, 1997).

[17] See, especially, Justice Scalia's dissent in *Lee v. Weisman* 505 US 577, 631–46 (1992) and his concurrence in *Lamb's Chapel v. Center Moriches Union Free School District* 508 US 384, 397–401 (1993).

[18] Accommodationists have particularly praised *Witters v. Washington Department of Service for the Blind* 474 US 481 (1986); *Zobrest v. Catalina Hills School District* 509 US 1 (1993); *Agostini v. Felton* 521 US 203 (1997); and *Rosenberger v. the Rector and Visitors of the University of Virginia* 515 US 819 (1995). For the accommodationist viewpoint, see Cord, R., 'Church-State Separation: Restoring the "No Preference" Doctrine of the First Amendment', 9 *Harvard Journal of Law and Public Policy* 129 (1986); Murray, W., *Let Us Pray: A Plea for Prayer in Our Schools* (New York: William Morrow & Co., Inc., 1995); Presser, S., 'Some Realism About Atheism'; Rice, C., *The Supreme Court and Public Prayer: The Need for Restraint* (New York: Fordham University Press, 1964); Robertson, M. G. 'Pat', 'Squeezing Religion Out of the Public Square – The Supreme Court, Lemon, and the Myth of the Secular Society', 4 *William and Mary Bill of Rights Journal* 223 (1995).

[19] See Esbeck, C., 'Myths, Miscues, and Misconceptions: No-Aid Separationism and the Establishment Clause', 13 *Notre Dame Journal of Law, Ethics and Public Policy* 285 (1999); Monsma, S., *When Sacred and Secular Mix: Religious Nonprofit Organizations and Public Money* (Lanham, Maryland and London: Rowman & Littlefield Publishers, Inc., 1996); Volokh, E., 'Equal Treatment is Not Establishment', 13

Notre Dame Journal of Law, Ethics and Public Policy 341 (1999); Howe, M.D., *The Garden and the Wilderness: Religion and Government in American Constitutional History* (Chicago: University of Chicago Press, 1965).

[20] The strength of strict separationism is in its understanding of history, neutrality provides a potential for understanding how to balance secular and sectarian needs and demands, and accommodation is strongest when arguing for the need to recognize the changing requirements of modern society.

[21] See, for example, Berger, R., *Government By Judiciary: The Transformation of the Fourteenth Amendment* (Cambridge, Massachusetts and London: Harvard University Press, 1977); Bork, R., 'Neutral Principles and Some First Amendment Problems', 47 *Indiana Law Review* 1 (1971); Dworkin, R., *Taking Rights Seriously* (London: Gerald Duckworth & Co. Ltd., 1977).

[22] Segal, J., and H. Spaeth, *The Supreme Court and the Attitudinal Model* (New York: Cambridge University Press, 1993) and *The Supreme Court and the Attitudinal Model Revisited* (Cambridge: Cambridge University Press, 2002) provide the clearest and most detailed introduction to this model.

[23] Murphy, W., *Elements of Judicial Strategy* (Chicago: University of Chicago Press, 1964); Maltzman, F., J. Spriggs II, and P. Wahlbeck, *Crafting Law on the Supreme Court: The Collegial Game* (Cambridge and New York: Cambridge University Press, 2000).

[24] See in particular Fisher, L., *Constitutional Dialogues: Interpretation as Political Process* (New Jersey: Princeton University Press, 1988).

[25] Fisher tends towards the former approach. For the latter, see Murphy, W., *Elements of Judicial Strategy* and Dahl, R., 'Decision Making in a Democracy: The Supreme Court as a National Policy Maker', 6 *Journal of Public Law* 279 (1957).

[26] The Court's subsequent Establishment Clause decisions followed the rationale established in *Agostini*. See in particular *Mitchell v. Helms* 530 US 793 (2000) (allowing provision of instructional materials other than books to students in religious schools) and *Zelman v. Simmons-Harrris* 536 US 639 (2002) (upholding Cleveland's school voucher programme).

Part One

[1] Benjamin Franklin, letter to Richard Price, 9 October 1780, quoted in Lee, F. (ed.), *All Imaginable Liberty: The Religious Liberty Clauses of the First Amendment* (Lanham, Maryland, and London: University Press of America, 1995), p. 163.

[2] See Madison's *Memorial and Remonstrance Against Religious Assessments* and Jefferson's 'Bill for Establishing Religious Freedom'.

[3] 'No American state at the time maintained an establishment in the European sense of having an exclusive or state church designated by law'. Levy, L., *The Establishment Clause: Religion and the First Amendment* (London and New York: Macmillan Publishing Co., 1986), p. 8. The six states were: Connecticut, Massachusetts, New Hampshire, New Jersey, New York and Vermont.

[4] Morken, H., 'The New Common School – The Evangelical Response to *Everson*', in Formicola, J. and H. Morken (eds), *Everson Revisited: Religion, Education, and Law At the Crossroads* (Lanham, Maryland and Oxford: Rowman & Littlefield Publishers, Inc., 1997).

5. Binder, F., *The Age of the Common School, 1830–1865* (New York: John Wiley & Sons, Inc., 1974), pp. 64–70; Ravitch, D., *The Great School Wars, New York City, 1805–1973: A History of Public Schools as Battlefields of Social Change* (New York: Basic Books, 1974), especially pp. 4–84.
6. Principally, Lutherans and Catholics and some leading figures within the Methodist Episcopal Church, South and the Southern Baptist Convention. See Clegg, Jr., A., 'Church Groups and Federal Aid to Education, 1933–1939', *History of Education Quarterly*, Vol. 4 No. 3 (September 1964), pp. 137–54.
7. For an overview of these and other areas of federal involvement with education see *Federal Activities in Education* (Washington, DC: National Education Association and American Association of School Administrators, 1939).
8. See Clegg, Jr., A., pp. 139–144.
9. Clegg, Jr., A., p. 146.
10. Although many of the programmes challenged in the Court's cases provided aid to students or their parents rather than to the schools, the term 'school aid' is here used to refer to both types of cases.

Chapter 1

1. Fair, D., 'The *Everson* Case in the Context of New Jersey Politics', in Formicola, J., and H. Morken (eds), *Everson Revisited: Religion, Education, and Law at the Crossroads* (Lanham, Maryland and Oxford: Rowman & Littlefield, 1997), p. 7.
2. See *Everson v. Board of Education* 330 US 1, 14 (1947) (*per* Justice Black) and 330 US 1, 33 (1947) (Justice Rutledge, dissenting). See also letter to Thomas Mulroy from Justice Rutledge, 19 March 1947 ('My own effort, as I am sure you characteristically sensed, was to keep the problem entirely free from sectarianism of any sort . . . I wanted my treatment and the expression of my views to be applicable to all sects alike.'), Justice Wiley Rutledge Papers (hereafter Rutledge Papers), Box 143. Changes in Black's opinion indicate his awareness of the issue. A passage on the 'wisdom' of New Jersey's legislation was removed from an early draft, possibly because it might be interpreted as being anti-Roman Catholic given the atmosphere. The passage read: 'So far as the transportation of school children generally at state expense is concerned, we repeat that: "With the wisdom of such legislation and the soundness of . . . the policy involved we are not concerned. Whether it will result in ultimate good or harm, it is not within our province to inquire"'. Undated draft, Rutledge Papers, Box 144. In the final opinion this read: 'While we do not mean to intimate that a state could not provide transportation only to children attending public schools' 330 US 1, 16 (1947).
3. By the time *Everson* reached the Supreme Court at least sixteen states (California, Illinois, Indiana, Kansas, Kentucky, Louisiana, Maryland, Massachusetts, Michigan, Missouri, Montana, New Hampshire, New Jersey, New York, Oregon and Rhode Island) had similar bus transportation laws, the result, in part, of litigation by the Catholic Church after the success of *Pierce v. Society of Sisters* 268 US 510 (1925). Courts in California, Illinois, Kentucky, Louisiana, Maryland and New Jersey had all upheld bus transportation laws; in the other ten states no court challenges had been brought. In Delaware, Oklahoma, South Dakota, Washington

and Wisconsin they had been struck down. See 'Note: Catholic Schools and Public Money,' 50 *Yale Law Journal* 917 (1941). In *Pierce v. Society of Sisters* the Supreme Court ruled that Oregon could not limit education to public schools only, recognizing the right of religious schools to exist and the right of parents to send their children to them.

[4] *Cantwell v. Connecticut* 310 US 296 (1940) incorporated the Free Exercise Clause into the Fourteenth Amendment in a case holding that Jehovah's Witnesses could not be required to obtain a permit before proselytizing on the street.

[5] Given that this is what makes *Everson* significant, it is disconcerting to discover that the Fourteenth Amendment claim was added to the brief as an afterthought, last on a list of reasons for challenging the transportation law sent to Roger Baldwin, executive director of the ACLU in August 1943. Fair, D., pp. 1, 8.

[6] *Everson v. Board of Education* 330 US 1, 18 (1947).

[7] *Everson v. Board of Education* 330 US 1, 18 (1947).

[8] *Everson v. Board of Education* 330 US 1, 15–16 (1947).

[9] In his first draft, Black wrote: 'No tax can be levied to support the religious tenets or the modes of worship of any religious sect', allowing a much broader range of activities to remain outside the limitation than the final draft which makes reference to 'religious activities'. In the second draft, Black appeared to allow for the possibility of non-discriminatory aid when he wrote: 'Neither can pass laws which prefer one religion over another', an option foreclosed in the final opinion. Rutledge Papers, Box 144.

[10] Quoted in Berg, T., 'Anti-Catholicism and Modern Church-State Relations', 33 *Loyola University of Chicago Law Review* 121, 127 (2001).

[11] See Berg, T., pp. 123–32. Also, Blum SJ, V., *Catholic Parents, Political Eunuchs* (St Cloud, Minnesota: Media and Materials, 1972) who sees anti-Catholicism in actions and decisions in this area as late as the 1970s.

[12] *Everson v. Board of Education* 330 US 1, 6–7 (1947). The brief for the school board suggested that these changing conditions were the health and safety of children and equal treatment of all at a time of changing ideas about the duty of the state to its citizens. Several *amicus* briefs mentioned the 'motor age' as an influencing factor while the National Councils of Catholic Men and Women in a joint brief suggested the influence of the growing idea of the school role as *parens patriae*.

[13] In 1875 James G. Blaine, Speaker of the House of Representatives, proposed an amendment to the US Constitution that would prevent the use of federal funds by religious schools. Although defeated, thirty-five states consequently enacted similar provisions in their constitutions, either by choice or as a precondition to admission to the Union. In most cases the wording of the amendments is far stricter than the Court's interpretation of the First Amendment. On the Blaine Amendment see O'Brien, F. W., 'The Blaine Amendment, 1875–1876', 41 *University of Detroit Law Journal* 137 (1963). On the state Blaine Amendments see DeForrest, M., 'An Overview and Evaluation of State Blaine Amendments: Origins, Scope, and First Amendment Concerns', 26 *Harvard Journal of Law and Public Policy* 551 (2003).

[14] See 'Note: Catholic Schools and Public Money.' With regards to bus transportation, sixteen states and the District of Columbia permitted provision of such services to private school pupils (see n.3), Colorado and Minnesota allowed for

transportation under the decisions of state attorneys general, and Connecticut, Ohio and West Virginia provided transportation by local practice with no legal ruling. However, fourteen states specifically limited bus services to public school students only (Alabama, Delaware, Florida, Georgia, Idaho, Nebraska, New Mexico, North Carolina, Ohio, Oklahoma, Pennsylvania, South Carolina, Tennessee and Virginia).

15. However, in following the legislatures, Black frequently overlooked actions by the courts striking down similar provisions. In New York, for example, the bus transportation law was only put into place by constitutional amendment after the Court of Appeals struck down the original legislation. See *Judd et al v. Board of Education* 278 NY 200, 15 N.E. (2d) 576 (1938). Similar events occurred in South Dakota and Wisconsin.

16. For the public purpose argument see *Borden v. Louisiana State Board of Education* 168 La. 1005, 123 So. 655 (1929); *State ex rel. Johnson v. Boyd* 28 N.E. (2d) 256 (Ind. Sup. Ct., 1940). See also Brief for Appellees, pp. 18–27, 37, and brief of the National Conferences of Catholic Men and Catholic Women, pp. 5–8, 14–21. For the opposite argument, see Brief for Appellant, pp. 6–19, and brief of the General Council of Seventh Day Adventists and Baptist Joint Conference Committee on Public Relations. For the 'indirect benefit' argument, see *Dunn v. Chicago Industrial Schools* 280 Ill. 613, 117 N.E. 735 (1917) and *Borden v. Louisiana State Board of Education* 168 La. 1005 (1929). Opposition to the argument was expressed in *Smith v. Donahue* 202 App. Div. 656, 195 NY Supp. 715 (1922); *State ex rel. Van Straten v. Milquet* 180 Wis. 109, 192 N.W. 392 (1923); *Traub v. Brown* 172 Atl. 835 (Del. 1934). Justice Douglas quoted by Justice Rutledge, Rutledge Papers, Box 143.

17. *Everson v. Board of Education* 330 US 1, 29 (1947) (Justice Rutledge, with Justices Frankfurter, Jackson and Burton, dissenting).

18. Justice Harold Burton Papers (hereafter Burton Papers), Box 138, Folder 11.

19. Rutledge also included as an appendix to the opinion Madison's *Memorial and Remonstrance Against Religious Assessments* and the *Virginia Bill for Religious Freedom*, authored by Thomas Jefferson, reinforcing his argument.

20. *Everson v. Board of Education* 330 US 1, 63 (1947) (Justice Rutledge et al, dissenting).

21. Justice Frank Murphy passed in conference but eventually joined the majority. Burton wrote to Rutledge on 8 January 1947: 'Please include me in this dissent. I am deeply indebted to you for its exposition of the meaning of "an establishment of religion" as used in the First Amendment'. Rutledge Papers, Box 143. With regards to a change of wording to indicate that New Jersey's law fell within the scope of Madison and Jefferson's intended restrictions, Jackson wrote: 'I did not think so originally but I am convinced it is'. Rutledge Papers, Box 144.

22. Letter to H. Meek from Justice Rutledge, 11 March 1948. Rutledge Papers, Box 144. See also letters to Irving Dillard, 19 February 1947; Ernest Kirschten, 20 February 1947; Luther Smith, 10 March 1947; Thomas Mulroy, 19 March 1947; and Justice Armstead Brown, 4 April 1947. Rutledge Papers, Box 143. Of the fifteen states in which cases were brought in the half century following *Everson*, the child benefit theory was accepted in two (Pennsylvania and Ohio) and rejected in five (Alaska, Delaware, Hawaii, Washington and Wisconsin, although the last was overturned by constitutional amendment). The police powers argument was rejected

in four states (Alaska, Oklahoma, Washington and Wisconsin) and accepted in four (Connecticut, Minnesota, Pennsylvania and West Virginia). Other states employed a variety of alternative arguments. By 1997, bus transportation was operating in California, Connecticut, Idaho, Illinois, Kentucky, Maryland, Massachusetts, Minnesota, New Jersey, Ohio and Pennsylvania. Statutes had been rejected in Alaska, Delaware, Hawaii, Oklahoma and Washington (Kentucky, New York and Wisconsin courts struck down statutes but were overturned by constitutional amendments in the latter two and a later court decision in the first).

[23] Illustrating the extent of these problems, see testimony before the House Subcommittee No. 1 of the Committee on Education and Labor, Hearings on Bills having for their Object the Granting of Federal Aid for Educational Purposes, 80th Congress, 1st Sess., 29 April–29 May 1947 (hereafter House Hearings [1947]). A February 1948 report by the National Education Association, 'Still Unfinished Business in American Education', indicated average national expenditure for schools was $99 per pupil, a level below which nearly half the states fell. The report noted specifically the problem of education inequalities across the nation: New York's per pupil expenditure was $234 in 1946–7; Arkansas' expenditure was $37 per pupil. 'Still Unfinished,' *NEA Journal*, Vol 33, No. 3 (March 1948), pp. 143–6. A further report in May updated the figures, indicated the same problems, and asserted that most states' unallocated resources would not be sufficient to raise expenditure to the national average. 'States' Surpluses for School Aid Hit', *New York Times* (hereafter *NYT*), 25 May 1948, A31.

[24] *Federal Aid to Education: A Review of Pertinent Facts* (Washington, DC: NEA, 1942); *Still Unfinished: Our Educational Obligation to America's Children* (Washington, DC: NEA, 1948); *National Policy and the Financing of Public Schools* (Washington, DC: NEA, 1959).

[25] Reported in *NEA Journal*, Vol. 35, No. 6 (September 1946).

[26] In a speech to the conference, Senator Robert Taft (R-Ohio), sponsor of the main aid to education bill before Congress in 1947, referred to education as essential to economic welfare and as the only defence of liberty against totalitarianism. 'Federal Aid Urged to Better Schools', *NYT*, 4 March 1947, A27; Kizer, G., 'Federal Aid to Education: 1945–1963', *History of Education Quarterly*, Vol. 10 No. 1 (Spring 1970), p. 84. Speaking the day before, Assistant Secretary of State William Benton had also mentioned national defence as a consideration. 'US Urged to Spend More for Schools', *NYT*, 4 March 1947, A21. For general coverage of the conference see the *NYT*, 4–8 March 1947.

[27] 'Federal Aid Urged to Better Schools', *NYT*, 7 March 1947, A27. Before the House subcommittee, Representative John Allen (R-Cal) estimated between thirty-two and thirty-five states would be covered. House Hearings (1947), p. 245.

[28] Speech to the AASA, 6 March 1947, reprinted in *NEA Journal*, Vol. 36, No. 5 (May 1947), pp. 361–3. Taft did not think that Catholics would support the bill. Asked about the possibility after his conference speech he replied: 'No, I do not think it will [receive the support of Catholic groups]. I understand they want direct aid and this bill does not provide it.' 'Taft Urges Federal Aid to Schools to Raise Standards in 33 States', *NYT*, 7 March 1947, A44. See also Taft's comments in Senate debate, 24 March 1948, *Congressional Record* (hereafter *Cong. Rec.*), 80th Congress, 2nd Sess., pp. 3346–52.

29 House Hearings (1947). See also US Congress. Senate. Subcommittee of the Committee on Labor and Public Welfare. Hearings on Bills relative to Federal Aid to Education, 80th Congress, 1st Sess., 9 April–2 May 1947.

30 'Parochial Aid Hit By Presbyterians', *NYT*, 21 May 1947, A4. For explicitly anti-Catholic positions see testimony of John Cowles and Elmer Rogers of the Ancient and Accepted Scottish Rite of Freemasonry, Southern Jurisdiction, House Hearings (1947), pp. 326–52. For slightly less offensive but still anti-Catholic views see testimony of Dr Frederick Fowler of the National Association of Evangelicals, pp. 525–32.

31 'Out in the Open', *Christian Century*, LXV (8 December 1948), pp. 1327–9, quoted in Kizer, G., p. 86. For a discussion of the influence of anti-Catholic thinking in this period see Berg, T., pp. 123–151 (2001).

32 'Parochial Schools Made Issue at NEA', *NYT*, 11 July 1947, A17.

33 *Cong. Rec.*, 80th Congress, 2nd Sess., 31 March 1948, pp. 3789–98, and 1 April 1948, pp. 3804, 3908.

34 Justice Stanley Reed dissented on the grounds released time was less advantageous to schools than *Everson* had been.

35 Quoted in 'School Aid Bills Cleared to Senate', *NYT*, 19 March 1949, A13.

36 Kizer, G., pp. 87–8.

37 'Spellman Denounces Author of School Aid As Bigot', *NYT*, 10 June 1949, A1, 20.

38 Mrs Roosevelt did not mention any particular bills by name, discussing the issue generally, and her only reference to Spellman was to point out his leadership of the movement to support federal aid to religious schools. She wrote: 'If we desire our children to go to schools of any particular kind, be it because we think they should have religious instruction or for any other reason, we are entirely free to set up those schools and to pay for them'. In a later column she repeated this sentiment and added, 'I do not want the public school system to be dominated by the Federal Government ... But neither do I want Church groups controlling the schools of our country. They must remain free', further explaining that those who believed in the right of individuals to believe and worship according to conscience 'cannot be accused of prejudice when we do not want to see public education connected with religious control of the schools, which are paid for by taxpayers' money'. Reprinted in *NYT*, 23 July 1949, A26.

39 An early contemporary example was Herbert Lehman, former Governor of New York and Democratic candidate for Senator who, less than a month after Spellman's attacks, openly opposed the Barden Bill and supported Spellman's position at a time when he was unpopular among the state's Catholics, despite having previously supported Eleanor Roosevelt's argument.

40 *Zorach v. Clauson* 343 US 306, 313 (1952). Technically *Zorach* did not overrule *McCollum* but distinguished between on-campus and off-campus instruction which would become an important part of the Court's school aid jurisprudence. However, to a general audience it appeared that by allowing released time programmes, the Court had reversed the *McCollum* decision.

41 See Rothman, S., 'The Politics of Catholic Parochial Schools: An Historical and Comparative Analysis', *Journal of Politics*, Vol. 25, No. 1 (February 1963), p. 71. Also, Carey, P., *The Roman Catholics* (Westport, Connecticut and London: Greenwood Press, 1993), pp. 93–114.

[42] Berg, T., pp. 152–8.
[43] Berg, T., pp. 153–4.
[44] The National School Lunch Act (1946) included participation by private school pupils; the National Defense Education Act (1958) authorized low-interest loans to religious elementary and secondary schools for equipment for science, mathematics and foreign language classes; and the Higher Education Facilities Act (1963) allowed religious colleges to receive federal construction grants.
[45] This had been a minor issue in the 1947 House hearings. See testimony of Irma Smith King, Supervisor of Negro Schools (pp. 150–8), Leslie Perry of the NAACP (pp. 394–408), Alexander Ginsburg, American Jewish Congress (pp. 589–601), and the frequent questions of Representative Thomas Owens (R-Il) (pp. 167–8, 376, 563–5, 572–3).
[46] Kizer, G., p. 92 (see pp. 90–2 for discussion of the provisions of the defeated bills). For an overview of the debates, see Bendiner, R., *Obstacle Course on Capitol Hill* (New York: McGraw-Hill Book Co., 1964), pp. 119–39.
[47] See, for example, *Griffin v. County School Board* 377 US 218 (1964) (striking down private school subsidies) and *Green v. County School Board* 391 US 430 (1968) (striking down a 'freedom of choice' plan).
[48] Quoted in *NYT*, 6 February 1967. For discussion of some of these problems see Smith, S., 'Parochial Schools in the Black Cities', *Journal of Negro Education*, Vol. 42, No. 3 (Summer 1973), pp. 379–91.
[49] Dallek, R., *John F. Kennedy: An Unfinished Life* (London: Penguin Books, 2004), pp. 146–7. See also Graham, H., *The Uncertain Triumph: Federal Education Policy in the Kennedy and Johnson Years* (Chapel Hill and London: University of North Carolina Press, 1984), pp. 3–25.
[50] See, for example, Kennedy's response to questions about his school aid bills at a 1 March 1961 press conference, *Public Papers of the President: John F. Kennedy, 1961* (Washington, DC: United States Government Printing Office, 1962), pp. 107–11, also p. 156; *NYT* Editorial, 20 June 1961.
[51] Graham, H., pp. 26–40.
[52] In a 1968 speech, Johnson added to Franklin Roosevelt's 'Four Freedoms' a fifth: freedom from ignorance. McGuinn, P. and F. Hess, 'Freedom From Ignorance?: The Great Society and the Evolution of the Elementary and Secondary Education Act of 1965', in Milkis, S. and J. Mileur (eds), *The Great Society and the High Tide of Liberalism* (Amherst and Boston: University of Massachusetts Press, 2005), pp. 289–319. *Public Papers of the President of the United States: Lyndon B. Johnson* (Washington, DC: US Government Printing Office, 1966–70) (hereafter *Public Papers: Johnson*) pp. 63–4, 372, 183.
[53] Graham, H., pp. 70–5; Jeffrey, J., *Education for Children of the Poor: A Study of the Origins and Implementation of the ESEA of 1965* (Columbus, Ohio: Ohio State University Press, 1978), pp. 59–72.
[54] Quoted in Jeffrey, J., p. 70.
[55] Quoted in Jeffrey, J., p. 73.
[56] *Engel v. Vitale* 370 US 421 (1962) and *Abington School District v. Schempp* 374 US 203 (1963) were the Warren Court's school prayer rulings.
[57] Justice William Douglas Papers, Box 1399 (hereafter Douglas Papers); Justice William Brennan Papers (hereafter Brennan Papers), Box I:161, Folder 1.

[58] *Board of Education v. Allen* 392 US 236, 241–2 (1968). White did make use of the 'purpose and primary effect' test established in *Schempp* but only insofar as it applied to the *Everson* ruling.

[59] *Board of Education v. Allen* 392 US 236, 247–8 (1968). See also 244 n.6 and 248 for discussion of the paucity of the record before the Court.

[60] See especially *Board of Education v. Allen* 392 US 236, 250, 251 (1968) (Justice Black, dissenting).

[61] *Board of Education v. Allen* 392 US 236, 253 (1968) (Justice Black, dissenting).

[62] Douglas also switched from the majority in *Everson* to dissent in *Allen*. However, in *Engel* in 1962 he had repudiated his earlier stance, and in *Schempp* issued a stinging attack on the possibility of public funds being used by religious institutions. As such, his *Allen* opinion was consistent. The reasons for Black's shift remain obscure as his papers were destroyed shortly before his death. However, one possible reason may have been simply that when *Everson* was decided only a few similar programmes existed and were limited to bus transportation and textbooks; by the time *Allen* reached the Court the type and scope of the programmes had expanded exponentially, making the risk of total funding of religious schools appear increasingly possible. Alternatively, given Black's comment about making the ruling in *Everson* 'tight', it may have been that he was sympathetic to Rutledge's arguments generally but did not see in *Everson* the same kind of danger perceived by Rutledge.

Chapter 2

[1] *Lemon* was the Pennsylvania case. It is noteworthy that the statute covered only mathematics, foreign languages, physical sciences and physical education, the same subjects covered by the National Defense Education Act of 1958. Similar arrangements existed in Connecticut (struck down by federal court in *Johnson v. Sanders* 319 F.Supp. 433 [Conn. 1970]), Louisiana (held unconstitutional by the state Supreme Court), Ohio and Michigan (ended by state referendum) at the time *Lemon* was decided.

[2] *Earley* and *Robinson* were the cases from Rhode Island. Because they were combined with *Lemon* for decision, all three cases are collectively referred to as *Lemon*.

[3] *Lemon v. Kurtzman* 403 US 602, 612–3 (1971) (internal references and quotation marks omitted).

[4] *Lemon v. Kurtzman* 403 US 602, 612 (1971).

[5] *Lemon v. Kurtzman* 403 US 602, 614 (1971).

[6] Memoranda between the justices in the period March to June 1971 indicate that the wording and structure of the opinions was crucial to the final alignment. See Justice Thurgood Marshall Papers (hereafter Marshall Papers), Box 69, Folder 1; Justice William Brennan Papers (hereafter Brennan Papers), Box I:238, Folder 8.

[7] *Lemon v. Kurtzman* 403 US 602, 617 (1971).

[8] *Lemon v. Kurtzman* 403 US 602, 614 (1971).

[9] *Lemon v. Kurtzman* 403 US 602, 614 (1971).
[10] Black, Douglas, Potter Stewart and Blackmun voted to reverse, John Marshall Harlan and White to affirm. The passes came from Burger and Brennan, while Thurgood Marshall did not participate due to NAACP involvement in the litigation.
[11] See Thomas, J. A. and R. Wimpelberg (eds), *Dilemmas in School Finance* (Chicago: Midwest Administration Center, University of Chicago, 1978); Jordan, K. F. and N. Cambron-McCabe (eds), *Perspectives in State School Support Programs* (Cambridge, Massachusetts: Ballinger Publishing Co., 1981); Leggett, S. (ed.), *Managing Schools in Hard Times* (Chicago: Teach 'em Inc., 1981).
[12] 'Schools in N.J. May Need More Than Money', *NYT*, 20 June 1976, E6; 'Maine Officials Seeking Substitute for Repealed School-Finance Tax', *NYT*, 7 December 1977, A20; 'Schools in Cleveland Permitted to Borrow Money for Salaries', *NYT*, 7 December 1977, A20. See *Review of Existing State School Finance Programs: A Commission Staff Report* (Report to the President's Commission on School Finance, 1972) for discussion of the range and type of proposals considered by the states.
[13] On the problems of inner city schools see Rosenfeld, G., *'Shut Those Thick Lips!': A Study of Slum School Failure* (New York: Holt, Rinehart and Winston, Inc., 1971); Iannaccone, L., *Political, Social, and Cultural Constraints Upon Financing Improved Urban Education and Proposals to Overcome Them* (Report to the President's Commission on School Finance, 1972); Marcus, S. and P. Vairo (eds), *Urban Education: Crisis or Opportunity?* (Metuchen, New Jersey: The Scarecrow Press, 1972); Rist, R., *The Urban School: A Factory for Failure* (Cambridge, Massachusetts, and London: MIT Press, 1974).
[14] 'New York Crisis Forcing Schools to Stress the 3Rs', *NYT*, 22 June 1976, A46.
[15] *United States Catholic Elementary and Secondary Schools 2003–2004: The Annual Statistical Report on Schools, Enrolment and Staffing* (Washington, DC: National Catholic Educational Association, 2004), pp. 2–3.
[16] For a statistical analysis of these trends see Barteau, E., 'Costs and Revenues of Nonpublic Elementary and Secondary Education: The Past, Present, and Future of Roman Catholic Schools', in *Economic Problems of Nonpublic Schools: A Report to the President's Commission on School Finance* (1972), pp. 211–82.
[17] For a detailed survey see Larsen, M., *When Parochial Schools Close: A Study in Educational Financing* (Washington, DC and New York: Robert B. Luce, Inc., 1972). For discussion of the impact on a single school system, see Gurash, J., *The Report of the Archdiocesan Advisory Committee on the Financial Crisis of Catholic Schools in Philadelphia and Surrounding Counties* (Philadelphia: 1972).
[18] Berg, T., 'Anti-Catholicism and Modern Church-State Relations', 33 *Loyola University of Chicago Law Journal* 121 (2001), pp. 156–7. Brown, A. and A. Greeley, *Can Catholic Schools Survive?* (New York: Sheed and Ward, Inc., 1970); Greeley, A., W. McCreedy and K. McCourt, *Catholic Schools in a Declining Church* (Kansas City: Sheed and Ward, Inc., 1974); Plude, F., *The Flickering Light: What's Happening to Catholic Schools?* (New York: William H. Sadler, Inc., 1974). For the influence of socio-economic factors in parents' school choices, see Fahey, F. and R. Kiekbusch, 'Attitudes Toward Nonpublic Education', in *Economic Problems of Nonpublic Schools*, pp. 1–154.

[19] Quoted in Smith, S., 'Parochial Schools in the Black Cities', *Journal of Negro Education*, Vol. 42, No. 3 (Summer 1973), p. 385.
[20] 'Troubled Catholic Schools Seeking Ways to Survive', *NYT*, 1 July 1973, A1, 15.
[21] In 1969, the Jewish Day School movement reported 80,000 students in 388 schools. Feuerstein, S., 'Torah Umesorah, 1944–1969: A Quarter of a Century', in Kaminetsky, J., *Hebrew Day School Education: An Overview* (New York: Torah Umesorah, 1970). See Larson, M., pp. 153–67, discussing Lutheran, Seventh Day Adventist, Missouri Synod Lutheran, and Church of the Nazarene schools, among others. Arthur Corazzini identified similar groups in his 1972 report, *The Non-Catholic Private Schools*, for the 1972 President's Commission on School Finance.
[22] 'Church Schools Lose Jersey Aid', *NYT*, 6 April 1973, A45. Thomas Schwartz estimated the cost of such absorption to be between $1,348,655,147 and $3,176,371,885 in 1971, with New York facing the highest cost and New Jersey the fourth highest. 'The Estimated Marginal Costs of Absorbing all Nonpublic Students into the Public School System', in *Economic Problems of Nonpublic Schools*, pp. 301–50.
[23] A *NYT* article in mid-1973 implied that Nixon and Rockefeller 'sought to win favor with anxious Catholic parents by devising aid programs to slip past the Constitutional obstacles'. 'The Court Reverses a Trend', *NYT*, 1 July 1973, E7.
[24] The Court ultimately found the Pennsylvania programme unconstitutional on other grounds.
[25] *Wolman v. Walter* 433 US 229, 233 (1977).
[26] See 'New Jersey's Plan for Private School Aid is Invalidated', *NYT*, 3 June 1979, E7.
[27] *Meek v. Pittenger* 421 US 349 (1975).
[28] *Wolman v. Walter* 433 US 229 (1977) and *CPERL v. Regan* 444 US 646 (1980).
[29] Both *Wolman v. Walter*.
[30] *Roemer v. Maryland Public Works Board* 426 US 736 (1976); *Americans United for the Separation of Church and State v. Blanton* 433 F. Supp. 97 (M.D.Tenn., 1977) aff'd. mem., 434 US 39 (1977).
[31] *Mueller v. Allen* 463 US 388 (1983).
[32] *CPERL v. Nyquist* 413 US 756 (1973).
[33] *CPERL v. Nyquist*.
[34] *CPERL v. Nyquist*.
[35] *Meek v. Pittenger and Wolman v. Walter*.
[36] *Meek v. Pittenger*.
[37] *Wolman v. Walter*.
[38] *New York v. Cathedral Academy* 434 US 125 (1977).
[39] *CPERL v. Nyquist* 413 US 756, 761 (1973) (internal quotation marks omitted).
[40] *Meek v. Pittenger* 421 US 349, 356, 363 (1975) (emphasis added). See also *CPERL v. Nyquist* 413 US 756, 767–9, 782 (1973) and *Wolman v. Walter* 433 US 229, 234 (1977). The one exception was in *Mueller v. Allen*, but as Rehnquist determined the tax deduction to be indirect aid, the character of the school did not become an issue in the case.
[41] The exceptions to this only serve to reinforce the point. In *Tilton v. Richardson* 402 US 672 (1971), the Supreme Court, in a 5:4 decision, upheld the constitutionality of carefully limited construction grants to colleges and universities. One of the main grounds for this decision was that, unlike schools, institutions

of higher education were less 'pervasively sectarian'. In *Hunt v. McNair* 413 US 734 (1973), the Court upheld lower interest rates in South Carolina for religious schools on similar grounds.
[42] *CPERL v. Nyquist* 413 US 756, 774 (1973) (these grants were struck down with an 8:1 majority, Justice White the only dissenter; the tuition reimbursement and tax deduction statutes also challenged in the case were held unconstitutional by a vote of 6:3).
[43] Powell, however, did not explicitly acknowledge this as a foundation for his argument, claiming instead that the direct link between the financial benefit and school expenditures distinguished *Nyquist* from earlier cases.
[44] Justices Brennan, Douglas and Marshall objected to the textbook loan programme, which was upheld, but supported the rejection of the other three programmes. Chief Justice Burger and Justices William Rehnquist and White argued to uphold all four programmes in question. This left only Justices Blackmun, Powell and Stewart (who wrote the opinion) to form the plurality.
[45] In *Wolman*, the Court upheld the textbook loan programme and testing services with a 6:3 majority, the diagnostic services with an 8:1 vote and therapeutic services with a 7:2 majority. The loan of instructional materials was struck down with a 6:3 majority and the field trips with a 5:4 vote.
[46] *Wolman v. Walter* 433 US 229, 247 (1977).
[47] But see Stevens in *Wolman*, Marshall in *Mueller*, and Brennan in *Meek*, arguing that any benefit to religious organizations frees funds to be used for other, potentially religious, activities.
[48] *McCollum v. Board of Education* 333 US 203, 210 (1948).
[49] *Zorach v. Clauson* 343 US 306, 308–9 (1952).
[50] *Zorach v. Clauson* 343 US 306, 316 (1952) (Justice Black, dissenting).
[51] *Mueller v. Allen* 463 US 388, 397 (1983).
[52] *Mueller v. Allen* 463 US 388, 405 (1983) (Justice Marshall, with Justices Brennan, Blackmun and Stevens, dissenting).
[53] The argument was also advanced by Congress in the 1940s and 1950s when enacting legislation allowing indirect benefits to flow to religious schools and their students as a result of general education programmes. The argument was rejected by Powell in *Nyquist* because the programmes challenged went directly to the schools and were financial in nature. Thus 'child benefit' could only be argued with reference to indirect, non-financial aid.
[54] See Blasi, V. (ed.), *The Burger Court: The Counter-Revolution That Wasn't* (New Haven and London: Yale University Press, 1983).
[55] Although these figures apply to all Establishment Clause cases, the voting patterns are sufficiently close to voting patterns in school aid cases to make them applicable. Figures taken from Kobylka, J., 'Leadership on the Supreme Court of the United States: Chief Justice Burger and the Establishment Clause', *Western Political Science Quarterly*, Vol. 42, No. 4 (December 1989), p. 551. Exact figures showing the justices' percentage of votes for accommodationist results: Rehnquist, 91 per cent; White, 86 per cent; Burger, 74 per cent; O'Connor, 73 per cent; Powell, 46 per cent; Harlan, 40 per cent; Stewart, 38 per cent; Blackmun, 37 per cent; Black, 20 per cent; Marshall, 15 per cent; Brennan, 14 per cent; Stevens, 12 per cent; Douglas, 0 per cent.

56 To 1972, Brennan, Marshall and Blackmun (who Stevens replaced) agreed in 83 per cent of cases; Burger, Rehnquist, and White in 80 per cent. Figures taken from Kobylka, J., p. 555.
57 Kobylka, J., p. 555.
58 Powell wrote in *Nyquist*, Stewart in *Meek*, and Blackmun in *Wolman*.
59 *CPERL v. Nyquist* 413 US 756, 777, n.33 (1973).
60 *Meek v. Pittenger* 421 US 349, 358–9 (1975). This echoed Burger's own warning, stated in *Lemon* at 403 US 602, 614 (1971).
61 *Wolman v. Walter* 433 US 229, 263 (1977) (Justice Powell, concurring in part and dissenting in part).
62 See *CPERL v. Nyquist* 413 US 756, 775–6 (1975). Providing little reasoning for the claim, Powell also attempted to turn the 'primary effect' test of *Lemon* into a 'direct and immediate effect' test, thus blurring, at least temporarily, the scope of *Lemon* (at 783).
63 *Mueller v. Allen* 463 US 388, 398, 396 (1983).
64 These were arguments that had once been made specifically against religious schools, echoing the debates of the 1940s and 1950s, but the religious element was now only a minor part of the debate. Similar arguments have since been made about school vouchers. In favour of tax credits see Coleman, J., T. Hoffer, and S. Kilgore, *High School Achievement: Public, Catholic, and Private Schools Compared* (New York: Basic Books, 1982); 'Tuition Tax Credits: Now or Never', *America*, 13 December 1980, pp. 380–1. Organizations taking this position included: National Institute for Education, American Enterprise Institute, Council for American Private Education, and the Heritage Foundation. In opposition to tax credits see Catteral, J., and H. Levin, 'Public and Private Schools: Evidence on Tuition Tax Credits', *Sociology of Education*, Vol. 55, No. 2/3 (April–July 1982), pp. 144–51; Gordon, A., 'The Three Cs on Tax Credits', *NYT*, 3 October 1982, CN24; 'Segregating Schools: The Foreseeable Consequences of Tuition Tax Credits', 89 *Yale Law Journal* 168 (1979/80); Wood, Jr., J., 'Tuition Tax Credits for Nonpublic Schools', 23 *Journal of Church and State* 5 (1981). Organizations which opposed tax credits included: National Education Association, National Coalition for Public Education, Americans United for the Separation of Church and State, and the American Jewish Committee.
65 See Brennan Papers reproduced in Dickson, D. (ed.), *The Supreme Court in Conference (1940–1985)* (New York: Oxford University Press, 2001), pp. 415–7.
66 See adverts in *NYT*, 10 May 1982, A10 and 16 May 1982, E24.
67 See 'Honor Thy Bill of Rights', *NYT*, 19 August 1984, E19; 'Political and Religious Shifts Rekindle Church-State Issue', *NYT*, 2 September 1984, A1, 20; 'Thoughts of an Infidel', *NYT*, 8 September 1984, A21; 'Voters Found Uneasy Over Religion as Issue', *NYT*, 19 September 1984, B9.
68 'Clergy Sees Danger in State Religion', *NYT*, 6 September 1984, B13.
69 Speech reprinted in *NYT*, 7 September 1984, A14: 'No President should attempt to transform policy debates into theological disputes. He must not let it be thought that political dissent from him is unchristian. And he must not cast opposition to his programs as opposition to America . . . I don't doubt Mr. Reagan's faith, his patriotism and his family values. And I call on him and his supporters to accept and respect mine'.

[70] However, the poll also showed this had little effect on the way people were likely to vote in the election. The controversy appeared to increase sensitivity to the religious issue without changing voters' fundamental beliefs. See 'Voters Found Uneasy Over Religion As Issue', *NYT*, 19 September 1984, B9.
[71] Although superseded by Chapter I of the Education Consolidation and Improvement Act of 1981, 20 U.S.C. § 3801, the provisions were virtually identical and the Supreme Court continued to use 'Title I' to refer to the statute in question.
[72] In 1985, 20,000 students were served in 253 non-public schools at a cost of $30 million. In total, New York's Title I programme served 178,595 students eligible under the income and educational limitations requirements. 'Education Board Faulted on Parochial Aid Stance', *NYT*, 22 January 1985, B1, 3.
[73] *Aguilar* was decided 5:4, *Ball* was decided 7:2. The two votes difference were those of Chief Justice Burger (arguing the result in *Aguilar* disadvantaged students and the Court had not adequately considered the context of New York's programme) and Justice O'Connor (arguing against the on-campus/off-campus distinction and the use of entanglement).
[74] 'The Top Court Will Have More to Say on Religion', *NYT*, 5 May 1985, E5.
[75] The cases were *Wallace v. Jaffree* 472 US 38 (1985), striking down an Alabama moment of silence statute, and *Estate of Thornton v. Caldor* 472 US 703 (1985), which rejected a Connecticut law requiring employers to give workers a weekly day off for their Sabbath.
[76] *Aguilar v. Felton* 473 US 402, 404 (1985). Burger, O'Connor and White also made reference to their *Aguilar* opinions when writing in *Ball* where minor differences between the cases were discussed. Burger and O'Connor concurred in part and dissented in part in *Ball*; White filed one opinion dissenting in both cases.
[77] *Grand Rapids School District v. Ball* 473 US 373, 383 (1985). This passage caused some debate among the justices of the majority. Originally conceived as a longer passage acknowledging criticism of the *Lemon* test, it was shortened to the final version. Originally, however, 'should' read 'must'. It was altered at the suggestion of Justice Powell, whose long-standing pragmatism in such cases led him to object to the restraints of the word 'must'. He wrote to Brennan: 'I shy away from using the word "must," however, as it is stronger than necessary. Bearing <u>Marsh v. Chambers</u> [in original] in mind, it occurs to me that none of us can foresee whether in some future case application of the <u>Lemon</u> [in original] test alone would not be dispositive.' Memorandum from Justice Powell to Justice Brennan, 16 May 1985. Marshall Papers, Box 362, Folder 8. *Marsh* involved an Establishment Clause challenge to legislative chaplains which the Court had rejected by relying on history rather than employing the *Lemon* test.
[78] *Grand Rapids School District v. Ball* 473 US 373, 383 (1985).
[79] *Grand Rapids School District v. Ball* 473 US 373, 395 (1985).
[80] The move was partially successful: O'Connor wrote separately but concurred in the decision with regards to Community Education, drawing specifically on symbolic union analysis.
[81] *Walz v. Tax Commission of the City of New York* 397 US 664, 669 (1970). That *Walz* employed entanglement to uphold a challenged programme makes it unusual among the Court's aid cases and that Burger employed the test in a positive fashion, as a way to praise New York's policy, suggests that the Court's subsequent

negative, suspicious employment of it was a change in emphasis. This subtle difference has been overlooked, unsurprisingly given Burger's role as architect of the *Lemon* test the following year, but it is intriguing, suggesting the possibility that a far different Establishment Clause jurisprudence might have developed on the Court.

[82] *Lemon v. Kurtzman* 403 US 602, 614 (1971).

[83] *Aguilar v. Felton* 473 US 402, 420–1 (1985) (Justice Rehnquist, dissenting) (internal citations omitted).

[84] 'Nominee for High Court: A Record Defying Labels', *NYT*, 12 July 1981, A22.

[85] 'The O'Connor Record Proves Surprising to Fans and Foes', *NYT*, 11 July 1982, E4.

[86] '[I]t is difficult to understand why a remedial reading class offered on parochial school premises is any more likely to supplant the secular course offerings of the parochial school than the same class offered in a portable classroom next door to the school'. *Aguilar v. Felton* 473 US 402, 426 (1985) (Justice O'Connor, with Justice Rehnquist, dissenting).

[87] Norman Redlich, speaking for the American Jewish Congress, quoted in 'Ruling Means Cities Must Work Out How to Get Help to Parochial Pupils', *NYT*, 2 July 1984, A14.

[88] *NYT*, 2 July 1984, A14.

[89] *NYT*, 2 July 1984, A14. For discussion of local approaches to *Aguilar* and *Ball* along with Department of Education guidelines see *After* Aguilar v. Felton*: Chapter 1 Services to Nonpublic Schoolchildren, A Report Prepared for the House Subcommittee on Elementary, Secondary, and Vocational Education of the Committee on Education and Labor* (March 1986).

[90] 'Bennett Assails Justices on "Disdain for Religion"', *NYT*, 5 September 1985, A24. See Vitullo-Martin, T. and B. Cooper, *Separation of Church and Child: The Constitution and Federal Aid to Religious Schools* (Indianapolis: The Hudson Institute, 1987) advocating a variety of methods to circumvent *Aguilar*.

[91] See, for example, the difference between textbooks in *Allen* and *Meek* and instructional materials in *Meek* and *Wolman*; also, compare *Everson* and *Allen* with *Lemon* and *Wolman* for the significance of aid provided to individuals compared to benefits provided to institutions.

[92] In *Everson* and *Allen* the school aid issue was so new to Establishment jurisprudence that it is difficult to evaluate the relative importance of factions as compared to other factors.

[93] Douglas Papers, Box 1509.

Chapter 3

[1] The Washington State Supreme Court found no reason to address the issue of entanglement, having held that the aid resulted in the unconstitutional effect of advancing religion by funding the religious studies of Larry Witters. 102 Wash.2d 624, 629; 689 P.2d 53, 56 (1984).

[2] This was Justice Thurgood Marshall's intent. See Memorandum from Justice Marshall to Justice Powell, 3 January 1986. Thurgood Marshall Papers (hereafter Marshall Papers), Box 384, Folder 8.

[3] *Witters v. Washington Department of Services for the Blind* 474 US 481, 485 (1986).
[4] Memorandum from Justice Marshall to Justice Powell, 3 January 1986. See generally Marshall Papers, Box 384, Folder 8.
[5] *Witters v. Washington Department of Service for the Blind* 474 US 481, 490 (1986) (Justice Powell et al., concurring). Justices White and O'Connor also noted their agreement with this view in separate opinions.
[6] *Zobrest v. Catalina Hills School District* 509 US 1, 18, 22 (1993).
[7] It should, however, be noted that *Zobrest* allowed but did not require such aid to disabled students, leaving local school districts substantial leeway to interpret their own constitutions. See *KR by MR v. Anderson Community School Corporation* (7th Cir., 1997) and *Russman v. Board of Education of the Enlarged City School District of the City of Watervliet* (NDNY, 2000) limiting aid available to religious school students. But see also *KDM by WJM v. Reedsport School District* (9th Cir., 1999) and *John T. by Paul T. and Joan T. v. Delaware County Intermediate Unit* (ED Pa, 2000). *Zobrest* was not the first time that public employees had been allowed by the Court onto religious school campuses to perform certain tasks. Where *Zobrest* is significant is in the extensive relationship between the signer and the student and the lack of external restrictions placed on the signer by the Court.
[8] The trend continued in *Mitchell v. Helms* 530 US 793 (2000) with Scalia's plurality opinion (see 809).
[9] The dissenters believed this was the majority's position. *Zobrest v. Catalina Hills School District* 509 US 1, 20 (1993) (Justice Blackmun, with Justice Souter, dissenting).
[10] In addition to the argument discussed here, the dissenters also objected to the majority raising constitutional questions when statutory interpretation was available. The procedural question was the only one addressed by O'Connor and Stevens, who refused to even consider the constitutional question (see 509 US 1, 23–4). Blackmun also raised this issue but challenged the majority on the substantive questions too.
[11] *Zobrest v. Catalina Hills School District* 509 US 1, 19 (1993) (Justice Blackmun, with Justice Souter, dissenting).
[12] *Lee v. Weisman* 505 US 577 (1992) (striking down prayers at graduation services).
[13] 'More Non-Catholics Using Catholic Schools', *NYT*, 28 November A25, 26; 'Enrolment Rising in Catholic Schools', *NYT*, 15 May 1988, NJ18, 19; 'Catholic Schools Reach Out to Serve and to Borrow', *NYT*, 13 September 1988, A1, 25; *The Non-Catholic in the Catholic School* (Washington, DC: Department of Religious Education, National Catholic Educational Association, 1987). But see O'Keefe SJ, J., 'No Margin, No Mission', in McLaughlin, T., J. O'Keefe SJ, and B. O'Keeffe, *The Contemporary Catholic School: Context, Identity, and Diversity* (Washington, DC and London: The Falmer Press, 1986), pp. 177–97, and Murnion, P., 'The Future of the Church in the Inner City', *America*, 15 December 1990, pp. 478–85 for some of the problems caused by this trend.
[14] Greeley, A., *Catholic High Schools and Minority Students* (New Brunswick, New Jersey and London: Transaction Books, 1982, 2nd edn., 2002); Coleman, J., T. Hoffer, and S. Kilgore, *High School Achievement: Public, Catholic, and Private Schools Compared* (New York: Basic Books, 1982); Martin, S., 'Is Catholic Schooling Providing Something Public Schools Cannot?' *America*, 26 May 1990, pp. 520–2.

[15] 'Enrolment Rising in Catholic Schools', *NYT*, 15 May 1988, NJ18, 19.
[16] See Bryk, A., V. Lee, and B. Holland, *Catholic Schools and the Common Good* (Cambridge, Massachusetts and London: Harvard University Press, 1993) (hereafter Bryk, Lee, and Holland) discussing exactly this issue. Also 'Fortress Days Are Over', *NYT*, 4 February 1973, E9; 'Catholic Colleges in US Debate Academic Freedom Amid Disputes', *NYT*, 8 October 1986, A1, D23; 'The Lessons of St. Joe's', *NYT*, Sunday Magazine, 5 February 1989, pp. 34–7; McLaughlin, T. et al., *The Contemporary Catholic School* (although several articles in this volume deal with British Catholic schools, many of the principles discussed are relevant to changes in US Catholic schools); Youniss, J., J. Convey, and J. McLellan, *The Catholic Character of Catholic Schools* (Notre Dame, Indiana: University of Notre Dame Press, 2000).
[17] A 1997 study of Jewish school finance noted, 'the statistics of American Jewish education are generally not reliable', but estimated that there were 200,000 students in more than 600 K-12, Reform, Orthodox and Liberal schools. Schick, M. and J. Dauber, *The Financing of Jewish Day Schools* (New York: Rabbi Jacob Joseph School, 1997). For a good introduction to the philosophy of Jewish Day Schools see Kaminetsky, J. (ed.), *Hebrew Day School Education: An Overview* (New York: Torah Umesorah, 1970) and Kramer, D. Z., *The Day Schools and Torah Umesorah: The Seeding of Traditional Judaism in America* (New York: Yeshiva University Press, 1984) (although this is more a history of Torah Umesorah and the Day School Movement, there are some useful insights into the philosophy of Jewish education).
[18] National Center for Education Statistics' figures quoted in 'Private Schools Look to Bright Future', *NYT*, 4 January 1981, Educ. 1, 14. For an insight into the culture of Christian schools see Billings, R., *A Guide to the Christian School* (Washington, DC: The New Century Foundation Press, 1983); Bramblet, J., *An Introduction to the Christian School* (Tacoma, Washington: James M. Bramblet, 1985); Peshkin, A., *God's Choice: The Total World of a Fundamentalist Christian School* (Chicago: University of Chicago Press, 1986); Parsons, P., *Inside America's Christian Schools* (Macon, Georgia: Mercer University Press, 1987); Menendez, A., *Visions of Reality: What Fundamentalist Schools Teach* (Buffalo, New York: Prometheus Books, 1993) (highly critical review of fundamentalist textbooks).
[19] Lupu, I., 'The Increasingly Anachronistic Case Against School Vouchers', 13 *Notre Dame Journal of Law, Ethics, and Public Policy* 375, 375 (1999); Berg, T., 'Anti-Catholicism and Modern Church-State Relations', 33 *Loyola University of Chicago Law Journal* 121 (2001), pp. 163–4.
[20] Bryk, Lee, and Holland, p. 69. See also, Greeley, A., *Catholic High Schools and Minority Students*; *America*, 29 March 1980 special volume titled 'Black Catholics and their Church'.
[21] 'Black Churches Renew a Mission: Education', *NYT*, 7 August 1991, A1,19.
[22] 'African-Americans Turning to Christian Academies', *NYT*, 4 August 1996, Educ. Life, pp. 26–9. But see Parsons, P., pp. 16–17, 113–26.
[23] The estimated costs and numbers of students affected are quoted in *Agostini v. Felton* 521 US 203, 213–4 (1997) from appellants' brief. The numbers include both public and religious school students.
[24] *Agostini v. Felton* 521 US 203, 216, 240 (1997).
[25] *Agostini v. Felton* 521 US 203, 240 (1997).

[26] McCarthy, M., 'Religion and Education: Whither the Establishment Clause?' 75 *Indiana Law Journal* 123 (2000); Waite, J., '*Agostini v. Felton*: Thickening the Establishment Clause Stew', 33 *New England Law Review* 81 (1998); Mozer, G., 'The Crumbling Wall Between Church and State: *Agostini v. Felton*, Aid to Parochial Schools, and the Establishment Clause in the Twenty-First Century', 31 *Connecticut Law Review* 337 (1998).

[27] In particular, see *Mitchell v. Helms* 530 US 793 (2000) and *Zelman v. Simmons-Harris* 536 US 639 (2002).

[28] Critics also failed to note that of the three justices involved in *Aguilar* who were still on the Court in 1997, none had altered their position. Justice Stevens had been part of the five-member majority in *Aguilar* but found himself in equally silent dissent in *Agostini*. Rehnquist and O'Connor had both dissented in 1985; Rehnquist, now chief justice, was one of the five-member majority in *Agostini*, while O'Connor wrote the majority opinion, drawing on a number of arguments made in her *Aguilar* dissent.

[29] *Zobrest v. Catalina Hills School District* 509 US 1, 13 (1993).

[30] *Agostini v. Felton* 521 US 203, 226–7 (1997).

[31] See Transcript of Oral Argument (*Agostini v. Felton*) pp. 39–40. Stanley Geller appeared on behalf of the private respondents.

[32] *Agostini v. Felton* 521 US 203, 224 (1997).

[33] *Agostini v. Felton* 521 US 203, 227 (1997).

[34] *Agostini v. Felton* 521 US 203, 232–3 (1997). (Internal references and quotation marks omitted).

[35] *Agostini v. Felton* 521 US 203, 234 (1997).

[36] See *Everson v. Board of Education* 330 US 1, 18, 17 (1947) and *Agostini v. Felton* 521 US 203, 228–9, 232 (1997).

[37] Warpula, C., 'The Demise of Demarcation: *Agostini v. Felton* Unlocks the Parochial School Gate to State-Sponsored Educational Aid', 33 *Wake Forest Law Review* 465, 508 (1998). Arguably the best indicator of the theory's potency and continued vitality is *Zelman v. Simmons-Harris* 563 US 639 (2002). Rehnquist's repeated emphasis that Cleveland's tuition voucher scheme was designed to benefit low income and minority families leaves little doubt that the majority viewed this as one of the most important factors resulting in approval of the programme.

[38] 'After Years of Classes in Vans, It's Back to School', *NYT*, 24 June 1997, B9. One student was not so impressed with the ruling, remarking that he would miss 'the fun' of the vans: air-conditioning in the summer and 'get[ting] to play in the snow on the way to class' in the winter.

[39] *Agostini v. Felton* 521 US 203, 240–54 (Justice Souter, dissenting) and 255–60 (Justice Ginsburg, dissenting). See 'Public Teachers in Parochial Schools', *NYT*, 24 June 1997, A18.

[40] 'Religious Freedom and Common Sense', *NYT*, 24 June 1997, A18.

[41] *Board of Education of Kiryas Joel v. Grumet* 512 US 687 (1994). The case involved a New York State law which created a special public school district encompassing only the town of Kiryas Joel, home to Satmar Hasidic Jews, in order to provide public aid to the community's disabled students in their own, religious, schools.

[42] At least until 1993 when Justice White retired and Justice Ginsburg was appointed. After 1993, the accommodationists required *both* swing votes for a majority.

Part Two

[1] Binder, F., *The Age of the Common School, 1830–1865* (New York: John Wiley & Sons, Inc., 1974), p. 71.
[2] Binder, F., pp. 64–66; Ravitch, D., *The Great School Wars, New York City, 1805–1973: A History of Public Schools as Battlefields of Social Change* (New York: Basic Books, 1974), especially pp. 4–84.
[3] Binder, F., pp. 67–71.
[4] "The Court Decision and the School Prayer Furore," *Newsweek*, 9 July 1962, p. 44.
[5] *Abington School District v. Schempp* 374 US 203 (1963).

Chapter 4

[1] Shayer, E., 'Approaches to Religious Teaching', *Phi Delta Kappan* (hereafter *PDK*), Vol. 28, No. 4 (December 1946), p. 170. The *PDK* was a magazine written for and by the nation's educators, both well known and unknown. As such, it reflects many of the attitudes and ideas of educators at the time.
[2] Religious leaders made this argument with some frequency. See sermons of Reverend Dr Norman Peale and Reverend Dr Eugene Flipse, published in the *New York Times* (hereafter *NYT*), 3 December 1951, A21, and those of Reverend Dr John Bonnell and Reverend Hugh McCandless, in *NYT*, 12 October 1953, A24. Also, Dulles, J. F., *Faith of Our Fathers* (Washington, DC: Department of State, 1954).
[3] Committee on Religion and Education, *The Relation of Religion to Public Education: The Basic Principles* (Washington, DC: American Council on Education, 1947). See also *Moral and Spiritual Values in the Public Schools* (Washington, DC: NEA and AASA, 1951) in which the National Education Association and the American Association of School Administrators concurred with this view. For an introduction to the range of sources available to teachers see Politella, J., *Religion in Education: An Annotated Bibliography* (New York: American Association of Colleges for Teacher Education, 1956) and Hunt, M. G., *Values Resources Guide: Annotated for the Elementary School Teacher* (New York: American Association of Colleges for Teacher Education, 1958). For a practical discussion of teaching about religion and some of the problems of doing so, see Brown, N. (ed.), *The Study of Religion in the Public Schools: An Appraisal* (Washington, DC: American Council on Education, 1957).
[4] Reverend James Pike quoted in 'Foes of Religion in Schools Scored', *NYT*, 21 April 1952, A18. Ball, W., 'The School Prayer Case: The Dilemma of Disestablishment', 8 *Catholic Lawyer* 182 (1962) and 'The School Prayer Case: What Course for the Future?' 8 *Catholic Lawyer* 286 (1962).
[5] Grafflin, D., 'Religious Education for Public Schools', *PDK*, Vol. 28, No. 4 (December 1946), p. 175; Read, G., 'Concerns for Religion and Education', *PDK*, Vol. 36, No. 7 (April 1955), pp. 267–8.
[6] Leavell, U., 'On Teaching Spiritual Values,' *PDK*, Vol. 27, No. 4 (December 1945), pp. 99–102. 'The aim is not to produce children who are merely informed and

skilled but without moral and religious commitments. The aim of education is rather to produce the citizen of deep and intelligent convictions. This is the heart of the public schools' task, and without question it involves implications that are moral and religious in nature'. Statement of the Protestant Teachers' Association of New York published in *NYT*, 16 November 1952, A81.

[7] See Statement of the Protestant Teachers' Association of New York published in *NYT*, 16 November 1952, A81; Harner, N., *Religion's Place in General Education* (Richmond, Virginia: John Knox Press, 1949): 'A flat, one-dimensional character education, which never dares to mention the will of God as the final source and resource of all attempts at ethical living, is like the play of *Hamlet* without Hamlet'. (p. 35).

[8] The heavily Christian-centric nature of the debate can, however, appear as sectarian to a modern audience. See, for example, Fleming, W. S., *God in Our Public Schools* (Pittsburgh, Pennsylvania: National Reform Association, 1947). Fleming's less than tolerant views of Jews, Catholics, and other 'alien minorities' are offensive to modern sensibilities but his argument reveals clearly the Christian-centric way in which some contributors to this debate in the 1940s and 1950s viewed the situation. 'Religious doctrines are those on which the Christian sects agree. Sectarian doctrines are those on which the Christian sects do not agree.' (p. 170). For a more recent view of this from a Jewish perspective see Feldman, S., *Please Don't Wish Me A Merry Christmas: A Critical History of the Separation of Church and State* (New York and London: New York University Press, 1997).

[9] Smith, H. L., 'A Program for Character Education,' *PDK*, Vol. 31, No. 5 (January 1950), p. 248. Also, Smith, H., R. McElhinney, and G. Steele, *Character Development Through Religious and Moral Education in the Public Schools of the United States* (Bloomington, Indiana: Bureau of Cooperative Research, Indiana University, 1937).

[10] Mayer, F., 'Goodness Cannot be Coerced', *PDK*, Vol 36, No. 6 (March 1954), p. 234 (italics in original).

[11] Thayer, V. T., 'Our Secular Schools and Religion', *PDK*, Vol. 34, No. 9 (June 1953), p. 394. See also Thayer, V.T., *The Attack Upon the American Secular School* (Boston: The Beacon Press, 1951).

[12] 'Faith' came bottom in a list of items emphasized after cooperation, honesty, respect for law, responsibility, kindness, appreciation, loyalty, generosity, good will, reverence and courage. In a list of activities and techniques employed, prayers, Bible reading and the use of religious literature received little attention when compared with cooperative planning of classroom activities, democratic organization of the classroom and teamwork activities. Although this survey does not indicate the extent to which religion was employed implicitly in these ostensibly secular activities, the lack of an explicit emphasis on religion and religious themes and practices serves to illustrate the point. See 'Will the Golden Rule Work?' *PDK*, Vol 30, No. 4 (December 1948), pp. 107–8. For Kentucky's results, see *Moral and Spiritual Values in Education* (Frankfort, Kentucky: Department of Education, Vol. XVIII, No. 8, October 1950). Also Bower, W., *Moral and Spiritual Values in Education* (Lexington: University of Kentucky Press, 1952).

[13] Brown, F., 'Studies of Religion in Public Education', *PDK*, Vol. 36, No. 7 (April 1955), p. 256.

14. Edington, A., 'Bible Teaching Policies in the Public Schools', *PDK*, Vol. 31, No. 8 (April 1950), pp. 394–5.
15. Figures taken from Brown, F., p. 253 and Bower, W., p. 29. Also, Smith, H. et al., *Character Development Through Religious and Moral Education in the Public Schools of the United States* (Bloomington, Indiana: Bureau of Cooperative Research, Indiana University, 1937). For a survey of state court actions prior to *Engel* see 'Note: A Daily Prayer in Public Schools', 7 *Catholic Lawyer* 334 (1961); 'Note: School Prayer and the Becker Amendment', 53 *Georgetown Law Journal* 192 (1964/5).
16. Brown, F., p. 256.
17. Hunt, R., 'Religion in Public Education', *PDK*, Vol. 36, No. 7 (April 1955), p. 243.
18. Regents' Prayer from *Engel v. Vitale* 370 US 421, 422 (1962). For a history of the Regents' actions, see the testimony of William Daiker, attorney for the school board, before the House Committee on the Judiciary, Hearings on Proposed Amendments to the Constitution Relating to Prayers and Bible Reading in the Public Schools, 88th Congress, 2nd Sess., 1964, pp. 1388–93.
19. *Engel v. Vitale* 370 US 421, 425 (1962).
20. See *Engel* conference notes: William Brennan Papers, Box 1:61 Folder 1 (hereafter Brennan Papers); William Douglas Papers, Box 1276 (hereafter Douglas Papers).
21. 'Neutrality' implies something non-neutral about the alternatives, in this instance allowing claims of the Court's hostility towards religion and its exercise.
22. See *West Virginia State Board of Education v. Barnette* 319 US 624 (1943) where the Court addressed the required participation of all students in a daily flag salute and recitation of the Pledge of Allegiance. No student was allowed to be excused from the ritual, regardless of religious objections.
23. *Engel v. Vitale* 370 US 421, 424, n. 2 (1962).
24. See *Engel v. Vitale* 370 US 421, 444–50 (Justice Stewart, dissenting). See Costanzo, J., 'Prayer in Public Schools', 8 *Catholic Lawyer* 269 (1962); Rice, C., *The Supreme Court and Public Prayer: The Need for Restraint* (New York: Fordham University Press, 1964); Ferrera, P., *Religion and the Constitution: A Reinterpretation* (Washington, DC: Free Congress Research and Education Foundation, 1983). See also testimony of Bishop James Pike, Episcopal Bishop of California (pp. 56, 65–6) and Representative Frank Becker (R-NY) before the Senate Committee on the Judiciary, Hearings on Prayer in Public Schools and Other Matters, 87th Congress, 2nd Sess. (1962), and of Governor George Wallace of Alabama (p. 845) and Robert Cook of the National Association of Evangelicals (pp. 968–9) before hearings of the House Judiciary Committee in 1964.
25. Schwartz, B., with S. Lesher, *Inside the Warren Court, 1953–1969* (Garden City, New York: Doubleday & Co., Inc., 1983), p. 181.
26. *Engel v. Vitale* 370 US 421, 435 (1962).
27. See *Engel v. Vitale* 370 US 421, 432, 435 (1962). The sentiment was reinforced by Black's comments from the bench. After reading the opinion, he commented: 'The prayer of each man from his soul must be his and his alone. That is the genius of the First Amendment ... If there is any one thing clear in the First Amendment it is that the right of people to pray in their own way is not to be

controlled by the election returns'. Quoted in Loren, J., *Engel v. Vitale: Prayer in the Public Schools* (San Diego, California: Lucent Books, 2001), p. 54.

28 See, for example, the Statement by the Roman Catholic Bishops of the USA (1952) (reprinted in the *NYT*, 16 November 1952, A80) and 'Letter to the Christian People of America' from the National Council of Churches in Christ (1952) (reprinted in *NYT*, 13 December 1952, A17).

29 For example, see *Donahoe v. Richards* 38 Me. 379 (1854); *Spiller v. Inhabitants of Woburn* 94 Mass. (12 Allen) 127 (1866); *Moore v. Monroe* 64 Iowa 367, 20 NW 475 (1884); *Hackett v. School District* 120 Ky 608, 87 SW 792 (1905); *Church v. Bullock* 104 Tex. 1, 109 SW 115 (1908); *People v. Stanley* 81 Colo. 276, 255 Pac. 610 (1927) upholding prayer and Bible reading. For cases striking down similar practices see *Board of Education v. Minor* 23 Ohio St. 211 (1872); *State v. District Board of School District No. 8* 76 Wis. 177, 44 NW 967 (1890); *State v. Sheve* 65 Neb. 853, 91 NW 846 (1902); *Herold v. Parish Board of School Directors* 136 La. 1034, 60 So. 116 (1915); *Evans v. Selma Union High School District* 193 Cal. 54, 222 Pac. 801 (1924). But see Laubach, J., *School Prayers: Congress, the Courts and the Public* (Washington DC: Public Affairs Press, 1969), p. 24: 'The pro's and con's of school religion already being well developed in state judicial reports, it merely remained for the Supreme Court to choose its options'.

30 Released time programmes allowed students to be excused from their normal classes during the school day to receive religious instruction with the permission of their parents. In *McCollum*, this instruction took place on public school grounds. In 1952, the Court upheld such programmes when conducted off school premises in *Zorach v. Clauson* 343 US 306 (1952), but the argument about 'secular' public schools continued.

31 Black's omission of legal principle was not simply an oversight since the Brief for Petitioners relied heavily on *McCollum*, while the Brief for Respondents made significant use of *Zorach* to support their respective arguments. See Brief for Petitioners, pp. 22–4; Brief for Respondents, pp. 14–16. Douglas made use of both in his concurrence, suggesting the absence of any reference to them in the majority opinion was designed to make a specific point.

32 This approach had been employed by the Court in *Brown v. Board of Education of Topeka, Kansas* 347 US 483 (1954) when holding racially segregated schools unconstitutional.

33 Douglas Papers, Box 1276; Brennan Papers, Box 1:61 Folder 1. Given the relative paucity of constitutional precedent for *Engel*, the cases could only have been *Everson*, *McCollum* and *Zorach*. General principles to be drawn from these cases were that the state could not give direct aid to religion and that religious exercises could not be conducted on public school campuses. Since the Regents' Prayer was conducted during the school day, on campus, and was clearly an aid to religion, Harlan's respect for precedent led him to support the majority. However, it was support based on the specific facts of the case rather than broad philosophical support for strict separation.

34 He had already noted his vote at conference. Douglas's memorandum to Black, dated 11 June 1962, reads: 'As you know, I have had troubles with No. 468 – Engel v. Vitale [in original] . . . I am inclined to reverse if we are prepared to disallow public property and public funds to be used to finance a religious exercise.

If, however, we would strike down a New York requirement that public school teachers open each day with prayer, I think we could not consistently open each of our sessions with prayer. That's the kernel of my problem.' Douglas Papers, Box 1276.

35. The earlier opinions were in *Zorach v. Clauson* 343 US 306 (1952) and *McGowan v. Maryland* 366 US 420 (1961).
36. See in particular Douglas Papers, Drafts 2 and 3, Box 1276.
37. Douglas Papers, Box 1276.
38. Simon, J., *The Center Holds: The Power Struggle Inside the Rehnquist Court* (New York: Simon & Schuster, 1995), pp. 176–7.
39. *Engel v. Vitale* 370 US 421, 445 (Justice Stewart, dissenting).
40. *Engel v. Vitale* 370 US 421, 446 (1962) (Justice Stewart, dissenting). For Stewart, that the Court began its sessions with an invocation of God, that Congress opened each day with a prayer, the national anthem and Pledge of Allegiance contained references to the Deity, and presidents from George Washington to John Kennedy had frequently invoked God, were all more important indicators of the status of religion in contemporary society than any debate about the dangers of religion from two hundred years earlier.
41. *Engel v. Vitale* 370 US 421, 449–450 (Justice Stewart, dissenting – emphasis added). In reality this is a misreading of Stewart's opinion, taking no consideration of his fundamental view of judicial activity or the fact that he based his opinion so heavily on the Free Exercise Clause, both of which lead to a different interpretation of the meaning of these assertions than that provided by most commentators.
42. See *Engel v. Vitale* 370 US 421, 435, n. 21 (1962).
43. Quoted in Pfeffer, L., *Religion, State and the Burger Court* (Buffalo, New York: Prometheus Books, 1984), p. 85.
44. 'Clerics, Politicians Hit Court Prayer Decision', *Washington Post*, 26 June 1962, A8.
45. 'Religious Exercises in Area Held in Doubt', *Washington Post*, 26 June 1962, A1; 'In Behalf of Education', *Washington Post*, 26 June 1962, A12. See also Kik, J. M., *The Supreme Court and Prayer in the Public School* (Philadelphia: Presbyterian and Reformed Publishing Co., 1963).
46. 'The Court Decision and the School Prayer Furore', *Newsweek*, 9 July 1962, p. 45.
47. *Congressional Record* (hereafter *Cong. Rec.*), 108th Congress, 26 June 1962, pp.11,675; *Washington Post*, 29 June 1962, A8. It is difficult to state conclusively whether these statements, and others like them, were the genuine views of the speakers or simply political manoeuvring. That many Congressmen who made statements shortly after *Engel* was handed down later retracted them or altered their stance on school prayer suggests they were at least made based on misleading, or limited, information about the Court's stance. However, these were the reactions initially reported in the newspapers, shaping public reaction to the ruling, and herein lies their significance.
48. *Cong. Rec.*, 108th Congress, 26 June 1962, pp. 11,719, 11,844.
49. *Cong. Rec.*, 108th Congress, 26 June 1962, pp. 11,844, 11,708 (for additional quotes, see 11,839–45 and 11,707–13); *Newsweek*, 9 July 1962, p. 43.
50. *Cong. Rec.*, 108th Congress, 29 June 1962, p. A4590; *Washington Post*, 26 June 1962, A8.

[51] Beaney, W. and E. Beiser, 'Prayer and Politics: The Impact of *Engel* and *Schempp* on the Political Process', 13 *Journal of Public Law* 475, 479 (1964) (hereafter Beaney and Beiser).

[52] Quoted in *Washington Post*, 26 June 1962, A8.

[53] 'Court Edict on Prayer is Decried', *Washington Post*, 27 June 1962, A6; *Newsweek*, 9 July 1962, p. 44.

[54] *Washington Post*, 27 June 1962, A6; *Newsweek*, 9 July 1962, p. 43.

[55] Quoted in *Washington Post*, 26 June 1962, A8.

[56] 'TRB from Washington', *The New Republic*, 9 July 1962 (Vol. 147, No. 2) p. 2.

[57] US Senate. Committee on the Judiciary. Hearings on Prayer in Public Schools and Other Matters, 87th Congress, 2nd Sess. (1962). Senators Philip Hart (D-Mich) and Roman Hruska (R-Neb) were the two notable exceptions to this trend. It is worth noting that of the ten witnesses providing oral testimony at the hearings, not one spoke in favour of *Engel* and only one, Bishop James Pike of San Francisco, was a non-Congressman.

[58] Quoted in Schwartz, B., p. 19.

[59] *Brown* was the notable exception to this trend. Powe, L., *The Warren Court and American Politics* (Cambridge, Massachusetts: Belknap Press, 2000), p. 104; Simon, J., pp. 62–3.

[60] McCloskey, R., *The Modern Supreme Court* (Cambridge, Massachusetts: Harvard University Press, 1972), p. 160.

[61] Powe, L., p. 85. On 17 June 1957, subsequently dubbed 'Red Monday' by critics, the Court handed down four such cases: *Watkins v. US* 354 US 178 (Due Process Clause of Fifth Amendment violated by conviction under the Smith Act for refusing to answer questions about other persons involved in the American Communist Party); *Sweezy v. New Hampshire* 354 US 234 (charge of contempt for refusing to answer questions about other members of the state Progressive Party violated Due Process Clause of the Fourteenth Amendment); *Yates v. US* 354 US 298 (overturned convictions under the Smith Act of leaders of the Communist Party in California); *Service v. Dulles* 354 US 363 (questioned discharge of Foreign Service official as a 'security risk' and for disloyalty). See also *Slochower v. Board of Education* 350 US 551 (1956) (discharge of teacher for failure to answer questions about Communist Party membership violated Due Process Clause of Fourteenth Amendment).

[62] For the text of the Attorneys General resolution, see *Cong. Rec.*, 85th Congress, 2nd Sess., p. 10,534. For the text of the ABA resolutions see *Cong. Rec.*, 85th Congress, 1st Sess., p. 15,970 and 86th Congress, 1st Sess., pp. 3361–80.

[63] Murphy, W., *Congress and the Court: A Case Study in the American Political Process* (Chicago: University of Chicago Press, 1962), p. 116.

[64] Schwartz, B., p. 104. Schwartz's comment may be overstated but Warren was sufficiently well known to attract criticism. See comments by Representatives Davis (D-Ga), Flynt (D-Ga), and Andrews (D-Ala) (*Cong. Rec.*, 85th Congress, 1st Sess., pp. 9887–96). For earlier criticism, see *Cong. Rec.*, 83rd Congress, 2nd Sess. (1954), pp. 6742–50. However, in defence of Warren, see comments by Senators Neuberger (D-Ore), Clark (D-Penn), Morse (D-Ore), and Douglas (D-Il) and editorials in the *NYT*, *Portland Oregonian* and *Christian Science Monitor* (*Cong. Rec.*, 85th Congress, 1st Sess., pp. 10,295–7, 11,954, 12,072).

[65] Powe, L., p. 209.
[66] Powe, L., p. 211.
[67] White turned out to be a more conservative justice than had been expected on his appointment. In 1962, however, his philosophy was unknown.
[68] *Mapp v. Ohio* 367 US 643 (1961) extended to the states the Fourth Amendment exclusionary rule, forbidding the use at trial of evidence obtained in violation of the requirements for a proper search and seizure.
[69] Only California, Illinois, Louisiana, Nebraska, South Dakota, Washington and Wisconsin outlawed all forms of religious exercise in schools. A Delaware law required five verses of the Bible to be read daily with a fine of $25 for a first failure and revocation of the teaching credentials of any teacher who refused to participate a second time. In Arkansas the Lord's Prayer, or any prayer, could be offered, but failure to comply after two warnings was grounds for dismissal. In Alabama public funds could be withheld from a school if the teachers' reports failed to show daily Bible reading. Mitau, G. T., *Decade of Decision: The Supreme Court and the Constitutional Revolution, 1954–1964* (New York: Charles Scribner's Sons, 1967), pp. 119–20. A 1960 survey showed Bible reading occurring in 80 per cent of Southern school districts, 62 per cent of Eastern districts, 28 per cent of Mid-Western districts, and 14 per cent of Western districts. Quoted in Loren, J., p. 24.
[70] *Abington School District v. Schempp* 374 US 203, 223 (1963). Again, Stewart was the lone dissenter.
[71] 374 US 203 *Records and Briefs*: Brief for Appellants, testimony of Dr. Charles H. Boehm, Superintendent of Public Instruction of Pennsylvania, p. 19.
[72] This represented almost a third of their combined length. 374 US 203 *Records and Briefs: Murray v. Curlett*, Petitioners' Brief, pp. 11–18; *Abington School District v. Schempp*, Brief for Appellees, pp. 15–17, 23–33.
[73] *Schempp*, Brief for Appellants, pp. 15–19, 30, 32; *Murray*, Brief of Respondents, pp. 12–16.
[74] *Abington School District v. Schempp* 374 US 203, 209–211, 224 (1963).
[75] In conference, Warren argued that 'unless we reverse <u>Vitale</u> [in original] we must reverse here – [this] case is stronger than it', Goldberg suggested, 'this is a much more religious prayer than the one in <u>Vitale</u>, [in original]' and even Stewart held that 'this is more of an Establishment case . . . this is sectarian'. Warren and Stewart in *Murray v. Curlett* conference, Douglas Papers, Box 1281; Goldberg in *Schempp* conference, Douglas Papers, Box 1295.
[76] Early drafts of the opinion reveal that Clark toyed with the idea of excluding the Murrays' atheism from discussion, possibly to avoid claims that the Court was 'godless' or establishing 'secularism' in American society. Although he ultimately did not exclude the Murrays, Clark's thinking shows his awareness of the potential controversy resulting from the case. Mengler, T., 'Public Relations in the Supreme Court: Justice Tom Clark's Opinion in the School Prayer Case', 6 *Constitutional Commentary* 331, 340–1 (1989).
[77] Remarks to the Commonwealth Club of San Francisco, 3 August 1962. See 'Critics of Prayer Rule Misguided, Clark Says', *Washington Post*, 4 August 1962, A4. See Mengler, T., 'Public Relations in the Supreme Court . . .'.

78 *Abington School District v. Schempp* 374 US 203, 226 (1963). Clark used the term at least half a dozen times throughout the opinion, referring to it at one point as 'wholesome neutrality' (at 222).
79 *Murray* Conference, Douglas Papers, Box 1281.
80 *Abington School District v. Schempp* 374 US 203, 222 (1963).
81 Nevertheless, Clark's two-part test drew heavily on *Engel*. See *Abington School District v. Schempp* 374 US 203, 224–5 (1963). The two-part test did not end the Court's problems, however. Clark never clearly defined exactly what constituted an unconstitutional purpose or effect, leaving them open to interpretation by future Courts. In 1971, Chief Justice Warren Burger added the entanglement prong to Clark's earlier test to create what became known as the *Lemon* test (*Lemon v. Kurtzman* 403 US 602 [1971]). Its significance in *Schempp*, however, was that the Court recognized the need for a clear test and sought to provide one.
82 *Schempp* Conference, Douglas Papers, Box 1295.
83 Other instances where this was employed by the Court were *Cooper v. Aaron* 358 US 1 (1958) and *US v. Nixon* 418 US 683 (1974).
84 The concurrences of Douglas, Brennan and Goldberg created a nice, though inadvertent, symmetry that may have gone some way towards dispelling criticism: a Protestant, a Catholic and a Jew respectively, all arguing against the practice of Bible reading implied that whatever one's belief, the Constitution meant no religious exercises in the schools. See *NYT*, 18 June 1963, A1.
85 See US House of Representatives. Committee on the Judiciary. Hearings on Proposed Amendments to the Constitution Relating to Prayers and Bible Reading in the Public Schools, 88th Congress, 2nd Sess. (1964) (hereafter Becker Hearings). For a good introduction to these hearings see Laubach, J, *School Prayers*, pp. 47–97.
86 They were: Robert Leggett (D-Cal) (pp. 1770–8), Abraham Multer (D-NY) (pp. 2069–88), B.F. Sisk (D-Cal) (pp. 533–45) and Robert Stephens (D-Ga) (pp. 2148–52).
87 Quoted in Laubach, J., pp. 49–50. Also, Becker Hearings, pp. 212, 223–4.
88 Beaney and Beiser, pp. 496–500.
89 In his study of the Becker Hearings, John Laubach noted that Reverend Dean Kelley was 'surprised to discover how many Congressmen shared the views of the *ad hoc* group', he chaired and sought to provide them with sufficient 'ammunition' during the hearings to challenge claims of godlessness against them. See Laubach, J, pp. 48–9. The fear of appearing to oppose God was clearly a major factor in some support for Becker; the ability of the anti-Becker forces to provide an alternative interpretation was thus crucial in encouraging support to their side.
90 Committee members also raised similar issues. See Emanuel Celler (D-NY), James Corman (D-Cal), Don Edwards (D-Cal) and Roland Libonati (D-Il).
91 Becker Hearings, p. 937. Also, see testimony of Paul Freund (pp. 1651–71), Wilbur Katz (pp. 813–9), Paul Kauper (pp. 1683–1704) and Philip Kurland (pp. 2152–9).
92 Becker Hearings, pp. 2483–4.
93 Quoted anonymously in Laubach, J., p. 67.

[94] *Cong. Rec.*, 22 March 1966, p. 6478; US Senate. Subcommittee on Constitutional Amendments of the Committee on the Judiciary, Hearings on SJ Res. 148 Relating to Prayer in the Public Schools, 89th Congress, 2nd Sess. (1966), p. 13.

[95] See, for example, testimony of Fr Robert Drinnan (pp. 7–23), Professor Paul Freund (pp. 23–32), and Dr David Hunter (pp. 33–50). For discussion of the Dirksen Hearings, see Laubach, J., pp. 141–54.

[96] For an overview and analysis of the 1966 and 1971 debates and their political context from someone sympathetic to the Supreme Court decisions, see Alley, R., *School Prayer: The Court, the Congress, and the First Amendment* (Buffalo, New York: Prometheus Books, 1994).

[97] Sixth Annual Gallup Poll of Public Attitudes Towards Religion, published in *PDK*, Vol. 56, No. 1 (September 1974), pp. 20–32.

[98] 'Prayer Hearing Begins in House', *NYT*, 23 April 1964, A14.

[99] Quoted in Beaney and Beiser, p. 495.

[100] See Laubach, J., pp. 84–97 and Beaney and Beiser, pp. 499–503.

[101] Mitau, G. T., p. 145. See Birkby, R., 'The Supreme Court and the Bible Belt: Tennessee Reaction to the *Schempp* Decision', *Midwest Journal of Political Science*, Vol. 10 (August 1966), pp. 304–15; Muir, Jr, W., *Prayer in the Public Schools* (London and Chicago: University of Chicago Press, 1967); Dolbeare, K. and P. Hammond, *The School Prayer Decisions: From Court Policy to Local Practice* (Chicago: University of Chicago Press, 1971).

[102] Muir, Jr, W., p. 120.

[103] *Chamberlain v. Dade County Board of Public Instruction* 171 So. 2d 535 (1964), 377 US 402 (1964). The other cases were *Johns v. Allen* 231 F.Supp. 852 (1964); *Adams v. Engelking* 232 F.Supp. 666 (1964); *Attorney General v. School Committee of North Brookfield* 199 N.E. 2d 553 (1964); *Read v. Van Houen* 237 F. Supp. 48 (1965); *Sills v. Board of Education of Hawthorne* 200 A. 2d 615 (1964); *Stein v. Oshinsky* 382 US 957 (1964), 348 F.2d 999 (1965); *James N. Snavely et al v. Cornwall-Lebanon Suburban Joint School District*, Civil Action No. 8355, US District Court for the Middle District of Pennsylvania, Lewisburg, Pennsylvania (the case was eventually dismissed after the Board of Education agreed to end Bible reading and prayer activities in classrooms).

[104] *DeSpain v. DeKalb County Community School District No. 428* 285 F.Supp. 655 (1966) (striking down a prayer from which all references to God had been removed); *Commissioner of Education v. School Committee of Leyden* 267 NE 2d 226 (Mass., 1971) and *State Board of Education v. Board of Education of Netcong* 270 A.2d 412 (NJ, 1970) (striking down student-initiated school prayer and prayer activities); *La Rocca v. Board of Education of Rye City School District* 406 NYS 2d 348 (App. Div., 1978); *Lynch v. Indiana State University Board of Trustees* 378 NE 2d 900 (Ind. App., 1978) *cert. denied* 441 US 946 (1979) (in which teachers violating the Court rulings were disciplined or dismissed).

[105] See, for example, *La Rocca v. Board of Education of Rye City School District* 406 NYS 2d 348 (App. Div., 1978); *Lynch v. Indiana State University Board of Trustees* 378 NE 2d 900 (Ind. App., 1978) *cert. denied* 441 US 946 (1979).

[106] 'Bay State Governor Vetoes Bill Allowing School Prayer', *NYT*, 4 August 1973, A26. Note, however, that his veto was overridden by the Massachusetts House and the bill was ultimately upheld by the Supreme Court in 1979. The challenge

in New Hampshire was dropped when the state attorney general said he would not take a direct role in the case because the state was not named in the suit. The New Hampshire attorney general in question was David Souter, now Justice Souter. For analysis of compliance in New York see Belmar, W., 'School Prayer – Still an Unsettled Controversy', 1 *Columbia Journal of Law and Social Problems* 100 (1965).

[107] Press conference proceedings reported in *Washington Post*, 28 June 1962, A18.

[108] Transcript of President Carter's press conference published in *NYT*, 11 April 1979, A16.

Chapter 5

[1] For example, having student-led prayers at the start of the day, abandoning county-wide policies for prayer and Bible reading provisions but unofficially encouraging teachers as individuals to continue the practice. See Dolbeare, K. and P. Hammond, *The School Prayer Decisions: From Court Policy to Local Practice* (Chicago: University of Chicago Press, 1971); Muir, Jr., W., *Prayer in the Public Schools* (London and Chicago: University of Chicago Press, 1967).

[2] See also *Ring v. Grand Forks Public School District* 483 F.Supp. 272 (D.N.D., 1980).

[3] A notation at the bottom of the poster stated: 'The secular application of the Ten Commandments is clearly seen in its adoption as the fundamental legal code of Western Civilization and the Common Law of the United States'. *Stone v. Graham* 449 US 39, 40 (1980).

[4] *Stone v. Graham* 449 US 39, 41 (1980).

[5] This approach elicited two procedural dissents, from Potter Stewart and Burger. Justice William Rehnquist's dissent was the only one to engage with the substantive issues raised.

[6] Senator Jesse Helms (R-NC) introduced a bill into Congress that would abolish the jurisdiction of the US Supreme Court and all federal courts over state laws dealing with 'voluntary prayers in public schools'.

[7] *Congressional Record* (hereafter *Cong. Rec.*), 97th Congress, 1st Sess., especially pp. 27,488–96, 27,895–7.

[8] Reprinted in *Cong. Rec.*, 97th Congress, 1st Sess., 6 November 1981, pp. 26,961–2.

[9] Remarks published in *NYT*, 30 October 1981, A22.

[10] Speaking to the American Bar Association in January 1982, Smith also sought to appeal to conservative lawyers, suggesting all the Administration was attempting to do was 'secure the independence of the judiciary, not undermine it', and thus to protect the legal system and the courts. 'Bar Urged to Join Fight on Politics in the Courts', *NYT*, 26 January 1982, B8.

[11] W. Bright quoted in 'Evangelist Calls for Restoration of Prayer in US Public Schools', *NYT*, 3 July 1980, A14 and 'The Churches Are at Odds Over Yet Another School Prayer Bill', *NYT*, 3 August 1980, E20. It is likely that Bright meant school-sponsored, vocal prayer activities which had been barred by *Engel* and *Schempp*. However, his language did not make that distinction, reinforcing the older perception that the Court had banned even private, silent prayer.

[12] 'Evangelist Calls for Restoration of Prayer in US Public Schools,' *NYT*, 31 July 1980, A14.

[13] See Murray, W., *Let Us Pray: A Plea for Prayer in Our Schools* (New York: William Morrow & Co., Inc., 1995).

[14] 'Bill on School Prayer Stirs Strong Criticism by Religious Leaders', *NYT*, 30 July 1980, A22 and 'Churches at Odds . . .'. What is interesting to note is that both drew heavily on language used by the Supreme Court, implicitly supporting those rulings.

[15] Quoted in *NYT*, 3 August 1980, E20.

[16] See Alley, R., *School Prayer: The Court, the Congress, and the First Amendment* (Buffalo, New York: Prometheus Books, 1994), pp. 187–94. Also important was the shift of the Southern Baptist Convention, long an opponent of such measures, to support a school prayer amendment in 1982. See 'Baptist Meeting Backs School Prayer Amendment', *NYT*, 18 June 1982, B8; 'Southern Baptists Assailed on School Prayer Vote', *NYT*, 25 June 1982, A10; 'The Baptist Switch', *NYT*, 22 June 1982, A27.

[17] Charles Rice, Notre Dame Law School, quoted in 'Congressional Assault on High Court', *NYT*, 30 May 1981, A8; Robert Bork, Yale Law School, quoted in 'The Congress vs. the Courts', *NYT*, 16 March 1981, A16.

[18] See 'The Bar Weighs in as a Friend of the Courts', *NYT*, 16 August 1981, E7 and 'Leading Lawyers Defend the Courts', *NYT*, 25 January 1982, A19.

[19] 'Prayer: An Issue Without an Amen', *NYT*, 20 April 1980, Educ. 3. For Dierenfield's studies see *Religion in American Public Schools* (Washington, DC: Public Affairs Press, 1962); 'The Impact of the Supreme Court Decisions on Religion in Public Schools', *Religious Education*, Vol. 62, No. 5 (September–October 1967), pp. 445–51; 'Religion in Public Schools: Its Current Status', *Religious Education*, Vol. 68, No. 1 (January–February 1973), pp. 96–114.

[20] *NYT*, 20 April 1980, Educ. 3.

[21] 'I know I'm not supposed to', she said, 'but there are so many evil things I've seen in the schools, violence and drugs. When I see a fight about to start, I think it helps to get them to just sit and be calm for a minute. Sometimes I make them say the "Our Father" prayer after me. Sometimes I say just think of the Supreme Being and how much more beautiful it is to live and love'. *NYT*, 20 April 1980, Educ. 3.

[22] 'Prayer in Schools Still At Issue 17 Years After Ruling', *NYT*, 26 December 1980, A20.

[23] See, for example, *Collins v. Chandler Unified School District* 470 F.Supp. 959 (D. Ariz., 1979) (student-initiated prayer in assemblies); *Kent v. Commissioner of Education* 402 N.E. 2d 1340 (Mass., 1980) (daily student-led prayers); *Bradon v. Board of Education of the Guilderland Central School District* (1981) (student-organized prayer groups before the school day); *Lubbock Civil Liberties Union v. Lubbock Independent School District* 669 F. 2d 1038 (5th Cir., 1982) (voluntary prayer); *May v. Cooperman* (1983) (New Jersey moment of silence statute).

[24] 'The First Amendment – Words and Meaning,' *NYT*, 17 February 1980, E19.

[25] Justices Stevens and Powell quoted in 'Three High Court Justices Speak to Lawyers But Shun Controversy', *NYT*, 10 August 1981, A10.

[26] The Helms Amendment was defeated by a 51:48 vote on 24 September 1982, the majority several votes short of the required two-thirds, following two separate filibusters between late August and the end of September 1982 led by Senators Bob Packwood (R-Ore) and Lowell Weicker, Jr (R-Conn).
[27] Transcript of speech published in *NYT*, 7 May 1982, B10.
[28] Quoted in 'Reagan Endorses Voluntary Prayer', *NYT*, 7 May 1982, B10.
[29] 'Sixty Second Debate', *NYT*, 9 May 1982, E5.
[30] *NYT*, 7 May 1982, B10.
[31] Joint statement by the Baptist Joint Committee on Public Affairs, National Coalition for Public Education and Religious Liberty, National Council of Churches, Synagogue Council of America and National Jewish Advisory Council. Quoted in 'Doubts on School Prayer', *NYT*, 8 May 1982, A10.
[32] See 'Baptist Meeting Backs School Prayer Amendment', *NYT*, 18 June 1982, B8; 'Southern Baptists Assailed on School Prayer Vote', *NYT*, 25 June 1982, A10; 'The Baptist Switch,' *NYT*, 22 June 1982, A27.
[33] 'Why should we give Jesse Helms a vote to target people with?' asked David Landau, a lobbyist for the ACLU. Quoted in 'School Prayer Bill Brings New Filibuster in Senate', *NYT*, 17 September 1982, A20.
[34] Reagan's action on tax exemptions was determined by the Supreme Court which upheld the IRS's withholding of tax-exempt status from religious schools which discriminated on racial grounds. See *Bob Jones University and Goldsboro Christian School v. US* 461 US 574 (1983).
[35] Speech reprinted in *Cong. Rec.*, 3 February 1983, pp. 1646–8.
[36] 'US Shuns Clash Over Prayer', *NYT*, 1 March 1983, B4.
[37] In addition, if Congress defeated the measure, Reagan could blame the failure on Congress without losing support for his Administration.
[38] See *Cong. Rec.*, 98th Congress, 2nd Sess., pp. 4318–45.
[39] 'Prayer Campaign Going to Capitol', *NYT*, 4 March 1984, A29.
[40] *Cong. Rec*, 5 March 1984, pp. 4319, 4333, 4342. In response to Weicker, Senator Roger Jepsen (R-Iowa) inadvertently defeated his own argument when he commented: 'If a child can pray in school, then I do not know what we are doing here. We are misinformed and everyone in this body is misinformed and the whole debate is uncertain' (p. 4586).
[41] 'Senate Backers Agree to Wording Changes in Prayer Amendment', *NYT*, 7 March 1984, A11.
[42] 'Strongest Effort Yet to Put Organised Prayer in Schools', *NYT*, 8 March 1984, B18.
[43] 'Alabama Governor Signs Bill on School Prayer', *NYT*, 14 July 1982, A16. The law replaced a statute permitting a moment of silence in the state's public schools.
[44] See 'Mobile Board Opposes School Prayer Lawsuit', *NYT*, 2 August 1982, A10; 'US Judge Bars Alabama School Prayer Law', *NYT*, 10 August 1982, B11; 'Alabama Governor Vows to Ignore Prayer Law', *NYT*, 16 September 1982, A18. For his blatant opposition, James was charged with criminal contempt, see 'Governor of Alabama Charged With Contempt', *NYT*, 27 September 1982, A10.
[45] 'Kean Vetoes Bill on Silent Period in Public Schools', *NYT*, 8 December 1982, B2.

46 Quoted in Irons, P., *The Courage of their Convictions: Sixteen Americans Who Fought Their Way to the Supreme Court* (New York: Penguin, 1990), p. 363.
47 I. Jaffree in Irons, P., p. 375. For Jaffree's recollections of the entire case see pp. 368–378. Jaffree's experience was not unusual; for detailed and disturbing accounts of similar experiences from 1946 to 1996 see Alley, R., *Without A Prayer: Religious Expression in Public Schools* (Amherst, New York: Prometheus Books, 1996).
48 Taken from 'The Question of Silence Raises Voices', *NYT*, 8 December 1982, B1, 4.
49 For supportive statements and the text of the opinion, see *Cong. Rec.*, 98th Congress, 2nd Sess., 26 January 1983, pp. 869–80.
50 'Why Kimmelman is Silent', *NYT*, 6 February 1983, NJ1, 6.
51 Seventeen years, if counting the time between *Schempp* and *Stone* rather than *Jaffree*. See *Gaines v. Anderson* 421 F.Supp. 337 (D. Mass, 1976) (upholding moments of silence); *Duffy v. Las Cruces Public Schools* 557 F.Supp. 1013 (1983); *Beck v. McElrath* 548 F.Supp. 1161 (1982), *May v. Cooperman* 572 F.Supp. 1561 (1983) (striking down moments of silence).
52 In 1985, twenty-five states required or permitted moments of silence in class: Alabama, Arizona, Arkansas, Connecticut, Delaware, Florida, Georgia, Illinois, Indiana, Kansas, Louisiana, Maine, Maryland, Massachusetts, Michigan, New Jersey, New Mexico, New York, North Dakota, Ohio, Pennsylvania, Rhode Island, Tennessee, Virginia and West Virginia. On the background to such laws see Drakeman, D., 'Prayer in Schools: Is New Jersey's Moment of Silence Constitutional?' 35 *Rutgers Law Review* 341 (1982/3).
53 *Wallace v. Jaffree* 472 US 38 (1985).
54 *Wallace v. Jaffree* 472 US 38, 60 (1985).
55 Justices Powell and O'Connor filed concurrences, O'Connor concurring only in the judgment. Dissents were filed by Justices Burger, White and Rehnquist.
56 *Wallace v. Jaffree* 472 US 38, 67–84 (1985) (Justice O'Connor, concurring). *Lynch v. Donnelly* 465 US 688 (1984) involved a challenge to a city-sponsored display of a crèche as part of a more general Christmas display. The Court held that it did not violate the Establishment Clause.
57 *Lynch v. Donnelly* 465 US 668, 690 (1984) (Justice O'Connor, concurring). In the increasingly complex area of Establishment Clause jurisprudence, 'endorsement' came to be known as O'Connor's personal contribution to the debate.
58 Undated draft of Stevens's opinion in Thurgood Marshall Papers (hereafter Marshall Papers), Box 362, Folder 2 (emphasis added).
59 *Wallace v. Jaffree* 472 US 48, 56 (1985) (internal references omitted; emphasis added). Letter from Justice Stevens to Justices Brennan, Marshall, and Blackmun, 8 May 1985, Marshall Papers, Box 362, Folder 2.
60 Memorandum from Chief Justice Burger to Justice Stevens, 28 February 1985. Marshall Papers, Box 362, Folder 2.
61 'Although there is nothing definite at this point', wrote Stevens, 'I think there is a strong possibility that this change would enable Lewis [Powell] to change his vote and to join our opinion'. Memorandum from Justice Stevens to Justices Brennan, Marshall, and Blackmun, 8 May 1985. Marshall Papers, Box 362, Folder 2.

[62] In his dissent, Rehnquist wrote: 'The purpose prong means little if it only requires the legislature to express any secular purpose and omit all sectarian references...', a position not that far from Powell's on this issue. *Wallace v. Jaffree* 472 US 38, 108 (1985).

[63] See *Wallace v. Jaffree* 472 US 38, 55–6 (1985). This was important in light of the District Court's 'remarkable conclusion that the Federal Constitution imposes no obstacle to Alabama's establishment of a state religion'. *Wallace v. Jaffree* 472 US 38, 48 (1985).

[64] *Wallace v. Jaffree* 472 US 38, 63, n. 3 (1985) (Justice Powell, concurring).

[65] Lewis, A., 'Foreword' to Blasi, V. (ed.), *The Burger Court: The Counter-Revolution That Wasn't* (New Haven and London: Yale University Press, 1983), p. ix; Maltz, E., *The Chief Justiceship of Warren Burger, 1969–1986* (Columbia, South Carolina: University of South Carolina Press, 2000), p. 21.

[66] *Wallace v. Jaffree* 472 US 38, 92 (1985) (Justice Rehnquist, dissenting). Lewis, A., p. ix.

[67] *Wallace v. Jaffree* 472 US 38, 106 (1985) (Justice Rehnquist, dissenting); for the full historical debate see 91–106. For this interpretation Rehnquist drew heavily on information provided by James McClellan who argued the case in the District Court. See Irons, P., p. 364.

[68] Marshall's comment reads: 'Unadulterated B.S.!!' Marshall Papers, Box 362, Folder 2. Rehnquist's activism was also evident in the second part of his opinion which challenged the *Lemon* test: although his arguments were similar to those of Burger, Rehnquist was far more direct in his criticism. He noted that '[o]ur Establishment Clause cases have been neither principled nor unified', and suggested, 'the *Everson* "wall" has proved all but useless as a guide to sound constitutional adjudication . . . It should be frankly and explicitly abandoned'. *Wallace v. Jaffree* 472 US 38, 107 (1985) (Justice Rehnquist, dissenting).

[69] *Wallace v. Jaffree* 472 US 38, 82 (1985) (Justice O'Connor, concurring in judgment – internal quotation marks omitted).

[70] Simon, J., *The Center Holds: The Power Struggle Inside the Rehnquist Court* (New York: Simon & Schuster, 1995), p. 227.

[71] Stewart, who dissented in *Schempp*, was also still on the Court in 1980 for *Stone*, where he again dissented, but he had retired by the time *Jaffree* was decided in 1985.

[72] Simon, J., pp. 143–6. See also *Newsweek*, 27 April 1970, p. 28.

[73] See, for example, Blackmun's opinion for the majority in *Roe v. Wade* 410 US 113 (1973).

[74] Schwartz, B., *A History of the Supreme Court* (New York and Oxford: Oxford University Press, 1993), p. 317; Maltz, E., p. 22.

[75] *Wallace v. Jaffree* 472 US 38, 62, 65–6 (1985) (Justice Powell, concurring) and 72–9 (Justice O'Connor, concurring in judgment).

[76] Blasi, V. (ed.), p. 211.

[77] 'Plaintiff in Prayer Suit Says the Suit Hurt His Children', *NYT*, 5 June 1985, B5.

[78] See 'High Court Rules Cities May Put Up Nativity Displays', *NYT*, 6 March 1984, A1, B7; 'Embracing Volatile Church-State Issues', *NYT*, 9 March 1984, A16; 'Church-State Issues to be Sharpened', *NYT*, 6 August 1984, A16. See Cannon III, J., 'First Amendment I', 1984 *Annual Survey of American Law* 265; Levinson, R.,

'Separation of Church and State: And the Wall Came Tumbling Down', 18 *Valparaiso Law Review* 707 (1984); Van Alstyne, W., 'Trends in the Supreme Court: Mr. Jefferson's Crumbling Wall – A Comment on *Lynch v. Donnelly*', 1984 *Duke Law Journal* 770; Katz, N., '*Lynch v. Donnelly*: One Giant Step Over the Wall', 5 *Pace Law Review* 91 (1984/5); 'Leading Cases of the 1983 Term: Establishment of Religion', 98 *Harvard Law Review* 174 (1984).

[79] 'The Court's New Line on Religion Isn't So New', *NYT*, 9 June 1985, E5.

[80] 'Meese, in Bar Group Speech, Criticizes High Court', *NYT*, 10 July 1985, A13.

[81] *NYT*, 10 July 1985, A13.

[82] See *Abington School District v. Schempp* 374 US 203, 237–242 (1963) (Justice Brennan, concurring).

[83] Text of Justice Brennan's speech published in *NYT*, 13 October 1985, A36.

[84] In particular, he referred to the Civil War and the post-war amendments. Excerpts from Justice Stevens's speech published in *NYT*, 26 October 1985, A11.

[85] See 'Newest Judicial Activists Come From the Right', *NYT*, 8 February 1985, E24; 'Not Many Judges Practice What the President Preaches', *NYT*, 29 November 1987, E4; Silverstein, M. and B. Ginsberg, 'The Supreme Court and the New Politics of Judicial Power', *Political Science Quarterly*, Vol. 102, No. 3 (Autumn 1987), pp. 371–88; Maltz, E., 'The Prospects for a Revival of Conservative Activism in Constitutional Jurisprudence', 24 *Georgia Law Review* 629 (1989/90); Glennon, R., 'Will the Real Conservatives Please Stand Up?' 76 *American Bar Association Journal* 49 (1 August 1990); Schwartz, H., 'Is the Rehnquist Court Activist? Yes: A Definite Agenda', 76 *American Bar Association Journal* 32 (1 August 1990). But see Tomasi, T. and J. Veloria, 'All the President's Men? A Study of Ronald Reagan's Appointments to the US Courts of Appeals', 87 *Columbia Law Review* 766 (1987).

Chapter 6

[1] 'Educators Urge Turn to Studies About Religion', *New York Times* (hereafter *NYT*), 2 July 1987, A16.

[2] 'Trend Gaining in Public Schools to Add Teaching About Religion', *NYT*, 19 March 1989, A1, 30.

[3] Rehnquist was elevated to chief justice on the retirement of Burger in 1986.

[4] *Karcher v. May* 484 US 72 (1987). The justices, in an opinion by Justice Sandra Day O'Connor, held that the two legislative leaders who had appealed the lower court decisions had no standing since they were no longer in these positions by the time they filed the suit.

[5] 'Bible and Constitution Clash in a Liberal Land', *NYT*, 27 August 1990, A12.

[6] 'Professors Seek End to Prayers at Ceremonies', *NYT*, 2 December 1990, A60, 62; 'Religion Notes', *NYT*, 21 September 1991, A8.

[7] 'Student Gains in Fight to Bar Pregame Prayer', *NYT*, 8 January 1989, A16; 'Football Prayer Ban Stirring Anger in South', *NYT*, 2 September 1989, A1, 8.

[8] See, for example, *Weist v. Mount Lebanon School District* 320 A.2d 362 (Pa., 1974) *cert. denied* 419 US 967 (1974) (upholding invocation and benediction at graduation ceremonies); *Grossburg v. Deusebio* 380 F.Supp. 285 (E.D. Va., 1974) (prayer at graduation); *Goodwin v. Cross County School District* 394 F.Supp. 417 (E. D. Ark.,

1973) and *Chamberlain v. Dade County Board of Public Instruction* 160 So. 2d 97 (Fla., 1964) (upholding baccalaureate services); *Miller v. Cooper* 244 P.2d 520 (N.M., 1952) (allowing commencement activities to take place in a church).

[9] McCarthy, M., *A Delicate Balance: Church, State, and the Schools* (Bloomington, Indiana: Phi Delta Kappan Educational Foundation, 1983), p. 41.

[10] Justices William Brennan, Thurgood Marshall and Lewis Powell were the three from the *Jaffree* majority who had retired by the time *Lee* reached the Court. The fourth retiree was Chief Justice Burger. The significance of the case can be seen in the fact that thirty-five religious, political and educational organizations filed or joined *amicus* briefs in the case.

[11] 'The concerns that have been raised about [the *Lemon* test] naturally provoke a search, not only perhaps for a different test of the standard which we think we are applying today, but a deeper re-examination about the very concept behind the Establishment Clause. But if I were to go to the Court, I would not go with a personal agenda to foster that; neither would I go in ignorance of the difficulty which has arisen in the administration of *Kurtzman*'. Testimony of David Souter, quoted in 'Supreme Court to Take Fresh Look at Disputed Church-State Boundary', *NYT*, 19 March 1991, A16.

[12] *NYT*, 19 March 1991, A16 and 'The Fight Over God's Place in America's Legacy', *NYT*, 1 November 1991, B10.

[13] However, it should be noted that in oral argument Starr agreed that classroom prayers would be unconstitutional because of the element of coercion present, distinguishing the graduation prayers at issue from such an environment. This was a huge compromise towards those who opposed all school prayer and fundamentally accepted the premise of *Engel* and *Schempp*. Transcript of oral argument of *Lee v. Weisman*, 6 November 1991.

[14] *Marsh v. Chambers* 463 US 783 (1983) (upholding the opening of state legislative sessions with a prayer based on the long history and traditional nature of the practice). The vote was 6:3 with Justices Brennan, Marshall and Stevens dissenting.

[15] *Engel v. Vitale* 370 US 421, 425 (1962) quoted in *Lee v. Weisman* 505 US 577, 588 (1992).

[16] *Lee v. Weisman* 505 US 577, 596 (1992).

[17] Couple, M., 'Not Just a Prayer', *National Law Journal*, Vol. 14, No. 10 (11 November 1991), p. 26, taken from the Harry Blackmun Papers, Box 586, Folder 10 (hereafter Blackmun Papers).

[18] Memorandum from Justice Kennedy to Justice Blackmun, 30 March 1992. See also a memo from Kennedy to Rehnquist confirming the situation to him, also 30 March 1992. Blackmun Papers, Box 586, Folder 6. This was Kennedy's only explanation for his shift. It suggests that he was influenced by *stare decisis* and the strength of the Court's earlier rulings. This implies that despite vocal opposition to the Court's prayer rulings, the principles they embodied had been broadly accepted.

[19] Memorandum from Justice Kennedy to Justice Blackmun, 30 March 1992.

[20] See, for example, *West Virginia Board of Education v. Barnette* 319 US 624 (1943) and *Sherbert v. Verner* 374 US 398 (1963).

[21] *Lee v. Weisman* 505 US 577, 587 (1992).

22 *Lee v. Weisman* 505 US 577, 587 (1992).

23 It was also a way of overlooking Kennedy's dissent in *Allegheny County v. ACLU*, 492 US 573 (1989) in which he had been critical of the *Lemon* test. By ignoring *Lemon*, Kennedy was free to consider *Lee* on its merits rather than procedural issues which allowed him to shift from his apparent accommodationist stance in the earlier case.

24 *Lee v. Weisman* 505 US 577, 589 (1992).

25 See *Lee v. Weisman* 505 US 577, 589–90 (1992). *Abington School District v. Schempp* 374 US 203, 284-7 (1963) (Justice Brennan, concurring).

26 This was in response to a request by O'Connor whose previous opinions had advocated modifying *Lemon*. Blackmun agreed to remove the specific reference to the test. See memoranda between Justice Blackmun and Justice O'Connor, 15 June 1992. Blackmun Papers, Box 586, Folder 6.

27 'Souter Anchoring the Court's New Center', *NYT*, 3 July 1992, A1, 16.

28 See Reverend L. McCausland, quoted in 'Unchanged But Growing as a Justice', *NYT*, 3 July 1992, A16; 'Souter Anchoring the Court's New Center', *NYT*, 3 July 1992, A1, 16.

29 *Lee v. Weisman* 505 US 572, 612, especially n.3 (1992) (Justice Souter, concurring). See also 611 (discussing precedent) and 612 (discussing the 'nonpreferentialist' position).

30 This was Souter's intent. In a memorandum to Justice Kennedy, he wrote: 'I'm happy to join your opinion. Since this is my first Establishment case, I expect to follow my original plan of filing a separate opinion to show where I stand on some, though hardly all, of the points on which such cases turn'. Memorandum from Justice Souter to Justice Kennedy, 15 April 1995. Blackmun Papers, Box 586, Folder 6.

31 *Lee v. Weisman* 505 US 577, 632 (1992) (Justice Scalia, dissenting).

32 *Lee v. Weisman* 505 US 577, 636 (1992) (Justice Scalia, dissenting – internal references omitted).

33 It soon became clear that *Lee* had not definitively answered the question of student prayer at graduation ceremonies. Lower courts divided on the constitutionality of student-initiated prayer. See *Jones v. Clear Creek Independent School District* 930 F2d 416 (5th Cir., 1991) and *Adler v. Duvall County School Board* 206 F3d 1070 (11th Cir., 2000), 250 F3d 1330 (11th Cir., 2001) (finding such prayers constitutional). But see *Doe v. Santa Fe Independent School District* 930 F2d 806 (5th Cir., 1999), *ACLU of New Jersey v. Black Horse Pike Regional Board of Education* 84 F3d 1471 (3rd Cir., 1996), and *Harris v. Joint School District* 41 F3d 447 (9th Cir., 1994) (holding prayers unconstitutional).

34 Among others, the Court rejected appeals in *Roberts v. Madigan* 921 F.2d 1047 (10th Cir., 1990) (fifth-grade teacher in Denver could not keep a Bible on his desk and read it during recess and during students' fifteen-minute silent-reading periods); *Village of Crestwood v. Doe* 917 F.2d 1476 (7th Cir., 1990) (Illinois town that sponsored an Italian-language mass as part of an Italian cultural festival violated the Establishment Clause); *Bishop v. Delchamps* 926 F.2d 1066 (11th Cir., 1991) (University of Alabama could warn a professor to stop telling students about his religious beliefs, including the assertion that the human body was designed by God); *Chabad-Lubavitch et al. v. City of Burlington* 936 F.2d 109

Notes 243

(2nd Cir., 1991) (display of a menorah in a public park in Vermont violated the Constitution because it could not be viewed with other, secular, displays); *Cammack et al. v. Waihee* 944 F.2d 466 (9th Cir., 1991) (twelve states' decision to hold Good Friday as a public holiday did not violate the Constitution); *Costangy v. North Carolina Civil Liberties Union* 947 F.2d 1145 (4th Cir., 1991) (judge in Richmond, Virginia could not issue his own religious invocation at the start of each session).

[35] 'Prayer in Public Schools? It's Nothing New For Many', *NYT*, 22 November 1994, A1, 21.

[36] Challenges included graduation prayers in Illinois, advocated by Pat Robertson; prayer over the school intercom at the beginning of the day in Jackson, Mississippi, where the dismissal of the school principal led to mass student walk-outs, prayer protests and demonstrations outside the state Capitol; a Virginia attempt to use the Bible to teach grammar, history and literature; graduation prayers in New Jersey; and moments of silence in Georgia.

[37] 'Gingrich May Delay School Prayer Vote', *NYT*, 22 November 1994, B7.

[38] In debate on 3 February 1994, Senator Dale Bumpers (D-Ark) argued: 'Everyone knows what these amendments are about. They are designed for political embarrassment to everybody who votes no, so the next time their opponents can say, he voted against voluntary prayer in schools'. *Cong. Rec.*, 103rd Congress, 2nd Sess., p. 1093.

[39] 'Clinton Reaches Out to G.O.P on School Prayer Amendment', *NYT*, 16 November 1994, A1, 16.

[40] 'Clinton Backs off School Prayer Proposal', *NYT*, 23 November 1994, A18.

[41] Clinton suggested the root of the 'misinterpretation' was that he and reporters alike were worn out from weeks of travel when he addressed the prayer issue in Jakarta.

[42] 'Clinton Reaches Out to G.O.P on School Prayer Amendment', *NYT*, 16 November 1994, A1,16.

[43] See reactions from groups including the ACLU, People for the American Way and the United Methodist Church in 'Clinton May Seek Neutral Solution', *Washington Post*, 17 November 1994, A1, 10; 'Some on Right See Tactical Misstep on School Prayer', *NYT*, 19 November 1994, A1, 10; 'Clinton Backs Off School Prayer Proposal', *NYT*, 23 November 1994, A18.

[44] See, for example, the lists provided by Senator Helms in debate on 23 January 1992 (*Cong. Rec.*, 102nd Congress, 2nd Sess., pp. 353–4) and 27 July 1994 (*Cong. Rec.*, 103rd Congress, 2nd Sess., pp. 18,223–4).

[45] The full text of the guidelines can be accessed from the Department of Education website at: http://www2.ed.gov/Speeches/08-1995/religion.html (accessed 5 August 2011). See also Clinton's Memorandum on Religious Expression in the Schools published in *NYT*, 13 July 1995, B10.

[46] Clinton's Memorandum on Religious Expression in the Schools published in *NYT*, 13 July 1995, B10.

[47] 'President Defends a Place for Religion in the Schools', *NYT*, 13 July 1995, A1, B10; 'Clinton Defines Religion's Role in US Schools', *NYT*, 26 August 1995, A1, 8; 'Clinton Says Schools Can't Bar Religion', *Washington Post*, 13 July 1995, A1, 16.

[48] 'School Prayer Anxieties', *NYT*, 13 July 1995, A22.

[49] Quoted *NYT*, 26 August 1995, A1, 8.
[50] Clinton, Bill, *My Life* (London: Hutchinson, 2004), pp. 558–9.
[51] Groups such as the ACLU and Americans United had periodically issued their own guidelines.
[52] Clinton's personal pride in his achievement was obvious in his memoirs: 'When the booklet was issued, it substantially reduced conflict and lawsuits, and in doing so won support across the religious and political spectrum. I had long been working on the issue, having established a White House liaison to faith communities, and signed the Religious Freedom Restoration Act. Near the end of my second term, Professor Rodney Smith, an expert on the First Amendment, said my Administration had done more to protect and advance religious liberty than any since James Madison's. I don't know if that's accurate, but I tried'. Clinton, Bill, p. 661.
[53] Following *Lee*, in 2000 the Court struck down prayer before varsity football games. *Santa Fe Independent School District v. Doe* 530 US 290 (2000).

Chapter 7

[1] The record reveals no clear reason for the University's change in policy regarding Cornerstone since the regulation relied on was passed in 1972. Both sides, however, found support in lower federal court cases: *Keegan v. University of Delaware* 349 A.2d 14 (Del., 1975) favoured Cornerstone's position, *Dittman v. Western Washington University* no. C79-1189V (W.D. Wash., 1980) and *Johnson v. Huntington Beach Union High School District* 68 Cal. App. 3d 1 *cert. denied* 434 US 877 (1977) favoured that of the University.
[2] *Widmar v. Vincent* 454 US 264, 276 (1981). Although the result was 8:1, with Justice White dissenting, Justice Stevens wrote a separate concurrence in which he agreed with the result but disputed what he saw as unnecessary federal intrusion into the University's right to make decisions governing the use of its own facilities.
[3] *Widmar v. Vincent* 454 US 264, 273 n.13 (1981). Justice Harry Blackmun commented on Justice Powell's explicit refusal to address the constitutional clash: 'Well, he tightrope walks fairly well.' Justice Harry Blackmun Papers, Box 342, Folder 6 (first draft, November 1981) (hereafter Blackmun Papers).
[4] *Widmar v. Vincent* 454 US 264, 267 (1981). Powell made it clear, however, that this was not an open public forum as had been used in prior cases, for example, public parks and streets, but that within the limits imposed by the University (that the forum was for students only) the forum was an open one. The distinction would become important in later debates over equal access legislation.
[5] The 'public forum' concept was written into constitutional law by Justice Roberts in *Hague v. Committee for Industrial Organisations (CIO)* 307 US 496 (1937) and extended to university campuses in *Cox v. Louisiana* 379 US 563 (1965); *Police Department of Chicago v. Mosely* 408 US 92 (1972); and *Healy v. James* 408 US 169 (1972). However, the Court has allowed for 'time, place, and manner' restrictions when public spaces are being used, see *Cox v. New Hampshire* 312 US 569 (1941); *Heffron v. International Society for Krishna Consciousness* 455 US 252 (1981); and

Ward v. Rock Against Racism 491 US 781 (1989). For Court protection of students' free speech rights on school grounds see *West Virginia State Board of Education v. Barnette* 319 US 624 (1943) (students may not be required to salute the flag) and *Tinker v. Des Moines* 393 US 503 (1969) (students permitted to wear black armbands in protest against the Vietnam War).

[6] That the case did not do so was further reinforced near the end of the opinion when Powell wrote, 'the State interest asserted here ... is limited by the Free Exercise Clause and in this case by the Free Speech Clause as well. In this constitutional context, we are unable to recognise the State's interest as sufficiently "compelling" to justify content-based discrimination against respondents' religious speech'. *Widmar v. Vincent* 454 US 264, 272 (1981).

[7] *Widmar v. Vincent* 454 US 264, 271 (1981).

[8] *Widmar v. Vincent* 454 US 264, 272, n.11 (1981). For the Eighth Circuit opinion see *Chess v. Widmar* 635 F.2d 1310, 1318 (CA8, 1980). See Leparulo, L., 'The Rights of Student Religious Groups Under the First Amendment to Hold Religious Meetings on the Public University Campus', 33 *Rutgers Law Review* 1008, 1039–40 (1980/1).

[9] See *US v. Seeger* 380 US 163 (1965) and *Welsh v. United States* 398 US 333 (1970). Also, *US v. Ballard* 322 US 78 (1944) (the truth or falsity of religious beliefs may not be judged by a jury at trial).

[10] *Widmar v. Vincent* 454 US 264, 274 (1981).

[11] Although Powell narrowed the scope of this later in the opinion: 'At least in the absence of empirical evidence that religious groups will dominate UMKC's forum, we agree with the Court of Appeals that the advancement of religion would not be the forum's primary effect'. *Widmar v. Vincent* 454 US 264, 275 (1981). Should religious groups constitute a larger proportion of those using the forum, this ruling could be in doubt.

[12] See, for example, *Cantwell v. Connecticut* 310 US 296 (1940); *Murdock v. Commonwealth of Pennsylvania* 319 US 105 (1943); and *Martin v. Struthers* 319 US 141 (1943), all dealing with the rights of Jehovah's Witnesses. Also, *Nietmotko v. Maryland* 340 US 268 (1951); *Sherbert v. Verner* 374 US 398 (1963); and *Thomas v. Review Board of Indiana Employment Security Division* 450 US 707 (1981).

[13] See, for example, *Tilton v. Richardson* 403 US 672 (1971). In *Widmar* the Court expressly refused to address the applicability of their ruling to high school students.

[14] Chief Justice Burger and Justices Thurgood Marshall, William Rehnquist, Stevens and Powell clearly argued for a free speech analysis in conference, while William Brennan and Sandra Day O'Connor raised it in conjunction with other issues. Comments regarding Establishment were made by Burger, O'Connor and Stevens. Blackmun Papers Box 342, Folder 6.

[15] *Widmar v. Vincent* 454 US 264, 282–9 (1981) (Justice White, dissenting); Blackmun Papers Box 342, Folder 6. However, White's argument that religious speech is substantially different from secular speech because of its content, a fact recognized, he claimed, by the Establishment Clause, foreshadowed the debate in *Rosenberger v. the Rector and Visitors of the University of Virginia* 515 US 819 (1995) fourteen years later.

[16] See Blackmun Papers, Box 342, Folder 6.

[17] *Widmar v. Vincent* 454 US 264, 276 ('We limit the holding to the case before us'), 277 ('The basis for our decision is narrow'), 271 n.10, 273, n.13 (1981).

[18] *Congressional Record*, 98th Congress, 1st Sess., 1983, p. 1645 (hereafter *Cong. Rec.*). The bill was S.425. In April, Denton introduced S.1059, a bill similar to the earlier one except providing recourse to the judicial system rather than a cut off of federal funds in instances of violation as proposed in the earlier bill.

[19] *Cong. Rec.*, 98th Congress, 1st Sess., 1983, p. 9811.

[20] Hearings were held by the Senate Committee on the Judiciary on 28 April and 3 August 1983 (hereafter Senate Hearings). House hearings took place on 16 June and 18–20 October 1983, and 28 March 1984 before the Subcommittee on Elementary, Secondary, and Vocational Education (hereafter House Hearings). HR.5345, the version of the bill amended after the committee hearings, was supported in the House 270:151. However, debate was heard under suspension of the rules and a two-thirds majority was required for passage: HR.5345 was eleven votes short.

[21] For debate see *Cong. Rec.*, 98th Congress, 2nd Sess., 1984, pp. 19,211–52.

[22] *Cong. Rec.*, 98th Congress, 2nd Sess., 1984, p. 19,225.

[23] See *Engel v. Vitale* 370 US 421, 435–6 (1962) and *Abington School District v. Schempp* 374 US 203, 224–6 (1963).

[24] House Hearings (1984), p. 35. Traditionally a separationist organization, the Baptist Joint Committee supported a carefully drawn measure that would ensure equal access for truly voluntary student groups.

[25] Senate Hearings, pp. 238, 242–3.

[26] House Hearings, pp. 5–6. Perkins made similar comments throughout the hearings, making clear his opinion that while equal access was acceptable, there was nothing wrong with school prayer either.

[27] House Hearings, pp. 189–97; Senate Hearings pp. 125–30. For Denton's comments see Senate Hearings pp. 2, 29–30, 68.

[28] *Cong. Rec.*, 98th Cong., 2nd Sess., 1984, p. 12,104.

[29] House Hearings, p. 161. See also testimony of Marc Pearl for the American Jewish Congress (p. 18), Francis Zwenig for People for the American Way (p. 54) and Rev. W. W. Finlater for the North Carolina Civil Liberties Union (pp. 84–6).

[30] The first version was found in HR.2732 and S.1079, the second in S.815.

[31] *Cong. Rec.*, 98th Congress, 2nd Sess., 15 May 1984, p. 12,216. See also statements by Representatives William Lehman (D-Fl) and Gary Ackerman (D-NY), p. 22,219. Once again politicians proved unable to debate the issue of religion without recourse to rhetoric. While the tone of the hearings was mostly moderate and thoughtful, in the House debates one of the most common arguments made against the bill was that it would allow 'cults' in schools. Mentioned by name were the Moonies, Hare Krishnas, Satanists, the Ku Klux Klan, witches, pagans, Charles Manson and voodoo. See, for example, comments by Representatives John Weber (R-Minn.) p. 12,062; Sala Burton (D-Cal.) p. 12,216; Don Edwards (D-Cal.) p. 20,937; Parren Mitchell (D-Md) p. 12,217; Gary Ackerman (D-NY) p. 22,219. Ackerman further stated: 'This bill opens the door so wide that not only prayer but the entire church could be moved inside' (p. 22,219).

[32] House Hearings, p. 18. See also Senate Hearings, pp. 255–7.

[33] 'The Unequal Access Bill', *Washington Post*, 6 April 1984, reprinted in *Cong. Rec.*, 98th Congress, 2nd Sess., 11 April 1984, p. 9045.
[34] House Hearings, especially pp. 9–11, 85.
[35] *Cong. Rec.*, 98th Congress, 2nd Sess., 27 June 1984, p. 19,227. See also testimony from the National Education Association before the Senate committee, pp. 201–2.
[36] Senate Hearings, p. 92.
[37] See House Hearings, pp. 166–7. For example, in *Lubbock Independent School District v. Lubbock Civil Liberties Union* 669 F.2d 1068 (1982) the equal access policy came after a decade of school-sponsored religious activities that were challenged by the Lubbock Civil Liberties Union. In *Brandon v. Board of Education* 635 F.2d 971 (2nd Cir., 1980) the court found there was no open forum and the activities occurred during school hours.
[38] House Hearings, p. 43.
[39] See, in particular, testimony by Dean Kelley on behalf of the National Council of Churches (pp. 96–7) and Senator Hatfield p. 2 (House Hearings [1984]). See also Laycock, D., 'Equal Access and Moments of Silence: The Equal Status of Religious Speech By Private Speakers', 81 *Northwestern Law Review* 1 (1986).
[40] House Hearings (1984), p. 2.
[41] House Hearings, p. 104. See also testimony of Representative Trent Lott: 'The equal access concept gives those students who voluntarily so choose the opportunity to discuss the spiritual and moral aspects of their education and their lives' (p. 4).
[42] Senate Hearings, pp. 38–83.
[43] Senate Hearings, pp. 56–7.
[44] See Senate Hearings, pp. 38–83, 148–51, 212–3.
[45] *Cong. Rec.*, 98th Cong., 2nd Sess., 14 May 1983, p. 12,066. But see Green, S., 'The Misnomer of Equality Under the Equal Access Act', 14 *Vermont Law Review* 369, 384 (1989/90).
[46] House Hearings, pp. 35–9; Senate Hearings, pp. 38–83. In fact, no student who opposed equal access testified before either committee: whether this was because none were called or simply that none were willing to testify is unclear from the record.
[47] Senate Hearings, p.38. She made a similar argument in the House Hearings, see p. 39. *Lubbock Independent School District v. Lubbock Civil Liberties Union* 669 F.2d 1038 (1982) (holding that high school was not a public forum and stating: '[w]hile students have First Amendment rights to political speech in public school, sensitive Establishment Clause considerations limit their right to air religious doctrines', at 1048).
[48] See also testimony of Secretary of Education Terrel Bell, Senate Hearings, pp. 26–32.
[49] For testimony of Thornton see House Hearings, pp. 39–40. For Ocker see House Hearings, pp. 16–17 and Senate Hearings, pp. 51–5. See also testimony of Bonnie Bailey, Lisa Bender and Sarah Scanlon, Senate Hearings, pp. 38–50, 62–5.
[50] L. Buzzard on behalf of the Christian Legal Society and Center for Law and Religious Freedom, Senate Hearings, p. 111.

[51] *Brandon v. Board of Education* 635 F.2d 971 (2nd Cir., 1980) (holding the Establishment Clause justified the school's refusal to allow groups to meet and the school did not operate an open forum); *Lubbock Independent School District v. Lubbock Civil Liberties Union* 669 F.2d 1068 (1982) (holding a long history of defiance of the Supreme Court's prayer rulings indicated an unconstitutional purpose behind the equal access policy); *Bender v. Williamsport Area School District* (M.D.Pa, May 12, 1983, slip op. 82-0697) (equal access did not violate the Establishment Clause).

[52] Although there is no direct evidence in the House or Senate hearings, school officials' actions may also have been influenced by concern to avoid expensive lawsuits brought by parents with a misunderstanding of the scope and application of *Engel* and *Schempp*, aided by lawyers looking to challenge the Court's rulings. Officials may have seen their actions or policies as attempts to avoid both unnecessary expense and the community division that was portrayed as extensive after the prayer cases. Claims of 'confusion' were just as likely to have been a cover for such concerns as for attempts to obtain a new ruling from the courts.

[53] House Hearings, p. 19. The need for legislation to provide guidance to lower courts and school officials was expressed to the House subcommittee by Representatives Trent Lott (R-Miss), William Goodling (R-Penn) and Ron Packard (R-Cal). Before the Senate committee the issue was raised by Senators Mark Hatfield (R-Ore) and Strom Thurmond (R-SC) as well as Secretary of Education Bell. In debate on the Senate floor the argument was made most eloquently by Senator Patrick Leahy (D-Vt) *Cong. Rec.*, 89th Cong., 2nd Sess., 27 June 1984, pp. 12,221-2.

[54] See House Hearings, pp. 95–7 (National Council of Churches) and pp. 169–88 (American Lutheran Council).

[55] House Hearings, pp. 17–18, 20–1 (American Jewish Congress), pp. 42–3 (Americans United), pp. 161–3 (American Civil Liberties Union). Senate Hearings, p. 260 (American Jewish Congress), pp. 87–90 (ACLU).

[56] See especially House Hearings, pp. 199–220 and testimony of Marc Pearl (American Jewish Congress), pp. 20–3. Also, testimony of Jack Novick (ACLU), Senate Hearings, pp. 87–92. Although such statements hold no legal significance, they provide an insight into the thinking and intention of those involved in creating the Equal Access Act, which is available to anyone wishing to interpret its meaning. Such statements are the type of evidence McNollgast argued could be taken into account when seeking to understand original intent. McNollgast, 'Legislative Intent: The Use of Positive Political Theory in Statutory Interpretation', 57 *Law and Contemporary Problems* 3 (1994).

[57] See especially testimony of Professor Laurence Tribe, House Hearings (1984), pp. 45–52.

[58] Even the ACLU, one of the staunchest defenders of the Establishment Clause, conceded that on its face the final bill was essentially neutral. Barry Lynn, executive director, wrote: 'it is a very significant improvement over earlier proposals, both in its sensitivity to potential establishment clause problems with religious meetings in public schools and its new protections for a variety of non-religious student groups'. Letter to Senator Hatfield reprinted in *Cong. Rec.*, 98th Congress,

2nd Sess., 27 June 1984, p. 19,232. Although not supporting the bill, and reserving the right to challenge specific applications of it, the ACLU did not actively oppose the Equal Access Act.

[59] As such, compromise might lead to more criticism, not less, as those with strong views on equal access might interpret compromise as 'selling out'.

Chapter 8

[1] See *Brandon v. Board of Education* 635 F.2d 971 (2nd Cir., 1980); *Lubbock Independent School District v. Lubbock Civil Liberties Union* 669 F.2d 1068 (1982); *Bender v. Williamsport Area School District* (M.D.Pa, May 12, 1983, slip op. 82-0697) (equal access did not violate the Establishment Clause); *Nartowicz v. Clayton County School District* 736 F2d. 646 (11th Cir., 1984).

[2] This was not the first case to challenge the constitutionality of the Act. In 1986 the Court heard argument in *Bender v. Williamsport* 475 US 534 (1986) but ultimately rejected the case for lack of standing, never reaching the substantive issues raised.

[3] Chief Justice William Rehnquist, and Justices Harry Blackmun, O'Connor and Byron White formed the plurality in favour of constitutionality, joined in concurrence by Justices Anthony Kennedy and Antonin Scalia. Thurgood Marshall and William Brennan agreed the Act could be constitutional within certain limits. In dissent, Justice John Paul Stevens addressed the issue briefly but asserted that as he decided the case on statutory grounds it was unnecessary to reach the constitutional issue.

[4] The vote on constitutionality was 6:2:1 with Justices Marshall and Brennan concurring only in the result and Justice Stevens in dissent; on applicability the vote was 8:1, again with Stevens in dissent.

[5] *Board of Education of the Westside Community Schools v. Mergens* 496 US 226, 248 (1990).

[6] *Board of Education of the Westside Community Schools v. Mergens* 496 US 226, 250 (1990).

[7] *Board of Education of the Westside Community Schools v. Mergens* 496 US 226, 261 (1990) (Justice Kennedy, with Justice Scalia, concurring in part and in judgment).

[8] *Board of Education of the Westside Community Schools v. Mergens* 496 US 226, 262 (1990) (Justice Marshall, with Justice Brennan, concurring in judgment).

[9] 'Thus the underlying difference between this case and *Widmar* is not that college and high school students have varying capacities to perceive the subtle differences between toleration and endorsement, but rather that the University of Missouri and Westside actually choose to define their respective missions in different ways'. *Board of Education of the Westside Community Schools v. Mergens* 496 US 226, 267 (1990) (Justice Marshall, with Justice Brennan, concurring in judgment).

[10] A school disclaimer of support for any student groups allowed to meet has been argued as sufficient to overcome students' misperceptions of school policy by several commentators. See, for example, Laycock, D., 'Equal Access and Moments of

Silence: The Equal Status of Religious Speech By Private Speakers', 81 *Northwestern Law Review* 1 (1986); Grossman, T., 'The Constitutionality of Student Initiated Religious Meetings on Public School Grounds', 50 *University of Cincinnati Law Review* 740 (1981).

[11] *Board of Education of the Westside Community Schools v. Mergens* 496 US 226, 237 (1990). See Laycock, D., pp. 36–41.

[12] *Board of Education of the Westside Community Schools v. Mergens* 496 US 226, 239 (1990).

[13] *Board of Education of the Westside Community Schools v. Mergens* 496 US 226, 240, 239 (1990) (emphasis in original).

[14] *Board of Education of the Westside Community Schools v. Mergens* 496 US 226, 276 (1990) (Justice Stevens, dissenting).

[15] *Board of Education of the Westside Community Schools v. Mergens* 496 US 226, 276, 291 (1990) (Justice Stevens, dissenting).

[16] Malcolm Stewart, law clerk to Justice Harry Blackmun, summarized the differences in a memo to Blackmun on 21 May 1990, suggesting, 'the Equal Access Act makes a lot more sense as JPS construes it', given the potential for federal intrusion into local school matters and the breadth of alternative definitions. But, he noted, 'at brute dictionary level ... SOC's reading of the word (or nonword) "noncurriculum" is the more plausible'. Justice Harry Blackmun Papers (hereafter Blackmun Papers), Box 549, Folder 9.

[17] But see O'Connor's comment at 496 US 226, 241 (1990): 'Congress clearly sought to prohibit schools from discriminating on the basis of the content of a student group's speech, and that obligation is the price a federally funded school must pay if it opens its facilities to noncurriculum-related student groups'.

[18] The need to ensure religion was not favoured was one of the biggest concerns of the concurrence by Marshall and Brennan. See 496 US 226, 262–70 (1990) (Justice Marshall, with Justice Brennan, concurring).

[19] *Lamb's Chapel v. Center Moriches Union Free School District* 508 US 384 (1993).

[20] *Lamb's Chapel v. Center Moriches Union Free School District* 508 US 384, 389 (1993).

[21] *Lamb's Chapel v. Center Moriches Union Free School District* 508 US 384, 393–4, 392–3 (1993).

[22] In fact, since the case was ostensibly decided on free speech grounds the result alone has little value for a study of the Establishment Clause.

[23] *Lamb's Chapel v. Center Moriches Union Free School District* 508 US 384, 398–9 (1993) (Justice Scalia, with Justice Thomas, concurring in judgment). White's response to Scalia in Footnote 7 read: 'While we are somewhat diverted by Justice Scalia's evening at the cinema ... we return to the reality that there is a proper way to inter an established decision and *Lemon*, however frightening it may be to some has not been overruled' (at 395).

[24] *Lamb's Chapel v. Center Moriches Union Free School District* 508 US 384, 395 (1993).

[25] Scalia wrote to White on 6 May 1993: 'I could not disagree more with John's [Stevens] assertion that it is "settled law" that the endorsement of "religion in general" violates the Establishment Clause. Old dicta may say that, but recent cases hold to the contrary'. Stevens replied to Scalia the same day: 'You may not agree with the reasoning in *Wallace v. Jaffree* ... (1985) but I do not think it

is fairly characterised as "old dicta."' Blackmun Papers, Box 618, Folder 5. The significance of the exchange was brought to the attention of Justice Blackmun by his law clerk who wrote: 'I had not thought it important for you to join the fray, but Justice Souter's clerk asked me to convey to you Justice Souter's concern that Justice White may give in to the Scalia/Thomas/Kennedy position. Your joinder would give Justice White a court and make him far less likely to accept changes'. Similar concerns had clearly been expressed to Justice O'Connor as on 10 May both she and Blackmun wrote to White expressing support for the existing language, even though O'Connor had already joined the majority opinion. This gave White the majority he needed.

[26] See 795 F. Supp. 175, 181–2 (WD Va, 1992) (District Court) and 18 F.3d 269, 279–81 (1994) (Fourth Circuit). For early speculation on how such a case might be handled see Howarth, D. and W. Connell, 'Students' Rights to Organise and Meet for Religious Purposes in the University Context', 16 *Valparaiso Law Review* 103, 141–3 (1981).

[27] *Rosenberger v. The Rector and Visitors of the University of Virginia* (hereafter *Rosenberger v. . . . University of Virginia*) 515 US 819, 845 (1995).

[28] However, of the four filed opinions in the case, only Justice O'Connor in concurrence accepted that *Rosenberger* represented such a clash, arguably making hers the stronger, and more honest, of the opinions. See *Rosenberger v. . . . University of Virginia* 515 US 819, 847 (1995) (Justice O'Connor, concurring).

[29] *Rosenberger v. . . . University of Virginia* 515 US 819, 830–2 (1995). Kennedy's approach also had implications for the Court's free speech jurisprudence. For an introduction, see Waring, R., 'Wide Awake or Half Asleep? Revelations from Judicial Tailings Found in *Rosenberger v. University of Virginia*', 17 *Northern Illinois University Law Review* 223 (1997).

[30] *Rosenberger v. . . . University of Virginia* 515 US 819, 835, 838–9 (1995).

[31] *Rosenberger v. . . . University of Virginia* 515 US 819, 840 (1995).

[32] *Rosenberger v. . . . University of Virginia* 515 US 819, 842 (1995).

[33] *Rosenberger v. . . . University of Virginia* 515 US 819, 840, 842–4 (1995).

[34] It also made it possible for the Court to sidestep, again, the issue of a clash between First Amendment principles by focusing on one to the exclusion of the other. See Bycroft, H., 'Ready – Aim – Fire! The Supreme Court Continues its Assault on the Wall of Separation in *Rosenberger*', 31 *Tulsa Law Journal* 533 (1996) (criticizing this approach).

[35] *Rosenberger v. . . . University of Virginia* 515 US 819, 868 (1995) (Justice Souter et al., dissenting). The distinction between secular speech and religious speech had earlier been raised by White in dissent in *Widmar*.

[36] See *Rosenberger v. . . . University of Virginia* 515 US 819, 865–76 (1995). See Brown, B., 'A Jeffersonian Nightmare: The Supreme Court Launches a Confused Attack on the Establishment Clause', 31 *Harvard Civil Rights and Civil Liberties Law Review* 257 (1996); Nault, C., 'Bridging the Separation of Church and State: How *Rosenberger* Threatens Religious Liberty', 70 *Southern California Law Review* 1049 (1997).

[37] *Rosenberger v. . . . University of Virginia* 515 US 819, 886 (1995) (Justice Souter et al., dissenting). Unlike the majority, the dissenters did not consider payment to the printer to be a break in the chain between state and religion since the

funds were specifically for printing *Wide Awake* and could not be used for any alternative purpose unlike, for example, the tax deduction in *Mueller*. See 880–9, also rejecting the claim that the Student Activities Fund was like a public forum or street corner since dollars, unlike street corners, are not available to all.

[38] See Bycroft, H., pp. 533–5, 555–7.

[39] In Justice Black's Papers at the Library of Congress, the files on *Engel* contain five boxes of letters sent to the Justice in response to the case (Boxes 354–8). Justice Blackmun's Papers include two boxes of heavily critical responses to the Court's decision in *Lee* despite the fact that he did not write the opinion (Boxes 586–7). In equal access cases there is barely a handful of responses to the rulings.

[40] This is not to suggest that there was no opposition to the Court's rulings. The Anti-Defamation League and the American Jewish Congress opposed Reagan's signing of the Equal Access Act: Theodore Mann, president of the AJC, pledged to bring a lawsuit if the Act became law (see 'Senate Backs Religious Meetings in High Schools', *NYT*, 28 June 1984, A13); both groups and the ACLU filed *amicus* briefs in *Mergens* supporting the school; and many strict separationist groups spoke out about the ruling in *Rosenberger* (see 'Ruling on Religion', *NYT*, 30 June 1995, A1, 24 and 'Victory on Religion Rulings Was Limited, Groups Say', *NYT*, 1 July 1995, A7), but none of it was of the scale and scope of opposition to school prayer and school aid decisions.

[41] See *NYT*, 1 July 1995, A7. For example, Jay Sekulow, legal counsel for the conservative American Center for Law and Justice, argued that the Court should have provided more specific protections for religious activities by students.

[42] Admittedly the results may have been the consequence of the justices' philosophical positions, but the results generally receive most attention and thus divert attention away from the reasoning.

Conclusion

[1] Mr Dooley, created by Finlay Peter Dunne, quoted in Levy, L., *The Establishment Clause: Religion and the First Amendment* (London and Chapel Hill: University of North Carolina Press, 2nd edn., revised, 1994), p. xiv.

[2] Specifically, compare Justice Black's majority opinion in *Everson v. Board of Education* (330 US 1 [1947]) with his dissent in *Board of Education v. Allen* (392 US 236, 250 [1968]) and compare both to Justice White's majority opinion in *Allen* 392 US 236 (1968). Also see *Allen* where five separate opinions were filed.

[3] See *Everson* 330 US 1, 6–7 (1947) ('Changing local conditions create new local problems . . .') and *Allen* 392 US 236, 247–8 (1968) ('. . . the continued willingness to rely on private school systems . . . strongly suggests that a wide segment of informed opinion . . . has found that those schools do an acceptable job of providing secular education to their students.').

[4] *Abington School District v. Schempp* 374 US 203, 222 (1963).

[5] In addition, growing opposition to student demonstrations and anti-war protests and the election of Richard Nixon as president in November 1968 indicated

that the country was becoming more conservative and moving away from the liberalism of the decade.

[6] Justices Rehnquist and White and Chief Justice Burger were sympathetic to accommodationist ideas; Justices Brennan, Marshall and Stevens advocated separationism. This left Justices Blackmun, Powell and Stewart in the centre. The importance of this moderate group is clear from the cases decided: they wrote the majority opinion or held the balance of the majority in 5:4 decisions in *Stone v. Graham* 449 US 39 (1980), the Ten Commandments case; *Widmar v. Vincent* 454 US 263 (1981) on equal access; and all the school aid cases except *Mueller v. Allen* 463 US 388 (1983). Powell wrote for the majority in *Committee for Public Education and Religious Liberty v. Nyquist* 413 US 756 (1973) (constitutionality of tuition reimbursement to parents of religious school students and maintenance and repair grants to religious schools) and *Widmar*, Stewart in *Meek v. Pittenger* 421 US 349 (1975) (textbook loans, loans of instructional materials, provision of auxiliary services, and the loan of instructional equipment to religious schools and their students) and Blackmun in *Wolman v. Walter* 433 US 229, 244 (1977) (textbook loans, testing and scoring services, diagnostic, therapeutic, guidance and remedial services, loans of instructional materials and equipment and reimbursement for the cost of field trips). In *Stone, Lemon v. Kurtzman* 403 US 602 (1971) (salary reimbursement and purchase of secular services programmes), *Aguilar v. Felton* 473 US 402 (1985) (remedial education services to religious school students) and *Grand Rapids School District v. Ball* 473 US 373 (1985) (remedial and enrichment classes held on religious school grounds) the three voted together to guarantee the majority. In *Mueller*, Powell supported the tax deduction while Blackmun opposed it.

[7] See almost any of the Burger Court's school aid cases and *Widmar v. Vincent* 454 US 264 (1981) for the Court's discussion of the significance of the age of the students and the balance of religious and secular groups on the University campus. This approach also continued the Court's refusal to accept strict separation: under that approach, no such analysis would have been required.

[8] The on-campus/off-campus debate was particularly important in school aid cases where the justices were always mindful of the religious nature of the schools receiving the aid. The idea of religious schools as 'pervasively sectarian' was expressed frequently in these cases.

[9] As on the Burger Court, central to both *Rosenberger* and *Agostini*, were the two swing votes: Justice Kennedy wrote for the majority in *Rosenberger*, Justice O'Connor in *Agostini*.

[10] Memorandum from Justice Kennedy to Justice Blackmun, 30 March 1992. See also a memo from Kennedy to Rehnquist confirming the situation to him, also 30 March 1992. Justice Harry Blackmun Papers, Box 586, Folder 6.

[11] This seems especially likely in light of Scalia's sharp dissent in *Lee* (505 US 577, 631–46): it is unlikely that such language would have been present in a majority opinion.

[12] *Wolman v. Walter* 433 US 229, 263 (1977) (Justice Powell, concurring in part and dissenting in part).

[13] *Lemon v. Kurtzman* 403 US 602, 614 (1971).

[14] This is especially clear when considering that the Court never found an unconstitutional purpose behind a challenged school aid programme even when striking down the same programme because of an unconstitutional effect.

[15] See *Clark v. Dallas Independent School District* 806 F.Supp. 116 (N.D. Texas 1992); *Sease v. School District of Philadelphia* 811 F.Supp. 183 (E.D. Pa 1993); *Bronx Household of Faith v. Community School District No. 10* 127 F3d 207 (2d Cir. 1997).

Bibliography

Primary Sources

Archive Resources

(Courtesy of the Manuscript Division, Library of Congress, Washington, DC)
Justice Harold Burton Papers
Justice Harry Blackmun Papers
Justice Hugo Black Papers
Justice Thurgood Marshall Papers
Justice Wiley Rutledge Papers
Justice William Brennan Papers
Justice William Douglas Papers

Government Hearings

Federal – House

US Congress. House of Representatives. Subcommittee No. 1 of the Committee on Education and Labor. Hearings on Bills having for their object the granting of federal aid for educational purposes. 80th Congress, 1st Sess. (1947).

US Congress. House of Representatives. Committee on the Judiciary. Hearings on Proposed Amendments to the Constitution Relating to Prayers and Bible Reading in the Public Schools. 88th Congress, 2nd Sess. (1964).

US Congress. House of Representatives. Subcommittee on Elementary, Secondary, and Vocational Education of the Committee on Education and Labor. Hearings on HR.2732: To provide access and opportunity to students in public schools and public colleges and universities who wish to meet voluntarily for religious purposes. 98th Congress, 1st Sess. (1983).

US Congress. House of Representatives. Subcommittee on Elementary, Secondary, and Vocational Education of the Committee on Education and Labor. Hearings on HR.4996: To provide that no federal education funds may be obligated or expended to any state or local educational agency which discriminates against any meetings of students in public secondary schools who wish to meet voluntarily for religious purposes. 98th Congress, 2nd Sess. (1984).

Federal – Senate

US Congress. Senate. Subcommittee of the Committee on Labor and Public Welfare. Hearings on Bills relative to federal aid to education. 80th Congress, 1st Sess. (1947).

US Congress. Senate. Subcommittee on Constitutional Amendments of the Committee on the Judiciary, Hearings on SJ Res. 148 Relating to Prayer in the Public Schools. 89th Congress, 2nd Sess. (1966).

US Congress. Senate. Committee on the Judiciary. Hearings on S.815 and S.1059, bills addressing the statutory protection of the right of students to meet voluntarily on public school grounds during extracurricular periods for religious purposes. 98th Congress, 1st Sess. (1983).

Government Reports

Federal

Congressional Record (1947–1998).

After Aguilar v. Felton: *Chapter 1 Services to Nonpublic Schoolchildren, A Report Prepared for the House Subcommittee on Elementary, Secondary, and Vocational Education of the Committee on Education and Labor* (March 1986).

Corazzini, Arthur, *The Non-Catholic Private Schools* (Report to the President's Commission on School Finance, 1972).

Economic Problems of Nonpublic Schools: A Report to the President's Commission on School Finance (1972).

Iannaccone, L., *Political, Social, and Cultural Constraints Upon Financing Improved Urban Education and Proposals to Overcome Them* (Report to the President's Commission on School Finance, 1972).

The Notre Dame Report to the President's Commission on School Finance (1972).

President Clinton's Guidelines on Religious Expression in Public Schools (1995).

Review of Existing State School Finance Programs: A Commission Staff Report (Report to the President's Commission on School Finance, 1972).

State

Moral and Spiritual Values in Education (Los Angeles City Schools Publication, No. 402, 1944–1945).

Moral and Spiritual Values in Education (Frankfort, KY: Department of Education, Vol. XVII, No. 11, January 1950).

Moral and Spiritual Values in Education (Frankfort, KY: Department of Education, Vol. XVIII, No. 8, October 1950).

Moral and Spiritual Values in Education (Albany, NY: University of the State of New York, 1951).

Moral and Spiritual Values in the Public Schools (Frankfort, KY: Department of Education, Vol. XIX, No. 12, February 1952).

Nickell, Vernon, *Supreme Court Decisions Concerning Reading of the Bible and Religious Education in the Public Schools* (Springfield, IL: Superintendent of Public Instruction and Board of Education, 1952).

Page, Ray, *Supreme Court Decisions Concerning Reading of the Bible and Religious Education in the Public Schools* (Springfield, IL: Superintendent of Public Instruction and Board of Education, 1963).

Promising Practices in Kentucky Schools (Frankfort, KY: Department of Education, Vol. XIX, No. 6, August 1951).

Religion in the Curriculum: A Report from the ASCD Panel on Religion in the Curriculum (Alexandria, VA: Association for Supervision and Curriculum Development, 1987).

Newspapers, Magazines, and Journals

New York Times (1940–2000)
Phi Delta Kappan (1940–1998)
Washington Post (1940–2000)

Individual Articles

Deedy, J., "Should Catholic Schools Survive?" *The New Republic*, 13 March 1971.

Degler, C., "Why Not Aid to Parochial Schools?" *Vassar Alumnae Magazine*, 47, February 1963, 2–7.

"Has the Church Lost Its Soul?" *Newsweek*, 4 October 1971.

Martin, S., "Is Catholic Schooling Providing Something Public Schools Cannot?" *America*, 162(20), 26 May 1990, 520–2.

Murnion, P., "The Future of the Church in the Inner City," *America*, 163(19), 15 December 1990, 478–85.

"Still Unfinished Business in American Education," *NEA (National Education Association) Journal*, 33(3), March 1948, 143–6.

"The Court Decision and the School Prayer Furore," *Newsweek*, 9 July 1962, 44.

"TRB from Washington," *The New Republic*, 147(2), 9 July 1962, 2.

"Tuition Tax Credits: Now or Never," *America*, 13 December 1980, 380–1.

Legal References

Oral Argument

Agostini v. Felton, 15 April 1997.
Lee v. Weisman, 6 November 1991.

Briefs (US Records and Briefs . . .)

330 US 1 Everson v. Board of Education of Ewing Township
Brief for Appellant
Brief for Appellees
Brief on behalf of the General Council of 7th Day Adventists and Baptist Joint Committee on Public Relations

Brief on behalf of the National Councils of Catholic Men and Women
370 US 421 (1962) *Engel v. Vitale*
Brief for Petitioners
Brief of Respondents
374 US 203 (1963) *Abington School District v. Schempp*
Brief for Appellants (*Schempp*)
Brief for Appellees (*Schempp*)
Brief of Respondents (*Murray v. Curlett*)
Petitioners' Brief (*Murray v. Curlett*)
472 US 38 *Wallace v. Jaffree*
Brief of Appellant
515 US 819 (1995) *Rosenberger v. the Rector and Visitors of the University of Virginia*
Brief of Respondents

Secondary Sources

Articles

Adams, T. Jonathan, "Interpreting State Aid to Religious Schools Under the Establishment Clause: *Zobrest v. Catalina Foothills School District*," 72 *North Carolina Law Review* 1039 (1994).

Areen, Judith, "Public Aid to Nonpublic Schools: A Breach in the Sacred Wall?" 22 *Case Western Reserve Law Review* 230 (1970–1971).

Audi, Robert, "The Place of Religious Argument in a Free and Democratic Society," 30 *San Diego Law Review* 677 (1993).

Avins, Alfred, "Incorporation of the Bill of Rights: The Crosskey-Fairman Debates Revisited," 6 *Harvard Journal on Legislation* 1 (1968).

Baer, Jr., Richard, "The Supreme Court's Discriminatory Use of the Term 'Sectarian'," 6 *Journal of Law and Politics* 449 (1990).

Ball, William, "The School Prayer Case: The Dilemma of Disestablishment," 8 *Catholic Lawyer* 182 (1962).

Ball, William, "The School Prayer Case: What Course for the Future?" 8 *Catholic Lawyer* 286 (1962).

Beaney, William, and Edward Beiser, "Prayer and Politics: The Impact of *Engel* and *Schempp* on the Political Process," 13 *Journal of Public Law* 475 (1964).

Bellah, Robert, "Civil Religion in America," *Daedalus* 40–56 (Winter 1967) reprinted in 34(4) (Fall 2005).

Belmar, Warren, "School Prayer – Still an Unsettled Controversy," 1 *Columbia Journal of Law and Social Problems* 100 (1965).

Bennett, Robert, "Judicial Activism and the Concept of Original Intent," 69 *Judicature* 219 (1985/1986).

Benson, John, "The Polls: A Rebirth of Religion?" 45(4) *Public Opinion Quarterly* 576–585 (Winter 1981).

Berg, Michael, "The Religious Right, Constitutional Values, and the Lemon Test," 37 *Annual Survey of American Law* 37 (1995).

Berg, Thomas, "Religion Clause Anti-Theories," 72 *Notre Dame Law Review* 693 (1997).

Berg, Thomas, "Anti-Catholicism and Modern Church-State Relations," 33 *Loyola University of Chicago Law Journal* 121 (2001).

Berger, Raoul, "Original Intent: Bittker v. Berger," 1991 *Brigham Young University Law Review* 1201 (1991).

Birkby, Robert, "The Supreme Court and the Bible Belt: Tennessee Reaction to the "Schempp" Decision," 10(3) *Midwest Journal of Political Science* 304–319 (1966).

Bishop, George, "Trends: Americans' Belief in God," 63(3) *Public Opinion Quarterly* 421–434 (Autumn 1999).

Bittker, Boris, "The Bicentennial of the Jurisprudence of Original Intent: The Recent Past," 77 *California Law Review* 235 (1989).

Black, Hugo, "The Bill of Rights," 35 *New York University Law Review* 865 (1960).

Bork, Robert, "Neutral Principles and Some First Amendment Problems," 47 *Indiana Law Review* 1 (1971).

Boucher, Jr., Robert, and Jeffrey Segal, "Supreme Court Justices as Strategic Decision Makers: Aggressive Grants and Defensive Denials on the Vinson Court," 57(3) *The Journal of Politics* 824–837 (1995).

Brennan, T., "Natural Rights and the Constitution: The Original "Original Intent"," 15 *Harvard Journal of Law and Public Policy* 965 (1992).

Brenner, Saul, and Marc Steir, "Retesting Segal and Spaeth's Stare Decisis Model," 40(4) *American Journal of Political Science* 1036–1048 (1996).

Brown, Ben, "A Jeffersonian Nightmare: The Supreme Court Launches a Confused Attack on the Establishment Clause," 31 *Harvard Civil Rights and Civil Liberties Law Review* 257 (1996).

Bycroft, Howard, "Ready – Aim – Fire! The Supreme Court Continues its Assault on the Wall of Separation in *Rosenberger*," 31 *Tulsa Law Journal* 533 (1996).

Calinger, Adam, "Original Intent and the Ten Commandments: Giving Coherency to Ten Commandments Jurisprudence," 3 *Georgetown Journal of Law and Public Policy* 257 (2005).

Cannon III, John, "First Amendment I," *Annual Survey of American Law* 265 (1984).

Catteral, James and Henry Levin, "Public and Private Schools: Evidence on Tuition Tax Credits," 55(2/3) *Sociology of Education* 144–151 (1982).

Chadsky, Mark, "State Aid to Religious Schools: From *Everson* to *Zelman*, A Critical Review," 44 *Santa Clara Law Review* 699 (2003).

Chaves, Mark, "Religious Congregations and Welfare Reform: Who Will Take Advantage of 'Charitable Choice'?" 64(6) *American Sociological Review* 836–846 (1999).

Choper, Jesse, "The Free Exercise Clause: A Structural Overview and an Appraisal of Recent Developments," 27 *William and Mary Law Review* 943 (1986).

Chopko, Mark, "Religious Access to Public Programs and Governmental Funding," 60 *George Washington Law Review* 645 (1992).

Chopko, Mark, "Vouchers Can Be Constitutional," 31 *Connecticut Law Review* 945 (1999).

Clegg, Jr., Ambrose, "Church Groups and Federal Aid to Education, 1933–1939," 4(3) *History of Education Quarterly* 137–154 (1964).

Conkle, Daniel, "Different Religions, Different Politics: Evaluating the Role of Competing Religious Traditions in American Politics and Law," 10 *Journal of Law and Religion* 1 (1993/1994).

Cord, Robert, "Church-State Separation: Restoring the "No Preference" Doctrine of the First Amendment," 9 *Harvard Journal of Law and Public Policy* 129 (1986).

Costanzo, Joseph, "Prayer in Public Schools," 8 *Catholic Lawyer* 269 (1962).

Coyle, P., "The Prayer Pendulum," 81 *ABA Journal* 62–66 (1995).

Curtis, Michael, "Still Further Adventures of the Nine-Lived Cat: A Rebuttal to Raoul Burger's Reply on Application of the Bill of Rights to the States," 62 *North Carolina Law Review* 517 (1984).

Dahl, Robert, "Decision Making in a Democracy: The Supreme Court as a National Policy Maker," 6 *Journal of Public Law* 279 (1957).

Davis, Jerome, "The Social Action Pattern of the Protestant Religious Leader," 1(1) *American Sociological Review* 105–114 (1936).

DeForrest, Mark, "An Overview and Evaluation of State Blaine Amendments: Origins, Scope, and First Amendment Concerns," 26 *Harvard Journal of Law and Public Policy* 551 (2003).

Dent, Jr., George, "Religious Children, Secular Schools," 61 *Southern California Law Review* 864 (1988).

Devins, Neal, "Fundamentalist Christian Educators v. State: An Inevitable Compromise," 60 *George Washington Law Review* 818 (1992).

Dierenfield, Richard, "The Impact of the Supreme Court Decisions on Religion in Public Schools," 62(5) *Religious Education* 445–451 (1967).

Dierenfield, Richard, "Religion in Public Schools: Its Current Status," 68(1) *Religious Education* 96–114 (1973).

Dolgin, Janet, "Religious Symbols and the Establishment of a National 'Religion'," 39 *Mercer Law Review* 495 (1988).

Dorsen, Norman and Charles Simms, "The Nativity Scene Case: An Error of Judgment," *University of Illinois Law Review* 837 (1985).

Drake, William, "God-State Idea in Modern Education," 3(2) *History of Education Quarterly* 81–98 (1963).

Drakeman, Donald, "Prayer in Schools: Is New Jersey's Moment of Silence Constitutional?" 35 *Rutgers Law Review* 341 (1982/1983).

Epstein, Lee, Andrew Martin, Kevin Quinn, and Jeffrey Segal, "Ideological Drift Among Supreme Court Justices: Who, When, and How Important?" 101 *Northwestern University Law Review* 1483 (2007).

Esbeck, Carl, "A Constitutional Case for Governmental Cooperation With Faith-Based Social Service Providers," 46 *Emory Law Journal* 1 (1997).

Esbeck, Carl, "Myths, Miscues, and Misconceptions: No-Aid Separationism and the Establishment Clause," 13 *Notre Dame Journal of Law, Ethics and Public Policy* 285 (1999).

Fairman, Charles, "Does the Fourteenth Amendment Incorporate the Bill of Rights?" 2 *Stanford Law Review* 1 (1949).

Farnsworth, Ward, "The Use and Limits of Martin-Quinn Scores to Assess Supreme Court Justices, with Special Attention to the Problem of Ideological Drift," 101 *Northwestern University Law Review* 1891 (2007).

Ferejohn, John, and Barry Weingast, "A Positive Theory of Statutory Interpretation," 12 *International Review of Law and Economics* 263 (1992).

Formicola, Jo Renee, "*Everson* Revisited: 'This Is Not . . . Just a Little Case Over Bus Fares'," 28(1) *Polity* 49–66 (Fall 1995).

Frankfurter, Felix, "Memorandum on 'Incorporation' of the Bill of Rights into the Due Process Clause of the Fourteenth Amendment," 78 *Harvard Law Review* 746 (1965).
Freund, Paul, "Public Aid to Parochial Schools," 82 *Harvard Law Review* 1680 (1969).
Furth, Alexandra, "Secular Idolatry and Sacred Traditions: A Critique of the Supreme Court's Secularization Analysis," 146 *University of Pennsylvania Law Review* 579 (1998).
Galloway, Jr., Russell, "The October 1984 Term: A Court Watcher's Perspective," 26 *Santa Clara Law Review* 355 (1986).
Garver, Eugene, "Why Should Anybody Listen? The Rhetoric of Religious Argument in Democracy," 36 *Wake Forest Law Review* 353 (2001).
Garvey, John, "Freedom and Equality in the Religion Clauses," 193 *Supreme Court Review* 198–209 (1981).
Garvey, John, "Another Way of Looking at School Aid," *Supreme Court Review* 61 (1985).
Giannella, Donald, "Religious Liberty, Nonestablishment and Doctrinal Development. Part II. The Nonestablishment Principle," 81 *Harvard Law Review* 513 (1968).
Giannella, Donald, "*Lemon* and *Tilton*: The Bitter and the Sweet of Church-State Entanglement," *Supreme Court Review* 147 (1971).
Glennon, Robert, "Will the Real Conservatives Please Stand Up?" 76 *American Bar Association Journal* 49 (1990).
Gordon, Glenn, "*Lynch v. Donnelly*: Breaking Down the Barriers to Religious Displays," 71 *Cornell Law Review* 185 (1985/1986).
Green, Steven, "The Misnomer of Equality Under the Equal Access Act," 14 *Vermont Law Review* 369 (1989/1990).
Greenawalt, Kent, "*Quo Vadis*: The Status and Prospects of 'Tests' Under the Religion Clauses," *Supreme Court Review* 323 (1995).
Greene, Abner, "The Political Balance of the Religion Clauses," 102 *Yale Law Journal* 1611 (1993).
Greenhouse, Linda, "Justices Who Change: A Response to Epstein et al." 101 *Northwestern University Law Review* 1885 (2007).
Grossman, Thomas, "The Constitutionality of Student Initiated Religious Meetings on Public School Grounds," 50 *University of Cincinnati Law Review* 740 (1981).
Hamilton, Marci, "Power, the Establishment Clause, and Vouchers," 31 *Connecticut Law Review* 807 (1999).
Hammack, David, "Private Organizations, Public Purposes: Nonprofits and Their Archives," 76(1) *Journal of American History* 181–191 (1989).
Hersman, Nancy, "*Lynch v. Donnelly*: Has the *Lemon* Test Soured?" 19 *Loyola of Los Angeles Law Review* 133 (1986).
Hopkins, John, "State Transportation of Students to Parochial Schools: The *Everson* Case," 36 *Kentucky Law Journal* 328 (1947/1948).
Howarth, Don, and William Connell, "Students' Rights to Organise and Meet for Religious Purposes in the University Context," 16 *Valparaiso Law Review* 103, 141–143 (1981).

Hudson, Carol, "From *Everson* to *Davey*: The Road is Long, With Many a Winding Turn, That Leads us to Who Knows Where, Who Knows When," 40 *Tulsa Law Review* 343 (2004/2005).

Hutson, James, "The Creation of the Constitution: The Integrity of the Documentary Record," 65 *Texas Law Review* 1 (1986).

Kalir, Erez, "Book Note: Is the Constitution "Godless" Or Just Nondenominational?" 106 *Yale Law Journal* 917 (1996).

Karst, Kenneth, "Equality As a Central Principle in the First Amendment," 43 *University of Chicago Law Review* 20 (1975).

Kaselonis, Jr., Raymond, "*Everson* and "The Wall of Separation Between Church and State": The Supreme Court's Flawed Interpretation of Jefferson's Letter to the Danbury Baptists," 17 *Regent University Law Review* 101 (2004/2005).

Katz, Naomi, "*Lynch v. Donnelly*: One Giant Step Over the Wall," 5 *Pace Law Review* 91 (1984/1985).

Kauper, Paul, "*Everson v. Board of Education*: A Product of the Judicial Will," 15 *Arizona Law Review* 307 (1973).

Kauper, Paul, "The Supreme Court and the Establishment Clause: Back to *Everson*?" 25 *Case Western Reserve Law Review* 107 (1974–1975).

Kemerer, Frank, "Reconsidering the Constitutionality of Vouchers," 30 *Journal of Law and Education* 435 (2001).

Kirby, James, "*Everson* to *Meek* to *Roemer*: From Separation to Détente in Church-State Relations," 55 *North Carolina Law Review* 563 (1976/1977).

Kizer, George, "Federal Aid to Education: 1945–1963," 10(1) *History of Education Quarterly* 84–102 (Spring 1970).

Knight, Jack, and Lee Epstein, "The Norm of Stare Decisis," 40(4) *American Journal of Political Science* 1018–1035 (1996).

Kobylka, J., "Leadership on the Supreme Court of the United States: Chief Justice Burger and the Establishment Clause," 42(4) *Western Political Science Quarterly* 545–568 (1989).

Kurland, Philip, "Of Church and State and the Supreme Court," 29 *University of Chicago Law Review* 1, 96 (1961).

Lardner, Lynford, "How Far Does the Constitution Separate Church and State?", 45(1) *American Political Science Review* 110–132 (1951).

Laycock, Douglas, "Equal Access and Moments of Silence: The Equal Status of Religious Speech By Private Speakers ," 81 *Northwestern Law Review* 1 (1986).

Laycock, Douglas, ""Nonpreferential" Aid to Religion: A False Claim About Original Intent," 27 *William and Mary Law Review* 875 (1985/1986).

Laycock, Douglas, "Freedom of Speech That Is Both Religious and Political," 29 *University of California-Davis Law Review* 793 (1996).

Laycock, Douglas, "The Underlying Unity of Separation and Neutrality," 46 *Emory Law Journal* 43 (1997).

"Leading Cases of the 1983 Term: Establishment of Religion," 98 *Harvard Law Review* 174 (1984).

Leparulo, Linda, "The Rights of Student Religious Groups Under the First Amendment to Hold Religious Meetings on the Public University Campus," 33 *Rutgers Law Review* 1008, 1039–1040 (1980–1981).

Levinson, Rosalie Berger, "Separation of Church and State: And the Wall Came Tumbling Down," 18 *Valparaiso Law Review* 707 (1984).

Lugg, Elizabeth, and R. Andrew Lugg, "Vouchers As School Choice: An Analysis of *Jackson v. Benson* – The Milwaukee Parental Choice Program," 29 *Journal of Law and Education* 175 (2000).

Lupu, Ira, "The Increasingly Anachronistic Case Against School Vouchers," 13 *Notre Dame Journal of Law, Ethics, and Public Policy* 375 (1999).

Macedo, Stephen, "Liberal Civic Education and Religious Fundamentalism: The Case of God v. John Rawls?" 105(3) *Ethics* 468–496 (1995).

Mahon, J. Patrick, "*Mergens*: Is the Equal Access Issue Settled?" 19 *Journal of Law and Education* 543 (1990).

Maltz, Earl, "The Prospects for a Revival of Conservative Activism in Constitutional Jurisprudence," 24 *Georgia Law Review* 629 (1989/1990).

Mansfield, John, "The Religion Clauses of the First Amendment and the Philosophy of the Constitution," 72 *California Law Review* 847 (1984).

Marshall, William, "We Know It When We See It": The Supreme Court and Establishment," 59 *Southern California Law Review* 495 (1986).

Marshall, William, "What is the Matter With Equality? An Assessment of the Equal Treatment of Religion and Nonreligion in First Amendment Jurisprudence", 75 *Indiana Law Journal* 193 (2000).

Marshall, William, and Douglas Blomgren, "Regulating Religious Organizations Under the Establishment Clause," 47 *Ohio State Law Journal* 293 (1986).

McAndrews, Lawrence, "Late and Never: Ronald Reagan and Tuition Tax Credits," 42 *Journal of Church and State* 467 (2000).

McCarthy, Martha, "Religion and Education: Whither the Establishment Clause?" 75 *Indiana Law Journal* 123 (2000).

McConnell, Michael, "Coercion: The Lost Element of Establishment," 27 *William and Mary Law Review* 933 (1985/1986).

McConnell, Michael, "The Selective Funding Problem: Abortions and Religious Schools," 104 *Harvard Law Review* 989 (1991).

McConnell, Michael, "Religious Freedom at a Crossroads," 59 *University of Chicago Law Review* 115 (1992).

McGarry, Daniel, "Tuition Tax Credits: Their Advantages and Constitutionality," 2 *Public Law Forum* 101 (1982).

McNollgast, "Legislative Intent: The Use of Positive Political Theory in Statutory Interpretation," 57 *Law and Contemporary Problems* 3 (1994).

Mengler, Thomas, "Public Relations in the Supreme Court: Justice Tom Clark's Opinion in the School Prayer Case," 6 *Constitutional Commentary* 331 (1989).

Mirsky, Yehudah, "Civil Religion and the Establishment Clause," 95 *Yale Law Journal* 1237 (1986).

Moraski, Byron, and Charles Shipman, "The Politics of Supreme Court Nominations: A Theory of Institutional Constraints and Choices," 43 *American Journal of Political Science* 1069 (1999).

Morgan, Richard, "The Establishment Clause and Sectarian Schools: A Final Installment?" *Supreme Court Review* 57 (1973).

Mozer, Gary, "The Crumbling Wall Between Church and State: *Agostini v. Felton*, Aid to Parochial Schools, and the Establishment Clause in the Twenty-First Century," 31 *Connecticut Law Review* 337 (1998).

Nault, Casey, "Bridging the Separation of Church and State: How *Rosenberger* Threatens Religious Liberty," 70 *Southern California Law Review* 1049 (1997).

"Note: A Daily Prayer in Public Schools," 7 *Catholic Lawyer* 334 (1961).
"Note: Catholic Schools and Public Money," 50 *Yale Law Journal* 917 (1941).
"Note: Constitutional Law – Higher Education Facilities Act – Constitutionality of Federal Financial Aid to Church-Related Colleges," 77 *Harvard Law Review* 1353 (1964).
"Note: Government Neutrality and Separation of Church and State: Tuition Tax Credits," 92 *Harvard Law Review* 696 (1978/1979).
"Note: Rethinking the Incorporation of the Establishment Clause: A Federalist View," 105 *Harvard Law Review* 1700 (1992).
"Note: School Prayer and the Becker Amendment," 53 *Georgetown Law Journal* 192 (1964/1965).
Nuechterlein, Jonathan, "The Free Exercise Boundaries of Permissible Accommodation Under the Establishment Clause," 99 *Yale Law Journal* 1127 (1990).
O'Brien, F. William, "The Blaine Amendment, 1875–1876," 41 *University of Detroit Law Journal* 137 (1963).
Otero-Ziegler, W., "The Remains of the Wall: *Everson v. Board of Education* to *Strout v. Albanese* and Beyond," 10 *Temple Political and Civil Rights Law Review* 207, 221 (2000/2001).
Paul, Jeremy, "Losing Our Religion," 28 *Connecticut Law Review* 269 (1996).
Paulsen, Michael, "Religion, Equality, and the Constitution: An Equal Protection Approach to Establishment Clause Adjudication," 61 *Notre Dame Law Review* 311, 318–322 (1986).
Perry, Michael, "Why Political Reliance on Religiously Grounded Morality is not Illegitimate in a Liberal Democracy," 36 *Wake Forest Law Review* 217 (2001).
Powell, H. Jefferson, "The Original Understanding of Original Intent," 98 *Harvard Law Review* 885 (1985).
Presser, Stephen, "Some Realism About Atheism: Responses to the Godless Constitution," 1 *Texas Review of Law and Politics* 87 (1997).
"Proceedings of the Annual Judicial Conference of the Tenth Judicial Circuit of the United States," 34 Federal Rules Decisions (F.R.D.) 29 (1963).
Robertson, M.G., "Pat", "Squeezing Religion Out of the Public Square – The Supreme Court, *Lemon*, and the Myth of the Secular Society," 4 *William and Mary Bill of Rights Journal* 223 (1995).
Rodriguez, Raul, "God Is Dead: Killed By Fifty Years of Establishment Clause Jurisprudence," 23 *St. Mary's Law Journal* 1155 (1992).
Rothman, Stanley, "The Politics of Catholic Parochial Schools: An Historical and Comparative Perspective," 25(1) *The Journal of Politics* 49–71 (1963).
Rotstein, Andrew, "Note: Good Faith? Religious-Secular Parallelism and the Establishment Clause," 93 *Columbia Law Review* 1763 (1993).
Schneider, Ronna G., "Getting Help With Their Homework: Schools, Lower Courts, and the Supreme Court Justices Look For Answers Under the Establishment Clause," 53 *Administrative Law Review* 943 (2001).
Schwartz, Herman, "Is the Rehnquist Court Activist? Yes: A Definite Agenda," 76 *American Bar Association Journal* 32 (1990).
Segal, Jeffrey and Harold Spaeth, "Norms, Dragons, and Stare Decisis," 40(4) *American Journal of Political Science* 1049–1063 (1996).

"Segregating Schools: The Foreseeable Consequences of Tuition Tax Credits," 89 *Yale Law Journal* 168 (1979/1980).

Servín-Gonzáles, Mariana, and Oscar Torres-Reyna, "Trends: Religion and Politics," 63(4) *Public Opinion Quarterly* 592–621 (Winter 1999).

Silverstein, Mark, and Benjamin Ginsberg, "The Supreme Court and the New Politics of Judicial Power," 102(3) *Political Science Quarterly* 371–388 (Autumn 1987).

Smith, Christopher, "The Supreme Court in Transition: Assessing the Legitimacy of the Legal Institution," 79 *Kentucky Law Journal* 317 (1990/1991).

Smith, Rodney King, "Getting Off on the Wrong Foot and Back on Again: A Reexamination of the History of the Framing of the Religion Clauses of the First Amendment and a Critique of the *Reynolds* and *Everson* Decisions," 20 *Wake Forest Law Review* 569 (1984).

Smith, Sandra, "Parochial Schools in the Black Cities," 42(3) *Journal of Negro Education* 379–391 (Summer 1973).

Songer, Donald, "The Relevance of Policy Values for the Confirmation of Supreme Court Nominees," 13 *Law and Society Review* 927 (1979).

Songer, Donald, and Stefanie Lindquist, "Not the Whole Story: The Impact of Justices' Values on Supreme Court Decision Making," 40(4) *American Journal of Political Science* 1049–1063 (1996).

Spaeth, Harold, and David Peterson, "The Analysis and Interpretation of Dimensionality: The Case of Civil Liberties Decision Making," 15(3) *Midwest Journal of Political Science* 415–441 (1971).

Stern, Marc, "School Vouchers – The Church-State Debate That Really Isn't," 31 *Connecticut Law Review* 977 (1999).

Stevens, John Paul, "The Bill of Rights: A Century of Progress," 59 *University of Chicago Law Review* 15 (1992).

Sullivan, Kathleen, "Religion and Liberal Democracy," 59 *University of Chicago Law Review* 195 (1992).

Sullivan, Kathleen, "Parades, Public Squares, and Voucher Payments: Problems of Government Neutrality," 28 *Connecticut Law Review* 243 (1996).

Teitel, Ruti, "The Supreme Court's 1984–85 Church-State Decisions: Judicial Paths of Least Resistance," 21 *Harvard Civil Rights-Civil Liberties Law Review* 651 (1986).

Tomasi, Timothy, and Jess Veloria, "All the President's Men? A Study of Ronald Reagan's Appointments to the US Courts of Appeals," 87 *Columbia Law Review* 766 (1987).

Tushnet, Mark, "Following the Rules Laid Down: A Critique of Interpretivism and Neutral Principles," 96 *Harvard Law Journal* 781 (1983).

Tushnet, Mark, "The Emerging Principle of Accommodation of Religion," 76 *Georgetown Law Journal* 1691 (1988).

Underkuffler, Laura, "Vouchers and Beyond: The Individual as Causative Agent in Establishment Clause Jurisprudence", 75 *Indiana Law Journal* 167 (2000).

Valente, William, "Aid to Church-Related Education – New Directions Without Dogma," 55 *Virginia Law Review* 579 (1969).

Van Alstyne, William, "Trends in the Supreme Court: Mr. Jefferson's Crumbling Wall – A Comment on *Lynch v. Donnelly*," *Duke Law Journal* 770 (1984).

Volokh, Eugene, "Equal Treatment is Not Establishment," 13 *Notre Dame Journal of Law, Ethics and Public Policy* 341 (1999).

Waite, Jason, "*Agostini v. Felton*: Thickening the Establishment Clause Stew," 33 *New England Law Review* 81 (1998).

Waldron, Jeremy, "Religious Contributions in Public Deliberation," 30 *San Diego Law Review* 817 (1993).

Waring, Robert, "Wide Awake or Half Asleep? Revelations from Judicial Tailings Found in *Rosenberger v. University of Virginia*," 17 *Northern Illinois University Law Review* 223 (1997).

Warpula, Christian Chad, "The Demise of Demarcation: *Agostini v. Felton* Unlocks the Parochial School Gate to State-Sponsored Educational Aid," 33 *Wake Forest Law Review* 465 (1998).

Weisenberger, Andrew, "Cleveland Program Could Lead to Definitive Supreme Court Precedent on School Vouchers," 30 *Journal of Law and Education* 564 (2001).

Weishaar, Peter, "School Choice Vouchers and the Establishment Clause," 58 *Albany Law Review* 543 (1994).

Wofford, John, "The Blinding Light: The Uses of History in Constitutional Interpretation," 31 *University of Chicago Law Review* 502 (1964).

Wood, Jr., James, "Tuition Tax Credits for Nonpublic Schools," 23 *Journal of Church and State* 5 (1981).

Wright, J.S., "The Judicial Right and the Rhetoric of Restraint: A Defense of Judicial Activism in an Age of Conservative Judges," 14 *Hastings Constitutional Law Quarterly* 487 (1986/1987).

Young, David, "Constitutional Validity of State Aid to Pupils in Church-Related Schools – Internal Tension Between the Establishment and Free Exercise Clauses," 38 *Ohio State Law Journal* 783 (1977).

Books

Abraham, Henry, *The Judiciary: The Supreme Court on the Governmental Process* (Boston, MA: Allyn & Bacon, Inc., 4th Ed., 1977).

Abraham, Henry, *Freedom and the Court: Civil Rights and Liberties in the United States* (New York: Oxford University Press, 4th Ed., 1982).

Adams, Arlin and Charles Emmerich, *A Nation Dedicated to Religious Liberty: The Constitutional Heritage of the Religion Clauses* (Philadelphia, PA: University of Pennsylvania Press, 1990).

Alley, Robert, (Ed.), *The Supreme Court on Church And State* (New York and Oxford: Oxford University Press, 1988).

Alley, Robert, *School Prayer: The Court, the Congress, and the First Amendment* (Buffalo, NY: Prometheus Books, 1994).

Alley, Robert, *Without a Prayer: Religious Expression in Public Schools* (Amherst, New York: Prometheus Books, 1996).

Audi, Robert and Nicholas Wolterstorff, *Religion in the Public Square: The Place of Religious Convictions in Political Debate* (Lanham, MD and London: Rowman and Littlefield, Inc., 1997).

Barr, David, and Nicholas Piediscalzi (Eds.), *The Bible in American Education: From Source Book to Textbook* (Philadelphia and Chico, California: Fortress Press and Scholars Press, 1982).

Barton, David, *A Guide to the School Prayer and Religious Liberty Debate* (Aledo, TX: Speciality Research Associates, 1995).
Beach, Waldo (Ed.), *Church, State, and Education* (Chapel Hill, NC: University of North Carolina at Chapel Hill, 1985).
Becker, Theodore (Ed.), *The Impact of Supreme Court Decisions* (New York: Oxford University Press, 1969).
Bendiner, R., *Obstacle Course on Capitol Hill* (New York: McGraw-Hill Book Co., 1964).
Berger, Raoul, *Government By Judiciary: The Transformation of the Fourteenth Amendment* (Cambridge, MA and London: Harvard University Press, 1977).
Bickel, Alexander, *The Least Dangerous Branch: The Supreme Court at the Bar of Politics* (New Haven, CT and London: Yale University Press, 2nd Ed., 1986).
Billings, Robert, *A Guide to the Christian School* (Washington, DC: The New Century Foundation Press, 1983).
Binder, Frederick, *The Age of the Common School, 1830–1865* (New York: John Wiley & Sons, Inc., 1974).
Blasi, Vincent (Ed.), *The Burger Court: The Counter-Revolution That Wasn't* (New Haven, CT and London: Yale University Press, 1983).
Blum SJ, Virgil, *Catholic Parents – Political Eunuchs* (St. Cloud, MN: Media and Materials, 1972).
Bosmajian, Haig (Ed.), *Freedom of Religion: The First Amendment in the Classroom Series* (New York: Neal-Schuman Publishers, Inc., 1987).
Bower, William, *Moral and Spiritual Values in Education* (Lexington, KY: University of Kentucky Press, 1952).
Boyer, Paul, *Urban Masses and Moral Order in America, 1820–1920* (Cambridge, MA and London: Harvard University Press, 1978).
Bradley, Martin, Norman Green, Jr., Dale Jones, Mac Lynn, and Lou McNeil, *Churches and Church Membership in the United States: An Enumeration by Region, State, and County* (Atlanta, GA: Glenmary Research Center, 1992).
Bramblet, James, *An Introduction to the Christian School* (Tacoma, WA: James M. Bramblet, 1985).
Brannen, Daniel, and Richard Clay Haynes, *Supreme Court Drama: Cases That Changed America, Volume 1* (New York and London: UXL, 2001).
Brown, Nicholas (Ed.), *The Study of Religion in the Public Schools: An Appraisal* (Washington, DC: American Council on Education, 1958).
Brown, William, and Andrew Greeley, *Can Catholic Schools Survive?* (New York: Sheed & Ward, Inc., 1970).
Bryk, Anthony, Valerie Lee, and Peter Holland, *Catholic Schools and the Common Good* (Harvard University Press, 1993).
Carey, Patrick, *The Roman Catholics* (Westport, CT and London: Greenwood Press, 1993).
Carter, Stephen, *The Culture of Disbelief: How American Law and Politics Trivialize Religious Devotion* (New York: Basic Books, 1993).
Clinton, Bill, *My Life* (London: Hutchinson, 2004).
Coleman, James, Thomas Hoffer, Sally Kilgore, *High School Achievement: Public, Catholic, and Private Schools Compared* (New York: Basic Books, 1982).
Cookson, Jr., Peter, *School Choice: The Struggle for the Soul of American Education* (New Haven, CT and London: Yale University Press, 1994).

Cooper, Phillip, *Battles on the Bench: Conflict Inside the Supreme Court* (Lawrence, KS: University Press of Kansas, 1995).
Craycraft, Jr., Kenneth, *The American Myth of Religious Freedom* (Dallas, TX: Spence Publishing Co., 1999).
Crosskey, William, *Politics and The Constitution in the History of the United States* (Chicago, IL: University of Chicago Press, 2 vols., 1953).
Curry, Thomas, *The First Freedoms, Church and State in America to the Passage of the First Amendment* (New York: Oxford University Press, 1986).
Curry, Thomas, *Farewell to Christendom: The Future of Church and State in America* (New York: Oxford University Press, 2001).
Dallek, Robert, *John F. Kennedy: An Unfinished Life* (London: Penguin Books, 2004).
Dart, John, and Jimmy Allen, *Bridging the Gap: Religion and the News Media* (Nashville, TN: The Freedom Forum First Amendment Center at Vandebilt University, 1993).
Dickson, D. (Ed.), *The Supreme Court in Conference (1940–1985)* (New York: Oxford University Press, 2001).
Dierenfield, Bruce, *The Battle Over School Prayer: How* Engel v. Vitale *Changed America* (Lawrence, KS: University Press of Kansas, 2007).
Dierenfield, Richard, *Religion in American Public Schools* (Washington, DC: Public Affairs Press, 1962).
Dionne Jr., E.J. and John DiIulio, Jr. (Eds.), *What's God Got To Do With the American Experiment?* (Washington, DC: Brookings Institution Press, 2000).
Dolan, Jay P., *The Immigrant Church: New York's Irish and German Catholics, 1815–1865* (Baltimore, MD and London: The Johns Hopkins University Press, 1975).
Dolbeare, Kenneth, and Philip Hammond, *The School Prayer Decisions: From Court Policy to Local Practice* (Chicago, IL: University of Chicago Press, 1971).
Donovan, Teresa, Marcella Donovan, and Joseph Piccione, *Voluntary School Prayer: Judicial Dilemma, Proposed Solutions* (Washington, DC: Free Congress Research and Education Foundation, 1984).
Douglas, William O., *The Bible and the Schools* (Boston, MA: Little, Brown & Co., 1966).
Dudley, Mark, *Engel v. Vitale(1962): Religion and the Schools* (New York: Twenty-First Century Books, 2001).
Dulles, John Foster, *The Secretary of State on . . . Faith of Our Fathers* (Washington, DC: Department of State, 1954).
Dunne, Finley Peter, *Mr. Dooley's Opinions* (London: Heineman, 1902).
Dworkin, Ronald, *Taking Rights Seriously* (London: Gerald Duckworth & Co. Ltd., 1977).
Elam, Stanley, *How America Views its Schools: The PDK/Gallup Polls, 1969–1994* (Bloomington, IN: Phi Delta Kappan Educational Foundation, 1995).
Farish, Leah, *Lemon v. Kurtzman: The Religion and Public Funds Case* (Berkeley Heights, NJ and Aldershot, Hampshire: Enslow Publishers, Inc., 2000).
Federal Activities in Education (Washington, DC: National Educational Association and American Association of School Administrators, 1939).
Federal Aid to Education: A Review of Pertinent Facts (Washington, DC: NEA, 1942).
Feldman, Stephen, *Please Don't Wish Me A Merry Christmas: A Critical History of the Separation of Church and State* (New York and London: New York University Press, 1997).

Ferrara, Peter, *Religion and the Constitution: A Reinterpretation* (Washington, DC: Free Congress Research and Education Foundation, 1983).
Fisher, Louis, *Constitutional Dialogues: Interpretation as Political Process* (Princeton, NJ: Princeton University Press, 1988).
Fleming, William, *God in Our Public Schools* (Pittsburgh, PA: National Reform Association, 1947).
Flowers, Ronald B., *That Godless Court? Supreme Court Decisions on Church-State Relationships* (Louisville, KY: Westminster John Knox Press, 1994).
Foltin, Richard (Ed.), *Religious Liberty in the 1990s: The Religion Clauses Under the Rehnquist Court, A Consultation* (New York: The American Jewish Committee, 1994).
Formicola, Jo Renee, and Hubert Morken (Eds.), *Everson Revisited: Religion, Education, and Law at the Crossroads* (Lanham, MD and Oxford: Rowman & Littlefield, 1997).
Frankel, Marvin, *Faith and Freedom: Religious Liberty in America* (New York: Hill & Wang, 1994).
Funston, Richard, *Constitutional Counterrevolution? The Warren Court and the Burger Court: Judicial Policy Making in Modern America* (Cambridge, MA: Schenkman Publishing Co. Inc., 1977).
Funston, Richard, *A Vital National Seminar: The Supreme Court in American Political Life* (Palo Alto, CA: Mayfield Publishing Co., 1978).
Gallup, Jr., George, and Timothy Jones, *The Next American Spirituality: Finding God in the Twenty-First Century* (Colorado Springs, CO: Cook Communications, 2000).
Garman, Gene, *America's Real Religion: Separation Between Religion and Government in the United States of America* (Pittsburg, KS: America's Real Religion Publishing, 1991).
Gedicks, Frederick Mark, *The Rhetoric of Church and State: A Critical Analysis of Religion Clause Jurisprudence* (Durham, NC and London: Duke University Press, 1995).
Glenn, Charles, *The Ambiguous Embrace: Government and Faith-Based Schools and Social Agencies* (Princeton, NJ: Princeton University Press, 2000).
Graham, Hugh, *The Uncertain Triumph: Federal Education Policy in the Kennedy and Johnson Years* (Chapel Hill, NC and London: University of North Carolina Press, 1984).
Greeley, Andrew, William McCready, and Kathleen McCourt, *Catholic Schools in a Declining Church* (Kansas City, MO: Sheed & Ward, Inc., 1976).
Greeley, Andrew, *Catholic High Schools and Minority Students* (New Brunswick, NJ and London: Transaction Books, 1982, 2nd Ed, 2002).
Griffin, Leslie (Ed.), *Religion and Politics in the American Milieu* (The Review of Politics and the Office of Policy Studies, 1986).
Gurash, John, *The Report of the Archdiocesan Advisory Committee on the Financial Crisis of Catholic Schools in Philadelphia and Surrounding Counties* (Philadelphia, PA: 1972).
Haas, Carol, *Engel v. Vitale: Separation of Church and State* (Hillside, NJ: Enslow Publishers, Inc., 1994).
Hall, Verna, and Rosalie Slater, *The Bible and the Constitution of the United States of America* (San Francisco, CA: Foundation For American Christian Education, 1983).
Harner, Nevin, *Religion's Place in General Education* (Richond, VA: John Knox Press, 1949).

Horwitz, Morton, *The Warren Court and the Pursuit of Justice: A Critical Issue* (New York: Hill & Wang, 1998).

Howe, Mark DeWolfe, *The Garden and the Wilderness: Religion and Government in American Constitutional History* (Chicago, IL: University of Chicago Press, 1965).

Hunt, Mate Graye, *Values Resources Guide: Annotated for the Elementary School Teacher* (New York: American Association of Colleges for Teacher Education, 1958).

Irons, Peter, *The Courage of their Convictions: Sixteen Americans Who Fought Their Way to the Supreme Court* (New York: Penguin, 1990).

Irons, Peter, *Brennan vs. Rehnquist: The Battle for the Constitution* (New York: Alfred A. Knopf, 1994).

Jeffrey, Julie, *Education for Children of the Poor: A Study of the Origins and Implementation of the Elementary and Secondary Education Act of 1965* (Columbus, OH: Ohio State University Press, 1978).

Jennings, John, *National Issues in Education: Elementary and Secondary Education Act* (Bloomington, IN and Washington, DC: Phi Delta Kappan International and Institute for Educational Leadership, 1995).

Johnson, Douglas, Paul Picard, and Bernard Quinn, *Churches and Church Membership in the United States, 1971: An Enumeration by Region, State, and County* (Washington, DC: Glenmary Research Center, 1974).

Johnson, Richard, *The Dynamics of Compliance; Supreme Court Decision-Making From a New Perspective*, (Evanston, IL: Northwestern University Press, 1967).

Jordan, K. Forbis. and Nelda Cambron-McCabe (Eds.), *Perspectives in State School Support Programs* (Cambridge, MA: Ballinger Publishing Co., 1981).

Kaestle, Carl F., *The Evolution of an Urban School System, New York City, 1750–1850* (Cambridge, MA: Harvard University Press, 1973).

Kaminetsky, Joseph (Ed.), *Hebrew Day School Education: An Overview* (New York: Torah Umesorah, 1970).

Katz, Michael B., *Improving Poor People: The Welfare State, the "Underclass," and Urban Schools as History* (Princeton, NJ: Princeton University Press, 1995).

Kelley, Dean, *Public Funding of Social Services Related to Religious Bodies* (New York: The American Jewish Committee, 1990).

Keynes, Edward, with Randall Miller, *The Court vs. Congress: Prayer, Busing, and Abortion* (Durham, NC and London: Duke University Press, 1989).

Kik, Jacob, *The Supreme Court and Prayer in the Public Schools* (Philadelphia, PA: Presbyterian and Reformed Publishing Co., 1963).

Kniker, Charles, *Teaching About Religion in the Public Schools* (Bloomington, IN: Phi Delta Kappan Educational Foundation, 1985).

Kramer, Doniel Zvi, *The Day Schools and Torah Umesorah: The Seeding of Traditional Judaism in America* (New York: Yeshiva University Press, 1984).

Kramnick, Isaac, and R. Laurence Moore, *The Godless Constitution, The Case Against Religious Correctness* (New York and London: W.W. Norton & Co., 1996).

Kurland, Philip, *Politics, the Constitution, and the Warren Court* (Chicago, IL: University of Chicago Press, 1970).

LaNoue, George, *Public Funds for Parochial Schools?* (New York: National Council of Churches in Christ, 1963).

Larson, Martin, *When Parochial Schools Close: A Study in Educational Financing* (Chicago, IL: Robert B. Luce, Inc., 1972).

Laubach, John, *School Prayers: Congress, the Courts and the Public* (Washington, DC: Public Affairs Press, 1969).
Lazarus, Edward, *Closed Chambers: The Rise, Fall, and Future of the Modern Supreme Court* (London: Penguin Books, 2005).
Leahy, James, *The First Amendment, 1791–1991: Two Hundred Years of Freedom* (Jefferson, NC and London: McFarland & Co., Inc., 1991).
Lee, Francis (Ed.), *All Imaginable Liberty: The Religious Liberty Clauses of the First Amendment* (Lanham, MD and London: University Press of America, 1995).
Leggett, Stanton (Ed.), *Managing Schools in Hard Times* (Chicago, IL: Teach 'em Inc., 1981).
Levy, Leonard, *The Establishment Clause: Religion and the First Amendment* (New York: Macmillan, 1986).
Levy, Leonard, *The Establishment Clause: Religion and the First Amendment* (London and Chapel Hill, NC: University of North Carolina Press, 2nd Ed., revised, 1994).
Levy, Leonard, *Original Intent and the Framers' Constitution* (New York: Macmillan, 1988).
Loren, Julia, *Engel v. Vitale: Prayer in the Public Schools* (San Diego, CA: Lucent Books, 2001).
Lynn, Barry, Marc Stern, and Oliver Thomas, *The Right to Religious Liberty: The Basic ACLU Guide to Religious Rights* (Carbondale, IL and Edwardsville, IL: Southern Illinois University Press, 2nd Ed., 1995).
Malbin, Michael, *Religion and Politics: The Intentions of the Authors of the First Amendment* (Washington, DC: American Enterprise Institute for Public Policy Research, 1978).
Maltz, Earl, *The Chief Justiceship of Warren Burger, 1969–1986* (Columbia, SC: University of South Carolina Press, 2000).
Maltzman, Forrest, James Spriggs II, and Paul Wahlbeck, *Crafting Law on the Supreme Court: The Collegial Game* (Cambridge and New York: Cambridge University Press, 2000).
Marcus, Sheldon, and Philip Vairo (Eds.), *Urban Education: Crisis or Opportunity?* (Metuchen, NJ: The Scarecrow Press, 1972).
Marsden, George, *Religion and American Culture* (Orlando, FL: Harcourt Brace Jovanovich, Inc., 1990).
Mauro, Tony, *Illustrated Great Decisions of the Supreme Court* (Washington, DC: Congressional Quarterly Inc., 2000).
McCarthy, Martha, *A Delicate Balance: Church, State, and the Schools* (Bloomington, IN: Phi Delta Kappan Educational Foundation, 1983).
McCarthy, Martha, *Religion and Public Schools: Separation, Accommodation, or Advancement* (Bloomington, IN: Indiana University Press, 1984).
McCloskey, Robert, *The Modern Supreme Court* (Cambridge, MA: Harvard University Press, 1972).
McLaughlin, Milbrey, *Evaluation and Reform: The Elementary and Secondary Education Act of 1965, Title I* (Cambridge, MA: Ballinger Publishing Co., 1975).
McLaughlin, Terence, Joseph O'Keefe SJ, Bernadette O'Keeffe, *The Contemporary Catholic School: Context, Identity and Diversity* (Washington, DC and London: The Falmer Press, 1996).

Menendez, Albert, *Visions of Reality: What Fundamentalist Schools Teach* (Buffalo, NY: Prometheus Books, 1993).

Milkis, Sidney, and Jerome Mileur (Eds.), *The Great Society and the High Tide of Liberalism* (Amherst, MA and Boston, MA: University of Massachusetts Press, 2005).

Miller, Arthur, *The Supreme Court: Myth and Reality* (Westport, CT: Greenwood Press, 1978).

Miller, William L., *The First Liberty: Religion and the American Republic* (New York: Paragon House Publishers, 1985).

Mitau, G. Theodore, *Decade of Decision: The Supreme Court and the Constitutional Revolution, 1954–1964* (New York: Charles Scribners Sons, 1967).

Monk, Linda, *The First Amendment: America's Blueprint for Tolerance* (Alexandria, VA: Close Up Publishing, 1995).

Monsma, Stephen, *When Sacred and Secular Mix: Religious Nonprofit Organizations and Public Money* (Lanham, MD and London: Rowman & Littlefield Publishers, Inc., 1996).

Moral and Spiritual Values in the Public Schools (Washington, DC: National Educational Assocation and American Association of School Administrators, 1951).

Mr. Justice and Mrs Black: The Memoirs of Hugo L. Black and Elizabeth Black (New York: Random House, 1986).

Muir, Jr., William, *Prayer in the Public Schools* (London and Chicago, IL: University of Chicago Press, 1967).

Murphy, Walter, *Congress and the Court: A Case Study in the American Political Process* (Chicago, IL: University of Chicago Press, 1962).

Murphy, W., *Elements of Judicial Strategy* (Chicago, IL: University of Chicago Press, 1964).

Murray, William, *Let Us Pray: A Plea for Prayer in Our Schools* (New York: William Morrow & Co., Inc., 1995).

National Policy and the Financing of Public Schools (Washington, DC: NEA, 1959).

Neamon, Anne, *God and Country vs. Atheism: Exploitations of US Supreme Court Decisions on School Prayers in Threat to National Security* (McLean, VA: Citizens for God and Country, 1977).

New Catholic Schools, 1985–1995 (Washington, DC: National Catholic Educational Association, 1997).

Newman, William, and Peter Halvorson, *Atlas of American Religion: The Denominational Era, 1776–1990* (Lanham, MD and Oxford: Altamira Press, 2000).

O'Brien, David M., *Constitutional Law and Politics, Volume Two: Civil Rights and Liberties* (New York: W.W. Norton & Company, 3rd Ed., 1991).

O'Brien, D., *Storm Center: The Supreme Court in American Politics* (New York and London: W.W. Norton & Co., Ltd., 4th Ed., 1996).

Palmer, Jan, *The Vinson Court Era: The Supreme Court's Conference Votes; Data and Analysis* (New York: AMS Press, 1990).

Parsons, Paul, *Inside America's Christian Schools* (Macon, GA: Mercer University Press, 1987).

Peshkin, Alan, *God's Choice: The Total World of a Fundamentalist Christian School* (Chicago, IL: University of Chicago Press, 1986).

Peterson, Paul, and Bryan Hassel (Eds.), *Learning From School Choice* (Washington, DC: The Brookings Institution, 1998).

Pfeffer, Leo, *Religion, State and the Burger Court* (Buffalo, NY: Prometheus Books, 1984).
Piediscalzi, Nicholas, and William Collie (Eds.), *Teaching About Religion in Public Schools* (Niles, IL: Argus Communications, 1977).
Plude, Francis, *The Flickering Light: What's Happening to Catholic Schools?* (New York: William H. Sadler, Inc., 1974).
Politella, Joseph, *Religion in Education: An Annotated Bibliography* (New York: American Association of Colleges for Teacher Education, 1956).
Powe, Jr., Lucas, *The Warren Court and American Politics* (Cambridge, MA and London: Belknap Press, 2000).
Pritchett, C. Herman, *Civil Liberties and the Vinson Court* (Chicago, IL and London: University of Chicago Press, 2nd Impression, 1966).
Public Papers of the President: John F. Kennedy, 1961 (Washington, DC: United States Government Printing Office, 1962).
Public Papers of the President of the United States: Lyndon B. Johnson (Washington, DC: US Government Printing Office, 1966–1970).
Ravitch, Diane, *The Great School Wars, New York City, 1805–1973: A History of Public Schools as Battlefields of Social Change* (New York: Basic Books, 1974).
Rehnquist, William, *The Supreme Court: How It Was, How It Is* (New York: William Morrow, 1987).
Religion and Public Education: Proceedings of a Conference (Washington, DC: American Council in Education Studies, 1945).
Religion and the Constitution (Washington, DC: American Enterprise Institute for Public Policy Research, 1984).
Rice, Charles, *The Supreme Court and Public Prayer: The Need for Restraint* (New York: Fordham University Press, 1964).
Rist, Ray, *The Urban School: A Factory for Failure* (Cambridge, MA and London: The MIT Press, 1974).
Rosenfeld, Gerry, *"Shut Those Thick Lips!": A Study of Slum School Failure* (New York: Holt, Rinehart, & Winston, Inc., 1971).
Rudko, Frances, *Truman's Court: A Study in Judicial Restraint* (Westport, CT: Greenwood Press, Inc., 1988).
Ruthven, Malise, *The Divine Supermarket: Travels in Search of the Soul of America* (London: Chatto & Windus, 1989).
Savage, David, *Turning Right: The Making of the Rehnquist Supreme Court* (Chichester: John Wiley & Sons, Inc., 1993).
Schick, Martin, and Jeremy Dauber, *The Financing of Jewish Day Schools* (New York: Rabbi Jacob Joseph School, 1997).
Schick, Marvin, *A Census of Jewish Day Schools in the United States* (New York: Avi Chai Foundation, 2000).
Schwartz, Bernard, with Stephan Lesher, *Inside the Warren Court, 1953–1969* (Garden City, NY: Doubleday & Co., Inc., 1983).
Schwartz, Bernard (Ed.), *The Burger Court: Counter-Revolution or Confirmation?* (New York and Oxford: Oxford University Press, 1998).
Schwartz, Bernard, *A History of the Supreme Court* (New York: Oxford University Press, 1993).
Schwartz, Herman (Ed.), *The Burger Years: Rights and Wrongs in the Supreme Court, 1969–1986* (New York: Viking Press, 1987).

Segal, Jeffrey, and Harold Spaeth, *The Supreme Court and the Attitudinal Model* (New York: Cambridge University Press, 1993).
Segal, Jeffrey, and Harold Spaeth, *The Supreme Court and the Attitudinal Model Revisited* (Cambridge: Cambridge University Press, 2002).
Sheldon, Charles, *The Supreme Court: Politicians in Robes* (Beverley Hills, CA: Glencoe Press, 1970).
Sikorski, Robert (Ed.), *Prayer in Public Schools and the Constitution* (3 vols.: New York and London: Garland Publishing, Inc., 1993).
Simon, James, *The Center Holds: The Power Struggle Inside the Rehnquist Court* (New York: Simon & Schuster, 1995).
Smith, Henry Lester, Robert McElhinney, and George Steele, *Character Development Through Religious and Moral Education in the Public Schools of the United States* (Bloomington, IN: Bureau of Cooperative Research, Indiana University, 1937).
Smith, Kevin, and Kenneth Meier, *The Case Against School Choice: Politics, Markets and Fools* (Armonk, NY and London: ME Sharpe, Inc., 1995).
Smith, Michael, and Joseph Bryson, *Church-State Relations: The Legality of Using Public Funds for Religious Schools* (Topeka, KS: National Organisation on Legal Problems of Education, 1972).
Smith, Steven D., *Foreordained Failure: The Quest For a Constitutional Principle of Religious Freedom* (New York and Oxford: Oxford University Press, 1995).
Smith, Steven R., and Michael Lipsky, *Nonprofits For Hire: The Welfare State in the Age of Contracting* (Cambridge, MA and London: Harvard University Press, 1993).
Solomon, Stephen, *Ellery's Protest: How One Young Man Defied Tradition and Sparked the Battle Over School Prayer* (Ann Arbor, MI: University of Michigan Press, 2007).
Starr, Kenneth, *The David and Mary Eccles Centre for American Studies Second Annual Lecture, Equality and Autonomy: The Polarization of Constitutional Law* (London: The British Library, 1994).
Steamer, Robert J., *The Supreme Court: Constitutional Revision and the New "Strict Constructionism"*, (Minneapolis, MN: Burgess Publishing Company, 1973).
Still Unfinished: Our Educational Obligation to America's Children (Washington, DC: National Educational Association, 1948).
Swanson, Austin, and Joseph Igoe (Eds.), *Should Public Monies Be Used to Support Non-Public Education?: A Review of the Issues and Practices* (Danville, IL: The Interstate Printers and Publishers, Inc., 1967).
Thayer, V.T., *The Attack Upon the American Secular School* (Boston, MA: Beacon Press, 1951).
The Non-Catholic in the Catholic School (Washington, DC: Department of Religious Education, National Catholic Educational Association, 1987).
The Relation of Religion to Public Education: The Basic Principles (Washington, DC: Committee on Religion and Education, American Council on Education, Vol. XI, April 1947).
Thomas, J. Alan, and Robert Wimpelberg (Eds.), *Dilemmas in School Finance* (Chicago, IL: Midwest Administration Center, University of Chicago Press, 1978).
Tribe, Laurence, *God Save This Honorable Court: How the Choice of Supreme Court Justices Shapes Our History* (New York: New American Library, 1985).
Tucker, D.F.B., *The Rehnquist Court and Civil Rights* (Aldershot, Hampshire: Dartmouth Publishing Co., 1995).

Tushnet, Mark (Ed.), *The Warren Court in Historical and Political Perspective* (Charlottesville, VA and London: University Press of Virginia, 1993).

Twomley, Dale, *Parochiaid and the Courts* (Berrien Springs, MI: Andrews University Press, 1979).

Tyack, David, Robert Lowe, and Elisabeth Hansot, *Public Schools in Hard Times: The Great Depression and Recent Years* (Cambridge, MA and London: Harvard University Press, 1984).

United States Catholic Elementary and Secondary Schools 2003–2004: The Annual Statistical Report on Schools, Enrolment and Staffing (Washington, DC: National Catholic Educational Association, 2004).

Urofsky, Melvin I., *The Continuity of Change: The Supreme Court and Individual Liberties, 1953–1986* (Belmont, CA: Wadsworth Publishing Company, 1991).

Utter, Glenn, and John Storey, *The Religious Right: A Reference Handbook* (Santa Barbara, CA: ABC-CLIO, Inc., 2nd Ed., 2001).

Van Alstyne, William, *The American First Amendment in the Twenty-First Century: Cases and Materials* (New York: Foundation Press, 3rd Ed., 2002).

Van Dusen, Henry, *God in Education: A Tract for the Times* (New York: Charles Scribner's Sons, 1951).

Viteritti, Joseph, *Choosing Equality: School Choice, the Constitution, and Civil Society* (Washington, DC: The Brookings Institution, 1999).

Vitullo-Martin, Thomas, and Bruce Cooper, *Separation of Church and Child: The Constitution and Federal Aid to Religious Schools* (Indianapolis, IN: The Hudson Institute, 1987).

Wagstaff, Caroline, "Race, Class and Federalism: A History and Analysis of *San Antonio Independent School District v. Rodriguez* (1973)" (unpublished PhD thesis, University of Kent, 2001).

Ward, Leo, *Federal Aid to Private Schools* (Westminster, MD: The Newman Press, 1964).

Wellington, Harry H., *Interpreting the Constitution: The Supreme Court and The Process of Adjudication*, (New York: Yale University Press, 1990).

White, G. Edward, *The American Judicial Tradition: Profiles of Leading American Judges* (New York and Oxford: Oxford University Press, Expanded Ed., 1988).

Witte, Jr., John, *Religion and the American Constitutional Experiment: Essential Rights and Liberties* (Boulder, CO and Oxford: Westview Press, 2000).

Wood, Jr., James, *The First Freedom: Religion and the Bill of Rights* (Waco, TX: JM Dawson Institute of Church-State Studies, Baylor University Press, 1990).

Woodward, Bob, and Scott Armstrong, *The Brethren: Inside the Supreme Court* (New York; Simon and Schuster, 1979).

Yarbrough, Tinsley, *The Rehnquist Court and the Constitution* (Oxford: Oxford University Press, 2000).

Youniss, James, John Convey, Jeffrey Mclellan, *The Catholic Character of Catholic Schools* (Notre Dame, IN: University of Notre Dame Press, 2000).

Index

Bold type represents the key pages for the topic indicated.

AASA *see American Association of School Administrators*
ABA *see American Bar Association*
Abington School District v. Schempp (1963)   29–30, 34, 37, 85, **100–4**, 109, 114–15, 119, 121, 127, 129–34, 137–8, 140–1, 144–6, 154, 157, 163, 165, 168, 170, 172, 185, 187, 192–4, 197, 201, 203, 206
  Clark's opinion   101–3, 195, 202
  compliance   109–12, 118
  test   103, 194
accommodation   6, 52–3, 62, 74, 114, 130, 134, 178, 180, 182–4, 187, 192–3, 196–7, 199–200
  voting blocs   47, 55, 58, 66, 177, 182, 193
ACE *see American Council on Education*
ACLU *see American Civil Liberties Union*
ADL *see Anti-Defamation League*
Aguilar v. Felton (1985)   41, **51–6**, 57, 62, 69, 72, 81, 184–5
Agostini v. Felton (1997)   10, **69–73**, 74–5, 82, 183, 187, 196, 200
American Association of School Administrators   20–1
American Bar Association   100, 118–19, 135
American Center for Law and Justice   151
American Civil Liberties Union   15, 49, 56, 62, 73, 97, 105, 122, 140–1, 151, 164–6, 168, 170, 185
American Council on Education   20–1, 87
American Jewish Congress   50, 96, 99, 165, 170
Americans United for the Separation of Church and State   49, 62, 97–8, 105, 139, 151, 164, 166, 170
anti-Catholicism   9, 12, 18, 22, 24, 59, 61, 83–4, 203
anti-Communism   24–5, 86–7, 97, 105–6, 111, 146, 201
Anti-Defamation League   62, 99, 105, 117, 165
atheism   25, 87, 98, 105–6, 111, 146
Attitudinal Model   6

auxiliary services   40–1, 43

Baptist Joint Committee on Public Affairs   50, 97, 99, 105, 117, 163
Barden, Graham   23–4
Becker Amendment   105–9, 202
  opposition to   106–7
Becker, Frank   97, 112
  and prayer amendment   105–7
bible reading   25, 30, 83–5, 88, 90, 101, 104, 111, 119
Black, Hugo   5, 30–1, 34, 36, 45, 47, 75, 77–8, 91, 100, 102, 132, 154, 182
  and *Engel*   91–4, 102, 202
  and *Everson*   16–19, 46, 203, 210n. 2, 211n. 9
Blackmun, Harry   35, 40, 44, 47, 55, 58, 65, 79–80, 82, 129, 132–3, 142, 144, 146, 155, 161, 195
Blaine Amendments   18, 206, 211n. 13
B'nai B'rith   50, 117
Board of Education of the Westside Community Schools v. Mergens (1990)   158, **174–8**, 185–6, 189, 198
Board of Education v. Allen (1968)   **29–31**, 33, 42–4, 46–7, 62, 65, 77, 187, 194, 198
Bork, Robert   118, 137
Brandon v. Board of Education (1980)   167, 169
Brennan, William   34, 36, 47, 53, 55, 66, 78–81, 100, 104, 129–30, 132, 135–6, 154, 161, 175–6, 189, 193
  and *Aguilar*   52–4
  and *Ball*   52–4
Breyer, Stephen   73, 75, 82, 182, 184, 187, 189, 193, 197
Brown v. Board of Education (1954)   26, 99, 104
Burger Court   62, 66, 114–15, 187, 193–5, 199, 204–5

Index

centre bloc   47, 132–3, 140, 193, 195–6, 199, 206, 253n. 6
  and school aid   **41–9, 51–6**, 114, 205
  and tests for constitutionality   **42–6**, 57–8, 66, 196, 206
Burger, Warren   33, 35, 47, 52, 54–5, 59, 63, 77–81, 114, 129, 132–3, 155, 194, 198, 204
  and *Lemon*   34–5, 42–3, 54, 59, 196, 198, 204, 206
Burton, Harold   19, 77
bus transportation   12, 15, 17, 19, 30, 33, 42, 72, 75, 198, 210n. 3, 211n. 14
Bush, George H. W.   140, 142

Cahill, William T.   39, 61
Campus Crusade for Christ   117, 164
Cantwell v. Connecticut (1940)   2, 16
Carter, Jimmy   37, 111, 150
Catholic schools   14, 25, 38, 59, 61, 67–8, 84
  lay teachers   25, 38
  mission   38–9
  non-Catholics   67–8
  race   26, 67
centre bloc   47, 55, 58, 62, 131–3, 195–6, 205
child benefit   12, 28, 30, 34, 46, 72, 198
citizenship education
  religious   86–8
  secular   88–90, 227n. 12
civil religion   24–5, 121
Clark, Tom   101–2, 154
  and *Schempp*   101–3, 195, 202
Clinton, Bill   9, 148–52
  Memorandum on Religious Expression in Schools   150–1
Cochran v. Louisiana State Board of Education (1930)   12, 29, 46
coercion   92, 106, 141, 143–5, 147, 176
Cold War   9, 14, 24–5, 32, 61, 84, 86–7, 201, 204
Committee for Public Education and Religious Liberty   73
Committee for Public Education and Religious Liberty v. Nyquist (1973)   40–1, 43–5, 47–8, 51, 55, 62–3, 78, 187
construction costs   27, 41, 43, 48
court stripping   49, 107, 111, 116, 118, 121–2, 124, 135–6, 167
CPERL *see Committee for Public Education and Religious Liberty*
crèche   52, 134, 142

deference to legislature   18, 59, 204
Denton, Jeremiah   162, 164, 168, 171–2
dicta   17, 25, 48, 67

direct-indirect test   18–19, 33–5, 40–1, **42**, 43–5, 53, 63, 75, 176, 180, 183–4, 198
Douglas, William   30–1, 34, 36, 47, 77–9, 100, 104, 132, 154, 194
  and *Engel*   94–5, 96, 229n. 34
  and *Zorach*   25, 45, 152

economic concerns   9, 36–7, 57–9, 61, 204
educational materials   34, 40–1, 43, 74, 199–200
effect   53, 71, 160, 175–6
Elementary and Secondary Education Act (1965)   27–9, 204
  Title I   51, 56, 69
eligibility criteria   17, **45–6**, 63–5, 72, 74–5, 183–4, 187
  expansion of   67, 75
endorsement   128–9, 143, 146, 160, 175–6, 180
Engel v. Vitale (1962)   27, 29–30, 37, 85, 89, **90–6**, 102, 109, 110–11, 114–15, 119–21, 127, 131, 133–4, 137–8, 140–1, 143–6, 154, 157, 163, 165, 168, 170, 172, 185, 187, 192–4, 197, 201–3, 206
  Black's opinion   91–4, 103, 127–8, 202
  compliance with   109–12, 118
  Douglas's opinion   94–5
  reaction to   96–9, 102, 104–11, 109–11, 157–8, 163, 201–3
entanglement   35, 43–5, 52, 54–5, 62, 71
equal access   5, 9–10, 66, 118–19, 144–5, 183, 185, 196–9, 203, 205–6
Equal Access Act   158, **162–72**, 173–8, 185–8, 193, 198, 206
ESEA *see Elementary and Secondary Education Act*
Establishment Clause
  history   2, 4, 11
  scope of   1, 11, 17, 19
evangelicals   49, 117
Everson v. Board of Education (1947)   3, 10, 13–14, **15–20**, 22–3, 29–31, 33, 40, 43, 47, 69, 57, 61, 65, 72, 75, 77, 84, 130, 147, 182, 184, 187, 191, 194, 200, 203–4
  Black's opinion   16–19, 203
  Rutledge's dissent   16, 19–20, 194, 203
excusal remedies   91–2

facial neutrality   18, 31, 42, 64, 66, 72, 127, 160, 178, 183–4, 187, 196
Falwell, Jerry   50, 121
federal funding   12–15, 24, 86, 114, 203–4
  Catholic views   13, 23
  debates over   20–9, 32, 93, 203
  and desegregation   27–8
  Protestant views   13, 23

financial benefits   35, 53
  and non-financial aid distinction   34, 41, **43–4**, 46, 53, 63, 74, 183, 196, 198
flag salute   2, 120
Ford, Gerald   132
Fortas, Abe   30, 35, 77, 132
forum analysis   159–60, 175, 178, 182–3, 186
Founding Fathers   4, 17, 42, 92, 112
Frankfurter, Felix   19, 77, 91, 100
free exercise   66, 91, 131, 144, 158–9, 173, 185, 206
  and prayer   92, 95, 105–6, 121
Free Exercise Clause   161, 167–8, 192
  scope of   2, 92
free speech   66, 158–61, 173, 178, 181–3, 186–7
fundamentalists   49, 122

Ginsburg, Ruth Bader   73, 75, 82, 182, 184, 187, 189, 193, 197
Goldberg, Arthur   100, 103–4, 154
Graham, Billy   9, 98, 112
Grand Rapids School District v. Ball (1985)   41, **51–6**, 57, 61–2, 81

Hand, Brevard   125–6
Harlan, John Marshall   47, 58, 91, 94, 103–4, 132, 154
Hatfield, Mark   162–3, 167, 172
Helms Amendment   107, 111, 116–18, 122, 174
Helms, Jesse   9, 107, 112, 124, 135
Holmes, Oliver Wendell   47
House of Representatives
  Committee on Education and Labor   21–2
  Judiciary Committee   105–8, 116
  Subcommittee on Education   162, 164, 169–70

indirect benefit   19, 46, 59, 70
inconsistency   47–8, 69, 119, 199
  claims of   8, 14, 41, 53, 57, 133, 199
  rejection of   46, 53, 57–8, 133, 153, 199–200
incorporation   13, 16
interpretivists   4–5

Jackson, Robert   19, 77, 193
Jaffree, Ishmael   124–7, 134
Jefferson, Thomas   4, 11, 16, 86
Johnson, Lyndon B.   27
  and Elementary and Secondary Education Act (1965)   27–9

Kennedy, Anthony   66, 74–5, 142, 155, 175–6, 179–80, 182, 189, 196–7
  and *Lee*   142, **143–6**, 193, 196, 205
Kennedy, John Fitzgerald   26–8, 61, 110
Keppel, Francis   28–9

Lee v. Weisman (1992)   66, 135, **142–8**, 153, 155, 196–7
  Kennedy's opinion   143–6, 153, 193, 196, 205
Lamb's Chapel v. Center Moriches Union Free School District (1993)   **178–81**, 183, 185, 187, 189, 196, 198
Legal Model   6, 7, 193
Lemon Test   34, 36, 40, 47, 52, 54, 58, 61, 64, 128, 129–31, 142–3, 145, 148, 160, 163, 175–6, 179–80, 196–8, 200, 206
  decline of   131, 142, 145, 179–80
  and effect   53, 71, 160, 175–6
  and entanglement   35, 52–5, 71
  and purpose   53, 115, 127–9, 140, 160, 175
Lemon v. Kurtzman (1970)   **33–6**, 41–2, 54, 59, 63, 78, 129, 138, 180, 184, 195, 198, 204
Lubbock Independent School District v. Lubbock Civil Liberties Union (1982)   167, 169–70
Lynch v. Donnelly (1984)   52, 128, 134–5, 144

McCollum v. Board of Education (1948)   22–3, 45, 53, 77, 93, 194
Madison, James   5, 11, 19, 86, 93
Marshall, Thurgood   47, 55, 63, 66, 79–81, 129–30, 132–3, 175–7, 189, 193
Marsh v. Chambers (1983)   49, 143
Meek v. Pittenger (1975)   40, 42–3, 46–7, 51, 54, 62–5, 70, 74, 79
Meese, Edwin   5, 56, 135–6
moments of silence   117–19, 125, 127, 133–4, 140, 148, 238n. 52
  New Jersey debate over   125–6, 140
monitoring   35, 44, 52, 54–5, 65
Moral Majority   117, 120–1, 126
Mueller v. Allen (1983)   46, 48–9, 52, 63–4, 67, 69, 74, 80, 200
Murray v. Curlett (1963) *see Abington School District v. Schempp* (1963)
Murray O'Hair, Madalyn   101, 117
Murray, William   101, 117

NAACP *see National Association for the Advancement of Colored People*
National Association for the Advancement of Colored People   26, 99

Index

National Association of Evangelicals 105, 164, 167
National Council of Churches 50, 90, 117, 167, 170
National Education Association 20–2, 28–9, 165
NCWC *see National Catholic Welfare Conference*
NDEA *see National Defense Education Act*
NEA *see National Education Association*
neutrality 5–6, 16, 54, 91, 103, 121, 131, 147, 178, 181, 183–4, 192–3
New Deal 3, 12–13, 20
Nixon, Richard 37, 39, 131–2

O'Connor, Sandra Day 47, 53, 55–6, 63, 66, 69–71, 74–5, 81–2, 122, 129–31, 133–4, 138, 146, 155, 161, 175–9, 182, 189, 197
  and endorsement 128, 131, 176
  as swing vote 131, 142, 182–3, 193, 196–7
  on campus-off campus distinction 42, **45**, 53, 56, 75, 196, 198
  demise of 70–1, 75
original intent 4–6, 135–6

People for the American Way 49–50, 56, 139, 164
Perkins, Carl 164, 168
pervasively sectarian 10, 42, 45, 54–5, 64–5
  rejection of 56, 70–1
Pfeffer, Leo 96, 107, 118
Pledge of Allegiance 25, 87, 95–6, 120–1
Politics
  reaction to cases 96–9, 104–12, 201
  Supreme Court and 48, 112–13, 202–3
Powell, Lewis 41, 47–8, 55, 58, 63, 66, 78, 80–1, 119–20, 128–30, 132–4, 155, 161, 189, 193, 195, 200
  and *Widmar* 159–61
pragmatism 47, 53, 55, 58, 95, 132–3, 140, 193, 195–6, 200, 204
prayer
  constitutional amendment 97–9, **104–11**, 118, **120–4**, 137, 139, 149–50, 167, 171, 202–3
  and free exercise 92, 95, 105–6, 131
  graduation 141–3
  and morality 49, 106, 113, 117, 124, 137, 202
  and politics 49, 96–9, 104–12, 122–4, 135, 137–8, 148–50, 201–3, 246n. 31
  in schools 5, 8–9, 49, 83–5, 91, 101, 111, 118–19, 141, 164
  silent 117, 124, 148
  voluntary 119–20, 148
Protestants and Other Americans United for the Separation of Church and State *see Americans United for the Separation of Church and State*
public schools 25, 46, 48, 56, 88, 187, 203
  desegregation 26, 38, 100
  dissatisfaction with 38, 48, 59, 61, 73, 75, 204
  federal funds 23
  movement 11, 83–4
public opinion 50, 56, 108–9, 119
  on education 37, 38
  Supreme Court response to 92–4, 102, 112–13, 115, 131
purpose 40, 53, 63, 115, 127–9, 140, 160, 175, 183

Rational Choice theory 7, 193
Reagan Administration 48, 56, 73, 116, 136–7, 158
  and school aid 56, 73
  and school prayer **120–4**
Reagan, Ronald 5, 9, 49–50, 55, 136–7, 202–3
  and prayer amendment 49, **120–4**, 126, 162, 167
  and Religious Right 122–3, 138
Reed, Stanley 45, 77
Regents' Prayer *see Engel v. Vitale* (1962)
Rehnquist Court 14, 74, 153, 182, 193, 196–7, 199–200
Rehnquist, William 47, 54–5, 63, 74, 78–82, 130, 132, 138, 140, 142, 147, 155, 161, 179, 182, 193, 197
  and *Mueller* 46, 48, 52, 74, 200
  and *Zobrest* 64–5, 70
released time 22–3, 45, 85, 88, 93
religious colleges 28, 41, 54
religious displays 52, 134, 142, 147–8
religious exercises 9, 12, 25, 101–2, 143, 194, 199, 202, 232n. 69
Religious Right 9, 49–50, 117, 120, 138–9, 164, 167, 185, 192, 203
religious schools 9–10, 30–1, 38, 42, 59, 62, 64–5, 67–8, 70, 75, 198, 204
  and public funds 22
  and public purpose 19, 36, 39, 48, 59, 204
  and race 26, 67–8
remedial education 41, 49, 51, 53, 69
Republican Party 9, 116
Rockefeller, Nelson A. 39, 61
Rosenberger v. the Rector and Visitors of the University of Virginia (1995) **181–4**, 185, 187, 189, 193, 196, 198–200
Rutledge, Wiley 30, 77, 193
  and *Everson* 16, 19–20, 193, 203, 210n. 2

salary reimbursement 27, 33–4
Scalia, Antonin 5, 66, 74, 142, 147–8, 155, 175–6, 179–80, 182, 189, 193, 197
school aid 5, 9–10, 129, 185–7, 193, 197–9, 203–6
school prayer 5, 8–10, 25, 30, 49, 83, 85, 91, 101, 111, 119, 164, 167, 185–7, 197, 201
  history, nineteenth century 83–4
  challenges to 90–6, 118
  and constitutional amendment 49, **104–11, 120–4**, 137, 139, 149–50, 167, 171, 202–3
  support for 8, 97–8, 140–1, 148–50
schools
  Catholic 9, 12, 14, 25, 34, 38, 59, 61, 67–8, 84
  financial problems 20–1
  inner-city 38, 61, 67, 73, 75, 204
  Jewish 39, 59, 61, 68, 75
  Protestant 39, 59, 61, 68, 75
  public 25, 46, 48, 56, 88, 187, 203
  religious 9, 31, 36, 42, 64–5, 67, 70, 75, 198, 204
Second Vatican Council 9, 24–6, 32, 38–9, 61, 204
secularization 23, 37, 85, 137, 163, 201
Senate
  Committee on Education and Labor 21
  Committee on Labor and Public Welfare 23
  Judiciary Committee 98–9, 121, 162, 168–70
Smith, William French 116, 123
social welfare 3, 5, 13–14, 30
Souter, David 65–6, 73, 75, 82, 142, 146–7, 155, 182, 184, 187, 189, 193, 197
Southern Baptist Convention 22, 122
Spellman, Cardinal Francis 9, 24, 98, 203
  and Eleanor Roosevelt 24
stare decisis 6, 130, 193, 197
states
  courts 18, 93, 109–10, 127, 166
  financial difficulties 37, 59
  school aid policies 36, 39–40, 59, 204
states' rights 20, 106
Stevens, John Paul 47, 55, 73, 75, 79, 82, 119–20, 127–9, 132, 136, 142, 146, 155, 161, 175–8, 180, 182, 184, 187, 189, 193, 197
Stewart, Potter 42, 44, 47, 55, 58, 79, 92, 94–6, 104, 132, 154–5, 193, 195
Stone v. Graham (1980) **115–16**, 127–8, 131–2, 137, 155, 161, 202
Strict separation 5–6, 16–19, 29, 34, 48, 53, 56–7, 62–3, 70, 91, 114, 134, 144, 161, 176, 184, 187, 192–4, 197–8
  voting bloc 47, 55, 58, 66, 75, 182, 193

Taft, Robert 21–2
tax
  credit 39–41, 45, 49, 73, 123, 199
  deduction 41, 46, 48, 63, 199, 200
  exemption 18, 54
Ten Commandments 115, 161
tests 30–1, 57
textbooks 12, 29–30, 33, 40–1, 43–4, 46, 198–200
Thayer, V. T. 88–9
Thomas, Clarence 66, 74, 142, 148, 155, 179–80, 182, 189, 193, 197
Title I *see Elementary and Secondary Education Act*
tuition reimbursement 41, 43, 45

Vatican II *see Second Vatican Council*
viewpoint discrimination 179, 181
voluntariness 106, 120, 141, 157, 163, 206
voting blocs 47–8, 55, 58, 142, 219n. 55
vouchers 40, 56, 73–4

Wallace v. Jaffree (1985) 123, **124–31**, 134–5, 137–8, 140, 142, 145, 155
  Stevens's opinion 127–9, 133
wall of separation 16, 19, 22, 30, 33, 103, 121, 130, 204
Walz v. Tax Commission of the City of New York (1970) 34, 55, 77
Warren Court 99–101, 114, 131, 137, 153, 192, 195
Warren, Earl 30–1, 33, 35, 91, 99–100, 104, 132, 194
West Virginia State Board of Education v. Barnette (1943) 120, 145, 158
White, Byron 30–1, 35–6, 47, 55, 63, 74, 77–81, 100, 132–3, 142, 147, 155, 161, 179–80, 189
Widmar v. Vincent 158, **159–62**, 170–3, 176, 178–80, 185–7, 189
Witters v. Washington Department of Services for the Blind (1986) 62–3, **64**, 66, 69–71, 73–5, 81, 178, 183–4, 195
Wolman v. Walter (1977) 40, 44, 46–7, 51, 54–5, 62, 64, 74, 79–80, 161
World War Two 3, 14, 20, 32, 84

Zobrest v. Catalina Hills Independent School District (1993) **64–6**, 67, 69–71, 73–5, 82, 178, 183–4, 196
Zorach v. Clauson (1952) 25, 45, 53, 77, 93, 152, 194

CPSIA information can be obtained
at www.ICGtesting.com
Printed in the USA
LVHW030214130120
643322LV00005B/71/P

9 781472 522528